텝스 한달만 제대로 공부 해보자

Reading

Perfect TEPS

텝스 한 달만 제대로 공부해보자

Perfect TEPS *Reading*

초판1쇄 2009년 10월 20일 인쇄
초판2쇄 2010년 3월 15일 발행

지 은 이 이충훈 & J&L English Lab

펴 낸 곳 도서출판 이비컴
펴 낸 이 강기원

기획진행 김현호
디 자 인 이승현
편   집 김윤영 · 윤은정

마 케 팅 김동중 · 이은미

주   소 130-811 서울시 동대문구 신설동 97-1 302호
대표전화 (02) 2254-0658
팩   스 (02) 2254-0634
전자우편 help@bookbee.co.kr

등록번호 제 6-0596호
등록일자 2002.4.9
I S B N 978-89-6245-027-9 13740
웹사이트 http://www.bookbee.co.kr

값 18,000원

파본이나 잘못 인쇄된 책은 구입하신 서점에서 교환해 드립니다.

텝스 한달만 제대로 공부해보자

Reading

Perfect!
TEPS

이충훈 &
J&L English Lab 지음

이비톡

Preface

30 DAYS TEPS 800＋Final Sum-up

　　기타 여러 가지 공인영어시험들에 대한 변별성이 의심을 받으면서 그 대안으로 TEPS가 떠오르고 있는 추세이다. 해마다 응시인원의 수가 늘어나고 있으며, 더 많은 학교와 기업체들에서 수험자들의 영어실력에 대한 인증으로 TEPS를 채택하고 있다. 요령과 편법이 통하는 몇몇 기타 시험과는 다르게 TEPS는 문제가 정형화되거나 일반화되어 있지 않다는 특징이 있다. 특히 독해의 경우 다뤄지는 지문의 유형이 워낙에 광범위하고, 어휘 역시 그 난이도가 높기 때문에 수험자들의 기본 영어 실력이 뒷받침되어 있지 않다면 접근하기조차 어려운 시험이 TEPS인 것도 사실이다.

　　본인은 지난 몇 년간 영어연구원으로 근무하며 시중의 수많은 TEPS 도서들을 분석하고 연구한 경험과, TEPS 온라인사이트의 콘텐츠 검수와 튜터 역할을 통해 많은 수험생들로부터 받은 질문과 어려움에 답해주며 얻은 지식들을 기반으로 가장 간결하면서도 핵심을 다룬 TEPS 도서의 집필에 고민해왔다. 그리고 이제 그 결실로 3단계로 구성한 〈Perfect TEPS〉 시리즈를 수험생들에게 자신 있게 내놓는 바이다.

　　이 책의 장점은 총 3단계에 걸쳐서 철저하게 TEPS 독해 지문의 '유형'과 '주제'를 학습할 수 있도록 구성되어 있다는 점이다. 첫 번째 유형분석 섹션을 통해, TEPS 독해에 등장하는 8가지 유형의 접근법과 문제출제 방식을 살펴보고 세 번의 Pre-Test를 통해서 충분히 유형연습을 할 수 있도록 하였고, 각 Pre-Test의 문제는 총 8가지 유형이 하나씩 들어가도록 구성되어 모든 유형을 골고루 연습할 수 있도록 배려하였다.

　　두 번째 주제분석 섹션에서는, TEPS 독해에 가장 빈번히 등장하는 10가지 주제에 대해서 지문별 특성을 학습하고 각 주제별로 5개의 문항을 Mini-Test 형식으로 풀어봄으로써 지문에 대한 적응력을 높여줄 수 있도록 하였다. 각 주제별 5개의 문항은 어느 한 문항에 치우치지 않고 각 유형이 하나씩 들어가도록 하여 주제와 유형이라는 두 마리 토끼를 모두 잡도록 구성하였다. 각 주제별 문제풀이가 끝나면 Vocabulary 정리 코너를 두어 독해의 가장 핵심이라고 할 수 있는 어휘 실력을 점검해 보고 마무리할 수 있도록 하였다.

　　마지막으로 세 번째 섹션에서는 총 3회에 걸친 Actual Test를 통해서 앞서 학습한 내용들을 최종 정리하며 TEPS 독해 만점을 위한 최종 실전 대비를 할 수 있도록 했다.

　　이 책이 제시하는 〈유형별 Pre-Test → 주제별 Mini-Test 및 어휘학습 → Actual Test〉의 3단계 과정을 한 달이라는 시간 동안 철저히 준비한다면 여러분 모두 반드시 고득점을 획득할 수 있을 것이라고 확신한다.

　　끝으로 본 TEPS 시리즈가 출간될 수 있도록 도와주신 이비톡 사장님, 김현호 팀장님과 원고의 집필에 있어서 큰 힘을 보태준 팀원들에게 감사드린다. 마지막으로 나의 정신적 지주이자 나의 집필 인생에 있어서 영원한 동반자인 아내와 이곳 호주와 한국에서 저의 성공을 위해 항상 기도해 주시는 아버지, 어머니, 여동생 하나, 장모님과 처형, 처제, 그리고 마지막으로 대한민국의 모든 TEPS 수험생들에게 이 책을 바친다.

－ 이충훈 & J&L ENGLISH LAB －

이 책의 특성 및 학습 방법

> **Section 01** : 유형별 연습 + Pre-Test 3회분
> **Section 02** : 주제별 Mini-Test 각 5문항씩
> **Section 03** : Actual Test 3회분

본 〈Perfect TEPS〉 시리즈는 30일 간의 시간 동안 각 영역별로 실제 TEPS 시험에서 출제가 가능한 모든 '유형'과 '주제'별 문제들을 Pre-Test와 Mini-Test 형식으로 풀어 본 후, 총 3회에 달하는 Actual Test 로 마무리함으로써 실제 TEPS 시험에서 800점 이상의 고득점을 목표로 하는 수험자들이 원하는 점수대를 획득할 수 있도록 구성되었다.

각 Section별로 좀 더 구체적으로 설명하자면 다음과 같다.

유형을 확실히 알고 넘어가자!!

우선, Section 1을 통해서 학습자들은 독해시험을 구성하는 세 가지 Part의 총 8가지 문제유형에 대해서 확인해 볼 수 있다. 각 유형별 출제 특징을 문제를 통해서 확인해 본 후, 모든 유형을 담은 총 3회에 걸친 Pre-Test를 통해서 충분히 유형연습을 할 수 있도록 하였다.

학습한 유형을 토대로 주제별 집중 연습을 하자!!

그리고 Section 2에서는 독해시험에 출제되는 지문들을 총 10가지 주제로 분류하여, 각 주제별로 지문별 특성을 확인해 볼 수 있도록 하였고, 유형별로 출제된 5개의 문항을 Mini-Test 형식으로 풀어봄으로써 TEPS 시험에 대한 적응력을 높여줄 수 있도록 하였다. Mini-Test 학습이 끝나면 Vocabulary 정리 코너를 두어 독해의 가장 핵심이라고 할 수 있는 주제별 어휘 실력을 간략하게나마 점검해 볼 수 있도록 하였다.

충분한 실전테스트로 정기시험을 완벽하게 대비하자!!

마지막으로 Section 3에서는 총 3회분에 달하는 실전 독해 Actual Test를 통하여 학습자들이 실제 TEPS 시험에 충분히 적응할 수 있도록 배려하였다.

TEPS는 편법과 요령이 통하지 않는 시험이다. 특히 독해의 경우 1개의 지문에 1개 문제 출제라는 원칙으로 토익을 포함한 기타 시험처럼 한 문제의 해결을 통해, 다음 문제의 정답까지도 유추하거나 쉽게 찾아낼 수 있는 길을 애초에 막고 있다. 한 지문당 60초 정도의 짧은 시간에 이해를 하고 정답을 찾아내야 하는 현실에서 단계별로 세분화시켜 놓은 문제풀이 전략이 실전에서 무슨 소용이 있겠는가? 그러므로 학습자들은 다른 어떤 시험들보다도 풍부한 어휘력과 함께, 많은 지문을 읽고 빠르게 문제를 풀어보는 연습을 통해서 자신의 내공을 쌓아야지만 고득점을 획득할 수 있다.

그래서 본 TEPS 시리즈는 여타의 다른 도서들과는 다르게 쓸데없이 긴 문제풀이 전략 등은 과감히 배제하고 오직 '유형'과 '주제'라는 두 가지 대전제에 충실하여 충분한 수의 문제를 제공함으로써 학습자들이 시험을 대비할 수 있도록 하는 데 그 목표를 두고 있다.

문제 수로만 따진다면 본도서는 실전 독해 총 5회분에 달하는 문제풀이 연습을 학습자들에게 제공함으로써 충분히 고득점을 획득할 수 있는 발판이 되어 줄 수 있을 것이라고 확신한다.

TEPS란 이런 시험이다

30 DAYS TEPS 800 + Final Sum-up

1. TEPS 시험이란?

TEPS는 [Test of English Proficiency developed by Seoul National University]의 약자로 서울대학교 언어교육원에서 개발되어 서울대학교 TEPS 관리위원회가 주관하고 시행하는 영어능력검정시험입니다. 국내외 최고 수준의 영어 관련 전문가 100여 명이 문제를 출제하고 세계의 권위자로 구성된 자문위원회에서 출제된 문제들을 검토하여 그 신뢰도와 타당도가 입증된 시험이라고 할 수 있습니다.

2. TEPS 시험은 어떻게 출제되고 시험시간은 어떻게 되나?

청해, 문법, 어휘, 독해의 4가지 영역에 걸쳐 총 200문항이 출제되며 990점이 만점인 시험으로, 청해 60문항 55분, 문법 50문항 25분, 어휘 50문항 15분, 독해 40문항 45분의 시간이 주어집니다

3. TEPS 시험 당일 날 반드시 챙겨 가져가야 할 것은?

반드시 자신의 신분증을 지참해야 합니다. TEPS 관리위원회에서 인정하는 신분증에는 주민등록증, 운전면허증, 기간 만료 전의 여권, 공무원증 등이 있고, 기타 인정되는 신분증은 다음과 같습니다.
(1) 장교 – 장교신분증
(2) 사병 – TEPS 정기시험 신분확인증명서
(3) 주민등록증을 분실 시 – 동, 읍, 면사무소에 발급된 주민등록증 발급확인서

컴퓨터용 사인펜은 두 자루 이상 준비할 수 있도록 하고, 수정액은 사용할 수 없으므로 꼭 수정테이프를 챙겨가도록 합니다. 꼭 필요하지는 않지만 시험 당일 자신의 고사실을 쉽게 확인하기 위해서 수험표를 출력해 갈 수 있도록 합니다.

4. TEPS 시험 접수/취소 방법 및 시험점수 유예기간은?

보통 TEPS 관리위원회 공식 사이트인 www.teps.or.kr에 회원가입을 한 후, 접수신청란에 접수를 완료하면 됩니다. 접수 취소와 관련해서는 접수 기간 내에는 신청금액이 전액 환불되지만 그 이후에 시간이 지남에 따라 차등 지급된다는 점을 유념하십시오.

5. TEPS 시험 점수는 언제 알 수 있나?

정기시험의 성적은 시험일로부터 15일 이후에 위에서 언급된 TEPS 관리위원회의 홈페이지에서 확인이 가능합니다. 성적표는 보통 20일 안에 우편으로 지정된 주소로 발송이 되고, 특별 시험의 성적표는 시험일로부터 일주일 이내에 해당 단체나 기관으로 통보됩니다.

6. TEPS 성적 평균 분포도는?

보통 전체 인원의 80% 정도에 해당하는 응시자들이 2급과 3급 사이에 집중적으로 분포되어 있습니다. 이 중 가장 높은 2+급을 제외하고 3급, 3+급, 2급 각각에 전체 응시자의 20% 정도가 차지하고 있습니다.

TEPS 시험 각 영역별 구성

영역	파트		문항수	시간/배점
청해	Part I	문장 하나를 들은 후 이어질 응답 고르기	15	55분/396점
	Part II	3문장의 대화를 듣고 마지막 응답 고르기	15	
	Part III	6-8 문장의 대화를 들은 후 질문에 맞는 답 고르기	15	
	Part IV	화자에 의해 말해지는 지문을 듣고 질문에 맞는 답 고르기	15	
문법	Part I	A-B 대화문의 빈칸에 적절한 표현 고르기	20	25분/99점
	Part II	문장의 빈칸에 적절한 표현 고르기	20	
	Part III	대화문에서 어법상 틀리거나 어색한 것 고르기	5	
	Part IV	4문장으로 구성된 단문에서 문법상 틀리거나 어색한 것 고르기	5	
어휘	Part I	A-B 대화문의 빈칸에 적절한 어휘 고르기	25	15분/99점
	Part II	문장의 빈칸에 적절한 어휘 고르기	25	
독해	Part I	지문 중 빈칸에 들어갈 적절한 내용 고르기	16	45분/396점
	Part II	지문을 읽고 질문에 맞는 답 고르기	21	
	Part III	지문을 읽고 문맥상 어색한 것 고르기	3	
총계	13개 파트	총계 13개 파트	200	140분/990점

청해 (총 60문항)

- **Part 1**
  (15문항)

  청해 Part 1은 질의응답을 다루며 내용은 단 한 번만 들려준다. 짧은 문장에 내용 자체는 간단하고 기본적인 수준이지만 주어지는 선택지들이 헷갈리는 경우가 많으므로 짧은 순간에 상황을 판단하여 올바른 대답을 골라낼 수 있도록 연습해 두어야 한다.

  예제) *Listen and choose the most appropriate response to the statement.*

  > M: Is Mrs. Ferguson likely to be our teacher next year?
  > W: _____
  >
  > (a) That's what the forecast said.
  > (b) Not a chance.
  > (c) You guessed it right.
  > (d) No, she doesn't like it at all.

  정답 (b)

- **Part 2**
  (15문항)

  A-B-A-B순의 짧은 대화 문제로 내용은 단 한 번만 들려준다. 보통 A-B-A 중 마지막 A의 내용이 B의 내용을 고르는 데 있어서 핵심 역할을 한다.

  예제) *Listen and choose the most appropriate response to complete the conversation.*

TEPS 시험 각 영역별 구성

30 DAYS TEPS 800+Final Sum-up

M: I'm here to buy fishing rods.
W: You came to the right place. We have a variety of fishing rods.
M: You can give me a discount if I buy them in bulk, can't you?
W: _____

(a) Great. Then I will take this one.
(b) I'll go check with the manager.
(c) It's an offer you cannot refuse.
(d) You will not regret it.

정답 (b)

- **Part 3**
  (15문항)

보통 한 사람당 3번 이상씩 주고받는 형태의 다소 긴 대화문이 등장한다. 대신 대화 부분과 질문을 들려준 뒤 다시 한 번 반복해서 들려주기 때문에 늘어난 길이만큼 문제풀이가 어렵다고 할 수는 없다.

예제) *Listen and choose the option that best answers the question.*

M: We visited the Museum of Pyramids yesterday.
W: How was your visit?
M: It was very entertaining. We saw some oil paintings and marble carvings. They were really beautiful.
W: Sounds like you had a great fun.
M: Yes, I did. And I went on a guided tour around the museum that lasted a half hour.
W: Where is this museum located? I feel like going there.
M: It is in the downtown area, and it opens at 8 in the morning.

Q: What is correct according to the conversation?

(a) The woman visited the Museum yesterday.
(b) The museum exhibits sculptures.
(c) It takes about 30 minutes to get to the museum.
(d) The museum closes at 8 o'clock.

정답 (b)

- **Part 4**
  (15문항)

앞의 파트들이 대화문을 다루었다면 Part 4는 담화문을 다룬다. 다양한 주제와 관련된 내용의 지문이 등장하고 이를 근거로 주제, 세부사항, 사실 여부 및 추론들을 다룬 문제가 출제된다. 담화 부분과 질문을 두 번 들려준다.

예제) *Listen and choose the option that best answers the question.*

After meeting in Geneva the UN has agreed to phase out nine more persistent chemicals widely used in farming and industry. The nine pesticides and industrial chemicals join 12 substances targeted for elimination. The banned substances are considered extremely dangerous because they can damage reproduction, mental capacity and growth and cause cancer. The chemicals, which are worth billions and traded worldwide, accumulate in the food chain and takes years to degrade.

Q: What is the main topic of the talk?

(a) The development of new chemicals for farming and industry.
(b) The long lasting effects of chemicals on human health.
(c) Dangerous agents added to global prohibited list.
(d) The size of the chemical industry.

정답 (c)

문법 (총 50문항)

- **Part 1**
  (20문항)

  Part 1은 A-B의 짧은 대화를 통해서 다양한 문법적 이해력을 측정할 수 있도록 출제된다. 대화문 빈칸에 들어갈 적절한 표현을 고르는 형식이다.

  예제) *Fill in the blank with the most appropriate word or phrase.*

  A: It's already half past 10. It's high time you _____ home.
  B: Okay. Do you think you can give me a lift?

  (a) go
  (b) will go
  (c) went
  (d) would go

  정답 (c)

- **Part 2**
  (20문항)

  하나 또는 두 개의 문장으로 구성된 서술문 속의 빈칸을 채우는 문제유형으로 총 20문항이 출제된다. 문법 자체의 이해도와 함께 구문에 대한 이해력 역시 문제풀이에 있어서 중요하다.

  예제) *Fill in the blank with the most appropriate word or phrase.*

  A lot of people often forget that it takes _____ to work their up in the business world.

  (a) the time
  (b) a time
  (c) time
  (d) times

  정답 (c)

TEPS 시험 각 영역별 구성

30 DAYS TEPS 800➕Final Sum-up

• **Part 3**
(5문항)

A-B-A-B 순의 대화문이 주어지고, 이 중 어법상 틀리거나 어색한 부분이 포함되어 있는 문장을 정답으로 골라야 한다. 총 5문항이 출제된다.

예제) *Identify the grammatical error in the dialogue.*

(a) A: I have no idea who James Patrick is.
(b) B: Well, I know who he is. He's the most famous chefs in America.
(c) A: Oh, is he? No wonder my wife mentions his name a lot.
(d) B: So does my wife.

정답 (b)

• **Part 4**
(5문항)

한 문단이 주어지고 그 중 문법적으로 틀리거나 어색한 문장을 골라내는 문제유형으로 Part 3와 마찬가지로 총 5문항이 출제된다.

예제) *Identify the ungrammatical sentence in the passage.*

(a) Lisa was tired of her older sister treating her badly. (b) They were close until she became a teenager, and then her sister seemed to be jealous of the male attention she was attracting. (c) When she raised the issue with her mom, she just told her to go and sort it out. (d) However, she decided to put up with it and pretended not to care.

정답 (b)

어휘 (총 50문항)

• **Part 1**
(25문항)

구어체로 이루어진 A-B의 대화 중 빈칸에 가장 적절한 단어를 골라내는 문제로 총 25문항이 출제가 된다. 단어 자체의 단편적 의미로 접근하기보다는 문맥에서 사용되는 상대적 의미에 더 초점을 두어 문제를 해결해야 한다.

예제) *Choose the most appropriate word or expression for the blank in the conversation.*

A: How did my test results _____ out?
B: There is nothing to worry about. You're in good health.

(a) make
(b) turn
(c) break
(d) rule

정답 (b)

• **Part 2**
(25문항)

하나 또는 두 개의 문장으로 구성된 글 속의 빈칸에 의미상 가장 적절한 단어를 골라내는 문제유형으로 Part 1과 마찬가지로 총 25문항이 출제된다. 평소 단어를 개별적으로 외우

30 DAYS TEPS 800+Final Sum-up

지 말고 의미 단위로 통째로 외워두는 습관이 중요하다.

예제) *Choose the most appropriate word or expression for the blank in the statement.*

The patient has been complaining of a _____ pain in the upper left side of the abdomen.

(a) contrary
(b) constant
(c) constable
(d) converse

정답 (b)

독해 (총 40문항)

- **Part 1**
  (16문항)

지문의 초반, 중반 또는 후반에 빈칸이 들어가 있고 글의 흐름상 그 안에 들어갈 내용으로 가장 적절한 보기를 고르는 문제유형으로 총 16문항이 출제된다.

예제) *Read the passage and choose the option that best fits the blank.*

Living in the warm, humid tropics can only be made more pleasurable by wearing cool cotton. At Wicked Weaves, Vicky Johnson, a resort wear and tropical wedding specialist, offers a specialized service and advice to you to complement your body and find the style that _____.
Choosing the correct style can make a world of difference on how you look and feel. See the difference Ms Johnson can make by customizing your garments with design and style that will fit perfectly. American owned and operated by the designer herself, Ms Johnson has been in the trade for 20 years and now offers a personalized service available for after hour appointments.

(a) are favored by American customers
(b) is in vogue at the moment
(c) meets your budget
(d) best suits your shape

정답 (d)

- **Part 2**
  (21문항)

주어진 글의 내용을 이해한 후 주제나 대의, 세부 내용 파악 혹은 논리적 추론 등을 묻는 질문에 가장 적절한 보기를 선택하는 문제유형으로 총 21문항이 출제된다.

예제) *Choose the option that correctly answers the question.*

TEPS 시험 각 영역별 구성

30 DAYS TEPS 800＋Final Sum-up

A father used a kitchen knife to slash his son across the chest in a tragic family dispute. Michael Loman faced the first day of his District Court trial charged with one count of unlawful wounding after the alleged incident. Prosecutor Bob Coleman told the court a dispute arose after Mr. Loman's son went to the house to collect personal items and told his dad he did not want to see him any more. Mr. Loman allegedly lunged at his son twice, before using a kitchen knife to inflict the would, which later required 22 stitches. His son left the house after the alleged incident and started yelling abuse on his father's driveway before leaving the house by car.

Q: What is the best title for the news article?

(a) Spoiled teenagers these days
(b) A father who frequently abused his son.
(c) A rising trend of family disruption
(d) Domestic Violence resulting in injury

정답 (d)

• Part 3
(3문항)

한 문단의 글에서 내용의 흐름상 어색한 내용을 담고 있는 문장을 골라내는 문제유형으로 총 3문항이 출제된다.

예제) *Identify the sentence that least fits the context of the passage.*

One of the major reasons for drug use and abuse is the fact that the media glamorizes their use by such terms as "recreational" drugs and the newly-favored term, "party" drugs. (a) This kind of glamorization makes so many people fall victim to drug overdoses. (b) However, they cannot blame authorities, suppliers or society because the fault is their own. (c) Drugs are universally available and selling them genera tes all sorts of other crimes. (d) At the end of the day, the choice to use drugs rests with the individual.

정답 (c)

TEPS 시험 각 등급 구성

등급	점수	능력 검정 기준
1+등급	901-990	**외국인으로서 최상급 수준의 의사소통 능력** 교양 있는 원어민에 버금가는 정도로 의사소통이 가능하고 전문 분야 업무에 대처할 수 있음.
1급	801-900	**외국인으로서 거의 최상급 수준의 의사소통 능력** 단기간 집중 교육을 받으면 대부분의 의사소통이 가능하고 전문 분야 업무에 별 무리 없이 대처할 수 있음.
2+등급	701-800	**외국인으로서 상급 수준의 의사소통 능력** 단기간 집중 교육을 받으면 일반 분야 업무를 큰 어려움 없이 수행할 수 있음.
2급	601-700	**외국인으로서 중,상급 수준의 의사소통 능력** 중장기간 집중 교육을 받으면 일반 분야 업무를 큰 어려움 없이 수행할 수 있음.
3+등급	501-600	**외국인으로서 중급 수준의 의사소통 능력** 중장기간 집중 교육을 받으면 한정된 분야의 업무를 큰 어려움 없이 수행할 수 있음.
3급	401-500	**외국인으로서 중하급 수준의 의사소통 능력** 중장기간 집중 교육을 받으면 한정된 분야의 업무를 다소 미흡하지만 큰 지장은 없이 수행할 수 있음.
4+등급, 4급	201-400	**외국인으로서 하급 수준의 의사소통 능력** 장기간의 집중 교육을 받으면 한정된 분야의 업무를 대체로 어렵게 수행할 수 있음.
5+등급, 5급	10-200	**외국인으로서 최하급 수준의 의사소통 능력** 단편적인 지식만을 갖추고 있어 의사소통이 거의 불가능함.

Contents

30 DAYS TEPS 800 ✚ Final Sum-up

Preface	4
이 책의 특성 및 학습 방법	5
TEPS란 이런 시험이다	6
TEPS 시험 각 영역별 구성	7
TEPS 시험 각 등급 구성	13

Section 01
독해 8가지 유형별(Type) 접근법

Part 1 빈칸 채우기 유형 ········· 18
- **Type 01** 초반 빈칸 유형 ········· 19
- **Type 02** 중반 빈칸 유형 ········· 20
- **Type 03** 후반 빈칸 유형 ········· 21
- **Type 04** 접속(부)사 빈칸 유형 ········· 22

Part 2 내용 파악 유형 ········· 23
- **Type 05** 대의 파악 · 제목 찾기 유형 ········· 24
- **Type 06** 세부 내용 파악 유형 ········· 25
- **Type 07** 추론 유형 ········· 26

Part 3 내용 일관성 파악 유형 ········· 27
- **Type 08** 문맥 파악 유형 ········· 28

Pre-Test
- **Pre-Test 1** ········· 30
- **Pre-Test 2** ········· 34
- **Pre-Test 3** ········· 38

Contents

30 DAYS TEPS 800 + Final Sum-up

Perfect TEPS Reading

Section 02
독해 10가지 주제별(Theme) 접근법

Mini-Test & Vocabulary

Theme 01	광고(Advertisement)	44
Theme 02	안내 · 공고(Announcement)	55
Theme 03	편지 · 에세이(Letters · Essays)	66
Theme 04	뉴스(News)	77
Theme 05	정치 · 경제(Politics · Economics)	88
Theme 06	과학 · 기술 · 우주 (Science · Technology · Universe)	99
Theme 07	역사 · 인물(History · People)	110
Theme 08	환경 · 생물(Environment · Life)	121
Theme 09	건강 · 의학(Health · Medical Science)	132
Theme 10	사회 · 문화(Society · Culture)	143

Section 03
Reading Comprehension
Actual Test

- Actual Test · 1 ·········· 156
- Actual Test · 2 ·········· 178
- Actual Test · 3 ·········· 200

정답편

Pre-Test 1 · 2 · 3 ·········· 4
Actual Test 1 · 2 · 3 ·········· 16

Section 01

30 DAYS TEPS 800+Final Sum-up

독해 8가지 유형별(Type) 접근법

TEPS 독해 시험은 총 3가지 Part로 나뉘는데, 이들은 다시 세부적으로 총 8가지 유형으로 분류해 볼 수 있다.

따라서 각 유형별로 문제들이 어떻게 출제가 되는지 실제 문제를 통해서 확인해 보고, 각 유형별 문제를 해결함에 있어서 어떤 식으로 접근해야 하는지를 연습해 두는 것은 실전 시험을 대비해 학습자들이 반드시 거쳐야 하는 과정이다.

예를 들어, Part 1에 해당하는 초반 빈칸 유형의 문제를 접근하는 데 있어서 Part 2의 세부사항 파악과 같이 전체 지문을 다 읽으면서 문제를 푸는 방식을 선택한다면 결코 주어진 시간에 문제를 풀지 못하고 후반에 가서는 모든 문제를 소위 말하는 찍기 신공으로 해결할 수밖에 없는 최악의 사태가 벌어진다.

이번 Section에서는 각 파트별로 총 8가지 유형에 대한 접근방법을 살펴보고, 실전 문제를 통해서 이를 확인해 보는 시간을 갖도록 한다. 모든 유형에 대한 파악이 완료가 되면 Pre-Test 3회분을 풀어보도록 하는데 각 Pre-Test는 독해에서 출제되는 8가지 유형을 모두 담고 있으므로 학습자들은 최종적으로 독해 문제의 유형을 정리해 보는 기회를 가지며 자신감을 높일 수 있다.

Part 1 빈칸 채우기 유형
- **Type 01** 초반 빈칸 유형
- **Type 02** 중반 빈칸 유형
- **Type 03** 후반 빈칸 유형
- **Type 04** 접속(부)사 빈칸 유형

Part 2 내용 파악 유형
- **Type 05** 대의 파악·제목 찾기 유형
- **Type 06** 세부 내용 파악 유형
- **Type 07** 추론 유형

Part 3 내용 일관성 파악 유형
- **Type 08** 문맥 파악 유형

Pre-Test
- Pre-Test · 1
- Pre-Test · 2
- Pre-Test · 3

Part 1
30 DAYS TEPS 800+Final Sum-up

빈칸 채우기 유형

Part 1 (16문항) : 지문의 빈칸에 들어갈 적절한 표현을 찾는 형태의 문제유형이 Part 1에 해당하며 총 16문항이 출제된다. 총 4가지 형태로 나누어 구분할 수 있다.

1. 초반 빈칸 유형

이 유형의 문제는 대부분 빈칸에 해당하는 내용이 글의 주제문이고 그 이후의 내용은 주제문에 대한 예시 및 부연설명 등이 이어지므로 빠르게 글을 훑어보고 주제문의 내용을 파악하도록 한다.

2. 중반 빈칸 유형

주로 초반에 언급되는 주제에 대한 예시, 부연설명과 관련된 내용이나 글의 논리적 흐름과 관계되는 내용이 빈칸에 들어가야 한다. 그러므로 빈칸이 등장하기까지의 글들을 빠르게 읽어서 내용을 파악할 수 있는 독해력을 길러두어야 한다. 정답을 고르기 힘들다면, 선택지의 내용을 빠르게 대입시켜 앞뒤 문맥이 맞는 선택지를 고르도록 한다.

3. 후반 빈칸 유형

초반 빈칸 유형과 마찬가지로 끝부분에 등장하는 빈칸 역시 글의 주제문인 경우가 많다. 혹은 주제의 예시, 부연, 설명에 해당하기도 한다. 그러므로 지문의 초반을 자세히 읽어 주제문을 파악하고 그 후는 빠르게 속독하여 빈칸의 내용에 적절한 것을 고를 수 있도록 한다. 이때 주의할 것은, 중간에 연결사가 등장하는 경우인데, 보통 however, but 등의 역접의 접속사가 오는 경우 그 이후의 내용이 주제문이 되는 경우가 많다.

4. 접속(부)사 빈칸 유형

빈칸의 전후 문장을 잘 파악해 그 논리관계에 가장 적절한 보기를 고르도록 한다.

Type 01
초반 빈칸 유형

Check This Out!

Read the passage and choose the option that best fits the blank.

People who play action-packed video games may be _____. Researchers found that those who played action video games experienced significant improvements in their contrast sensitivity. This finding may help people with trouble seeing while they drive at night. Normally, improving contrast sensitivity requires glasses or surgery, but video games seem to train the brain to process visual information more efficiently. The study involved two groups, one playing action games, the other strategy playing games for 50 hours over the course of two months. At the end of the training, the action game players showed an average of 43% improvement in their ability to discern similar shades of grey, while the strategy players showed none.

(a) more susceptible to sensitivity
(b) improving their eyesight
(c) risking their lives with night-driving
(d) causing harm to their brains

해석

액션으로 가득한 비디오 게임을 하는 사람들은 시력을 향상시키고 있는 것일지도 모르겠습니다. 연구원들은 액션 비디오 게임을 하는 사람들이 그들의 대비감도에 있어서 중대한 향상을 경험했다는 것을 발견했습니다. 이러한 조사결과는 밤에 운전을 하는 동안 앞을 보는데 있어서 어려움을 겪는 사람들에게 도움을 줄 수 있을 것입니다. 보통은 대비감도를 향상시키기 위해서는 안경이나 수술을 필요로 합니다. 하지만, 비디오 게임들은 뇌가 시각적 정보를 좀 더 효율적으로 처리할 수 있도록 훈련시키는 것으로 보입니다. 이 조사는 한 그룹은 액션 게임을 하고, 다른 그룹은 전략 게임을 두 달 동안 50시간을 하도록 하는 두 가지 그룹을 포함시켰습니다. 훈련 후에, 액션 게임을 했던 사람들은 평균적으로 비슷한 명암의 회색을 구분하는 능력이 43% 향상된 반면, 전략 게임을 한 사람들은 아무런 변화를 보이지 못했습니다.

해설

단락의 첫 문장이 주제문이다. 이어지는 내용들은 주제문을 뒷받침하는 설명들이다. 빈칸 뒤의 문장에서 액션 게임을 하는 사람들은 대비감도가 향상되었다고 언급하고 있다. 글에 따르면 이 대비감도는 야간운전 시 앞을 보는 것을 도와주는데, 보통 대비감도를 높이기 위해선 안경이나 수술이 필요하다고 말하고 있으므로 결국 비디오 게임이 '시력을 향상시킬 수도 있다'는 (b)가 정답이 되어야 한다.

어휘

action-packed 액션으로 가득한
eyesight 시력
significant 중대한, 귀중한
contrast sensitivity 대비감도
finding 조사결과
normally 정상적으로, 보통은
process 처리하다
strategy 전략
discern 분별하다, 식별하다
shade 명암, 색조

Type 02
중반 빈칸 유형

Check This Out!

Read the passage and choose the option that best fits the blank.

Living in the warm, humid tropics can only be made more pleasurable by wearing cool cotton. At Wicked Weaves, Vicky Johnson, a resort wear and tropical wedding specialist, offers a specialized service and advice to you to complement your body and find the style that _____ _____. Choosing the correct style can make a world of difference on how you look and feel. See the difference Ms. Johnson can make by customizing your garments with design and style that will fit perfectly. American owned and operated by the designer herself, Ms. Johnson has been in the trade for 20 years and now offers a personalized service available for after hour appointments.

(a) is favored by American customers
(b) is in vogue at the moment
(c) meets your budget
(d) best suits your shape

> **해석**
> 따뜻하고 습기가 많은 열대에서 사는 것은 시원한 무명옷을 입음으로써만이 더 즐거워질 수 있습니다. Wicked Weaves의 피서지 의류와 열대 결혼식 전문가인 Vicky Johnson은 당신의 신체를 보완해 주고, 당신의 체형에 가장 잘 어울리는 스타일을 찾기 위해서 전문화된 서비스와 조언을 제공합니다. 올바른 스타일을 선택하는 것은 당신이 어떻게 보일지 그리고 어떻게 느낄지에 큰 차이점을 만들어 낼 수 있습니다. Johnson 씨가 당신에게 완벽하게 어울릴 스타일과 디자인의 의복을 개인에 맞추어 제작함으로써 만들어 낼 차이점을 보십시오. 미국인이 소유하고, 디자이너인 그녀 자신에 의해서 운영되는 이곳에서 Johnson 씨는 20년 동안 일해 왔고, 이제 폐점 시간 이후에도 개인 서비스를 제공하고 있습니다.

 해설

빈칸 앞뒤 문장의 흐름을 이해해야 한다. 빈칸이 포함된 문장에서 신체를 보완할 수 있는 조언과 서비스를 제공한다고 언급되고 있고, 뒤의 문장 중 'Ms. Johnson can make by customizing~fit perfectly'에서 Johnson이 제공하는 서비스는 개인의 신체에 가장 잘 맞고 어울리는 맞춤 의복을 제공한다는 것을 알 수 있다. 그러므로 정답은 (d)이다.

 어휘

tropic 열대(지방)의	garment 의복	suit 어울리다, 적합하다
specialized 전문의	personalize 개인화하다	favor 선호하다
complement 보완하다, 보충하다	in vogue 유행인	
customize 주문을 받아 만들다	budget 예산	

Type 03
후반 빈칸 유형

Check This Out!

Read the passage and choose the option that best fits the blank.

There's more to Hong Kong than shopping. The city has amazing natural beauty, with lush green hills and ocean outlooks. Even so, it's hard to get close to nature when you're in the heart of bustling Hong Kong city. So when someone invites you on a harbor boat trip to spot pink dolphins, you start to wonder if this is some kind of ruse. The species in question is the Indo-Pacific hump-back dolphin and they do still exist, albeit precariously, amid the floating rubbish, freeway-like boat traffic, and sewage of Hong Kong harbor. It doesn't usually take long to spot them. First, a pink beak pops up and appears to do a 360 degrees pirouette, then, out of the ocean flips a pink dolphin, followed by another. To see these cute creatures larking around the water is remarkable, _____
_____.

(a) a scene which has made Hong Kong famous
(b) a most unexpected side of Hong Kong
(c) the show which tourists visit Hong Kong for
(d) a view visitors can spot anywhere in Hong Kong

해석

홍콩은 쇼핑 이상의 것이 있습니다. 이 도시는 푸르게 우거진 녹색 언덕들과 바다 전경과 함께 놀라운 자연의 아름다움을 가지고 있지요. 그렇다고는 하나, 여러분들이 번잡한 홍콩시의 중심에 있을 때, 자연에 가까이 가는 것은 어려운 일입니다. 그래서 누군가가 여러분을 분홍색 돌고래를 보기 위한 항구 배 여행에 초대를 하면, 여러분은 뭔가 계략이 있지 않나 궁금해 하기 시작합니다. 이 의문의 종은 인도-태평양 혹등고래로, 이들은 비록 불안정하지만 홍콩 항구의 떠다니는 쓰레기, 다차선식 고속도로와 같은 보트 교통 그리고 하수 오물에 에워 쌓여서도 아직 존재하고 있습니다. 그들을 발견하는 것은 보통 그렇게 오래 걸리지 않습니다. 우선, 분홍색 주둥이가 불쑥 나오고 360도 회전을 하기 위해서 몸을 드러냅니다. 그리고서 바다 밖으로 핑크색 돌고래가 휙 튀어 나오고 다른 돌고래들도 이어집니다. 이 귀여운 생물들이 물 주위에서 장난치는 모습은 놀랍고, 홍콩의 가장 예상치 못했던 면이지요.

해설

쇼핑으로 유명한 홍콩 시티의 또 다른 볼거리인 항구의 돌고래에 관한 내용이다. 중간에 'you start to wonder ~ ruse' 에서 대부분의 사람들은 홍콩의 항구에 돌고래가 살고 있다는 사실에 대해서 모르는 것이 일반적이란 것을 알 수 있다. 그러므로 빈칸은 '홍콩의 가장 예상치 못했던 면'이라는 (b)가 정답이 된다.

어휘

lush 푸르게 우거진	albeit 비록 ~지만	lark 장난치다
bustling 번잡한	precariously 위험하게, 불안정하게	unexpected 예상치 못한
spot 발견하다	sewage 하수, 오물	
ruse 책략, 계략	spot 발견하다	

Type 04
접속(부)사 빈칸 유형

30 DAYS TEPS 800+Final Sum-up

Check This Out

Read the passage and choose the option that best fits the blank.

A government minister speeding down the ski slopes collided with another skier, killing her. Yet far from the accident wrecking his career, he got off with a fine and a slap on the wrist. The court's leniency—a $ 33,000 fine for involuntary manslaughter and the case heard behind closed doors—proves that those in the higher echelons can expect special treatment. _____, there are people who say it's only because he belongs to that hated breed of politician that he's getting a public pillorying. They say he wasn't drunk and an accident like that could happen to anyone, and insisting that politicians should be infallible is ridiculous. Anyway, the minister was badly hurt and is undergoing therapy, and must live with the guilt for the rest of his life. It seems the real question now is whether he is well enough for the job, not whether he is morally suited for it.

(a) Therefore
(b) As a result
(c) On the contrary
(d) For example

🔓 해석

스키 경사지를 빠르게 내려오던 정부 장관이 다른 스키를 타던 사람과 충돌하여 그녀가 사망하게 되었습니다. 이 사건으로 인해 그의 경력이 파괴되는 것과는 거리가 멀게, 그는 벌금과 가벼운 질책만으로 형벌을 면했습니다. 본의 아닌 살인에 따른 33,000달러의 벌금과 비공개로 재판이 진행이 되도록 한 법원의 관대함은 이러한 높은 계층의 사람들은 특별대우를 기대할 수 있다는 것을 증명합니다. 반면에, 몇몇 사람들은 그가 증오를 받는 종족이라고 할 수 있는 정치인이기 때문에 공개 비웃음거리가 되는 것이라고 말합니다. 그들은 그가 취했던 것도 아니고 이러한 종류의 사고는 누구에게나 일어날 수 있는 것이라 하며, 정치인들은 결코 잘못이 없어야 한다고 주장하는 것은 어리석은 짓이라고 말합니다. 어쨌든, 장관은 심하게 다쳤고 치료를 받고 있는 중입니다. 그리고 그의 남은 삶 동안 죄책감을 가지고 살아야 합니다. 이제 문제는 그가 도덕적으로 직책에 적합한지 그렇지 않은지가 아니라 그가 직책을 수행하기에 충분히 건강한지 그렇지 않은지로 보입니다.

🔓 해설

스키를 타던 중 사고로 사람을 죽이게 된 정치인이 비공개로 재판을 받고, 벌금형만을 선고 받은 것에 대한 두 가지 의견을 대조하여 제시하고 있다. 빈칸 앞의 내용은 이러한 내용이 높은 계층에 대한 특별대우라고 주장하는 의견이고, 빈칸 뒤는 정치인도 사람이며 이러한 사고는 누구에게나 일어날 수 있다고 주장하는 내용이다. 그러므로 빈칸에 들어갈 접속사는 (c)의 'on the contrary(이에 반하여)'가 정답이다.

🔍 어휘

minister 장관, 각료
speed down 빠른 속도로 내려오다
collide 충돌하다
yet 그럼에도 불구하고
wreck 파괴하다
get off with ~로 빠져나가다
manslaughter 과실치사
echelon 계층
pillory 웃음거리로 만들다
infallible 결코 잘못이 없는

Part 2
30 DAYS TEPS 800 + Final Sum-up

내용 파악 유형

Part 2 (21문항) : 주어진 지문을 읽고 질문에 적절한 답변을 찾는 문제 유형으로 총 21개의 문제가 출제된다. 먼저 질문을 빠르게 읽고 묻고 있는 내용이 무엇인지 파악한 후 이를 상기하며 지문을 읽어가도록 한다.

1. 대의 파악 및 제목 찾기 유형

대의 파악 또는 제목 찾기 문제유형은 모두 지문의 핵심주제가 무엇인지를 알아내는 것이 핵심이다. 일반적으로 글의 주제는 지문의 첫 부분 또는 끝 부분에서 들어남으로, 우선적으로 이 부분을 주의 깊게 읽어서 이해할 수 있어야 한다. 하지만, 앞서서 말한 내용을 뒤집어 버릴 수 있는 but, however, although, nevertheless 등의 역접, 상관, 양보의 접속사가 지문 중에 등장한다면, 그 뒤에 이어지는 부분이 주제문이 되는 경우가 있으니 주의하도록 한다.

2. 세부 내용 파악 유형

세부 내용 파악 유형의 문제는 지문을 읽어 내려가면서 적절히 (a)~(d)의 보기들과 비교하여 정답을 찾는 연습을 해놓는 것이 중요하다. 이 과정에서 명백히 오답인 보기는 X로 표시해 배제하여 오답율을 줄이고, 나머지 보기를 지문의 해당 부분과 자세히 진위 여부를 비교하여 정답을 골라 낼 수 있도록 한다. 보기의 선택지들은 절대 지문의 내용과 똑같이 문장이 제시되지 않고 paraphrasing 되어서 제시되니 헷갈리지 않도록 주의해야 한다.

3. 추론 유형

추론 유형의 문제는 세부 내용 파악 유형의 문제와 마찬가지로 지문을 읽어 내려가면서 적절히 (a)~(d)의 보기들과 비교하여 정답을 찾는 연습을 해놓는 것이 중요하다. 또는 반대로 선택지를 먼저 읽어 보고, 지문을 읽으면서 내용에서 벗어나는 보기들을 제거하며 정답을 좁혀나가는 것도 좋은 방법이 될 수 있다. 추론 문제를 해결함에 있어서 중요한 것은 주어진 내용을 바탕으로 지나치게 확대 해석하거나 논리적 비약의 보기를 정답으로 선택하지 않는 것이다.

Type 05
대의 파악·제목 찾기 유형

30 DAYS TEPS 800+Final Sum-up

Check This Out!

Choose the option that correctly answers the question.

A father used a kitchen knife to slash his son across the chest in a tragic family dispute. Michael Loman faced the first day of his District Court trial charged with one count of unlawful wounding after the alleged incident. Prosecutor Bob Coleman told the court a dispute arose after Mr. Loman's son went to the house to collect personal items and told his dad he did not want to see him any more. Mr. Loman allegedly lunged at his son twice, before using a kitchen knife to inflict the would, which later required 22 stitches. His son left the house after the alleged incident and started yelling abuse on his father's driveway before leaving the house by car.

Q: What is the best title for the news article?

(a) Spoiled teenagers these days.
(b) A father who frequently abused his son.
(c) A rising trend of family disruption.
(d) Domestic violence resulting in injury.

 해석

비극적인 가족 간의 다툼에서 아버지가 부엌칼로 아들의 가슴을 가로지르는 상처를 내었습니다. 본 사건 이후에 Michael Loman 씨는 아들에게 법이 용납할 수 없는 부상을 입힌 죄로 지방법원에서 재판 첫 날을 맞이했습니다. Bob Coleman 검사는 법원에서 Loman 씨의 아들이 개인용 물품을 가져가려고 집에 와서 그에게 더 이상 그를 보기 원치 않는다고 말하면서 다툼이 발생했다고 말했습니다. 알려진 바에 의하면, Loman 씨는 부엌칼을 이용해 그의 아들에게 22 바늘을 꿰매야 한 상처를 입히기 전, 두 번에 걸쳐서 그의 아들에게 달려들었다고 합니다. 그의 아들은 차를 타고 집을 떠나기 전에 그의 아버지 차고 앞 길에서 그의 아버지가 자신을 상처 입혔음을 소리쳤습니다.

질문유형

What is the passage about?
What is the main topic of the passage?
What is the main idea of the passage?
What is the best title for the passage?

 해설

아버지와 아들간의 다툼 끝에 아버지가 칼로 아들에게 깊은 상처를 입혔다는 내용의 뉴스 기사이다. 사건 전체의 내용을 판단해 봤을 때, '상처로 끝난 가정폭력'인 (d)가 정답이다. 기사 어디에도 아버지가 아들을 지속적으로 학대했다는 내용은 없으므로 (b)는 정답이 될 수 없으며, 이 한 사건으로 (c)의 '가정 붕괴의 증가추세'란 제목을 쓰는 건 지나친 비약이다.

 어휘

slash 베다, 상처를 입히다	alleged 주장되는, 추정되는	abuse 욕설
tragic 비극적인	lunge 찌르다, 돌진하다	disruption 분열
dispute 말다툼, 논쟁, 싸움	inflict (타격, 상처 등을) 입히다	spoiled 버릇없는
be charged with ~의 혐의를 받다	frequently 빈번하게	domestic 가정(의)

Type 06
세부 내용 파악 유형

PART 02

30 DAYS TEPS 800+Final Sum-up

Check This Out !

Choose the option that correctly answers the question.

Nannies, like registered child-care centers, must have qualifications or, at least, many years of experience caring for children and appropriate references. A nanny can come to your home daily or live-in to care for your children. The role of a nanny involves child-care education and development, nutrition and meals for the children, cleaning their bedrooms and play areas, nursery duties, such as changing diapers, and shopping for the children. Nannies are popular because they offer one-on-one care for your child, which is especially important in the early years. Babies can be held more often and comforted when crying. The children are cared for in a familiar environment, which means you can set the rules for them.

Q: Which of the following is correct according to the passage?

(a) There are no qualifications to become a nanny.
(b) It is the nanny's job to cook for the whole family.
(c) Paying close attention to children is very important.
(d) It is necessary to let nannies make their own rules.

해석

유모들은 등록된 보육원들과 마찬가지로 반드시 자격증을 가지고 있거나 또는 최소한 아이들을 돌봐온 수년간의 경력과 적절한 신원보증인들이 있어야만 한다. 유모는 매일 당신의 집을 방문할 수도 있고, 또는 아이들을 돌보기 위해서 거주를 하면서 일할 수도 있다. 유모의 역할은 육아교육 및 발달, 영양공급과 아이들을 위한 식사, 침실과 놀이장소의 청소, 귀저기를 갈아주는 것과 같은 육아임무와 아이들을 위한 쇼핑이 포함된다. 유모는 인기가 많은데 왜냐하면 그들은 아이들을 위해 일대일의 보살핌을 제공하기 때문이다. 이는 특히 아이들의 어린 시절에 중요하다. 아기들은 울음을 터트릴 때 좀 더 많이 안길 수 있고, 위로 받을 수 있다. 아이들은 친숙한 환경에서 보살핌을 받게 되므로 이는 곧, 여러분이 규칙을 정할 수 있다는 것을 의미한다.

질문유형
Which of the following is correct according to the passage?   Why did the man reject the company's offer?
Which of the following is correct about the heart cancer?

해설
보육원 대신에 직접 집에서 아이들을 돌봐줄 수 있는 유모와 관련한 내용을 담고 있는 지문이다. 끝에서 아이들이 어릴 때, 일대일의 보살핌이 중요하다고 했으므로, 보기 (c)의 '아이들에게 친밀한 관심을 주는 것은 매우 중요하다' 가 정답이다. 규칙을 정하는 것은 유모를 고용한 부모지 유모가 아니므로 (d)는 정답이 될 수 없다.

어휘
nanny 유모
registered 등록된
child-care 보육원(의)
qualification 자격(증), 조건
experience 경험하다
references 참조인, 신용보증인
nursery 육아, 탁아
one-on-one 일대일의

Type 07
추론 유형

Check This Out!

Choose the option that correctly answers the question.

Could fast food be the secret to long life? Probably not, but with cheese burgers as her favorite food, Vera Jackson, 98, hasn't let the burgers and fries get in her way. She also enjoys her coffee and biscuits, and at 98, why not? She eats fast food once or twice a week, but she said her secret to a long life was in her genes. And she might be on to something, with her grandfather living to 105—without the aid of fast food—and her sister living to 89. She says she also prays a lot and her strong faith has helped her. Ms Jackson had lived a normal life and followed a strict routine, also walked a lot. Her family says that she is very independent. She does everything for herself, and no one can do anything for her.

Q: What can be inferred from the passage?

(a) Vera Jackson lives long thanks to fast food.
(b) Vera Jackson outlived her grandfather.
(c) Vera Jackson comes of a long-lived family.
(d) Vera Jackson loves to do things unexpected.

해석

패스트푸드가 장수를 위한 비밀이 될 수 있을까요? 아마도 아니겠죠. 하지만 가장 좋아하는 음식이 치즈버거인 98살의 Vera Jackson 씨는 햄버거와 감자튀김이 그녀에게 (그녀의 건강에) 방해가 되지 못했습니다. 그녀는 또한 커피와 비스킷을 즐깁니다. 98살에 말이죠. 안될 게 뭐 있겠습니까? 그녀는 일주일에 한 번 또는 두 번 패스트푸드를 먹지만, 그녀는 자신의 장수의 비결이 그녀의 유전자에 있다고 말합니다. 그리고 그녀의 할아버지가 패스트푸드의 도움 없이 105살까지 사셨고, 그녀의 여동생이 89살까지 살았다는 것을 보면 그녀에게 무언가가 있을지도 모르겠습니다. 그녀는 그녀가 항상 기도를 많이 하고, 그녀의 강한 신앙이 그녀를 도와왔다고 말합니다. 그녀의 가족들은 그녀가 매우 독립적이라고 말합니다. 그녀는 스스로 모든 것을 하고 그 누구도 그녀를 위해 무언가를 할 수는 없다고 합니다.

질문유형
What can be inferred from the passage?
Which of the following can be inferred from the passage?
What is the next paragraph likely to be about?

해설
내용을 통해, Vera Jackson 뿐만이 아니라, 그녀의 할아버지와 그녀의 동생도 오랫동안 살았음을 알 수 있다. 이를 통해 '그녀는 장수하는 집안 출신이다' 라는 정답 (c)를 유추해 낼 수 있다.

어휘
get in one's way 방해되다
gene 유전자
aid 도움, 원조
pray 기도하다
routine 일상(의)
thanks to ~덕분에
outlive ~보다도 오래 살다
unexpected 예상치 못한

Part 3

30 DAYS TEPS 800 + Final Sum-up

내용 일관성 파악 유형

Part 3 (3문항) : 주어진 지문을 읽고 글을 구성하는 문장들 중에서 일관성이 떨어지는 것을 고르는 문제유형으로 총 3문제가 출제된다.

내용 일관성 유형의 경우 선택지에 포함되지 않는 지문의 첫 번째 문장에 전체 글의 주제가 드러나 있다. 이 주제를 바탕으로 보기 (a) ~(d)까지 세심하게 읽으며, 지문이 얘기하고자 하는 주제와 다소 동떨어진 내용이 등장한다거나 논리적 비약이 보이는 선택지를 고르면 된다. 예를 들어, '집에 일찍 들어가는 것의 중요성'을 주제로 '집에 일찍 들어가면 덜 피곤하다', '집에 일찍 들어가면 위험하지 않다' 등으로 이야기를 펼쳐 나가다 중간에 '야근이 있어서 집에 늦게 들어갔다'와 같은 보기가 주어진다면 바로 이것이 문맥상 일관성이 떨어지는 정답 선택지가 되는 것이다.

Type 08
문맥 파악 유형

Check This Out !

Identify the sentence that least fits the context of the passage.

One of the major reasons for drug use and abuse is the fact that the media glamorizes their use by such terms as "recreational" drugs and the newly-favored term, "party" drugs. (a) This kind of glamorization makes so many people fall victim to drug overdoses. (b) However, they cannot blame authorities, suppliers or society because the fault is their own. (c) Drugs are universally available and selling them generates all sorts of other crimes. (d) At the end of the day, the choice to use drugs rests with the individual.

해석

마약을 이용하고 남용하는 중요한 이유들 중 하나는 언론이 "기분전환용" 마약, 그리고 새롭게 애용되는 용어인 "파티" 마약이라는 용어들로 마약의 사용을 미화시키고 있다는 사실이다. (a) 이러한 종류의 미화가 엄청 많은 사람들이 마약 과다복용의 희생자가 되게끔 한다. (b) 하지만, 그들은 실수는 그들 자신의 것이기 때문에 당국이나, 공급자 또는 사회를 비난할 수 없다. (c) 마약은 도처에서 입수가 가능하고 그것들을 판매하는 것은 모든 종류의 다른 범죄들을 낳는다. (d) 결국, 마약을 사용하는 선택은 개인에게 달린 것이다.

 해설

마약이 이용되고 남용되는 이유 중 하나로 언론에 의한 마약의 미화를 전제로 이야기를 끌어가고 있다. (a)에서는 이러한 미화가 많은 사람들을 마약과다복용으로 이끌고, (b)에서는 하지만 그렇다고 해도 결국 잘못은 자신의 것이지 다른 이들을 비난할 수 없다는 것, (d)에서는 결국 선택은 자신의 몫이라고 이야기하고 있다. 반면, (c)는 전체 흐름과 관계없이 마약의 입수, 그리고 마약의 판매로 인한 범죄를 언급하고 있으므로 문맥에 어울리지 않는 문장이라고 할 수 있다. 정답은 (c)이다.

 어휘

abuse 남용, 오용
glamorize 미화하다
recreation 휴양, 기분전환
term 용어
generate 낳다, 발생시키다
fall a victim to ~의 희생자가 되다
blame 비난하다
overdose 과잉투여
authorities 당국, 권력기관
universally 보편적으로, 전 세계적으로

Pre-Test

30 DAYS TEPS 800 ✚ Final Sum-up

- **Pre-Test • 1**
- **Pre-Test • 2**
- **Pre-Test • 3**

Type 01 초반 빈칸 유형

Type 02 중반 빈칸 유형

Type 03 후반 빈칸 유형

Type 04 접속(부)사 빈칸 유형

Type 05 대의 파악 유형

Type 06 세부 내용 파악 유형

Type 07 추론 유형

Type 08 문맥 파악 유형

Pre-Test · 1

Type 01 초반 빈칸 유형

Have you noticed how tricky it is for American women to _____? American women talk about anything and everything, from our husbands' bald spots spreading, to the price of petrol rising, to the fungal infection we got from a pedicure. And that's what we discuss with the man who comes to fix the fridge. We simply don't feel feminie having a conversation about money. We can question the cost of a coffee and talk about the prices of supermarkets. We also enthuse about a bargain but we do it for the indignation or the envy, those vital ingredients for a satisfying life. Come to think of it, women seem to be perfectly happy to talk about money going out, but not about the money coming in.

(a) backbite other people
(b) talk about money
(c) maintain friendly relationships with others
(d) discuss daily routines

Type 02 중반 빈칸 유형

The Subaru Forester combines functionality and beauty to produce an outstanding driving experience. Premium styling and sweeping contemporary lines set a new standard in style. Intelligent use of interior space _____, functionality and flexibility to handle anything your weekday routine or weekend adventures can throw at it. Across the range, from the fully equipped Forester X through to the luxurious Forester XS, the engineering and superior safety philosophy for which Subaru is renowned is very evident.

(a) delivers exceptional car-like handling
(b) offers unbeatable speed and versatility
(c) provides electronic stability control
(d) offers greater seating comfort

Type 03 후반 빈칸 유형

Archaeologists and forensic experts believe they have identified the skeleton of Cleopatra's younger sister who was murdered more than 2000 years ago, says The Washington Post. Princess Arsinoe was put to death in 41 BC on the orders of Cleopatra and her Roman lover, Mark Antony, to eliminate her as a rival to the Egyptian throne. Arsinoe and Cleopatra were both descendants of Ptolemy, the Macedonian general who ruled Egypt after Alexander the Great, but they had different mothers. The remains were found in Turkey and, if genuine, indicate that Arsinoe's mother had African origins. The discovery challenges long-held beliefs about Cleopatra's family and suggests she, too, _____.

(a) lost her mother when she was young
(b) was a Turkish
(c) was probably of mixed race
(d) was put to death

Type 04 접속(부)사 빈칸 유형

Sugar is totally devoid of the protein, vitamins, minerals, essential fats, dietary fiber or any of the essential nutrients we need each day. It provides nothing except calories, making it the ultimate junk food. If you eat all the goodies the body needs and are active enough to also burn off the calories from sugar, the main problem it causes is its adverse effects on teeth. _____, for the two-thirds of American men, half of the women and a quarter of our children who are overweight or obese, sugar simply adds calories that are likely to contribute to weight problems.

(a) Likewise
(b) However
(c) For example
(d) As a result

Type 05 대의 파악 유형

A research shows that Americans collectively throw away more than three million tones of food each year, which means that one in every five bags of shopping is going straight in the bin. According to the American Institute, an independent public research center, food waste costs us more than 5 billion dollars annually, and the main food group going to waste is fresh fruit and vegetables. This means the billions of liters of water, fuel and other resources used to produce and deliver this food are also being wasted. Therefore, to start reducing your food waste, be mindful of how much you're throwing away and the impact that it's having on the environment, not to mention your wallet.

Q: What is the main idea of the passage?

(a) Americans are intentionally wasting lots of money by throwing away food.
(b) Americans are not eating recommended amount of fruit and vegetables.
(c) Americans should be aware of the consequences of food waste.
(d) Americans save money by buying less food.

Type 06 세부 내용 파악 유형

If you are a first home buyer you may be eligible for additional support from the Australian Government through the "First Home Owners Boost". To be eligible for up to $21,000, you must enter into a contract to purchase or construct a home between 12 November 2008 and 29 May 2009. If you are a first home buyer who purchases an existing home, you may receive an extra $7,000, taking the total payment to $14,000. If you are a first home buyer who constructs or purchases a new home, you may receive an extra $14,000, taking the total payment to $21,000. The Boost can be used to buy a property of any value. To be eligible for the Boost, you must be at least 18 years of age and be an Australian citizen, or permanent resident.

Q: Which of the following is correct according to the passage?

(a) Anyone who lives in Australia is eligible for the Boost.
(b) A person who entered into a contract in March 2009 is not eligible for the support.
(c) The maximum amount of money a person can get from the Boost is $28,000.
(d) The price of houses doesn't affect the eligibility of successful candidates.

Type 07 추론 유형

Often referred to as "Little Madrid", Buenos Aires is the vibrant, cosmopolitan capital of Argentina. European in flavor, it retains a South American swagger, where cobbled streets and old-time cafes compete with modern architecture. It all comes together to produce one fascinating city. Visitors will find fantastic shopping, an energetic nightlife, incredible antique markets, arguably the best steaks in the world, and cake shops and ice-creameries on every corner. The locals are mostly Italian and Spanish descent, which makes for good wine, great food and fiery people!

Q: What can be inferred from the passage?

(a) The city is located close to Madrid.
(b) Old coffee shops are strongly competing with new coffee chains.
(c) Visitors can enjoy dancing and drinking all night long.
(d) The local people are mixed bloods of Spanish and Italian.

Type 08 문맥 파악 유형

A new stem-cell technique can enlarge breasts while reducing the waistline. (a) The treatment for breast enlargement involves taking stem cells from excess fat on the butt, thigh or stomach, and then growing them in the breasts. (b) Doctors say that breasts treated with stem cells would feel more natural because the tissue has the same softness as the rest of the breast. (c) Implants are associated with long-term complications and require replacement. (d) Currently, the process can only make breasts one cup size bigger, but it is expected larger augmentations will be possible as the technique develops.

Pre-Test·2

Type 01 초반 빈칸 유형

Network your home with Sky Home Broadband, and then _____
_____ from anywhere in your home without messy wires. While you're downloading a movie in the study or researching holidays in the garden, the kids can be playing games in the family room or surfing the internet in the kitchen. Plus day or night helps is available on a wide range of queries, simply by phoning our award-winning 24/7 technical support center. All of which makes for a much happier household, and it costs less than you might think.

    (a) you can give your friends a call
    (b) everyone can watch their favorite programs on television
    (c) you can remote control all electric appliances
    (d) everyone can be online at the same time

Type 02 중반 빈칸 유형

Dog lovers often claim their dogs can communicate complex emotions and this idea lies at the heart of the novel Dog Boy. The dog boy of the title is Romochka, a four-year-old child abandoned by his parents in a Moscow flat. Starving and distressed, the child wanders onto the street and follows a large yellow dog to her hiding place. There he is adopted into a litter of suckling puppies, and _____.
Through Romochka's perspective, we catch a glimpse of what it might be like to switch species. The events of Dog Boy are rich in interest and ideas, and set down in strong, plain language.

    (a) learns how to love other creatures
    (b) trains them to follow people's commands
    (c) leaves on a journey to find his parents
    (d) begins to forget his human habits

Type 03 후반 빈칸 유형

A slump is never good news, whether it's happening to the global economy, or to your own body. Yet slumping, both seated and standing versions, has become so much a part of our postural habits that a recent study by The George Institute for International Health found more than 10 million Americans have recurrent back and neck problems. When your posture is all wrong, the disc of your vertebrae are strained and squashed, which can cause them to deteriorate. You also engage the wrong muscles, putting unnecessary stress on your neck, chest and shoulders, and even your jaw and throat. Slouching and slumping also compresses your rib cage, making it more difficult to take in deep breaths. The resulting shallow breathing _____ by not supplying enough oxygen through your entire body. No wonder you feel tired!

(a) affects your clear thinking
(b) makes you feel edgy
(c) makes you fatigued and sluggish
(d) completely paralyzes you

Type 04 접속(부)사 빈칸 유형

Internet is a remarkable invention. It is a valuable tool that provides people with opportunities for learning, getting in touch with friends by email, finding information, shopping and for chatting to other people with similar interests. _____, it is safe to say that the Internet is an adult environment, with few limits on what is posted on it, and where the information may not always be sound and reliable. As such, it is obvious that it can often be a very dangerous place for children to play. Most of young boys and girls at some stage will have some sort of contact with the Internet. That is why parents should understand the influence of the technology and monitor the Internet access of your children.

(a) However
(b) Furthermore
(c) For example
(d) In other words

Type 05 대의 파악 유형

A substance similar to hippopotamus sweat could one day protect us from sunburn. Hippos can stand in the hot sun all day without getting burnt thanks to a glandular secretion that contains microscopic particles to scatter light, protecting the animals from burns. Scientists hope to create a sunscreen product inspired by hippo sweat. Researcher Christopher Viney from the University of California is also attempting to replicate the antiseptic and insect repellent characteristics of the sweat. This would form the basis of a four-in-one product: sunscreen, sunblock, antiseptic and insect repellent. It would be an advertiser's dream as long as the product doesn't smell like a hippo.

Q: What is the passage mainly about?

(a) The importance of using sun protection.
(b) Scientists' effort to understand hippos.
(c) Positive properties of hippo sweat.
(d) The newly invented cosmetics made from hippo sweat.

Type 06 세부 내용 파악 유형

It is recommended that you sleep aboard the vessel the night before the voyage in order to let your body get used to the boat's motion. However, this may not be possible in small boats. Otherwise, you can take seasickness tablets, but be cautious as some may make you drowsy. If you feel seasick, you need to keep yourself busy and stay in the fresh air. You should avoid the head down position, as this aggravates illness. It is also helpful to nibble on a dry biscuit, chew gums or dried fruit. Ginger is also considered a good anti-seasickness remedy. Don't forget to stay out of enclosed areas where fumes from fuel and food odors may temporarily collect. Experienced sailors keep their diet free of greasy foods and alcohol both before going to sea and while aboard.

Q: Which of the following is correct according to the passage?

(a) Seasickness occurs due to the small size of vessels.
(b) Some of the seasickness pills may cause sleepiness.
(c) Dried fruit is considered to be an effective medicine for seasickness.
(d) Sailors supply refreshments for the people on board.

Type 07 추론 유형

Twenty-nine-year old Iranian blogger Omid Mirsayafi died in Iran's notorious Evin prison after taking an overdose of medication. Omid was suffering from depression. Another political prisoner, Dr. Hessam Firouzi, leaked news of the death and accused prison authorities of not taking Omid's illness seriously. The young blogger had been jailed for 30 months in February due to the post insulting the country's Supreme Leader, and the Islamic Republic's founder. Another political prisoner, Amir Saran, suffered a stroke and died earlier this month. His family also accused prison authorities of negligence.

Q: What can be inferred from the passage?

(a) Omid Mirsayafi died following the misprescription of drugs.
(b) Amir Saran died from a stroke despite treatment attempts.
(c) Officials in prison are not responsible for the death of the two people.
(d) Iranian internet users have no freedom of expression on the net.

Type 08 문맥 파악 유형

Early food experiences can set a life time of eating pattern and influence health status later in life. (a) The use of food as a reward can send inappropriate messages to our children that can adversely affect both their short and long term health. (b) Frequently, quick and easy rewards such as sweets and soft drinks given to our children encourages them to believe that these low nutritional foods and drinks are a more desirable choice than other healthier options. (c) The best time for sweets is prior to exercise or after a main meal. (d) Also, they begin to associate achievement and reward for good behavior with sweets when it should be understood that there is no connection between behavior and food.

Pre-Test·3

Type 01 초반 빈칸 유형

The Iowa Supreme Court unanimously upheld a lower court decision overturning as unconstitutional a state law that defined marriage as_____ _____. In doing so, the court made Iowa the third state in the US, with Massachusetts and Connecticut, in which gay and lesbian marriage will be legal. On the other hand, California legalized gay marriage in 2008 only to have it overturned by a referendum. A challenge to that result is now before the California Supreme Court. Meanwhile, votes in the New Hampshire and Vermont legislatures are moving those states closer to approving same-sex unions.

(a) a union between persons of the same race
(b) open to both opposite and same-gender couples
(c) a contract for the production of children
(d) exclusive to heterosexual partners

Type 02 중반 빈칸 유형

Helicobacter pylori is the bacteria that sometimes causes gastritis and stomach ulcers. They survive in the acidic environment of the stomach, and symptoms can include bloating, reflux, belching, nausea and abdominal pain. Medical treatment is two types of antibiotics and a stomach acid suppressor over one to two weeks. But, there's concern the bacteria are becoming resistant to antibiotics and treatment may cause bad side effects. On the other hand, _____ treating the bug with probiotics, unartificial alkalisers to reduce stomach acid, and other nutrients to improve stomach function.

(a) Synthetic drug treatment includes
(b) The faster way to cure stomach ulcers includes
(c) The most efficient treatment to eliminate the bug involves
(d) The natural approach involves

Type 03 후반 빈칸 유형

More renowned for smoothing the furrowed foreheads of stars, Botox can now be used to help people recover from a stroke. The treatment, which relaxes face muscles for cosmetic reasons, can also reduce upper limb spasticity, a stiffening of the muscles that can immobilize the arms and cause a victim's hands to clench permanently. Botox is now used for the treatment of moderate to severe cases of upper-limb spasticity, a common effect of stroke. Doctors can now offer the treatment when alternative muscle-relaxant drugs fail, or in conjunction with physiotherapy to help restore _____.

(a) brain damage due to stroke
(b) the ability to walk erect
(c) the use of stroke-affected limbs
(d) healthy and radiant skin

Type 04 접속(부)사 찾기 유형

The majority of pedestrian fatalities last year were elderly, young or intoxicated. Many pedestrian deaths are on roads signposted at 50~60 km/h. The 50 km/h limit will work if only drivers stick to it. _____, some drivers think pedestrian safety is not their concern. At 50 km/h, a pedestrian will probably still be killed, but an alert driver who brakes could save their life. If the suburban limit was dropped to 40 km/h, and the limit was policed, the death toll might drop. If you wait that extra five seconds rather than play chicken with traffic, it might drop. Develop one of your own action plan. Then, the life saved might be yours.

(a) In consequence
(b) For all that
(c) Similarly
(d) Unfortunately

Type 05 대의 파악 유형

A new kind of Automatic Teller Machine is being launched in America that can vary its transaction charges depending on the time of day, says The New York Times. The CashOut is being promoted as a way for pub owners to raise transaction fees at times when clients are more likely to be intoxicated. The company has suggested that on Saturday nights the charge to draw cash could go from $1.50 to $2 after 11 pm. " Most people will start not to care about the charge after that time", said the company. They are expecting to have 50 CashOut operating in pubs across New York by the end of the month.

Q: What is the best title for the passage?

(a) A rise in transaction fees of Automatic Teller Machines.
(b) How intoxication causes reckless behavior.
(c) An introduction of an innovative Automatic Teller Machine.
(d) A prospering future for pub owners.

Type 06 세부 내용 파악 유형

A meeting of more than 2,000 scientists and economists has warned that the 2007 worst-case predictions of the Intergovernmental Panel on Climate Change have been realized and that the continued failure of governments to act on global warming could see abrupt or irreversible climate shifts. They warned of consequent social and economic catastrophe. On the bright side, the meeting, in preparation for the United Nations Climate Change Conference in Copenhagen in December this year, emphasized that governments now had the technology to control climate change if they chose to act. Meanwhile, more than 600 climate change skeptics met in New York, challenging the view that global warming is linked to human activity.

Q: Which of the following is correct according to the passage?

(a) Economists and scientists fight against each other for different reasons.
(b) The UN Climate Change Conference will be held in December next year.
(c) Nations do not have the technology to control environmental change.
(d) People gathered in New York think humans do not affect global warming.

Type 07 추론 유형

It is hard to believe that biting into a peanut butter sandwich almost proved fatal for a young boy. The two-year-old toddler has since been diagnosed with a life threatening allergy to peanuts and tree nuts. It was one year ago when he took a bit of his sister's peanut butter sandwich and suffered anaphylaxis. His family have made significant lifestyle changes as a result of his allergy. Wherever the boy goes, there is an adrenaline auto-injector close by, ready to be administered should the toddler suffer an anaphylactic reaction. Then, there is grocery shopping and reading labels carefully to ensure products carry no traces of peanuts or tree nuts. And when the family dines out, it means verifying whether peanuts or tree nuts are part of any of the dishes.

Q: What can be inferred from the passage?

(a) Kids are more likely to develop peanut allergy.
(b) The boy inherited the allergy from his father.
(c) The boy is the only one who was the peanut allergy in his family.
(d) The boy is taken to the hospital when he needs to get an injection.

Type 08 문맥 파악 유형

Traditionally here in the UK, Sunday has always been the day of the week to enjoy a really good and hearty lunch. (a) With that in mind, this month's recipes are all about comforting, delicious food. (b) I've used one of my favourite birds—duck—and a roasted lamb shoulder in my arrosto misto recipe. (c) In some respects, slow cooking is quick cooking. (d) Arrost misto means 'mixed roast' and is a simple but wonderful Italian dish that includes different joints of meat roasted together.

Section 02

30 DAYS TEPS 800+Final Sum-up

독해 10가지 주제별(Theme) 접근법

TEPS 시험에 출제가 되는 독해 지문은 크게 10가지 정도의 주제로 분류해 볼 수 있다.

따라서 각 주제별로 어떤 종류의 지문들이 출제가 될 수 있는지 실전 문제를 통해서 확인해 보고, 관련된 어휘들을 정리하여 외워두는 것은 실전 시험을 대비해 학습자들이 반드시 거쳐야 하는 과정이다.

예를 들어 광고문이 출제된다면 어떠한 제품이 광고되고 있는지 제품의 특징은 무엇인지와 같은 큰 틀을 위주로 하여 문제가 출제될 수 있기 때문에 사전에 광고문들을 따로 모아서 앞에서 배운 각 유형별로 다양한 문제들을 풀어보고, 등장 가능한 필수 어휘들을 모아서 정리해 둔다면 분명 실전을 대비하는 데 있어서 큰 도움이 될 것이다.

이번 Section에서는 총 10가지 주제별로 유형을 달리한 문제들로 구성된 Mini-Test를 제공한다. 학습자들은 각 주제에 해당하는 서로 다른 유형의 문제들을 풀어봄으로써 실전 시험에 대한 적응력을 높이고, 간략한 어휘 정리를 통해서 자신감을 높일 수 있을 것이다.

- **Theme 01** 광고(Advertisement)
  - Mini-Test
- **Theme 02** 안내 공고(Announcement)
  - Mini-Test
- **Theme 03** 편지 에세이(Letters · Essays)
  - Mini-Test
- **Theme 04** 뉴스(News)
  - Mini-Test
- **Theme 05** 정치 경제(Politics · Economics)
  - Mini-Test
- **Theme 06** 과학 기술 우주(Science · Technology · Universe)
  - Mini-Test
- **Theme 07** 역사 인물(History · People)
  - Mini-Test
- **Theme 08** 환경 생물(Environment · Life)
  - Mini-Test
- **Theme 09** 건강 의학(Health · Medical Science)
  - Mini-Test
- **Theme 10** 사회 문화(Society · Culture)
  - Mini-Test

30 DAYS TEPS 800 + Final Sum-up

Theme 01
광고
Advertisement

1. 광고문에 등장할 수 있는 지문은 정말 다양하다. 일반 생필품, 전자제품의 광고에서부터 여행지에 대한 광고, 쇼핑몰에 대한 광고, 잡지에 대한 광고 등 다양한 상품 및 장소가 광고의 대상으로 등장한다.

2. 이러한 광고문은 Part 3를 제외한 Part 1과 Part 2의 지문으로 주로 등장하며, Part 1의 빈칸 채우기의 경우, 보통 광고문의 주제와 관련지어서 빈칸에 들어갈 영문을 골라야 하는 경우가 자주 등장한다. 그러므로 광고문은 우선 초반에 등장하는 내용을 자세히 읽어서 과연 어떠한 상품 또는 장소를 광고하려는 글인지를 명확히 파악하는 것이 핵심이다.

3. Part 2의 경우, 전반적인 내용을 묻는 질문들의 경우에는 대개 광고하는 대상의 특징이 무엇인지, 광고하는 제품에 대한 설명으로 올바른 것은 무엇인가와 같은 세부내용을 묻는 질문들이 자주 등장한다. 오답은 대부분 광고문 내의 일부 단어와 내용을 이용하여 혼동되는 문장을 제시하니 이에 현혹되지 않도록 주의해야 한다.

Theme 01
광고

Mini-Test

Read the passage and choose the option that best fits the blank. (1~3)

1. A cruising holiday offers much more than all-you-can-eat buffets. A good cruise successfully blends all the amenities you need at sea with an outstanding variety of cultures, sights and experiences on land. We're very happy to be able to offer you cruise options from around the world, all the way from the exciting islands of the Caribbean, the jungle-rimmed Amazon River and the Panama Canal, across the seas to China, Japan and Indonesia. From exotic and vibrant wildlife to some of the world's most delicious cuisine and stunning scenery, a cruise to these parts of the world _____.

    (a) is bound to become a calamity
    (b) remains unexplored
    (c) poses jeopardy for children
    (d) is sure to please

2. People who think they might miss out on a university place now _____. Smith Business School has a diploma course that allows students who miss out on university places to take an another path without repeating 12th grade. Smith Incorporated has launched Smith Business School New Zealand, a private provider of higher education business courses. The international education company is a subsidiary of the Washington Post newspaper, with more than 2 billion dollars in revenue from education interests in the US, UK, Asia and now in New Zealand. Its newly-launched Business School offers a one-year Diploma of Commerce, equivalent to the first year of a bachelor degree in business at university. On completion of the one-year diploma, students can apply for full credit of the first year in many bachelor degree courses at other universities and apply to go straight to second year of such courses with no time wasted.

    (a) get a chance to enter any school they want
    (b) can finish a four-year degree course at Smith Business School
    (c) have another study avenue to follow their career dream
    (d) have an opportunity to take university entry exams

3. Are you looking for travel, adventure or a change in your career? Perhaps you are dreaming of visiting exciting destinations around the world. Then a short course in TESOL(Teaching English to Speakers of Other Languages) with the University of Toronto will provide you with teaching skills and prepare you _____. English is the number one language being learnt around the world and the need for native English speakers to teach overseas is ever-growing. Besides running courses in Toronto, we have also extended our courses to a Study Overseas Program where our training will take place in great locations including Vietnam, China and Turkey. Students can learn to develop their teaching skills and then practice in real classrooms, with real students and meet with real employers to organize a contract.

(a) to become the best English teacher in Canada
(b) to have what it takes to live a stable life
(c) to speak English fluently enough to teach students
(d) to live and work overseas

Choose the option that correctly answers the question. (4~5)

4. Entertain Chicago is a full event management company specializing in fashion and entertainment coordination. From interior designs, food and beverage caterers, sound, lighting, stage and set technicians to photographers, allow our staff to help navigate you on the journey to your special day. Let us guide you through the overwhelming hassle, frustration, run-around and confusion that so frequently surrounds event planning. Whether you are hosting an event for 10 guests through to 1000, we will create the perfect occasion. Allow Entertain Chicago to ensure that your next company product launch or event, reception, gala, benefit or fund raiser will be flawless. With packages ranging from all inclusive event planning, to day-off coordination, you will find the perfect service to match your needs and budget.

Q: What is this passage advertising?

(a) A book publication
(b) A personal fashion coordinator
(c) A Full function organizer
(d) A variety of packaging service companies

Advertisement

5. What's the green, gold and very cool? It's the Sunday Newspaper's exclusive cooler bag—and it's free. Thanks to Foodland, the biggest grocery chain in the country, the Sunday Newspaper is giving 40,000 readers something to help keep cool this summer. The cooler bag is a practical and reusable option for carrying drinks and snacks to many events and throughout the warm summer months. Whether it's watching soccer games or baseball games, the bag is the coolest accessory to beat the heat. People who have given the bag a trial run gave it two thumbs up. With only 40,000 available, the bags are expected to go quicker than the famous cyclist Lanc Armstrong's time trial. The Sunday Newspaper's cooler bag is free with a coupon in next weekend's Sunday Newspaper. There are only 40,000 available, so be sure to get in quickly because stocks are limited.

   Q: What can be inferred from the passage?

   (a) Cooler bags are used to carry various types of accessories.
   (b) The famous cyclist Lanc Armstrong uses the cooler bag.
   (c) Cooler bags will be given to the Foodland's customers only.
   (d) The bags received positive reviews from early users.

Theme 01
광고

Mini-Test 1

A cruising holiday offers much more than all-you-can-eat buffets. A good cruise successfully blends all the amenities you need at sea with an outstanding variety of cultures, sights and experiences on land. We're very happy to be able to offer you cruise options from around the world, all the way from the exciting islands of the Caribbean, the jungle-rimmed Amazon River and the Panama Canal, across the seas to China, Japan and Indonesia. From exotic and vibrant wildlife to some of the world's most delicious cuisine and stunning scenery, a cruise to these parts of the world _____.

(a) is bound to become a calamity
(b) remains unexplored
(c) poses jeopardy for children
(d) is sure to please

  해석

배를 타고 여행하는 휴가는 무엇이든 다 먹을 수 있는 뷔페보다 더 많은 것을 제공합니다. 좋은 선박여행은 당신이 바다에서 필요로 하는 설비들과 눈에 띄는 다양한 문화들, 경치들 그리고 육지 위에서의 경험을 성공적으로 한데 어우러지게 합니다. 저희는 여러분에게 캐리비언의 흥분되는 섬들과 정글이 테를 두르고 있는 아마존 강 그리고 파나마 운하에서부터 중국, 일본, 그리고 인도네시아를 가로지르는 것까지, 전 세계로부터의 선박여행 선택권을 제공해 드릴 수 있게 되어서 기쁩니다. 이국적이고 힘찬 야생생물부터 세계에서 가장 맛있는 요리와 멋진 풍경까지, 세계의 이 지역들로의 선박여행은 분명 여러분을 기쁘게 해 드릴 겁니다.

 해설

선박여행과 관련한 광고문이다. 전체 지문에 걸쳐서 선박여행이 가져다주는 즐거움들과 선박여행을 통해 가게 되는 다양한 장소와 지명들이 언급되고 있다. 그러므로 이러한 지역들로의 여행은 분명히 즐거울 것이라는 의미의 (d)가 정답이 된다. 재난과 위험이 될 것이라는 보기 (a), (c)는 글의 주제와 일치하지 않고, 글에서 언급되는 지역들로의 선박여행이 탐험되지 않았다는 내용의 (b)는 글에서 언급된 바 없다.

 어휘

blend 섞다, 혼합하다
offer 제공하다
amenities 쾌적한 설비, 문화적 설비
cruise (배를 타고) 순항하다, 바다 위를 떠돌아다니다 n. 선박여행
canal 운하
exotic 이국적인
stunning 멋진, 매력적인
bound ~하지 않을 수 없는, (필연적으로) ~하게 되어 있는
cuisine 요리
calamity 재난, 재해
jeopardy 위험
remain ~대로이다, 남다
please 기쁘게 하다, 만족시키다

Advertisement

Mini-Test 2

People who think they might miss out on a university place now _____. Smith Business School has a diploma course that allows students who miss out on university places to take an another path without repeating 12th grade. Smith Incorporated has launched Smith Business School New Zealand, a private provider of higher education business courses. The international education company is a subsidiary of the Washington Post newspaper, with more than 2 billion dollars in revenue from education interests in the US, UK, Asia and now in New Zealand. Its newly-launched Business School offers a one-year Diploma of Commerce, equivalent to the first year of a bachelor degree in business at university. On completion of the one-year diploma, students can apply for full credit of the first year in many bachelor degree courses at other universities and apply to go straight to second year of such courses with no time wasted.

(a) get a chance to enter any school they want
(b) can finish a four-year degree course at Smith Business School
(c) have another study avenue to follow their career dream
(d) have an opportunity to take university entry exams

 해석

대학에 들어갈 기회를 놓쳤다고 생각할 사람들은 이제 그들의 성공의 꿈을 따라가기 위한 또 다른 학업의 길을 가지게 됩니다. Smith Business School은 대입입학의 기회를 놓친 학생들이 고등학교 12학년을 반복할 필요 없이 또 다른 길을 택할 수 있도록 해주는 학위 코스를 갖고 있습니다. Smith 법인은 비즈니스 고등교육 코스의 사교육 제공자로서 뉴질랜드 Smith Business School을 발진시켰습니다. 이 국제적인 교육 회사는 Washington Post 신문의 자회사로서 미국, 영국, 아시아 그리고 이제는 뉴질랜드에 이르기까지 교육 이익으로부터 2억불 이상의 수익을 얻고 있습니다. 새롭게 개시되는 Business School은 1년짜리 통상 학위를 수여하는데, 이는 대학에서의 비즈니스 전공 학사학위를 1년 동안 이수한 것과 동등한 것입니다. 1년짜리 학위를 완수하게 되면, 학생들은 다른 대학들의 많은 학사학위 코스에 첫 해에 해당하는 전 학점의 적용을 신청할 수 있고, 시간의 낭비 없이 그러한 과정들의 2학년으로 곧바로 들어가게끔 신청할 수 있습니다.

 해설

지문의 초반에 보통 전체 글의 주제가 드러나는 경우가 많다는 것을 기억하자. 빈칸이 포함되어 있는 문장 이하의 내용들을 통해서, 본 학교가 입학 학생들에게 1년간의 과정을 통해서 다른 대학의 2학년부터 입학을 할 수 있는 1년짜리 학위를 제공해 준다는 내용을 확인할 수 있다. 즉, 본문에 언급된 'take another path'란 말처럼, 대학을 못 간 학생들에게 성공을 위한 또 다른 길을 제공해 주는 것이 이 광고문이 말하고자 하는 주제문이므로 정답은 (c)이다. 학생들이 과정 이수 후, 신청을 통해서 다른 많은 대학의 정규과정에 편입을 하게 되는 것이지, 원하는 어떤 대학에도 들어갈 수 있는 기회를 얻는 것은 아니므로 (a)는 정답이 될 수 없다.

 어휘

miss out (on) 기회를 놓치다
avenue 길, 방법
diploma 졸업증서, 학위증서
allow 허락하다, 허가하다
incorporated 법인, 주식회사
launch 발진시키다, 시작하다
revenue 소득, 수익
equivalent 동등한, 대등한
opportunity 기회

Mini-Test 3

Are you looking for travel, adventure or a change in your career? Perhaps you are dreaming of visiting exciting destinations around the world. Then a short course in TESOL(Teaching English to Speakers of Other Languages) with the University of Toronto will provide you with teaching skills and prepare you _____. English is the number one language being learnt around the world and the need for native English speakers to teach overseas is ever-growing. Besides running courses in Toronto, we have also extended our courses to a Study Overseas Program where our training will take place in great locations including Vietnam, China and Turkey. Students can learn to develop their teaching skills and then practice in real classrooms, with real students and meet with real employers to organize a contract.

(a) to become the best English teacher in Canada
(b) to have what it takes to live a stable life
(c) to speak English fluently enough to teach students
(d) to live and work overseas

해석

당신의 경력에서 여행, 모험 혹은 변화를 찾고 계신가요? 아마도 당신은 세계 여러 재미있는 목적지들을 방문하는 것을 꿈꾸고 있을 겁니다. 그렇다면, 토론토 대학교의 TESOL(영어를 다른 언어 사용자들에게 가르치는 것) 단기과정이 여러분에게 수업기술을 제공하고, 해외에서 일하면서 살도록 준비시켜 드릴 겁니다. 영어는 전 세계에서 배우는 첫 번째 언어입니다. 그리고 해외에서 아이들을 가르치는 원어민 영어교사들에 대한 필요성은 어느 때보다도 증가하고 있습니다. Toronto에서 코스를 운영하는 것 이외에도, 저희는 코스들을 베트남, 중국, 터키를 포함한 세계의 멋진 장소들에서 진행될 수 있도록 해외 학업프로그램을 확대시켰습니다. 저희 학생들은 수업기술을 발전시키고 그것을 학생들과 실제 수업에서 실행하는 방식을 배울 수 있습니다. 그리고 계약을 맺기 위해 실제 고용주들과 만날 수도 있습니다.

 해설

글의 일관성이 문제 해결의 포인트로 빈칸이 포함된 문장의 앞뒤 내용의 관계를 잘 파악해야 한다. 토론토 대학에서 제공하는 TESOL 프로그램의 특징은 수업기술만을 가르치는 것이 아니라, 해외프로그램을 통해서 학생들이 세계 여러 나라로 가서 실제 환경에서 아이들을 가르치는 경험을 얻을 수 있다는 것이다. 그러므로 정답은 (d)임을 알 수 있다. 이미 원어민들을 대상으로 한 수업이므로 영어를 유창하게 해주도록 한다는 (c)는 오답이며, 모험과 여행, 변화를 찾는 사람들에게 안정적으로 살게끔 해준다는 (b) 역시 정답이 될 수 없다.

 어휘

destination 목적지, 도착지
provide A with B A에게 B를 제공하다
prepare 준비하다, ~를 준비시키다
need 수요, 필요성
extend 확장하다, 확대하다
take place 일어나다, 생기다
employer 고용주
stable 안정된
have what it takes to ~할 자격을 갖추고 있다

Advertisement

Mini-Test 4

Entertain Chicago is a full event management company specializing in fashion and entertainment coordination. From interior designs, food and beverage caterers, sound, lighting, stage and set technicians to photographers, allow our staff to help navigate you on the journey to your special day. Let us guide you through the overwhelming hassle, frustration, run-around and confusion that so frequently surrounds event planning. Whether you are hosting an event for 10 guests through to 1000, we will create the perfect occasion. Allow Entertain Chicago to ensure that your next company product launch or event, reception, gala, benefit or fund raiser will be flawless. With packages ranging from all inclusive event planning, to day-off coordination, you will find the perfect service to match your needs and budget.

Q: What is this passage advertising?

(a) A book publication
(b) A personal fashion coordinator
(c) A full function organizer
(d) A packaging service company

해석

Entertain Chicago는 패션과 파티 협조에 특화를 둔 이벤트 관리 회사입니다. 인테리어 디자인, 음식과 음료 공급, 사운드와 조명, 무대, 그리고 세트기술자에서부터 사진기사에 이르기까지 저희 스태프들이 여러분들의 특별한 하루를 향한 여정에 도움이 될 수 있도록 허락해 주십시오. 저희가 이벤트 계획 과정에서 빈번하게 발생하는 감당할 수 없는 복잡함과, 짜증, 여기저기 뛰어다니기, 그리고 혼란스러운 과정들에 있어서 여러분들을 이끌어 드릴 수 있게 해주세요. 여러분들이 10명을 위한 혹은 1000명을 위한 이벤트를 여시든 그 수에 관계없이, 저희는 완벽한 행사를 만들어 드리겠습니다. Entertain Chicago가 여러분의 다음 회사 상품 발진식 또는 행사, 환영회, 축제, 자선행사 또는 기금 모음 행사 등이 완벽할 수 있게끔 책임질 수 있도록 해주십시오. 총괄적인 행사 기획에서부터 휴일 협조에 이르는 상품들과 함께, 여러분의 필요와 예산에 일치하는 완벽한 서비스를 찾으실 수 있을 겁니다.

해설

지문이 광고하고 있는 것이 무엇인지 묻고 있다. 첫 문장에서 주제문이 이미 드러나 있다. Entertain Chicago라는 이벤트 관리 회사에 대한 광고문이다. 그러므로 정답은 (c)이다. 파티 협조와 함께, 패션에도 특화되어 있다고는 했지만, 본 지문이 광고하는 것은 개인 패션 코디네이터가 아니므로 (b)는 정답이 될 수 없고, (d)의 포장 서비스 회사 역시 지문의 주제에서 벗어나는 내용이므로 오답이다.

어휘

specialize 전문으로 다루다
entertainment 오락, 파티
coordination 조정, 협조
caterer (여흥, 음식 등의) 공급자, 진행자
overwhelming 압도적인, 저항할 수 없는
frequently 빈번히
host 접대하다

Mini-Test 5

What's the green, gold and very cool? It's the Sunday Newspaper's exclusive cooler bag—and it's free. Thanks to Foodland, the biggest grocery chain in the country, the Sunday Newspaper is giving 40,000 readers something to help keep cool this summer. The cooler bag is a practical and reusable option for carrying drinks and snacks to many events and throughout the warm summer months. Whether it's watching soccer games or baseball games, the bag is the coolest accessory to beat the heat. People who have given the bag a trial run gave it two thumbs up. With only 40,000 available, the bags are expected to go quicker than the famous cyclist Lanc Armstrong's time trial. The Sunday Newspaper's cooler bag is free with a coupon in next weekend's Sunday Newspaper. There are only 40,000 available, so be sure to get in quickly because stocks are limited.

Q: What can be inferred from the passage?

(a) Cooler bags are used to carry various types of accessories.
(b) The famous cyclist Lanc Armstrong uses the cooler bag.
(c) Cooler bags will be given to the Foodland's customers only.
(d) The bags received positive reviews from early users.

해석

초록색이고, 금색이고, 매우 시원한 것은 무엇일까요? 바로 Sunday 신문만의 독점적인 냉각 가방입니다. 게다가 공짜이지요. 나라에서 가장 큰 식료품 체인점인 Foodland 덕분에, Sunday 신문은 40,000명의 독자 여러분에게 이번 여름 시원하게 지내실 수 있는 무언가를 드리고 있습니다. 이 냉각 가방은 따뜻한 여름 동안, 음료수나 간식거리를 운반하기에 실용적이고 재활용이 가능한 옵션입니다. 축구를 보러 가든, 혹은 야구를 보러 가든, 이 가방은 더위를 무찌를 가장 시원한 부속물이지요. 이 가방을 시험용으로 사용해 보신 분들은 이미 이 가방에 대해 극찬을 했습니다. 단지 40,000개만이 있기에, 가방들은 유명한 싸이클리스트인 랜스 암스트롱의 시간 기록보다도 더 빨리 사라질 수 있습니다. Sunday 신문의 냉각 가방은 다음 주말에 발행될 일요일 신문 안에 쿠폰을 통해 공짜로 받으실 수 있습니다. 단, 40,000개만이 있습니다. 그러니, 서둘러 오시도록 하세요. 왜냐하면 물품이 제한적이기 때문이죠.

해설

지문의 전체 내용을 읽고, 주어진 사실로부터 추측할 수 있는 보기를 찾아야 한다. 9번째 줄 'People who have given~ gave it two thumbs up'이란 문장에서 최초로 가방을 사용해 본 사람들이 긍정적인 평가를 했다는 것을 알 수 있으므로 정답은 (d)가 된다. 냉각 가방은 사람들이 들고 다니기에 좋은 accessory라는 것이지, 여러 종류의 accessory를 들고 다니는데 사용된다는 것은 아니므로 (a)는 오답이고, (c)의 Foodland는 본 가방을 신문사의 경품으로 준 것이지, Fooldand의 고객들에게만 본 가방을 준다는 것은 취지와 맞지 않으므로 오답이다.

어휘

exclusive 독점적인, 한정적인
cooler 냉각기, 냉동기
thanks to ~덕분에
practical 실용적인
trial run 시운전, 시험
time trial 개인마다 시간을 재는 레이스
available 이용 가능한, 사용 가능한
stock 재고(품)
give two thumbs up 엄지손가락을 치켜들다
be limited 한정되어 있다
positive 긍정적인
review 평론, 비평

Vocabulary 광고

앞에서 학습한 지문들에 등장하는 TEPS 빈출 출제 어휘 및 표현들을 다시 한 번 확인하고 그 외 주제와 관련한 빈출 필수 어휘 및 표현들을 학습하고 넘어 갑시다.

- (1) _____ 제공하다
- amenities 쾌적한 설비, 문화적 설비
- exotic 이국적인
- cuisine 요리
- please 기쁘게 하다, 만족시키다
- avenue 길, 방법
- allow 허락하다, 허가하다
- (2) _____ 발진시키다, 시작하다
- equivalent 동등한, 대등한
- destination 목적지, 도착지
- prepare 준비하다, ~를 준비시키다
- extend 확장하다, 확대하다
- take place 일어나다, 생기다
- (3) _____ 고용주
- stable 안정된
- (4) _____ 전문으로 다루다
- entertainment 오락, 파티
- (5) _____ 조정, 협조

- caterer (여흥, 음식) 공급자, 진행자
- (6) _____ 압도적인
- frequently 빈번히
- host 접대하다
- create 창조하다, 만들어 내다
- occasion 축전, 행사
- flawless 완벽한, 흠 없는
- inclusive 일체를 포함한
- budget 예산
- (7) _____ 독점적인, 한정적인
- thanks to ~덕분에
- practical 실용적인
- trial run 시운전, 시험
- (8) _____ 이용 가능한, 사용 가능한
- (9) _____ 재고(품)
- be limited 한정되어 있다
- positive 긍정적인
- gala 축제

Advertisement

- user-friendly 사용이 편리한
- second-hand 중고의
- up-to-date 최신의
- supreme 최상의
- subscription 정기 구독
- sponsor 광고주
- special offer 특별 제안, 특별 조건
- quality 고급의
- home appliance 가전제품
- guarantee 보증하다, 보장하다
- competitive rate 경쟁력 있는 가격
- (10) _____ 무료로
- qualified 자격이 있는
- product 상품
- out of order 고장난
- monthly 월 1회의
- insurance 보험
- adventure 모험
- award-winning 수상경력이 있는
- incredible 엄청난, 믿을 수 없는
- durable 오래 견디는, 내구성이 있는
- a variety of 여러 가지의, 가지각색의
- fill out ~을 작성하다
- order 주문(서), 주문하다
- method 방법
- take care of ~을 처리하다, 해결하다
- discount 할인, 할인하다
- distinction 구별, 차이
- advertising 광고(업)
- consumer 소비자
- promotion 판매촉진
- book 예약하다
- effectively 효과적으로
- reduce 줄이다, 삭감하다
- category 범주, 종류
- complimentary 무료의

Answers (1) offer (2) launch (3) employer (4) specialize (5) coordination (6) overwhelming (7) exclusive (8) available (9) stock (10) free of charge

30 DAYS TEPS 800 + Final Sum-up

Theme 02
안내 · 공고
Announcement

1. 안내 및 공고문에 등장할 수 있는 지문들은 말 그대로 어떤 행사, 회의, 일정 등의 세부내용을 대중들에게 안내하고 공고해주는 글의 유형을 말한다.

2. 이러한 안내, 공고문의 경우, Part 1, 2, 3 전반에 걸쳐서 출제가 가능한 주제로 특정 내용을 알려주어야 한다는 점에서, 전체적인 지문의 흐름이 일관성을 띤다는 특징을 가지고 있다.

3. 안내나 공고문의 경우 대중들에게 명확하게 어떠한 사실을 전달해 주어야 한다는 점에서, Part 2의 세부사항을 파악하는 문제유형이 자주 등장한다. 그러므로 지문 내용을 꼼꼼히 챙겨서 읽고, 내용과 일치하지 않는 선택지들을 제거해가며 문제를 풀도록 한다.

Theme 02
안내 · 공고

Mini-Test

Choose the option that correctly answers the question. (1~2)

1. Welcome to the child-care center of the future: where toddlers can grow, pick fruit and vegetables, learn music, see a speech pathologist and hang out with their grand-parents. The ground-breaking center acts as a primary school and church, and includes a cafe, vegetable garden, health and welfare services-and even pilates classes. This community is believed to be one of America's first early education one-stop shops for families. It would foster a community environment that would support families across all generations from birth to school and beyond. As well as providing child-care and pre-school services for up to 350 families, the community will offer a range of other initiatives. These will include speech and physical development, nutrition talks, and a program where families are encouraged to bring in fruit and vegetables to share. There also will be immunizations and therapy programs for children.

   Q: What is the best title for the passage?

   (a) How to build a future child-care center.
   (b) A community for children's field activities.
   (c) An alternative school for home-schooling children.
   (d) The introduction of a new-concept facility.

Announcement

2. Ladies and gentlemen. This is surely the biggest weekend in the 57-year history of the Golden Globe Awards. Just like many awards shows, including the venerable Academy Awards, the Golden Globes have attracted only patchy TV ratings in recent years and they certainly could ill afford the ravages of last year's Writers Guild of America strike, which reduced what traditionally is one of Hollywoods glitziest nights to basically a glorified press conference with no big stars attending. The Globes need a new injection of the two ingredients for which they are famous—glamour and unpredictability. Tomorrow in Los Angeles, they are back in full force, trying to reclaim their place as "Hollywood's party of the year". Recession? What recession? Hollywood will be dressing up and partying down. But who will be leaving the LA Hilton Hotel Ballroom with one of the shining statuettes, as well as the now ubiquitous goodie bags?

   Q: What is the next paragraph likely to be about?

   (a) Reflection on the history of the Golden Globe Awards.
   (b) Efforts made by Hollywood to crawl back from the recession.
   (c) People who will leave the hotel after hitting a jackpot.
   (d) Names of possible award nominees.

Read the passage and choose the option that best fits the blank. (3)

3. Getting around New Zealand is easy for backpackers. Independent backpacker transport networks offer travellers a unique travel option with the convenience of express bus passes. _____, travelling by car or campervan is a great option, too. There are no restrictions other than those you impose on yourself. You have the freedom of the open road. If you don's t feel the length of your trip warrant buying a car, hiring is a good option, with car hire outlets in most major towns. Auckland is the easiest city to buy a car in, as it's where most tourists buy and sell. Don't buy a car that doesn't have a Warrant of Fitness(WOF) or a registration. You need a current WOF to register your vehicle in order to prove that it is actually roadworthy.

   (a) Therefore
   (b) On the other hand
   (c) In the end
   (d) As a result

Choose the option that correctly answers the question. (4~5)

4. Recently I had the privilege of attending the opening of the Domestic Violence Outreach Service in Campbelltown. The project is the inspiration of Reverend Dr. Gills Ambler of the Campbelltown Uniting Church, who has worked tirelessly to improve the lives of vulnerable women and new arrivals in our community. The services are offered at the newly redeveloped Campbelltown Uniting Church on North East Road and were developed with $10,000 funding from the Uniting Church Synod, a 65,000 grant from the State Government, and 25,000 from the Campbelltown City Council. It is a tranquil and safe retreat for those in our community experiencing domestic violence. The services are offered in conjunction with our local Eastern Domestic Violence Service, and includes personal counselling financial management courses, conflict resolution training and practical support including emergency food parcels.

   Q: What can be inferred from the passage?

   (a) The services are provided for the people who have recently arrived in town.
   (b) Reverend Dr. Ambler spent most of his life helping people suffering from poverty.
   (c) They successfully raised enough money to redevelop the church.
   (d) Victims of domestic violence can take shelter in the church.

5. Australia's 2008 National Coastal Safety Report has uncovered alarming trends relating to coastal drowning deaths. The annual report revealed that 88 lives were lost along the Australian coast during 2007 and 2008 due to a drowning death. This is a seven percent increase on the previous season. Summer is typically the busiest and most dangerous time on Australian beaches. Therefore, the government would like to remind all Australians of the need to be surf safe and to swim between the flags at all times. In order to stay this summer safe, you can pick up a Surf Safety wallet card from one of your local grocery stores which includes instructions for cardiac resuscitation and how to stop a rip.

   Q: Which of the following is correct according to the announcement?

   (a) The government's plan has resulted in a reduction in the number of deaths.
   (b) More people died in the water in 2008 than in 2007.
   (c) The safety card is designed to teach people how to avoid dehydration.
   (d) Eighty-eight people died due to suffocation in the water during 2007 and 2008.

Theme 02
안내 · 공고

Mini-Test 1

Welcome to the child-care center of the future: where toddlers can grow, pick fruit and vegetables, learn music, see a speech pathologist and hang out with their grand-parents. The ground-breaking center acts as a primary school and church, and includes a cafe, vegetable garden, health and welfare services—and even pilates classes. This community is believed to be one of America's first early education one-stop shops for families. It would foster a community environment that would support families across all generations from birth to school and beyond. As well as providing child-care and pre-school services for up to 350 families, the community will offer a range of other initiatives. These will include speech and physical development, nutrition talks, and a program where families are encouraged to bring in fruit and vegetables to share. There also will be immunizations and therapy programs for children.

Q: What is the best title for the passage?

(a) How to build a future child-care center.
(b) A community for children's field activities.
(c) An alternative school for home-schooling children.
(d) The introduction of a new-concept facility.

해석

아장아장 걷는 유아들이 자라서 과일과 야채를 줍고, 음악을 배우고, 언어 병리학자들에게 진찰을 받고, 아이들의 할아버지, 할머니와 함께 시간을 보낼 수 있는 미래의 보육센터에 오신 걸 환영합니다. 기공식을 갖는 본 센터는 초등학교와 교회의 역할을 하고, 카페, 식물정원, 건강과 복지 서비스, 그리고 필라테 교실까지 포함하고 있습니다. 이 공동체는 가족들을 위한 미국의 첫 번째 조기교육 원-스톱 숍들 중 하나로 생각되어지고 있습니다. 이곳은 출생에서부터 학교 그리고 그 이상까지 모든 세대에 걸쳐서 가족들을 지원하는 공동체 환경을 기를 것입니다. 350개 가정에 대한 육아와 취학 전 서비스뿐만이 아니라, 저희는 여러 가지 다른 발의내용들도 제공할 것입니다. 이 내용들은 언어와 신체 발달, 영양과 관련한 담화, 그리고 가족들이 서로 나눌 과일과 야채를 가져오도록 장려하는 프로그램을 포함할 것입니다. 아이들을 위한 면역성 및 치료 프로그램 또한 있을 예정입니다.

해설

지문은 새롭게 오픈하는 보육센터를 소개하며, 이 장소가 제공하는 새로운 서비스 내용들을 구체적으로 하나하나 진술해 주고 있다. 그러므로 제목으로 가장 적합한 보기는 '신 개념의 시설 소개' 인 (d)가 정답이다.

어휘

tropic 육아	ground-breaking 기공식을 갖는	support 지원하다, 후원하다
toddler (아장아장 걷는) 유아	welfare 복지	birth 출생
pathologist 병리학자	community 지역사회, 공동체	preschool 취학 전(의)
hang out ~와 어울리다	foster 기르다, 촉진하다	

Mini-Test 2

Ladies and gentlemen. This is surely the biggest weekend in the 57-year history of the Golden Globe Awards. Just like many awards shows, including the venerable Academy Awards, the Golden Globes have attracted only patchy TV ratings in recent years and they certainly could ill afford the ravages of last year's Writers Guild of America strike, which reduced what traditionally is one of Hollywoods glitziest nights to basically a glorified press conference with no big stars attending. The Globes need a new injection of the two ingredients for which they are famous—glamour and unpredictability. Tomorrow in Los Angeles, they are back in full force, trying to reclaim their place as "Hollywood's party of the year". Recession? What recession? Hollywood will be dressing up and partying down. But who will be leaving the LA Hilton Hotel Ballroom with one of the shining statuettes, as well as the now ubiquitous goodie bags?

Q: What is the next paragraph likely to be about?

(a) Reflection on the history of the Golden Globe Awards.
(b) Efforts made by Hollywood to crawl back from the recession.
(c) People who will leave the hotel after hitting a jackpot.
(d) Names of possible award nominees.

해석

신사 숙녀 여러분. 오늘은 분명 Golden Globe 시상식의 57년 역사상 가장 큰 주말일 겁니다. 존경받는 아카데미 시상식을 포함하여, 많은 수상식 쇼와 마찬가지로 Golden Globe 시상식은 최근에 단지 형편없는 텔레비전 시청률을 얻었습니다. 그리고 분명 작년의 미국 작가 노조의 파업의 손해를 거의 감당할 수 없었지요. Golden Globe는 그것이 유명한 이유인 두 가지 요소를 새롭게 투입할 필요가 있습니다. 바로 우아함과 예측할 수 없음이죠. 내일 로스앤젤레스에서 본 시상식은 "그 해의 할리우드 파티"로서 입지를 되찾기 위해서 만반의 준비를 하고 돌아옵니다. 경기침체라고요? 무슨 경기침체요? 할리우드는 옷을 화려하게 차려입고, 파티를 시작할 겁니다. 하지만, 누가 반짝거리는 트로피와 상금을 가지고 LA의 힐튼 호텔 연회장을 떠나게 될까요?

해설

지문의 마지막 줄에서 던지는 질문을 잘 음미하면 정답을 유추할 수 있다. 유명한 할리우드의 시상식인 Golden Globe에 대한 설명을 한 후에, 과연 누가 트로피와 상금을 들고 갈까라고 질문을 하는 것에서, 다음에 이어질 내용으로 가장 적합한 것은 수상 후보자들의 이름들. 즉 보기 (d)이다. Golden Globe의 역사에 대해선 이미 짧게나마 앞에서 언급을 했고, 'Recession? What recession?'이란 문장에서 경기 후퇴는 할리우드의 관심사항이 아님을 알 수 있으므로 (b) 역시 정답이 될 수 없다.

어휘

surely 확실히, 틀림없이	patchy 누덕누덕 기운	glamour 매력, 아름다움
award 수상, 상	TV rating 시청률	reclaim 재요구하다, 되찾다
venerable 존경받는	ravages 손해	party 파티를 하다, 파티
attract 끌어당기다, 매혹하다	glitz 현란한, 눈부시도록 화려한	statuette 작은 조상

Announcement

Mini-Test 3

Getting around New Zealand is easy for backpackers. Independent backpacker transport networks offer travellers a unique travel option with the convenience of express bus passes. _____, travelling by car or campervan is a great option, too. There are no restrictions other than those you impose on yourself. You have the freedom of the open road. If you don't feel the length of your trip warrant buying a car, hiring is a good option, with car hire outlets in most major towns. Auckland is the easiest city to buy a car in, as it's where most tourists buy and sell. Don't buy a car that doesn't have a Warrant of Fitness(WOF) or a registration. You need a current WOF to register your vehicle in order to prove that it is actually roadworthy.

(a) Therefore
(b) On the other hand
(c) In the end
(d) As a result

 해석

뉴질랜드를 돌아다니는 것은 배낭여행객들에게는 쉬운 일입니다. 독립 배낭여행 운송 네트워크는 여행객들에게 고속버스 승차권의 편리함과 함께 독특한 여행 선택권을 제공하고 있습니다. 반면에, 자동차나 캠퍼밴을 이용해 여행하는 것 역시 좋은 방법입니다. 여러분이 자신에게 내린 제한사항들을 제외하고는 전혀 걸릴 것이 없지요. 여러분은 쫙 펼쳐진 도로의 자유를 얻게 됩니다. 만약 여행 기간이 차를 구입할 만큼 길다고 느끼지 않으신다면, 자동차 대여점이 대부분의 주요 마을마다 있기에 차를 대여하는 것도 좋은 방법입니다. Auckland는 대부분의 여행객들이 차를 사고팔고 하는 곳이기 때문에 차를 구입하기 가장 쉬운 도시입니다. WOF(적합 보증서)를 가지고 있지 않은 자동차나 등록증이 없는 차는 사지 마세요. 여러분은 자동차가 실제로 운행할 만 하다는 것을 증명하기 위한 목적으로 자동차를 등록하기 위해서는 현재의 WOF를 가지고 있어야 합니다.

 해설

빈칸이 포함된 문장에서 'travelling by car or campervan'은 앞의 문장에서 언급되는 'the convenience of express bus passes'와는 대조되는 내용이다. 그러므로 대조/비교의 연결사에 해당하는 보기 (b)가 정답이다.

🔍 어휘

get around 돌아다니다	convenience 편의, 편리	hire 대여하다
backpacker 배낭여행객	impose 지우다, 부과하다	in order to ~을 위하여
pass 정액승차권	warrant 보증(보장)하다	prove 증명하다
unique 독특한	registration 등록(증)	roadworthy 도로에 적합한
restriction 제한, 제재	register 등록하다	

Mini-Test 4

Recently I had the privilege of attending the opening of the Domestic Violence Outreach Service in Campbelltown. The project is the inspiration of Reverend Dr. Gills Ambler of the Campbelltown Uniting Church, who has worked tirelessly to improve the lives of vulnerable women and new arrivals in our community. The services are offered at the newly redeveloped Campbelltown Uniting Church on North East Road and were developed with $10,000 funding from the Uniting Church Synod, a 65,000 grant from the State Government, and 25,000 from the Campbelltown City Council. It is a tranquil and safe retreat for those in our community experiencing domestic violence. The services are offered in conjunction with our local Eastern Domestic Violence Service, and includes personal counselling financial management courses, conflict resolution training and practical support including emergency food parcels.

Q: What can be inferred from the passage?

(a) The services are provided for the people who have recently arrived in town.
(b) Reverend Dr. Ambler spent most of his life helping people suffering from poverty.
(c) They successfully raised enough money to redevelop the church.
(d) Victims of domestic violence can take shelter in the church.

해석

최근에 저는 Campbelltown의 가정폭력 복지 서비스의 오프닝에 참석하는 특권을 갖게 되었습니다. 이 프로젝트는 Campbelltown의 통합교회 목사로서 힘없는 여성들과 저희 마을에 새롭게 이주하시는 분들의 삶을 향상시키기 위해서 피곤함도 모르게 일해 오신 Dr. Gills Ambler 목사님의 영감입니다. 이러한 서비스들은 North East Road에 위치한 새롭게 재건축된 Campbelltown 통합 교회에서 제공되어지고, 통합교회 총회의 10,000달러 기금과, 주정부의 65,000달러 보조금, 그리고 Campbelltown 시의회로부터의 25,000달러로 개발되어졌습니다. 이곳은 우리 공동체에서 가정폭력을 경험한 분들을 위한 조용하고 안전한 휴식처입니다. 본 서비스들은 지역 동쪽 가정 폭력 서비스와 함께 연계하여 제공되어지고 있으며 개인 상담, 재정관리 코스, 논쟁해결훈련과 비상식품소포를 포함한 실질적인 지원들을 포함하고 있습니다.

 해설

가정폭력의 피해자들을 도와주기 위해서 여러 기관들로부터 금전적 도움을 받아 교회를 재건축하였고 여러 가지 서비스들이 피해자들에게 제공되고 있다는 내용의 지문이다. 본문 중에 'It is a tranquil~domestic violence' 라는 문장에서, 재건축된 교회가 가정폭력 피해자들의 피신처로 이용되고 있음을 유추할 수 있다. 그러므로 (d)가 정답이다. 지문에서 언급되는 서비스들은 새롭게 마을로 이주한 사람들과는 관련이 없는 내용들이며, 지원된 돈으로 개발된 것은 피해자들에게 제공되는 서비스들이지 교회가 아니므로 (a)와 (c)는 정답이 될 수 없다.

 어휘

recently 최근에	tireless 지칠 줄 모르게	retreat 은신처, 묵상장소
privilege 특권	vulnerable 상처입기 쉬운	conflict 갈등, 충돌
attend ~에 참석하다	funding 자금조달	poverty 가난
outreach service 복지 서비스	grant 보조금	raise (돈을) 마련하다, 조달하다
domestic violence 가정폭력	tranquil 조용한, 평온한	take shelter 피난(대피)하다

Announcement

Mini-Test 5

Australia's 2008 National Coastal Safety Report has uncovered alarming trends relating to coastal drowning deaths. The annual report revealed that 88 lives were lost along the Australian coast during 2007 and 2008 due to a drowning death. This is a seven percent increase on the previous season. Summer is typically the busiest and most dangerous time on Australian beaches. Therefore, the government would like to remind all Australians of the need to be surf safe and to swim between the flags at all times. In order to stay this summer safe, you can pick up a Surf Safety wallet card from one of your local grocery stores which includes instructions for cardiac resuscitation and how to stop a rip.

Q: Which of the following is correct according to the announcement?

(a) The government's plan has resulted in a reduction in the number of deaths.
(b) More people died in the water in 2008 than in 2007.
(c) The safety card is designed to teach people how to avoid dehydration.
(d) Eighty-eight people died due to suffocation in the water during 2007 and 2008.

 해석

호주의 2008년 국가 해변 안전 보고서는 연안의 익사로 인한 사망과 관련하여 놀라운 동향을 털어놓았습니다. 이 연간 보고서는 2007년과 2008년에 걸쳐서 호주 해변에 걸쳐서 익사로 인해서 88명이 목숨을 잃었다고 밝히고 있습니다. 이것은 이전 시즌보다 7퍼센트가 증가한 것입니다. 여름은 호주의 해변에서 전형적으로 가장 바쁘고 가장 위험한 시간입니다. 그러므로 정부는 모든 호주인들에게 안전하게 서핑을 하고 항상 깃발들 사이에서 수영을 할 것을 상기시켜 드리고자 합니다. 올해 여름을 안전하게 보내기 위해서, 여러분은 심폐소생 방법과 찢어진 곳을 멈추는 방법 등을 담고 있는 서프 안전 지갑용 카드를 지역의 식료품점 한 곳에서 얻을 수 있습니다.

 해설

내용과 일치하는 보기를 고르는 문제유형이다. 88명이 익사(drowning deaths)로 죽었기 때문에, '88명이 물속에서 질식해 죽었다'는 (d)가 정답이다. 2008년과 2007년 사이에 죽은 사람들의 수가 그 이전 시즌보다 높은 것이지, 2008년에 죽은 사람이 2007년보다 많았는지 여부는 알 수 없으므로 (b)는 정답이 아니다.

어휘

uncover 폭로하다, 털어놓다	coastal 근해의, 연안의	suffocation 질식
alarming 놀라운, 불안하게 하는	drowning 익사하는	cardiac resuscitation 심폐소생(술)
trend 경향, 추세	remind A of B A에게 B를 상기시키다	be designed to ~하기 위해서 설계되어지다
relating to ~와 관련 있는	instructions 지시사항	

Vocabulary 안내·공고

앞에서 학습한 지문들에 등장하는 TEPS 빈출 출제 어휘 및 표현들을 다시 한 번 확인하고 그 외 주제와 관련한 빈출 필수 어휘 및 표현들을 학습하고 넘어 갑시다.

- □ hang out ~와 어울리다
- □ ground-breaking 기공식을 갖는
- □ (1) _____ 복지
- □ (2) _____ 지역사회, 공동체
- □ foster 기르다, 촉진하다
- □ (3) _____ 지지하다, 후원하다
- □ initiative 발의, 선창
- □ encourage 격려하다, 장려하다
- □ immunization 예방접종, 면역화
- □ (4) _____ 시설
- □ surely 확실히, 틀림없이
- □ (5) _____ 수상, 상
- □ venerable 존경받는
- □ (6) _____ 끌어당기다, 매혹하다
- □ reclaim 요구하다, 되찾다
- □ dress up 옷을 차려입다
- □ statuette 작은 조상
- □ glamour 매력, 아름다움

- □ get around 돌아다니다
- □ unique 독특한
- □ (7) _____ 편의, 편리
- □ impose 지우다, 부과하다
- □ (8) _____ 보증하다, 보장하다
- □ hire 대여하다
- □ in order to ~을 위하여
- □ prove 증명하다
- □ recently 최근에
- □ (9) _____ 특권
- □ attend ~에 참석하다
- □ funding 자금조달
- □ grant 보조금
- □ retreat 은신처, 묵상장소
- □ (10) _____ (돈을) 마련하다, 조달하다
- □ trend 경향, 추세
- □ remind A of B A에게 B를 상기시키다
- □ suffocation 질식

Announcement

- appropriate 적합한, 적절한
- summarize 요약해서 말하다
- propose 제안하다, 신청하다
- outcome 결과, 성과
- necessary 필요한, 필수의
- submit 제출하다
- competition 경쟁, 시합
- seek 구하다, 찾다
- participate 참가하다
- donate 기부하다
- regardless of ~와 상관없이
- join 합류하다, 참가하다
- be interested in ~에 관심이 있다
- in addition to ~에 덧붙여
- notify ~을 알리다, 발표하다
- recruit 신입을 모집하다
- approximately 대략

- currently 현재, 지금
- lead to ~로 이끌다
- purchase 구입하다, 구매하다
- eligible 적격의, 자격이 되는
- evaluate 평가하다, 측정하다
- consult ~의 의견을 듣다, 참고하다
- feature 특징, 특색
- obligation 의무, 강조
- enclose 동봉하다, 둘러싸다
- itinerary 여정, 여행일정
- move 이동하다, 움직이다
- announcement 공고, 발표
- on the increase 증가하고 있는
- report 보고하다, 알리다
- disclose 드러내다, 폭로하다
- respondent 응답자, 회답자
- apply 적용하다, 이용하다

Answers (1) welfare (2) community (3) support (4) facility (5) award (6) attract (7) convenience (8) warrant (9) privilege (10) raise

30 DAYS TEPS 800 + Final Sum-up

Theme 03
편지 · 에세이
Letters · Essays

1. 편지는 TEPS에서 출제되는 여러 가지 지문 유형들 중 광고문과 함께 내용이 가장 쉽고, 평이하다고 할 수 있다. TEPS 시험에서 매 시험 2문항 정도는 반드시 출제되는 주제유형이다.

2. 편지를 쓴다는 것은 어떤 특정한 목적을 전달하기 위해서이다. 예를 들어, 고객에게 상품을 구매해 준 것에 대한 감사편지, 승진이나 행사의 수상자로 선발된 것을 알리는 축하편지 등을 들 수 있다. 이처럼 대부분의 편지는 뚜렷한 목적(purpose)을 갖고 있으므로, 편지를 쓴 목적이 무엇인지 파악하는 것이 중요하다.

3. 에세이 글은 보통 화자가 "I"로 표현되어, 자기가 겪은 경험, 또는 자기 주변에서 벌어지는 상황들을 풀어나가는 글의 형식을 말한다. 에세이의 주제가 무엇인지, 에세이에서 언급되는 대상에 대한 필자의 태도는 어떠한지와 같은 유형들의 질문이 주로 출제된다.

Theme 03
편지 · 에세이

Mini-Test

Read the passage and choose the option that best fits the blank. (1)

1. Dear Mrs. Hwang,

   We're delighted you signed up to experience Myer Fun. Being a member turns everyday shopping at Myer into a world of rewards, special offers and exclusive shopping events. Whenever you shop at any Myer store, simply present your attached Myer Fun card and you'll receive 2 Myer Fun Shopping Credits for every dollar spent. Once you've earned 2000 Shopping Credits you'll receive a $20 Myer Fun Gift Card with the next Quarterly Member Update. If you _____, don't worry. Simply ask a Myer team member to call Myer Fun and obtain your membership number.

   Yours sincerely,

   (a) want to receive this Myer Fun card
   (b) would like to get a Myer Fun gift card
   (c) cannot find your Myer card at home
   (d) forget to take your shopping card with you

Choose the option that correctly answers the question. (2~3)

2. Dear Readers,

   I am writing in response to the article concerning teenage drug addiction these days. Hospitals in America are overrun with drug addicts wanting treatment for their stupidity and it seems there are more joining these queues. There is no end in sight to the major social and economic problems created by drug abuse. We need very heavy penalties and more time behind bars for drug-pushers. Drugs are the scourge of this country's future. I believe parents are the key to instilling some awareness and understanding of the consequences of long-term addiction and this is where governments must target their campaigns.

   Sincerely,

   Q: What is the purpose of this letter?

   (a) To criticize teenagers with drug addictions.
   (b) To suggest building more hospitals.
   (c) To render opinion on how to tackle drug issues.
   (d) To offer election campaign ideas.

3. People who advocate torture often say it's the only way to break hardened terrorists. But after personally conducting 300 interrogations and supervising more than 1000, I can tell you it just isn't true. I'm not some ivory-tower type, but when I got to Iraq in 2006 I was shocked to see some of my fellow interrogators use "fear and control" in a manner that crossed the line into "torture and abuse." I found this brutality inconsistent with American principles and sought instead to get information by building rapport with suspects, showing cultural understanding, and using good old-fashioned brainpower. It worked extremely well. Among my team's accomplishments was getting a captured terrorist to reveal the hiding place of a leader of al-Qaeda in Iraq.

   Q: What can be inferred from the passage?

   (a) There is no better way than torture to get information from terrorists.
   (b) It's almost impossible to persuade terrorists to reveal secret information.
   (c) Most of the terrorists have an incredible ego.
   (d) Non-violence is the key to deal with the most violent people.

Read the passage and choose the option that best fits the blank. (4)

4. Throughout my adult life, as a new year begins, I have reflected upon the past 12 months, and thought "Phew! That was a big year!" Events such as graduation, marriage, home-buying and the birth of a child, through to illness and the passing away of loved ones, made every year feel as if it was the biggest that life could dish up, and that everything should be plain sailing from then on. _____ each year presented its own unique set of challenges to be faced and, hopefully enjoyed. Taking on the editorship of this magazine presents just such a significant challenge, and a very welcome one: it's a role that draws upon many of the resources gained through experience—of life and of work—but which at the same time demands fresh and imaginative thinking.

   (a) In consequence
   (b) Furthermore
   (c) However
   (d) For example

Choose the option that correctly answers the question. (5)

5. Yesterday was one of those days when I seriously considered cryogenics for my children. My firstborn plunked himself at the kitchen counter that morning and proceeded to strike a match, pour some ethanol into a squashed down can and set the whole thing alight with little regard for my dawn fragility. Upon my feeble protests and concern for our wooden kitchen counter, which already has a variety of indelible marks created by our two children, both my sons have always have been resolute in their manner.

   Q: According to the passage, which best describes the writer's children?

   (a) Demanding
   (b) Capricious
   (c) Stubborn
   (d) Independent

Theme 03
편지 · 에세이

Mini-Test 1

Dear Mrs. Hwang,

We're delighted you signed up to experience Myer Fun. Being a member turns everyday shopping at Myer into a world of rewards, special offers and exclusive shopping events. Whenever you shop at any Myer store, simply present your attached Myer Fun card and you'll receive 2 Myer Fun Shopping Credits for every dollar spent. Once you've earned 2000 Shopping Credits you'll receive a $20 Myer Fun Gift Card with the next Quarterly Member Update. If you _____, don't worry. Simply ask a Myer team member to call Myer Fun and obtain your membership number.

Yours sincerely,

(a) want to receive this Myer Fun card
(b) would like to get a Myer Fun gift card
(c) cannot find your Myer card at home
(d) forget to take your shopping card with you

해석

저희는 귀하께서 Myer Fun을 경험하시기 위해 참가해 주셔서 기쁩니다. 저희 멤버가 되시는 것은 Myer에서의 매일 매일의 일상적인 쇼핑을 여러 가지 보상과, 특별 조건 그리고 독점적인 쇼핑행사들의 세계로 변화시켜드릴 겁니다. Myer 백화점에서 귀하께서 쇼핑을 하실 때마다, 간단하게 본 편지에 첨부되어 있는 Myer Fun 카드를 제시하세요. 그러면 매 1달러를 쓸 때마다, Myer Fun 쇼핑점수 2점을 받으실 수 있습니다. 일단 2000점의 쇼핑점수를 얻으시게 되면, 귀하께서는 다음 연 4회에 걸친 멤버 소식과 함께 20달러를 쓸 수 있는 Myer Fun 선물카드를 받으실 겁니다. 만약 쇼핑카드를 가지고 오시는 걸 잊으셨다면, 간단히 저희 Myer 직원에게 Myer Fun으로 전화를 해서 귀하의 멤버십 숫자를 얻으라고 요청하시면 됩니다.

해설

Myer Fun에 가입한 회원에게 감사의 내용을 전하며, Myer Shopping card를 편지와 함께 동봉했음을 내용을 통해 알 수 있다. 빈칸의 내용이 발생 시 걱정할 필요가 없다는 것과 함께, Myer 백화점 직원에게 Myer Fun으로 전화할 것을 요청하여 회원번호를 물으면 된다는 내용을 통해, 쇼핑 시 카드를 잊어버렸을 경우를 가정한 (d)가 정답임을 알 수 있다. (c)처럼 집에서 잃어버렸다면, 직접 Myer Fun에 새 카드를 신청하면 되지, 백화점 직원을 통해서 회원번호를 물으라는 것은 말이 되지 않는다.

어휘

delighted 아주 기쁜
sign up 참가하다, 등록하다
experience 경험하다
reward 보상, 보답
present 제출하다, 건네주다
attached 첨부되어 있는
shopping credit 쇼핑점수
quarterly 연 4회의
obtain 얻다, 획득하다
membership 회원, 회원자격

Mini-Test 2

Dear Readers,

I am writing in response to the article concerning teenage drug addiction these days. Hospitals in America are overrun with drug addicts wanting treatment for their stupidity and it seems there are more joining these queues. There is no end in sight to the major social and economic problems created by drug abuse. We need very heavy penalties and more time behind bars for drug-pushers. Drugs are the scourge of this country's future. I believe parents are the key to instilling some awareness and understanding of the consequences of long-term addiction and this is where governments must target their campaigns.

Sincerely,

Q: What is the purpose of this letter?

(a) To criticize teenagers with drug additions.
(b) To suggest building more hospitals.
(c) To render opinion on how to tackle drug issues.
(d) To offer election campaign ideas.

해석

저는 요즈음 십대들의 마약 남용과 관련한 기사를 보고 이렇게 편지를 씁니다. 미국의 병원들은 그들의 어리석음으로 인해 치료를 원하는 마약 중독자들로 넘쳐나고 있습니다. 그리고 더 많은 사람들이 이러한 행렬에 가담할 것으로 보입니다. 마약 남용으로 인해서 생겨나는 주요한 사회적 그리고 경제적 문제는 끝이 없습니다. 우리는 마약 밀매꾼들에 대한 더 심한 형벌을 내리고 더 오랜 시간 감옥에 갇혀 있게 할 필요가 있습니다. 마약은 이 나라의 미래에 두통거리입니다. 저는 부모들이 장기간의 중독이 가져올 결과에 대한 이해와 깨달음을 아이들에게 주입시키는 것이 해결 열쇠라고 믿습니다. 그리고 이 부분이 바로 정부가 사회운동의 목표로 삼아야 할 부분이라고 봅니다.

해설

마약 남용과 관련한 기사를 읽고 그에 대한 자신의 의견을 피력하는 내용의 편지이다. 마약 남용이 가져올 수 있는 내용들을 언급한 후, 그것을 해결할 수 있는 방법에 대한 자신의 의견을 전달하고자 하는 것이 목적이다. 그러므로 정답은 (c)이다. 마약 중독에 빠진 10대들의 어리석음을 이야기하고 있지만 비난 자체가 편지의 목적은 아니므로 (a)는 오답이다.

어휘

article 기사	penalty 형벌, 벌금	consequence 결과, 영향
concerning ~에 관하여	behind bars 감옥에 갇힌	target ~을 목표로 정하다
drug addiction 마약 중독	suit 어울리다, 적합하다	criticize 비판하다
overrun 범람하다, 넘쳐흐르다	drug-pusher 마약 밀매자	render 제출하다, 표현하다
addict 중독자	scourge 두통거리, 불행을 가져오는 것	tackle 달려들다, 맞싸우다
queue 열, 행렬	instill 주입시키다, 조금씩 가르치다	

Mini-Test 3

People who advocate torture often say it's the only way to break hardened terrorists. But after personally conducting 300 interrogations and supervising more than 1000, I can tell you it just isn't true. I'm not some ivory-tower type, but when I got to Iraq in 2006 I was shocked to see some of my fellow interrogators use "fear and control" in a manner that crossed the line into "torture and abuse." I found this brutality inconsistent with American principles and sought instead to get information by building rapport with suspects, showing cultural understanding, and using good old-fashioned brainpower. It worked extremely well. Among my team's accomplishments was getting a captured terrorist to reveal the hiding place of a leader of al-Qaeda in Iraq.

Q: What can be inferred from the passage?

(a) There is no better way than torture to get information from terrorists.
(b) It's almost impossible to persuade terrorists to reveal secret information.
(c) Most of the terrorists have an incredible ego.
(d) Non-violence is the key to deal with the most violent people.

  해석

고문을 옹호하는 사람들은 종종 그것이 단련된 테러리스트들을 꺾을 수 있는 유일한 방법이라고 말한다. 하지만 개인적으로 300건의 심문을 집행했고, 1000건이 넘는 심문을 감독한 후, 나는 그것이 사실이 아니라는 것을 당신에게 말할 수 있다. 내가 무슨 이상만 쫓는 그런 사람은 아니다. 하지만, 2006년도에 이라크에 도착했을 때, 나는 나의 동료 심문자들이 "공포와 통제"라는 선을 넘어 "고문과 학대"라는 수준에까지 이를 사용하는 것을 보고 충격을 받았다. 나는 이 잔혹성이 미국의 원칙과 일치하지 않는다고 생각하여, 대신에 혐의자들에게 문화적 이해를 보여주고 그들과 친밀한 관계를 유지함으로써 구식의 방법이라고 할 수 있는 두뇌싸움을 통해서 정보를 얻으려고 했다. 이 방법은 굉장히 잘 통했다. 내 팀의 성과 중에는 포획된 테러리스트를 통해서 알카에다 지도자가 이라크에 숨어있는 장소를 누설하도록 한 것이 포함된다.

 해설

고문을 실행했던 경험자로서 고문보다 더 좋은 방법은 용의자들과 문화적 배경을 바탕으로 한 유대관계를 형성하는 것이라는 내용의 지문이다. 지문 중 'I found this brutality inconsistent~It worked extremely well'까지의 내용을 통해서 비폭력적 방법이 대단히 좋은 결과를 내었다는 사실을 알 수 있다. 즉, 비폭력이 가장 폭력적이라고 할 수 있는 테러리스트들을 다루는 열쇠라고 말하는 (d)가 정답이다.

어휘

advocate 옹호하다	ivory-tower 이상만 쫓는 태도, 상아탑	rapport (친밀한) 관계, 조화
conduct 집행하다, 처리하다	fear and control 공포와 통제	old-fashioned 구식의
interrogation 질문, 심문	cross the line 정도를 넘어서다	reveal 알리다, 폭로하다
supervise 감독하다, 지휘하다	torture and abuse 고문과 학대	ego 자만심

Mini-Test 4

Throughout my adult life, as a new year begins, I have reflected upon the past 12 months, and thought "Phew! That was a big year!" Events such as graduation, marriage, home-buying and the birth of a child, through to illness and the passing away of loved ones, made every year feel as if it was the biggest that life could dish up, and that everything should be plain sailing from then on. _____ each year presented its own unique set of challenges to be faced and, hopefully, enjoyed. Taking on the editorship of this magazine presents just such a significant challenge, and a very welcome one: it's a role that draws upon many of the resources gained through experience—of life and of work—but which at the same time demands fresh and imaginative thinking.

(a) In consequence
(b) Furthermore
(c) However
(d) For example

해석

내 성인의 삶을 통하여, 새로운 해가 시작될 때, 나는 늘 지난 12개월을 회고해 보았고, "휴, 굉장한 한 해 였어"라고 생각해왔다. 졸업식, 결혼, 주택구매 그리고 아이의 출생 등에 이르는 여러 가지 행사들과 질병 그리고 사랑하는 이들의 죽음에 이르기까지 이 모든 것들은 매해가 마치 삶에 있어서 가장 큰 해이며 그 이후부터는 평탄한 삶이 될 것인 양 느끼게 만든다. 하지만 매년은 그 해의 직면해야 하고, 또 바라건데 즐길 수 있는 독특한 과제들을 내어놓는다. 본 잡지의 편집자 역할을 하는 것은 바로 그러한 중요한 도전들과 함께 매우 환영할 수 있는 일들을 제공한다. 이는 삶과 직업의 경험을 통해서 얻어지는 많은 자원들에 의존하게끔 하는 역할이지만, 동시에 신선하고 상상력이 넘치는 생각을 요구하는 직업이기도 하다.

해설

빈칸 앞에서는 매년 여러 가지 일들로 가득 찬 한 해가 끝나면 그 다음 해는 평탄할 것 같이 느껴진다고 말하고 있는 반면, 빈칸 뒤에서는 매년은 고유의 독특한 도전들을 내어 놓는다고 말하고 있다. 이 둘은 서로 상반되는 내용으로 정답은 (c)이다.

어휘

reflect upon ~을 회고하다
pass away 사망하다
as if 마치 ~인 것처럼
dish up 요리를 내놓다 (이야기를) 꺼내다
plain 평이한, 간단한
challenge 도전
face 직면하다
editorship 편집자(의 직위)
draw upon ~에 의존하다
demand 요구하다

Mini-Test 5

Yesterday was one of those days when I seriously considered cryogenics for my children. My firstborn plunked himself at the kitchen counter that morning and proceeded to strike a match, pour some ethanol into a squashed down can and set the whole thing alight with little regard for my dawn fragility. Upon my feeble protests and concern for our wooden kitchen counter, which already has a variety of indelible marks created by our two children, both my sons have always have been resolute in their manner.

Q: According to the passage, which best describes the writer's children?

(a) Demanding
(b) Capricious
(c) Stubborn
(d) Independent

해석

어제는 내가 진지하게 내 아이들을 냉동상태로 얼려버리고 싶다는 맘이 든 날 중의 하루였다. 첫째 아이는 내가 아침에는 기운이 없다는 것을 전혀 고려해 주지 않은 채 그날 아침에 부엌 카운터에 몸을 날리더니, 계속해서 성냥에 불을 붙이고 으깨진 깡통 안에 에탄올을 붓고 나서는 이 모든 것에 불을 붙였다. 이미 우리 두 아이에 의한 지워지지 않는 다양한 자국들이 생겨버린 나무로 된 부엌 선반에 대한 나의 걱정과 이에 대한 나의 기운 빠진 항의에도 불구하고, 두 아이는 그들의 태도를 고집스럽게 고수했다.

해설

필자는 자신의 요구에도 아랑곳하지 않고, 자신들이 하고 싶은 대로 하는 아이들에 대한 이야기를 하고 있다. 마지막 문장의 'both my sons~resolute in their manner'에서도 알 수 있듯이 아이들의 행동은 보기 (c), 즉 고집이 센 것으로 묘사되고 있다. 정답은 (c)이다.

어휘

seriously 진지하게	proceed 나아가다, 진행하다, 계속하다	indelible 지워지지 않는
cryogenics 냉동저온학, 사람을 냉동상태로 얼림	strike a match 성냥에 불을 붙이다	resolute 완고한, 단호한
	regard 고려, 마음 씀	demanding 요구하는 게 많은
firstborn 맨 처음 태어난 아이	fragility 연약함, 부서지기 쉬움	capricious 변덕스러운
plunk 홱 내던지다, 넘어뜨리다	feeble 연약한, 힘없는	stubborn 완고한, 고집 센

Vocabulary 편지·에세이

앞에서 학습한 지문들에 등장하는 TEPS 빈출 출제 어휘 및 표현들을 다시 한 번 확인하고 그 외 주제와 관련한 빈출 필수 어휘 및 표현들을 학습하고 넘어 갑시다.

- sign up 참가하다, 등록하다
- (1) _____ 경험하다
- reward 보상, 보답
- present 제출하다, 건네주다
- (2) _____ 첨부되어 있는
- quarterly 연 4회의
- obtain 얻다, 획득하다
- membership 회원, 회원자격
- (3) _____ ~에 관하여
- drug addiction 마약 중독
- behind bars 감옥에 갇힌
- scourge 두통거리, 불행을 가져오는 것
- instill 주입시키다
- (4) _____ 결과, 영향
- target ~을 목표로 정하다
- (5) _____ 비판하다
- render 제출하다, 표현하다
- tackle 달려들다, 맞싸우다

- advocate 옹호하다
- conduct 집행하다, 처리하다
- interrogation 질문, 심문
- (6) _____ 감독하다, 지휘하다
- cross the line 정도를 넘어서다
- rapport 친밀한 관계, 조화
- old-fashioned : 구식의
- seriously : 진지하게
- proceed 나아가다, 진행하다
- (7) _____ 고려, 마음 씀
- fragility 연약함, 부서지기 쉬움
- resolute 완고한, 단호한
- demanding 요구하는 게 많은
- (8) _____ 변덕스러운
- (9) _____ 완고한, 고집 센
- reflect upon ~을 회고하다
- pass away 사망하다
- as if 마치 ~인 것처럼

Letters · Essays

- plain 평이한, 간단한
- face 직면하다
- (10) _____ 요구, 요구하다
- draw upon ~에 의존하다
- awards ceremony 시상식
- confirm 확실히 하다, 확인하다
- attendance 참석, 출석
- be praised for ~으로 칭찬 받다
- contact 접촉하다, 연락하다
- paperwork 문서업무
- late delivery 배송지연
- reimbursement 상환, 변상
- refund 환불
- equipment 장비
- information 정보
- urge 재촉하다, 촉구하다
- inform ~에게 알리다
- overdue 연체된, 지체된

- credit standing 신용등급
- cancel 취소하다
- sales representative 판매직원
- account 계정, 계좌
- rectify 시정하다, 고치다
- disciplinary 징계의, 훈계의
- complain 불평하다, 불만
- appreciation 감사, 평가
- advise ~에게 충고하다
- recommend 추천하다
- solution 해결(방법)
- urgent 긴급한
- review 세밀히 조사하다, 재검토하다
- remain 남아 있다, ~한 대로이다
- hesitate 주저하다, 망설이다
- email address 이메일 주소
- opinion 의견
- identify 확인하다, ~의 신원을 밝히다

Answers (1) experience (2) attached (3) concerning (4) consequence (5) criticize (6) supervise (7) regard (8) capricious (9) stubborn (10) demand

30 DAYS TEPS 800+Final Sum-up

Theme 04
뉴스
News

1. 신문 또는 잡지에서 등장하는 다양한 주제의 뉴스기사들을 다룬 지문이 여기에 속한다.

2. 뉴스가 특정한 내용을 독자들에게 전달하는 것에 목적이 있는 만큼, 주로 뉴스의 주제가 무엇인지, 기사의 제목으로 가장 적절한 것이 무엇인지와 같은 질문들이 자주 출제된다.

3. 뉴스는 대부분 첫 문장에서 주제가 들어나지만, 간혹 전체의 내용을 종합해서 이해해야만 주제를 파악할 수 있는 글들이 등장하기도 한다. 이런 경우, 뉴스의 주제나 제목을 판단할 때, 지엽적인 선택지의 내용에 속지 말고, 전체를 포괄하는 선택지를 고를 수 있도록 주의한다.

Theme 04
뉴스

30 DAYS TEPS 800 **+**Final Sum-up

Mini-Test

Read the passage and choose the option that best fits the blank. (1~2)

1. Investors are bracing for a shaky start on the stock market tomorrow after a jump in unemployment _____. The US Dow Jones industrial average slid 143.28 points to end the week down nearly 5 percent at 8599. The Labor Department's much-anticipated report showed employers cut 524,000 jobs in December—fewer than forecast but still pushing the unemployment rate to a 16 year high of 7.3 percent. The report revealed the worst annual job losses since World War 2 and raised alarms the deepening recession's worst was yet to come. President-elect Barack Obama called December's jobs loss "a stark reminder of how urgently action is needed".

   (a) raised the prices of US stocks for the past six weeks
   (b) might lead to the possibility of more people buying US stocks
   (c) sent US share prices sharply lower on Wall Street
   (d) can be prevented by the efforts of the US government

2. The recession may have caused a 30% fall in the demand for cosmetic surgery in the US, says David Lazarus in the Los Angeles Times, but interest in hair transplants is soaring. An open house for the New Hair Institute was full of guys who were willing to spend as much as US$ 20,000 apiece to restore what nature is taking away. It seems the incentive now is not merely vanity, but the desire to _____. The Institute claims that when two people go for a job, the one with hair is considered to have more youth and vitality than the one who's partly bald.

   (a) gain credit from others
   (b) attract females with their better looks
   (c) be more competitive
   (d) get a substantial raise

Choose the option that correctly answers the question. (3~5)

3. Israeli forces pounded dozens of targets and edged closer to the north of Gaza City yesterday, killing 15 militants in heavy fighting. Its air force also dropped leaflets on the Gaza Strip warning residents it is planning to escalate its two-week-old offensive. The fliers said Israel is about to begin a new phase in the war on terror. Israel's military said its aircraft attacked more than 40 targets throughout Gaza yesterday, striking 10 rocket-launching sites, weapons stores, smuggling tunnels, and anti-aircraft missile launcher and gunmen. It said ground forces inside Gaza also engaged militants in a series of clashes. Flames and smoke could be seen rising into the sky over Gaza City. Eight members of the same Palestinian family, including a 12-year-old, were killed by Israeli fire. The fighting raged after both sides ignored a United Nations resolution calling for an immediate cease-fire.

    Q: What is the passage mainly about?

    (a) The failure of the UN efforts to stop the ongoing war.
    (b) The extent of damages caused by Israel's attack.
    (c) Israel's new stage of the war on terrorism.
    (d) How the two countries ended the war against each other.

4. Gemma Ward, the striking model who once captivated the international fashion scene, has gained a significant amount of weight as she continues to struggle with the death of her close friend. Ward, seen this week relaxing on a Byron Bay beach, is due back on the runway in February. The model has clearly added kilograms since her last catwalk appearance at shows in Paris in September 2007. Ward announced plans to take a year off following her friend's death to go trekking in Nepal and spend time with friends and family. In 2007, Ward earned 3 million dollars from her doll-face looks and was ranked by Forbes magazine as the 11th highest-paid model in the world. She is now based between Australia, Los Angeles and New York and has spent the past weeks in Byron Bay, renting a beachside mansion at Sufflok Park with her fellows.

    Q: Which of the following is correct about Gemma Ward?

    (a) She has been on a diet since she gained weight.
    (b) She decided to take a vacation because of the weight gain.
    (c) She is scheduled to do some running exercises in February.
    (d) She has been having a difficult time since her friend died.

5. The United States and China intensified their naval confrontation in the South China Sea, each sending an armed ship to the region. The conflict began when an unarmed US navy ship, used to monitor submarine movements, was harassed by five Chinese vessels. China claimed the ship had entered its territorial waters. The US rejected this and sent an armed destroyer escort to the area. China, in turn, despatched a patrol boat. The incident took place in waters subject to conflicting territorial claims by China and other nations.

Q: What can be inferred from the passage?

(a) The US navy destroyed the vessels sent by Chinese government.
(b) Some other countries are also claiming the sovereignty over the waters.
(c) Sporadic skirmishes are continuing in the South China Sea.
(d) China and other nations are forming an alliance against America.

Theme 04 뉴스

Mini-Test 1

Investors are bracing for a shaky start on the stock market tomorrow after a jump in unemployment _____ _____. The US Dow Jones industrial average slid 143.28 points to end the week down nearly 5 percent at 8599. The Labor Department's much-anticipated report showed employers cut 524,000 jobs in December—fewer than forecast but still pushing the unemployment rate to a 16 year high of 7.3 percent. The report revealed the worst annual job losses since World War 2 and raised alarms the deepening recession's worst was yet to come. President-elect Barack Obama called December's jobs loss "a stark reminder of how urgently action is needed".

(a) raised the prices of US stocks for the past six weeks
(b) might lead to the possibility of more people buying US stocks
(c) sent US share prices sharply lower on Wall Street
(d) was by the efforts of the US government

해석

실업률의 큰 상승이 월가의 주식가격을 폭락시킨 이후인 내일 투자자들이 주식 시장에서 위태로운 시작을 대비하고 있다. 미국 다우존스 산업 평균지수가 143.28 포인트 미끄러지며 거의 5퍼센트 하락한 8599에서 그 주를 마감하였다. 굉장히 많이 기대가 되었던 노동부의 보고서는 고용주들이 12월에 524,000개의 일자리를 없앴다고 밝혔다. 이는 예상되던 것보다는 낮지만 여전히 실업률을 16년간 최고수준인 7.3퍼센트로 올려놓았다. 보고서는 2차 세계대전 이후로 최악이라 할 수 있는 1년간의 직업감소를 나타내었고, 깊어지는 경기 후퇴 속에 아직 최악의 상황은 오지 않았다는 불안감을 높였다. 대통령으로 선출된 버락 오바마는 12월의 직업감소를 두고 "얼마나 긴급 행동이 필요한지를 알려주는 것"이라고 외쳤다.

해설

빈칸 뒤의 내용은 미국의 주식시장 지수가 실업률의 증가로 인해 급격하게 하락했다는 것을 말하고 있다. 즉, 빈칸은 실업의 급등이 미국 주식가격을 하락시킨 후에 투자자들이 위태한 시작을 대비해야 한다고 말해야 문맥이 이어진다. 고로 정답은 (c)이다.

어휘

investor 투자자
brace for ~을 대비하다
stock market 주식시장
unemployment 실업(상태)
US Dow Jones Industrial Average 미국 다우존스 공업평균지수
slide 미끄러지다
anticipate 기대하다, 예상하다
stark 강한, 엄한
lead to ~로 이끌다
possibility 가능성
share price 주식가격

Mini-Test 2

The recession may have caused a 30% fall in the demand for cosmetic surgery in the US, says David Lazarus in the Los Angeles Times, but interest in hair transplants is soaring. An open house for the New Hair Institute was full of guys who were willing to spend as much as US$ 20,000 apiece to restore what nature is taking away. It seems the incentive now is not merely vanity, but the desire to _____. The Institute claims that when two people go for a job, the one with hair is considered to have more youth and vitality than the one who's partly bald.

(a) gain credit from others
(b) attract females with their better looks
(c) be more competitive
(d) get a substantial raise

해석

경기후퇴가 미국에서의 성형수술에 대한 수요를 30퍼센트 감소시켰을 수도 있다고 로스앤젤레스 타임즈의 David Lazarus가 말합니다. 하지만 머리카락 이식술에 대한 관심은 증가하고 있는 중이지요. New Hair 협회의 공개행사는 자연의 섭리가 빼앗아가 버린 것을 복구하기 위해 한 사람당 미화 20,000달러까지도 쓸 의향이 있는 남자들로 넘쳐났습니다. 이제 이러한 동기는 단순히 허영심이 아니라 더 경쟁력 있게 되기를 원하는 욕망인 것처럼 보입니다. 협회는 두 명의 사람이 일자리를 얻으러 갈 때, 머리카락이 있는 사람이 부분적으로 머리가 대머리인 사람보다도 더 젊음과 활기를 가지고 있는 것으로 생각되어진다고 주장합니다.

해설

비싼 돈을 들여서라도 머리카락을 이식하고 싶어하는 남성들이 단순히 허영심 때문만이 아니라 이것 때문이라는 내용이 빈칸에 들어가야 한다. 뒤의 문장에서 구직을 하러 갈 때, 머리카락이 있는 사람이 그렇지 않은 사람보다 젊고 활기차 보인다는 내용에서, 빈칸의 내용은 '좀 더 경쟁력을 갖고 싶은'이란 (c)가 적절하다. 젊고 활기차 보인다는 것이 다른 이들로부터 신용을 얻는 것과는 다른 내용이기에 (a)는 정답이라고 보기 어렵다.

어휘

recession 경기후퇴
cause ~의 원인이 되다, 일으키다
cosmetic surgery 성형수술
transplant 이식, 옮겨 심다
soar 급등하다, 치솟다
open house 공개파티, 일반 공개일
willing to 기꺼이 ~을 하다
take away ~을 앗아가다
incentive 격려, 동기
vanity 허영심
gain credit 신용을 얻다
competitive 경쟁할 수 있는, 경쟁력 있는
substantial 실질적인
vitality 활기, 생명력

Mini-Test 3

Israeli forces pounded dozens of targets and edged closer to the north of Gaza City yesterday, killing 15 militants in heavy fighting. Its air force also dropped leaflets on the Gaza Strip warning residents it is planning to escalate its two-week-old offensive. The fliers said Israel is about to begin a new phase in the war on terror. Israel's military said its aircraft attacked more than 40 targets throughout Gaza yesterday, striking 10 rocket-launching sites, weapons stores, smuggling tunnels, and anti-aircraft missile launcher and gunmen. It said ground forces inside Gaza also engaged militants in a series of clashes. Flames and smoke could be seen rising into the sky over Gaza City. Eight members of the same Palestinian family, including a 12-year-old, were killed by Israeli fire. The fighting raged after both sides ignored a United Nations resolution calling for an immediate cease-fire.

Q: What is the passage mainly about?

(a) The failure of the UN efforts to stop the ongoing war.
(b) The extent of damages caused by Israel's attack.
(c) Israel's new stage of the war on terrorism.
(d) How the two countries ended the war against each other.

해석

이스라엘 병력이 어저께 12개 정도의 목표점을 맹렬히 폭격했고 격렬한 싸움에서 15명의 전투원을 사살하며 가자시 북쪽 근처에까지 근접했다. 이스라엘의 공군병력 역시 가자지구에 전단지를 떨어뜨리며 주민들에게 2주에 걸친 공격을 확대할 계획이라는 것을 경고했다. 전단지는 이스라엘이 테러와의 전쟁에서 새로운 단계를 막 시작할 것이라고 얘기하고 있다. 이스라엘 군대는 공군항공기가 어저께 가자 전체에 걸쳐서 10개의 로켓발사 장소와 무기 저장고, 밀수 터널과 대공 미사일 발사기 그리고 사격수들을 폭격하며, 40개 이상의 목표물을 공격했다고 말했다. 가자 내부의 지상병력들 또한 일련의 충돌에서 전투원들과 교전을 벌였다고 말했다. 화염과 연기가 가자시 위의 하늘로 올라가는 것을 볼 수 있다. 12살짜리를 포함해서 같은 팔레스타인 가족의 8명이 이스라엘의 포화로 사망했다. 본 전투는 양측이 유엔의 즉각적인 휴전을 요구하는 결의안을 무시하면서 더 사납게 휘몰아쳤다.

해설

대의를 묻는 문제이다. 지문을 꼼꼼히 읽고 기사에서 알려주고자 하는 내용이 무엇인지 파악해야 한다. 이스라엘의 가자시에 대한 폭격의 연장계획 및 공격의 대상이 된 목표물의 종류와 그로 인해 누가 죽었는지에 중점을 둬 기술되고 있다. 그러므로 '이스라엘의 공격으로 인한 피해의 범위'를 의미하는 (b)가 정답이다. 전쟁의 '새로운 단계'의 시작은 현재 벌어지는 상황 이후의 일이므로 보기 (c)는 정답이 될 수 없다.

어휘

force 병력, 군대
pound 맹렬히 폭격하다
edge 천천히 움직이다
militant 전투원
Gaza Strip 가자지구
leaflet 전단지
escalate 확대하다, 강화하다
flier 광고쪽지, 삐라
engage ~와 교전하다
rage 사납게 휘몰아치다, 격노하다
ignore 무시하다
resolution 결의(안)
cease-fire 휴전
extent 범위

Mini-Test 4

Gemma Ward, the striking model who once captivated the international fashion scene, has gained a significant amount of weight as she continues to struggle with the death of her close friend. Ward, seen this week relaxing on a Byron Bay beach, is due back on the runway in February. The model has clearly added kilograms since her last catwalk appearance at shows in Paris in September 2007. Ward announced plans to take a year off following her friend's death to go trekking in Nepal and spend time with friends and family. In 2007, Ward earned 3 million dollars from her doll-face looks and was ranked by Forbes magazine as the 11th highest-paid model in the world. She is now based between Australia, Los Angeles and New York and has spent the past weeks in Byron Bay, renting a beachside mansion at Sufflok Park with her fellows.

Q: Which of the folling is correct about Gemma Ward?

(a) She has been on a diet since she gained weight.
(b) She decided to take a vacation because of the weight gain.
(c) She is scheduled to do some running exercises in February.
(d) She has been having a difficult time since her friend died.

 해석

한때, 국제 패션계를 사로잡았던 멋진 모델인 Gemma Ward가 그녀의 친한 친구의 죽음을 극복하기 위해 계속 애쓰면서 체중이 크게 늘었다. Byron Bay 해변에서 이번 주에 쉬고 있는 모습을 보인 Ward는 2월에 패션쇼의 스테이지에 복귀하기로 예정되어 있다. 이 모델은 2007년도 9월에 파리의 쇼에서 마지막으로 무대에 선 이후로 분명히 살이 쪘다. Ward는 친구의 죽음 이후에 네팔에 트래킹을 가는 것과 친구와 가족들과 시간을 보내기 위해서 1년을 쉬겠다는 계획을 발표했었다. Ward는 그녀의 인형 같은 얼굴로 3백만 달러를 벌었고, Forbes 잡지에 의해서 세계에서 11번째로 높은 금액을 지급받는 모델로 순위가 매겨졌었다. 그녀는 지금 호주, 로스앤젤레스 그리고 뉴욕 사이를 기반으로 친구들과 Sufflok Park에 있는 해변 옆 맨션을 임대해 Byron Bay에서 지난 몇 주를 보내왔다.

 해설

세부사항 문제는 지문을 읽으며 틀린 보기를 배제해가며 정답을 찾아야 한다. 지문의 주인공인 Gemma Ward에 대한 내용 중 올바른 것을 찾아야 하는데, 본문 중 그녀가 가까운 친구의 죽음으로 계속해서 고군분투(struggle)하고 있다는 언급을 통해 그녀가 친구의 죽음으로 어려운 시간을 보내왔음을 알 수 있다. 고로 정답은 (d)이다. 2월에 그녀에게 예정되어 있는 일은 패션 스테이지인 runway로의 복귀이지 달리기 훈련이 아니므로 (c)는 오답이다.

어휘

striking 두드러진, 인상적인
captivate 현혹시키다, 매혹하다
struggle 허우적거리다, 고군분투하다
runway (패션쇼 등의) 스테이지
catwalk (패션쇼에서 모델이 걸어가는) 긴 통로
gain weight 살이 찌다

Mini-Test 5

The United States and China intensified their naval confrontation in the South China Sea, each sending an armed ship to the region. The conflict began when an unarmed US navy ship, used to monitor submarine movements, was harassed by five Chinese vessels. China claimed the ship had entered its territorial waters. The US rejected this and sent an armed destroyer escort to the area. China, in turn, despatched a patrol boat. The incident took place in waters subject to conflicting territorial claims by China and other nations.

 해석

미국과 중국은 각각 그 지역으로 무장된 선박을 보내면서 남중국해에서의 해군대치를 격렬히 높이고 있습니다. 본 충돌은 잠수함 움직임을 감시하는데 사용되어지는 비무장 미국 해군선박이 다섯 대의 중국 배에 의해서 방해를 받으며 시작되었습니다. 중국은 배가 자신들의 영해에 침범을 했다고 주장했습니다. 미국은 이 주장을 거부했고, 무장된 구축함 호위선을 보냈습니다. 중국은 이에 대응하여 순찰선을 급파했습니다. 본 사건은 중국과 다른 국가들에 의해서 영토 주장의 논쟁이 되고 있는 영해에서 발생했습니다.

Q: What can be inferred from the passage?

(a) The US navy destroyed the vessels sent by Chinese government.
(b) Some other countries are also claiming the sovereignty over the waters.
(c) Sporadic skirmishes are continuing in the South China Sea.
(d) China and other nations are forming an alliance against America.

 해설

마지막에서 사고가 발생한 영해는 중국과 다른 국가들에 의해서 영토 주장 충돌이 있는 곳이라고 언급되어 있다. 즉, '몇몇 다른 나라들이 그 영해에 대한 주권을 주장하고 있다'는 (b)가 정답이다. 미국과 중국은 서로 대치상태로 있는 것이지 실제로 전투가 일어난 것은 아니기에 (a), (c) 모두 정답이 될 수 없다.

어휘

intensify 증가하게 하다, 격렬하게 하다	conflict 충돌, 대립	waters 영해, 수역
naval 해군의	submarine 잠수함	reject 거절하다, 거부하다
confrontation 대결, 대치	harass 괴롭히다, 애먹이다	dispatch 급파하다
armed 무장한	territorial 영토의, 사유지의	sporadic 산발적인

Vocabulary 뉴스

앞에서 학습한 지문들에 등장하는 TEPS 빈출 출제 어휘 및 표현들을 다시 한 번 확인하고 그 외 주제와 관련한 빈출 필수 어휘 및 표현들을 학습하고 넘어 갑시다.

- ☐ investor 투자자
- ☐ brace for ~을 대비하다
- ☐ (1) _____ 주식시장
- ☐ unemployment 실업(상태)
- ☐ slide 미끄러지다
- ☐ (2) _____ 기대하다, 예상하다
- ☐ lead to ~으로 이끌다
- ☐ possibility 가능성
- ☐ share price 주식가격
- ☐ (3) _____ ~의 원인이 되다, 일으키다
- ☐ cosmetic surgery 성형수술
- ☐ transplant 이식, 옮겨 심다
- ☐ soar 급등하다, 치솟다
- ☐ (4) _____ 기꺼이 ~을 하는
- ☐ take away ~을 앗아가다
- ☐ incentive 격려, 동기
- ☐ (5) _____ 허영심
- ☐ vitality 활기, 생명력

- ☐ force 병력, 군대
- ☐ militant 전투원
- ☐ leaflet 전단지
- ☐ (6) _____ 확대하다, 강화하다
- ☐ rage 사납게 휘몰아치다, 격노
- ☐ (7) _____ 무시하다
- ☐ resolution 결의(안)
- ☐ cease-fire 휴전
- ☐ (8) _____ 범위
- ☐ captivate 현혹시키다, 매혹하다
- ☐ (9) _____ 고군분투하다, 허우적거리다
- ☐ gain weight 살이 찌다
- ☐ intensify 증가하게 하다, 격렬히 하다
- ☐ confrontation 대결, 대치
- ☐ armed 무장한
- ☐ conflict 충돌, 대립
- ☐ (10) _____ 괴롭히다, 애먹이다
- ☐ territorial 영토의, 사유지의

□ reject 거절하다, 거부하다	□ be sentenced to ~의 형을 받다
□ sporadic 산발적인	□ impersonate 흉내 내다, 분장하다
□ dispatch 급파하다	□ authorities 당국
□ allegedly 들리는 바에 의하면	□ federal judge 연방 판사
□ apparently 명백히, 분명히	□ attorney 변호사, 대리인
□ cite (내용을) 인용하다	□ by guilty of ~로 유죄이다
□ commentary 논평	□ greedy 탐욕스러운
□ coverage 보도, 취재	□ be prosecuted for ~로 기소당하다
□ flash 뉴스 특보	□ arrest 체포하다
□ follow-up 속보	□ sue 고소하다, 소송을 제기하다
□ quote (사람을) 인용하다	□ violate 어기다, 침해하다
□ reportedly 보도에 의하면	□ constitutional 헌법상의
□ sources 소식통	□ court 법원
□ unnamed 이름을 밝히지 않는	□ appeal 상고, 항소
□ likely 있음직한, 가능한	□ consent 검사
□ pretend ~인 척하다	□ be limited 한정되어 있다
□ frisk 소지품 검사를 하다	□ permit 허락하다, 허가하다
□ victim 피해자	□ liability 책임이 있음, 채무

Answers (1) stock market (2) anticipate (3) cause (4) willing to (5) vanity (6) escalate (7) ignore (8) extent (9) struggle (10) harass

30 DAYS TEPS 800+Final Sum-up

Theme 05
정치 · 경제
Politics · Economics

1. 정치 및 경제와 관련된 지문에서 Part 1의 빈칸 채우기의 경우 however, but, so 등의 연결어 뒤에 빈칸이 위치하는 경우가 많다. 그러므로 빈칸을 포함한 문장뿐 아니라, 앞뒤의 내용간의 연결 관계를 잘 파악해서 문제를 해결해야 한다.

2. 주제와 세부사항, 추론에 이르기까지 다양한 문제유형이 등장한다. 단, 추론문제를 풀 때에는 지문에서 주어진 내용을 바탕으로 너무 비약적인 유추를 한 선택지를 고르지 않도록 주의한다.

3. 주로 미국의 정치와 경제와 관련한 시사적인 지문들이 자주 등장하기 때문에, 평소에 타임즈, 뉴스위크 등의 잡지들을 많이 읽어 어휘 실력을 향상시켜 놓으면 시험 때 문제를 푸는 데 많은 도움이 된다.

Theme 05
정치 · 경제

Mini-Test

Read the passage and choose the option that best fits the blank. (1)

1. When you get up one day and find that your investment has plummeted in value, it's natural that you want to do something about it as soon as possible. However, the reality is that your best defense might be_____. You should remember that it's when investors join in and exit their investments en masse, that economic crises are made worse. Recovery can be encouraged by investors who continue to have confidence, wait out the volatility and gradually resume normal trading. Historically, even the most devastated financial markets have rebounded given time. Remember that selling investments hastily could turn a short-term paper loss into a real one. Waiting out periods of financial turbulence can mean you effectively avoid the crisis and continue to profit long-term.

    (a) doing as what others do
    (b) not investing in the first place
    (c) to look for other investments
    (d) not to act at all

Choose the option that correctly answers the question. (2~4)

2. The current US president signed an executive order lifting restrictions on federal government funding of stem cell research. In doing so he repudiated the policies of the former administration, which had applied conservative values to a range of scientific and medical questions including family planning and climate change. In another reversal, the president ordered federal officials to consult the attorney-general before relying on any of former president Bush's "signing statements". These were written instructions issued by Mr. Bush when signing a bill into law, defining how the legislation was to be implemented.

    Q: What is the main topic of the passage?

    (a) An innovative approach to biotechnology
    (b) The conflict between the former and current president
    (c) The changes made by the new administration
    (d) Challenges against the conservative points of view

3. Shares in airline Virgin Blue have fallen as low as 18 cents. The company's market capitalization now stands below 200 million dollars with the share price having fallen 37.7% since the beginning of the calendar year. Those losses are more than double the falls on the overall stock market and represent the worst share price decline for any airline in the Asia-Pacific region. Richard Branson remains the single largest shareholder in Virgin Blue with a 25% stake. The share price falls followed news that 2% fewer Australians took overseas trips in January despite the low airfares. Outbound business travel fell by 24.3% in January to reach its lowest level since 2003. The current share price is below the lowest analyst target of 27 cents.

   Q: What caused the company's share price to plummet according to the passage?

   (a) The world stock market plunge.
   (b) Reduced number of air passengers.
   (c) The increased price of gasoline.
   (d) Low profitability due to the low fares.

4. The US economy has congestive heart failure, says Thomas Friedman. Our heart—our banking system that pumps blood to our industrial muscles—is clogged and functioning below capacity. Nothing remotely compares to the importance of the urgent need to heal our banks. Economically, it's the morning after Pearl Harbor attack. Yet, we continue to dither. What is worse, the opposition party think they would rather see the country fail than the government succeed, so they've opted for catcalls. As for the new president Barak Obama, he's too relaxed under fire. Sure, he doesn't want to be held hostage to the banking crisis, but great crises are what create great presidents. The banking meltdown is Obama's shot at greatness. It won't be easy, and will mean giving more money to Wall Street. It may even involve nationalizing some banks. Above all, it will require boldness, persistence and persuasion.

   Q: What can be inferred from the passage?

   (a) The majority of Americans are suffering from heart ailments.
   (b) The government took immediate action against the financial crisis.
   (c) President Obama is not getting the support from the Opposition.
   (d) Some of the banks in America may go public in the future.

Identify the sentence that least fits the context of the passage. (5)

5. It's been a year since Kosovo gained its independence from Serbia but we can't call it truly independent. (a) The former Serbian province, home to ethnic Albanians, is tiny and surrounded by neighbours that are either still hostile or struggling themselves. (b) Its security depends on its Western backers, so if it's left to itself, it is not viable. (c) Many Kosovars have succeeded in other countries, mostly Germany and Austria. (d) Consequently, Kosovar politicians tend to make appeals, not decisions, and govern with an eye towards their Western overseers.

Theme 05
정치·경제 Answers

Mini-Test 1

When you get up one day and find that your investment has plummeted in value, it's natural that you want to do something about it as soon as possible. However, the reality is that your best defense might be _____ _____. You should remember that it's when investors join in and exit their investments en masse, that economic crises are made worse. Recovery can be encouraged by investors who continue to have confidence, wait out the volatility and gradually resume normal trading. Historically, even the most devastated financial markets have rebounded given time. Remember that selling investments hastily could turn a short-term paper loss into a real one. Waiting out periods of financial turbulence can mean you effectively avoid the crisis and continue to profit long-term.

(a) doing as what others do
(b) not investing in the first place
(c) to look for other investments
(d) not to act at all

해석

어느 날 아침에 일어나서 당신의 투자액의 가치가 수직으로 떨어져 있다는 것을 발견하게 되었을 때, 당신이 그것에 대해서 가능한 빨리 무언가를 하길 원하는 것은 자연스러운 일입니다. 하지만, 현실에서 당신이 취할 수 있는 최선의 방어책은 전혀 아무런 행동도 하지 않는 것이죠. 경제 위기가 더 심각해지는 것은 투자자들이 참여하여 한꺼번에 그들의 투자금액을 빼낼 때라는 것을 기억해야만 합니다. 경기회복은 지속적으로 자신감을 가지고, 돌발성을 참고 기다리며 천천히 정상적인 거래를 개시하는 투자자들에 의해서 조장될 수 있습니다. 역사적으로, 가장 많이 피폐화된 금융 시장도 시간과 함께 재반등했었습니다. 투자물을 급하게 팔아버리는 것은 단기간의 장부상의 손실을 실제 손실로 만들어 버릴 수 있다는 것을 기억하세요. 금융 혼란의 기간을 참고 기다리는 것은 여러분이 효과적으로 위기를 피하고 장기간 수익을 지속할 수 있음을 뜻합니다.

해설

빈칸이 포함된 문장은 however로 연결되기에, 앞에 위치한 문장과는 반대되는 내용이 나올 것임을 예상할 수 있다. 앞에서는 투자액의 가치가 하락을 하면 가능한 빨리 무언가를 하기를 원한다는 것이다. 그리고 지문의 마지막에서 가장 효과적으로 위기를 피할 수 있는 것은 기다리는 것이라고 말하고 있다. 즉, 빈칸은 (d) '전혀 행동하지 않는 것'이 가장 적절하다. 이미 투자를 한 상황을 가정하고 그에 대한 대응방법을 이야기하는 것이기에 (b)의 '애초에 투자를 하지 않는 것'은 정답이 될 수 없다.

어휘

investment 투자(금)
as soon as possible 가능한 빨리
en masse 한꺼번에, 집단으로
plummet 수직으로 떨어지다, 갑자기 내려가다
crisis 위기, 공항
recovery 회복
confidence 자신감
volatility 휘발성
gradually 점진적으로
resume 개시하다
devastate 유린하다, 황폐시키다
short-term 단기간의
financial 재정, 재무의
turbulence 소란, 동란

Politics · Economics

Mini-Test 2

The current US president signed an executive order lifting restrictions on federal government funding of stem cell research. In doing so he repudiated the policies of the former administration, which had applied conservative values to a range of scientific and medical questions including family planning and climate change. In another reversal, the president ordered federal officials to consult the attorney-general before relying on any of former president Bush's "signing statements". These were written instructions issued by Mr. Bush when signing a bill into law, defining how the legislation was to be implemented.

Q: What is the main topic of the passage?

(a) An innovative approach to biotechnology
(b) The conflict between the former and current president
(c) The changes made by the new administration
(d) Challenges against the conservative points of view

 해석

현재 미국 대통령이 줄기 세포 연구의 연방정부 자금조달 규제를 해지하는 대통령 명령에 서명을 했다. 그렇게 함으로써, 그는 가족계획과 기후 변화 등을 포함한 다양한 과학적 그리고 의학적 문제에 보수적 가치를 적용했던 이전 정부의 정책의 이행을 거부하게 되었다. 또 다른 반대의 움직임으로, 대통령은 연방 관료들에게 전 대통령인 부시의 "입법진술"에 의존하기 전에 법무장관의 의견을 들을 것을 명령했다. 이 입법진술들은 의안을 법으로 만들 때 부시에 의해서 발행된 서면 지시사항들로 법률제정이 이행되는 방식을 정의한 것들이다.

 해설

줄기세포 연구에 대한 제한 해제, 그리고 법률제정과 관련한 절차상의 변경, 이 두 가지를 지문에서 언급하고 있다. 이는 새로운 정부가 들어서면서 생긴 변화이므로 정답은 보기 (c)의 '새 정부에 의해 만들어진 변화들'이다.

어휘

executive order 대통령 명령	repudiate 거부하다, 받아들이지 않다	attorney-general (연방정부의) 법무장관
lift restrictions 제한을 없애다	administration 집행부, 행정부, 내각	signing statements 입법진술
stem cell 줄기 세포	conservative 보수적인	bill 법안, 의안
federal government 연방정부	reversal 반전, 역전	legislation 입법, 법률제정
funding 자금조달	official 공무원, 임원	implement 이행하다

Mini-Test 3

Shares in airline Virgin Blue have fallen as low as 18 cents. The company's market capitalization now stands below 200 million dollars with the share price having fallen 37.7% since the beginning of the calendar year. Those losses are more than double the falls on the overall stock market and represent the worst share price decline for any airline in the Asia-Pacific region. Richard Branson remains the single largest shareholder in Virgin Blue with a 25% stake. The share price falls followed news that 2% fewer Australians took overseas trips in January despite the low airfares. Outbound business travel fell by 24.3% in January to reach its lowest level since 2003. The current share price is below the lowest analyst target of 27 cents.

Q: What caused the company's share price to plummet according to the passage?

(a) The world stock market plunge.
(b) Reduced number of air passengers.
(c) The increased price of gasoline.
(d) Low profitability due to the low fares.

해석

Virgin Blue 항공사의 주식가격이 18센트 가까이 내려갔습니다. 회사의 시장 자본평가액은 올해 시작 이후로 37.7%가 하락해 현재 2억 달러 이하입니다. 이러한 손실은 전체 시장의 하락에 두 배에 달하며, 아시아 태평양 지역의 그 어떤 항공사와 비교해도 최악의 주식가격 폭락을 나타냅니다. Richard Branson은 25%의 주식을 보유하고 있어 단독 최대 주주로 남아 있습니다. 주식가격의 하락은 1월에 2% 적은 호주인이 해외여행을 갔다는 뉴스에 뒤따랐습니다. 외국으로 향하는 사업 여행도 1월에 24.3%가 하락해 2003년 이후 최저점에 도달했습니다. 현재 (Virgin Blue의) 주식가격은 애널리스트들이 가장 낮은 가격으로 전망한 27센트보다도 아래에 있습니다.

 해설

지문에 의하면 주식가격의 하락이 호주인들의 해외여행 하락으로 이어졌다고 언급하고 있다. 또한, 해외 비즈니스 여행객 역시 크게 하락했음을 언급하고 있다. 그러므로 '항공 승객수의 감소'라는 (b)가 정답이다. 싼 항공기 값에도 불구하고 승객수가 하락한 것이 이유이지, 싼 항공기 값으로 인한 저수익성이 직접적인 이유는 아니기에 (b)는 오답이다.

 어휘

share 주식	overall 전체적으로	airfare 항공료
capitalization 자본평가액)	represent 기술하다, 대표하다	outbound 외국으로 가는, 시외로 가는
calendar year 1년간	despite ~에도 불구하고	profitability 수익성

Mini-Test 4

The US economy has congestive heart failure, says Thomas Friedman. Our heart—our banking system that pumps blood to our industrial muscles—is clogged and functioning below capacity. Nothing remotely compares to the importance of the urgent need to heal our banks. Economically, it's the morning after Pearl Harbor attack. Yet, we continue to dither. What is worse, the opposition party think they would rather see the country fail than the government succeed, so they've opted for catcalls. As for the new president Barak Obama, he's too relaxed under fire. Sure, he doesn't want to be held hostage to the banking crisis, but great crises are what create great presidents. The banking meltdown is Obama's shot at greatness. It won't be easy, and will mean giving more money to Wall Street. It may even involve nationalizing some banks. Above all, it will require boldness, persistence and persuasion.

Q: What can be inferred from the passage?

(a) The majority of Americans are suffering from heart ailments.
(b) The government took immediate action against the financial crisis.
(c) President Obama is not getting the support from the Opposition.
(d) Some of the banks in America may go public in the future.

해석

미국 경제는 울혈성 심부전증을 앓고 있다고 Thomas Friedman이 말했다. 우리의 심장, 즉 다시 말해 산업이라는 근육에 피를 공급해주는 은행업 체계가 막혀버려서 함량미달로 작동중이다. 은행들을 치유해야 하는 긴급한 필요성의 중요도와 근접하게나마 비교되는 것은 아무것도 없다. 경제적 견지에서, 이는 진주만 공격을 당한 다음날의 아침이라고 할 수 있다. 그럼에도 불구하고, 우리는 계속해서 망설이고 있다. 더 최악인 것은 야당이 버락 오바마가 성공하는 것보다는 차라리 정부가 실패하는 것을 보는 게 낫다고 생각하여, 야유를 하는 것을 선택했다는 것이다. 현 대통령인 오바마에 대해서 말하자면, 그는 이런 포화를 받고도 너무 느긋하다. 물론, 그는 은행업 위기에 인질로 잡히는 것을 원치는 않을 것이다. 하지만, 위대한 대통령을 만드는 것은 중대한 위기들이다. 은행업의 붕괴는 위대함을 보여줄 수 있는 오바마의 기회이다. 쉽지는 않을 것이고 월스트리트에 더 많은 돈을 주어야 한다는 것을 의미할 것이다. 몇몇 은행들은 국유화해야 할 수도 있다. 무엇보다도 이는 대범함, 끈기 그리고 설득력을 요할 것이다.

해설
지문의 중간에서 '야당이 현 정부의 성공을 원하지 않으며, 야유하는 것을 선택했다'에서 현 대통령인 오바마가 야당의 지지를 받고 있지 못하다는 것을 추측할 수 있다. 그러므로 정답은 (c)이다.

어휘
congestive heart failure 울혈성 심부전증
heal 구제하다
economically 경제적 관점에서
dither 우유부단하게 행동하다, 망설이다
what is worse 더 최악인 것은
opposition party 야당
opt for ~을 선택하다
catcall 야유
relaxed 느긋한, 편안한
hostage 인질
nationalize 국유화하다
persistence 완고, 끈덕짐
go public (회사가) 주식을 공개하다

Mini-Test 5

It's been a year since Kosovo gained its independence from Serbia but we can't call it truly independent. (a) The former Serbian province, home to ethnic Albanians, is tiny and surrounded by neighbours that are either still hostile or struggling themselves. (b) Its security depends on its Western backers, so if it's left to itself, it is not viable. (c) Many Kosovars have succeeded in other countries, mostly Germany and Austria. (d) Consequently, Kosovar politicians tend to make appeals, not decisions, and govern with an eye towards their Western overseers.

해석

코소보가 세르비아로부터 독립한 지 1년이 되었지만, 우리는 코소보가 진정 독립되었다고 말할 수 없습니다. 전 세르비아의 지방이자 알바니아 인종의 고향인 이곳은 작고 여전히 그들에게 적대적이거나 혹은 국가 자체가 위태로운 이웃 국가들로 둘러싸여 있습니다. 코소보의 안전은 그들의 뒤를 봐주는 서방 국가들에 달려있습니다. 코소보가 홀로 남겨진다면, 이 나라는 살아남을 수가 없습니다. 많은 코소보인들이 독일 그리고 오스트리아 등의 다른 국가에서 성공을 했습니다. 따라서 코소보의 정치인들은 그들을 감독하는 서방국가들을 향해 눈을 맞춰 국민을 통치하고 있습니다.

해설

보기 중 전체 문맥 상 흐름에 어울리지 않는 것을 골라야 한다. 지문의 주된 내용은 세르비아로부터 독립한 코소보가 내부 상황과 여러 가지 주변 상황으로 인해 완전한 독립국가로서의 역할을 하고 있지 못한다는 내용이다. 단, (c)의 경우 '많은 코소보인들이 해외에서 성공했다' 내용인데, 이는 글의 전체 흐름인 독립성과 관련성이 떨어지며 (d)의 그 결과로 코소보 정치인들이 서방국가들의 눈치를 본다는 것은 인과관계가 맞지 않는다. 그러므로 정답은 (c)이다.

어휘

gain 얻다
province 지방
be surrounded by ~에 의해 둘러싸여 있다
ethnic 인종의, 민족의
neighbour 이웃
hostile 적대적인
security 안전, 안보
viable 살아갈 수 있는, 생명력이 있는
consequently 결과적으로
politician 정치인
govern 통치하다

Vocabulary 정치·경제

앞에서 학습한 지문들에 등장하는 TEPS 빈출 출제 어휘 및 표현들을 다시 한 번 확인하고 그 외 주제와 관련한 빈출 필수 어휘 및 표현들을 학습하고 넘어 갑시다.

- ☐ investment 투자(금)
- ☐ (1) _____ 수직으로 떨어지다, 하강하다
- ☐ (2) _____ 위기, 공항
- ☐ recovery 회복
- ☐ confidence 자신감
- ☐ gradually 점진적으로
- ☐ (3) _____ 개시하다
- ☐ devastate 유린하다, 황폐시키다
- ☐ short term 단기간의
- ☐ financial 재정의, 재무의
- ☐ turbulence 소란, 동란
- ☐ (4) _____ 제한을 없애다
- ☐ federal government 연방정부
- ☐ funding 자금 조달
- ☐ (5) _____ 행정부, 내각
- ☐ reversal 반전, 역전
- ☐ bill 법안, 의안
- ☐ implement 이행하다
- ☐ (6) _____ 주식
- ☐ capitalization 자본평가(액)
- ☐ overall 전체적으로
- ☐ represent 기술하다, 대표하다
- ☐ profitability 수익성
- ☐ create 창조하다, 만들어 내다
- ☐ be clogged 막혔다
- ☐ heal 구제하다
- ☐ economically 경제적 관점에서
- ☐ what is worse 더 최악인 것은
- ☐ (7) _____ 야당
- ☐ (8) _____ 국유화 하다
- ☐ persistence 완고, 끈덕짐
- ☐ go public (회사가) 주식을 공개하다
- ☐ gain 얻다
- ☐ (9) _____ 인종의, 민족의
- ☐ neighbor 이웃
- ☐ hostile 적대적인

Politics · Economics

- security 안전, 안보
- viable 살아갈 수 있는, 생명력 있는
- politician 정치인
- (10) _____ 통치하다
- overseer 감독관
- remittance 송금
- gross domestic product 국내총생산
- alleviate 경감하다
- boost 경기 활성화, 후원
- fraud 사기
- advent 도래, 출현
- currency 통화
- exceed 초과하다, 넘다
- bureaucratic 관료정치의, 관료의
- candidate (선거의) 후보자
- congress 의회, 국회
- constituent 선거구민, 구성 요소
- corrupt 타락시키다, 부패하다
- demonstrate 시위하다
- deputy 대리의, 부의
- dictator 독재자
- oppress 억압하다, 압제하다
- reform 개혁하다
- regime 정체, 정권, 사회 제도
- riot 폭동
- sanction 제재조치
- sovereignty 주권, 독립국
- suffrage 투표권, 참정권
- commodity 상품
- contract 계약(서), 계약하다
- depression 불경기, 불황
- expire 만기가 되다
- heavy industry 중공업
- infrastructure 산업기반
- manufacturer 제조업자
- tariff 관세

Answers (1) plummet (2) crisis (3) resume (4) lift restrictions (5) administration (6) share (7) opposition party (8) nationalize (9) ethnic (10) govern

30 DAYS TEPS 800 + Final Sum-up

Theme 06
과학·기술·우주
Science·Technology ·Universe

1. 이 주제의 지문은 전문적인 용어들이 빈번히 등장하여 다소 어렵게 느껴질 수 있다. 관련 어휘들을 평소에 많이 학습해 놓는다면 지문을 독해할 때 많은 도움을 준다.

2. Part 1, 2, 3 전반에 걸쳐서 출제가 되는 유형으로 Part 1의 경우 주제문과 관련한 곳에 빈 칸이 있는 경우가 많으니, 글이 말하고자 하는 핵심 내용이 무엇인가를 신경 쓰면서 읽는 것이 중요하다.

3. 지문 주제의 특성 상, 지문에서 나타난 특정 용어들이 보기 선택지에서도 등장시킨 후 서술어 부분을 paraphrasing하여 오답을 유도시키는 경우가 많다. 그 만큼, 지문 내용을 철저히 읽고 해석할 수 있는 능력이 요구된다.

Theme 06
과학·기술·우주

Mini-Test

Read the passage and choose the option that best fits the blank. (1~2)

1. Scientists may have _____. The high-tech sheet captures nearly every photon of all wavelengths of light, or up to 99% of the wavelengths that can be directly measured. By comparison, the blackest available paints and coatings absorb between 84% and 95% of all light. Therefore, this is the closest scientists have come to a black body, a hypothetical state of perfect light absorption. The sheet is made from a series of carbon nanotubes. Photons that aren't immediately absorbed by a single nanotube deflect away, but are absorbed by neighbouring tubes. The process repeats until light is almost completely absorbed.

   (a) found the darkest natural color
   (b) developed a sheet that illuminates light itself
   (c) created the blackest material in the universe
   (d) invented panels that could be painted in any color

2. Ever wonder how musicians manage to play in unison? It's their brain waves that make this possible. According to scientists who measured the electrical activity of their brains, musicians playing together synchronize their minds. Researchers at the Max Planck Institute monitored eight pairs of guitarists while they played a modern jazz piece. They found that the guitarists' brain waves _____ at points during the composition that demanded the most synchrony. The effect was most prominent in the frontal and central parks of the brain that regulates motor function. But just how this happens remains a mystery.

   (a) were not matched at all
   (b) were most aligned
   (c) were vibrating randomly
   (d) were most scattered

Science · Technology · Universe

Choose the option that correctly answers the question. (3~4)

3. Astronomers have discovered a new planet orbiting a red giant star in another solar system and it offers clues about what may happen to our own solar system. The planet, dubbed HD 102272, is about six times the mass of Jupiter and orbits 40% closer to its star than Earth does around the sun. Astronomers from Pennsylvania State University observed the red giant star wobbling from the gravitational pull of a nearby object, identified as the planet. Consequently, the planet has been drawn closer to the star. This observation shows that, five billion years from now, Earth is expected to be consumed by the heat when our much younger sun becomes a gigantic old red star.

   Q: What is the best title for the passage?

   (a) An accidental astronomical discovery in history.
   (b) HD 102272 in our solar system.
   (c) The foretold Earth's fate.
   (d) How the sun become a gigantic old red star.

4. Scientists must invent a way to save the Earth from collision with the asteroid Apophis. Apophis has a diameter of 330 meters, much smaller than the "dinosaur-killer" but large enough to create devastating tidal waves or a major crater. In 2029 it will pass just 25,600 km from the Earth. This approach may bump it into an orbit that will cause it to hit the Earth in 2036 or later this century. The odds of a collision are just one in 45,000, but a possible death toll in the tens of millions is exercising minds. If Apophis misses us, eventually something of a similar size will hit unless we can take defensive action.

   Q: What is the next paragraph likely to be about?

   (a) When the asteroid Apophis will make its close approach to Earth.
   (b) Possible methods to save the Earth from the collision.
   (c) The need for developing a comprehensive strategy for space exploration.
   (d) Ways to defend ourselves from further destruction.

Identify the sentence that least fits the context of the passage. (5)

5. British scientists are about to mount one of the boldest-ever missions. (a) They will search for organisms that survived in a frozen "lost world" beneath an ancient ice sheet. (b) The team of Antarctic scientists will drill through a 3km-thick sheet of ice that has sealed a sub-glacial lake from the rest of the biosphere for at least as long as Homo sapiens have walked the earth. (c) They are still searching for extra-terrestrial life on Europa, a moon of Jupiter where life is also thought to exist beneath a frozen ocean. (d) The scientists, from a consortium of universities including Bristol and Edinburgh, hope to find species that have survived below the ice sheet since it formed between 400,000 and two million years ago.

Theme 06
과학·기술·우주

Mini-Test 1

Scientists may have_____.
The high-tech sheet captures nearly every photon of all wavelengths of light, or up to 99% of the wavelengths that can be directly measured. By comparison, the blackest available paints and coatings absorb between 84% and 95% of all light. Therefore, this is the closest scientists have come to a black body, a hypothetical state of perfect light absorption. The sheet is made from a series of carbon nanotubes. Photons that aren't immediately absorbed by a single nanotube deflect away, but are absorbed by neighbouring tubes. The process repeats until light is almost completely absorbed.

(a) found the darkest natural color
(b) developed a sheet that illuminates light itself
(c) created the darkest material in the universe
(d) invented panels that could be painted in any color

해석

과학자들은 우주에서 가장 어두운 물질을 만들어 냈을 수도 있습니다. 이 하이테크 얇은 판은 거의 빛의 모든 파장의 광양자를 붙잡을 수 있습니다. 혹은 직접적으로 수치를 잴 수 있는 파장의 99%까지를 붙잡을 수 있습니다. 비교해보면, 이용 가능한 가장 어두운 페인트와 도료는 모든 빛의 84~95% 사이를 흡수합니다. 그러므로 이것은 과학자들이 가상의 완벽한 빛의 흡수 상태인 흑체에 가장 가깝게 근접한 물체라고 할 수 있겠습니다. 이 얇은 판은 일련의 탄소 나노관으로부터 만들어집니다. 하나의 나노관에 의해서 즉각적으로 흡수가 되지 않는 광양자들은 빗나가게 되지만, 근처에 있는 관들에 의해서 흡수가 되는 것이지요. 이 과정은 빛이 거의 완전히 흡수가 될 때까지 반복됩니다.

해설

빛을 거의 완벽히 흡수할 수 있는 새로운 물질에 관한 설명이다. 본문 상에서 본 물질이 '흑체(black body)에 가장 근접한 물질로 과학자들이 근접했다' 라는 설명을 통해서 빈칸은 '우주에서 가장 어두운 물질을 만들었을지도 모른다' 라는 (c)가 정답임을 알 수 있다.

어휘
capture 붙잡다, 포획하다
photon 광양자
wavelength 파장
absorb 흡수하다
blackbody 흑체 (모든 파장의 방사를 완전히 흡수하는 가상물체)
hypothetical 가설의, 가정의
carbon 탄소
deflect 빗나가다
repeat 반복하다

Mini-Test 2

Ever wonder how musicians manage to play in unison? It's their brain waves that make this possible. According to scientists who measured the electrical activity of their brains, musicians playing together synchronize their minds. Researchers at the Max Planck Institute monitored eight pairs of guitarists while they played a modern jazz piece. They found that the guitarists' brain waves _____ at points during the composition that demanded the most synchrony. The effect was most prominent in the frontal and central parks of the brain that regulates motor function. But just how this happens remains a mystery.

(a) were not matched at all
(b) were most aligned
(c) were vibrating randomly
(d) were most scattered

 해석

음악가들이 어떻게 조화를 이뤄 연주를 하게 되는지 궁금해 한 적 있나요? 이를 가능하게 하는 것은 그들의 뇌파입니다. 음악가들의 뇌의 전기활동을 측정한 과학자들에 의하면 함께 연주를 하는 음악가들은 그들의 마음을 일치시킨다고 합니다. Max Planck 연구소의 연구원들은 8쌍의 기타 연주가들이 현대 재즈곡을 연주하는 동안 그들을 관찰했습니다. 연구원들은 작곡 도중에 가장 높은 동시성이 요구되는 시점에 기타연주가들의 뇌파가 가장 정렬된다는 것을 발견했습니다. 이 결과는 운동기능을 조절하는 뇌의 앞과 중앙 부분에서 가장 두드러지게 나타났습니다. 하지만 이것이 어떻게 일어나는지는 여전히 불가사의로 남아 있습니다.

 해설

빈칸 안의 내용은 작품을 연주 중에 가장 동시성 높게 요구될 때, 어떠한 현상이 벌어지는 가에 대한 내용이 들어간다. 빈칸 앞에서도 음악가들은 연주 중 마음을 일치시킨다(synchronize their minds)라고 했기에 '뇌파가 가장 많이 일렬로 정렬된다' 라는 (b)가 정답임을 알 수 있다.

 어휘

unison 조화, 화합	synchronize 동시에 진행하다, 일치시키다	prominent 현저한, 두드러진
make possible 가능케 하다		vibrate 진동하다
according to ~에 의하면	brain wave 뇌파	randomly 닥치는 대로
electrical 전기의	align 정렬시키다	scatter 뿔뿔이 흩어져 버리다

Science · Technology · Universe

Mini-Test 3

Astronomers have discovered a new planet orbiting a red giant star in another solar system and it offers clues about what may happen to our own solar system. The planet, dubbed HD 102272, is about six times the mass of Jupiter and orbits 40% closer to its star than Earth does around the sun. Astronomers from Pennsylvania State University observed the red giant star wobbling from the gravitational pull of a nearby object, identified as the planet. Consequently, the planet has been drawn closer to the star. This observation shows that, five billion years from now, Earth is expected to be consumed by the heat when our much younger sun becomes a gigantic old red star.

Q: What is the best title for the passage?

(a) An accidental astronomical discovery in history.
(b) HD 102272 in our solar system.
(c) The foretold Earth's fate.
(d) How the sun become a gigantic old red star.

 해석

천문학자들은 또 다른 태양계에서 붉은 거대 별 주위를 도는 새로운 행성을 발견했다. 그리고 이것은 우리의 태양계에 무슨 일이 일어나게 될 것인가에 대한 실마리를 제공한다. HD 102272로 칭해진 이 행성은 목성 질량의 약 6배이고, 지구가 태양을 도는 것보다 40% 더 가깝게 그것의 항성을 돈다. 펜실베이니아 주립대학교의 천문학자들은 이 붉은 거대 별이 행성으로 확인된 다른 대상의 중력의 힘으로부터 흔들리는 것을 목격했다. 결과적으로, 이 행성은 별에게로 점점 더 가까이 당겨지고 있는 중인 것이다. 이 관찰은 지금으로부터 500억년 후, 훨씬 어린 우리의 태양이 거대한 늙은 붉은 별이 되었을 때, 지구는 열에 의해서 다 타버릴 것으로 예상되어짐을 보여준다.

 해설

지문은 초반에 다른 태양계에서 발견된 행성을 언급하고, 이어지는 문장인 'it offers clues about what may happen to our own solar system'을 통해 우리 태양계와의 관련성을 이야기 할 것임을 알 수 있다. 지문 마지막에 이는 500억년 후 지구가 태양열에 의해서 다 타버릴 것이라는 예상을 보여준다고 말하고 있다. 즉, 다른 태양계의 모습을 통해서 '미리 예견되어진 지구의 운명' (c)가 주제문이다.

어휘

astronomer 천문학자	star 별, 항성	wobble 흔들리다, 동요하다
discover 발견하다	solar system 태양계	gravitational 중력의 n. gravity 중력
planet 행성	dub ~라고 칭하다	accidental 우연한, 우발적인
orbit 궤도를 그리며 돌다	mass 질량, 부피	foretell 예언하다, 예시하다

Mini-Test 4

Scientists must invent a way to save the Earth from collision with the asteroid Apophis. Apophis has a diameter of 330 meters, much smaller than the "dinosaur-killer" but large enough to create devastating tidal waves or a major crater. In 2029 it will pass just 25,600 km from the Earth. This approach may bump it into an orbit that will cause it to hit the Earth in 2036 or later this century. The odds of a collision are just one in 45,000, but a possible death toll in the tens of millions is exercising minds. If Apophis misses us, eventually something of a similar size will hit unless we can take defensive action.

Q: What is the next paragraph likely to be about?

(a) When the asteroid Apophis will make its close approach to Earth.
(b) Possible methods to save the Earth from the collision.
(c) The need for developing a comprehensive strategy for space exploration.
(d) Ways to defend ourselves from further destruction.

  해석

과학자들은 소행성인 Apophis와의 충돌로부터 지구를 구할 수 있는 방법을 고안해 내어야 한다. Apophis는 330미터의 직경을 가지고 있고, 공룡을 멸종시켰던 그것보다 훨씬 크기가 작지만 강력한 해일을 불러일으키거나 지구에 거대한 분화구를 만들 만큼의 충분한 크기가 된다. 2029년에 이 소행성은 지구로부터 단 25,600km 떨어진 거리를 통과할 것이다. 이러한 접근은 궤도 내로 그것을 충돌시켜 2036년이나 이번 세기 후반에 지구와 충돌을 일으키게 될 것이다. 이 충돌이 일어날 확률은 45,000분의 일밖에 되지 않지만, 수천만 명에 달할 수도 있는 사망자 수는 충분히 마음을 걱정시킬 만하다. 만약 Apophis가 지구를 빗맞힌다면, 최종적으로는 우리가 방어적 행동을 취하지 않는 이상 비슷한 크기의 또 다른 무언가가 지구와 충돌할 것이다.

 해설

지문 다음에 이어질 내용으로 적절한 것을 찾아야 한다. 지문 초반 행성과의 충돌로부터 지구를 구할 수 있는 방법을 고안해 내어야 한다고 말했고, 지문 전반에 걸쳐서 구체적으로 어떤 식으로 충돌이 일어날 것으로 예상되며, 그 예상 피해를 알려주고 있다. 마지막에서도 우리가 취해야 할 방어적 행동의 중요성을 언급해주고 있으므로, 이 지문 다음에 이어질 내용은 '충돌로부터 지구를 구할 수 있는 가능한 방법들'이란 (b)가 가장 적절하다.

어휘

collision 충돌, 불일치	tidal wave 해일	death toll 사망자 수
asteroid 소행성	crater 분화구	eventually 최후에는, 결국에는
diameter 직경	approach 접근법, 해결방법	unless ~하지 않는 한
devastating 파괴적인, 강력한	odds 확률	exploration 탐험

Science · Technology · Universe

Mini-Test 5

British scientists are about to mount one of the boldest-ever missions. (a) They will search for organisms that survived in a frozen "lost world" beneath an ancient ice sheet. (b) The team of Antarctic scientists will drill through a 3km-thick sheet of ice that has sealed a subglacial lake from the rest of the biosphere for at least as long as Homo sapiens have walked the earth. (c) They are still searching for extra-terrestrial life on Europa, a moon of Jupiter where life is also thought to exist beneath a frozen ocean. (d) The scientists, from a consortium of universities including Bristol and Edinburgh, hope to find species that have survived below the ice sheet since it formed between 400,000 and two million years ago.

해석

영국 과학자들은 지금까지 가장 대담한 임무 중의 하나에 오를 예정에 있다. 그들은 고대 얼음장 밑에 있는 얼어버린 "잃어버린 세계" 안에서 살아남은 생물체들을 탐색할 것이다. 남극 과학자들의 팀은 최소한 호모사피엔스들이 지구를 걸어 다녔던 때만큼이나 오랜 시간 동안 나머지 생물권으로부터 하위 빙하의 호수를 밀폐시켜 둔 3km 두께의 얼음장에 구멍을 뚫을 것이다. 그들은 아직도 얼어붙은 해양 아래에 존재하고 있을 거라고 또한 여겨지는 목성의 달 유로파의 우주생명체를 찾고 있는 중이다. Bristol과 Edinburgh를 포함한 대학들의 조합으로 구성된 과학자들은 400,000만 년에서 2백만 년 사이에 형성된 얼음장 아래에서 살아남은 생명의 종들을 찾기를 바라고 있다.

해설

영국 과학자들의 새로운 임무에 관한 글이다. (a)에서 그 임무가 무엇인지 알려주고, (b)에서는 임무의 수행과 관련한 작업 방식을 설명해 주고 있다. (d)에서는 이러한 임무를 통해서 과학자들이 수백만 년 전 형성된 이 얼음장 아래에서 살아남은 생물체를 발견하기를 희망하고 있음을 말하고 있다. 반면, (c)는 지문에서 언급되는 남극의 얼음장과는 상관없는 목성 위성의 생명체 탐사 작업을 이야기하고 있음으로 문맥과 어울리지 않는다.

어휘

mount 오르다, 타다
mission 임무
organism 유기체, 생물체
Antarctic 남극의
drill 꿰뚫다, 구멍을 뚫다
seal 봉인하다, 가두어 놓다
glacial 얼음의, 빙하의
biosphere 생물권
homo sapiens 호모 사피엔스
extra-terrestrial 우주의, 외계인
Europa 목성 위성의 하나

Vocabulary 과학·기술·우주

앞에서 학습한 지문들에 등장하는 TEPS 빈출 출제 어휘 및 표현들을 다시 한 번 확인하고 그 외 주제와 관련한 빈출 필수 어휘 및 표현들을 학습하고 넘어 갑시다.

- capture 붙잡다, 포획하다
- photon 광양자
- (1) _____ 파장
- (2) _____ 흡수하다
- blackbody 흑체
- (3) _____ 가설의, 가정의
- carbon 탄소
- deflect 빗나가다
- make possible 가능케 하다
- electrical 전기의
- (4) _____ 동시에 진행하다, 일치시키다
- brain wave 뇌파
- align 정렬시키다
- (5) _____ 현저한, 두드러진
- vibrate 진동하다
- randomly 닥치는 대로의
- scatter 뿔뿔이 흩어져버리다
- (6) _____ 천문학자

- discover 발견하다
- planet 행성
- (7) _____ 궤도를 그리며 돌다
- solar system 태양계
- dub ~라고 칭하다
- mass 질량, 부피
- (8) _____ 중력의
- accidental 우연한, 우발적인
- (9) _____ 충돌, 불일치
- asteroid 소행성
- diameter 직경
- devastating 파괴적인, 강력한
- tidal wave 해일
- crater 분화구
- approach 접근법, 해결 방법
- odds 확률
- eventually 최후에는, 결국에는

Science · Technology · Universe

- exploration 탐험
- destruction 파괴, 파멸
- mount 오르다, 타다
- organism 유기체, 생명체
- glacial 얼음의, 빙하의
- biosphere 생물권
- (10) _____ 우주의, 외계인
- artificial intelligence 인공지능
- astronaut 우주비행사
- high-tech 첨단기술의
- satellite 인공위성, 위성
- sophisticated 정교한
- state-of the-art 최첨단 기술의
- virtual reality 가상현실
- retrieve 되찾다, 회수하다
- optical fiber 광섬유
- computerize 컴퓨터로 처리하다
- automate 자동화하다

- nucleus 핵
- flexibility 유연성
- optional 선택적인, 선택사양의
- measurement 측량, 치수
- chemist 화학자
- demonstrate 증명하다
- anthropologist 인류학자
- a myriad of 무수히 많은
- configuration 배열
- magnetic field 자기장
- mineral 광물
- impurity 불순물
- communication 통신
- partially 부분적으로
- transmit 보내다, 전송하다
- overflow 범람, 과잉
- galaxy 은하
- hub 중심

Answers (1) wavelength (2) absorb (3) hypothetical (4) synchronize (5) prominent (6) astronomer (7) orbit (8) gravitational (9) collision (10) extra-terrestrial

30 DAYS TEPS 800 + Final Sum-up

Theme 07
역사 · 인물
History · People

1. 전 세계 역사에서 벌어진 일들 중에 특히 미국의 역사와 관련한 지문이 자주 등장하고 보통 연대기적 서술 방식을 취한다.

2. 예술인, 시민운동가, 정치인 등 다양한 인물들을 소재로 그들의 삶과 업적 등에 관한 내용을 기술하는 글이 '인물' 주제에 해당한다. Part 1, 2, 3 전반에 걸쳐서 출제가 되는 편이고, 소개되는 인물에 대한 설명 내용들을 세심히 파악해야 한다.

3. 두 주제 모두 세부사항을 물어보는 문제의 경우, 본문의 단어를 이용해 일어난 사실들을 교묘하게 틀어서 오답으로 출제하는 경우가 많으니, 반드시 본문과의 철저한 대비를 통해서 정답을 고를 수 있도록 한다.

Theme 07
역사 · 인물

Mini-Test

Read the passage and choose the option that best fits the blank. (1)

1. Aborigines are people who lived in Australia before white convicts and settlers arrived. There were possibly 750,000 of them in Australia, who lived by gathering food, catching fish and killing kangaroos. They came into conflict with whites as sheep owners and Aborigines competed for the same land. The struggle _____, as spears were no match for firearms and the tribes did not unite but fought each other as well as the whites. The highest estimate of the number of Aborigines killed in conflict with the whites in the nineteenth century is 20,000.

    (a) seemed to have come out of nothing
    (b) evoked a less violent strain of militancy
    (c) was completely one-sided
    (d) took its toll on the settlers

Choose the option that correctly answers the question. (2~4)

2. John Quincy Adams was the sixth president of the USA. He was a son of the second President, John Adams, and a typical New England Puritan, with strong principles, yet self-righteous and overbearing. First, he became President Monroe's secretary of State between 1817 and 25. He was very successful: he made a treaty with Britain which fixed the borders with Canada as far west as the Rockies; he persuaded Spain to cede Spanish Florida to the USA in 1819. Nevertheless, his brilliant run of success came to an end when he became President in 1825. He appeared to be the best-qualified preisdential candidate to succeed Monroe but none of the candidates in the election had a majority. Adams became President only with the support of Henry Clay, whom he made his Secretary of State. This laid Adams open to the charge of being corrupt. His reputation was under attack and faced with a hostile Congress. He could do little as President and was defeated by Andrew Jackson in 1828.

    Q: What is the main topic of the passage?

    (a) A brief history of the Adams.
    (b) The successful path that were set for John Quincy Adams.
    (c) What made John Quincy Adams become president.
    (d) The bright and dark sides of Jone Quincy Adams' life.

3. Henry Ford was born on a Michigan farm. He became a watch-repairer and mechanic before building his first petrol-driven car, mainly from bicycle parts, in 1893. He formed the Ford Motor Company in 1903 and, at a time when automobiles were for the rich, conceived the idea of concentrating on one model and producing a cheap family car. His Model T was produced in 1909 and remained the best-selling car until 1926. In 1913, he introduced assembly-line techniques, which cut production time by 90 per cent. Work was planned so that each man and each machine do only one thing. The thing is to keep everything in motion and take the work to the man and not the man to the work. By 1925 Ford was producing a car every ten seconds and built fifteen million Model T between 1909 and 1927.

Q: Which of the following is correct according to the passage?

(a) Henry Ford made Model T using parts mainly from bicycles.
(b) The price of Model T was exorbitant.
(d) Model T is the most sold automobile in America.
(d) Assembly-line made possible the mass production of Model T.

4. American Civil War began because President Abraham Lincoln, elected in 1860, was determined to preserve the Union, which was threatened by the issue of Slavery. The North was growing rapidly in wealth and population, and it was clear to the Southern states that the North would eventually be strong enough to carry a constitutional amendment abolishing slavery. The Republican Party had been formed in 1854 to oppose slavery. Southern leaders decided that when a Republican President was elected, they should secede from the Union. Consequently, when Lincoln became President, seven states seceded, formed the Confederate States of America and elected Jefferson Davis as their president. On 12 April 1861, Confederates bombarded Fort Sumter and this marked the start of the Civil War.

Q: Which of the following can be inferred from the passage?

(a) People in Southern states were more affluent than those in northen states.
(b) The Republican Party was organized by anti-slavery activists.
(c) Confederate States of America was the name taken by Northern states.
(d) It was the North which started the American Civil War first.

Identify the sentence that least fits the context of the passage. (5)

5. Okinawa is the largest island of the Ryuku Islands between Taiwan and Japan. (a) The Americans intended to use it as a springboard for the invasion of Japan. (b) The invasion of Okinawa showed how high the cost of invading the Japanese mainland would be and may have influenced President Truman's decision to drop an atomic bomb on Hiroshima. (c) The Japanese had carefully prepared defensive lines, with deep dug-outs and well concealed artillery, so US progress was slow and costly. (d) The Japanese tried to destroy the invading fleet and American beachheads by air and sea suicide attacks.

Theme 07
역사 · 인물

Mini-Test 1

Aborigines are people who lived in Australia before white convicts and settlers arrived. There were possibly 750,000 of them in Australia, who lived by gathering food, catching fish and killing kangaroos. They came into conflict with whites as sheep owners and Aborigines competed for the same land. The struggle _____ _____, as spears were no match for firearms and the tribes did not unite but fought each other as well as the whites. The highest estimate of the number of Aborigines killed in conflict with the whites in the nineteenth century is 20,000.

(a) seemed to have come out of nothing
(b) evoked a less violent strain of militancy
(c) was completely one-sided
(d) took its toll on the settlers

해석

애보리진들은 백인 죄수들과 이주민들이 도착하기 전 호주에 살던 사람들이다. 음식을 모으고, 물고기를 잡고 캥거루를 죽이며 살았던 이들은 아마도 호주에 750,000명 정도가 있었다. 양 소유주들과 애보리진들은 같은 땅을 두고 경쟁을 했기에, 애보리진들과 백인들은 싸움을 하게 되었다. 이 전투는 창이 화기에 적수가 되지 못했고 각 부족들은 백인들뿐이 아니라, 부족들 간에도 싸움이 있어 서로 결합을 하지 못했기에 한 쪽으로 치우친 것이었다. 19세기 백인들과의 전투 중에 죽은 애보리진의 최고 예상 숫자는 20,000명이다.

 해설

빈칸 뒤에 'as spears~at the whites'가 문제 해결의 핵심이다. 애보리진들과 백인 이주민들 간의 싸움에 관한 내용인데, 창은 화기에 적수가 되지 못했고, 부족들은 백인들과의 전투뿐만이 아니라 부족들 간의 전투도 진행하며 통합이 되지 못했기 때문에 빈칸이 발생했다고 한다. 또한 죽은 애보리진들의 숫자로 미루어 봐서도 전투가 일방적이었다는 (c)가 문맥상 가장 적절하다.

어휘

aborigine (호주의) 원주민
convict 죄인, 죄수
settler 이주민
compete 경쟁하다
struggle 싸움, 전투
firearm 화기
tribe 부족
estimate 평가, 견적
evoke 불러일으키다
violent 폭력적인
militancy 교전상태, 호전성, 투쟁정신
one-sided 일방적인, 한쪽으로 치우친
take one's toll 손해(피해)를 끼치다

History · People

Mini-Test 2

John Quincy Adams was the sixth president of the USA. He was a son of the second President, John Adams, and a typical New England Puritan, with strong principles, yet self-righteous and overbearing. First, he became President Monroe's secretary of State between 1817 and 25. He was very successful: he made a treaty with Britain which fixed the borders with Canada as far west as the Rockies; he persuaded Spain to cede Spanish Florida to the USA in 1819. Nevertheless, his brilliant run of success came to an end when he became President in 1825. He appeared to be the best-qualified presidential candidate to succeed Monroe but none of the candidates in the election had a majority. Adams became President only with the support of Henry Clay, whom he made his Secretary of State. This laid Adams open to the charge of being corrupt. His reputation was under attack and faced with a hostile Congress,. He could do little as President and was defeated by Andrew Jackson in 1828.

Q: What is the main topic of the passage?

(a) A brief history of the Adams.
(b) The successful path that were set for John Quincy Adams.
(c) What made John Quincy Adams become president.
(d) The bright and dark sides of Jone Quincy Adams's life.

해석

존 퀸시 애덤스는 미국의 여섯 번째 대통령이다. 그는 미국의 두 번째 대통령인 존 애덤스의 아들이고, 강한 원칙을 가진 전형적인 뉴 잉글랜드 청교도인으로, 독선적이고 거만했다. 우선, 그는 1871년과 1825년 사이에 먼로 대통령의 국무장관이 되었다. 그는 로키산맥에 이르는 서쪽까지 캐나다와의 국경을 확정하는 조약을 영국과 맺었고, 1819년에는 스페인들의 Florida를 미국에 넘길 것을 설득시켰다. 그럼에도 불구하고, 그의 놀라운 성공의 일련들은 그가 대통령이 된 1825년에 끝이 났다. 그는 먼로를 이을 가장 적합한 대통령 후보로 보였지만, 후보들 중 아무도 선거에서 과반수를 얻지 못하였다. 애덤스는 그가 추후 그의 국무장관으로 만든 Henry Clay의 지지만으로 대통령이 되었을 뿐이다. 이는 애덤스를 부패라는 혐의를 받게 했다. 그의 명성은 공격을 받았고, 적대적의 의회를 마주하게 되었다. 그는 대통령으로 할 수 있는게 거의 없었고, 1828년에 Andrew Jackson에 의해서 패배하게 된다.

해설

John Quincy Adams에 대한 간략한 소개와 그가 대통령이 되기까지의 성공 과정을 설명해주고 있다. 또한, 그의 성공이 어떻게 끝을 보게 되었는지의 실패 과정 또한 언급해 주고 있다. 이 둘을 모두 담고 있는 것은 'John Quincy Adams의 삶의 양면'인 (d)이다. 이 글은 John Quincy Adams에 관한 내용이지, 아담스 가문의 역사에 관한 내용은 아니므로 (a)는 오답이다.

어휘

puritan 청교도(의)	treaty 조약, 협정	presidential candidate 대통령 후보
self-righteous 독선적인	cede 인도하다, 양보하다	election 선거
overbearing 거만한	come to an end 끝나다, 마치다	corrupt 부정한, 타락한
secretary of state 국무장관	appear ~로 보이다, ~로 생각되다	

Mini-Test 3

Henry Ford was born on a Michigan farm. He became a watch-repairer and mechanic before building his first petrol-driven car, mainly from bicycle parts, in 1893. He formed the Ford Motor Company in 1903 and, at a time when automobiles were for the rich, conceived the idea of concentrating on one model and producing a cheap family car. His Model T was produced in 1909 and remained the best-selling car until 1926. In 1913, he introduced assembly-line techniques, which cut production time by 90 per cent. Work was planned so that each man and each machine do only one thing. The thing is to keep everything in motion and take the work to the man and not the man to the work. By 1925 Ford was producing a car every ten seconds and built fifteen million Model T between 1909 and 1927.

Q: Which of the following is correct according to the passage?

(a) Henry Ford made Model T using parts mainly from bicycles.
(b) The price of Model T was exorbitant.
(d) Model T is the most sold automobile in America.
(d) Assembly-line made possible the mass production of Model T.

해석

헨리 포드는 미시간의 농장에서 태어났다. 그는 1893년 주로 자전거 부품을 활용해서 그의 첫 번째 가솔린으로 운행되는 자동차를 조립하기 이전에 시계수리공과 기계공이 되었다. 그는 포드 자동차 회사를 1903년도에 세웠고, 자동차가 부자들만을 위한 것이었던 시대에 하나의 모델에 집중하여 값싼 가족 자동차를 생산할 생각을 품었다. 그의 T모델은 1909년도에 생산되었고, 1926년도까지 가장 많이 팔린 차가 되었다. 1913년에 그는 일관작업기술을 소개하였는데, 이는 생산시간을 90 퍼센트 가까이 단축시켰다. 작업은 계획이 되었고 이로 인해, 각각의 사람들과 각각의 기계들은 오직 하나의 일만 하면 되었다. 핵심은 모든 것을 계속해서 운행하도록 하고 사람을 일로 데려가는 것이 아니라 일이 사람에게 전달되도록 하는 것이었다. 1925년이 되어, 포드는 매 10초마다 차를 생산하고 있었고, 1909년과 1927년 사이에 15,000만 대의 T모델을 만들어냈다.

해설

지문에서 Model T에 관해서 언급된 내용을 보기와 대조해가며 정답을 찾아내야 한다. 지문 중 'he introduced~90 percent work'를 통해서 일관작업기술로 인해서 생산량이 늘어났고, 이것이 마지막에서 언급되는 10초의 한 대 생산을 가능케 했음을 알 수 있다. 그러므로 정답은 (d)이다. Henry Ford가 자전거 부품을 이용해 만든 차는 Model T 이전에 제작되었으므로 (a)는 정답이 될 수 없다.

어휘

mechanic 기계공
part 부품
concentrate 집중하다
assembly-line 일관작업라인
exorbitant (가격 따위가) 터무니없는, 부당한
production 생산(량)

History · People

Mini-Test 4

American Civil War began because President Abraham Lincoln, elected in 1860, was determined to preserve the Union, which was threatened by the issue of Slavery. The North was growing rapidly in wealth and population, and it was clear to the Southern states that the North would eventually be strong enough to carry a constitutional amendment abolishing slavery. The Republican Party had been formed in 1854 to oppose slavery. Southern leaders decided that when a Republican President was elected, they should secede from the Union. Consequently, when Lincoln became President, seven states seceded, formed the Confederate States of America and elected Jefferson Davis as their president. On 12 April 1861, Confederates bombarded Fort Sumter and this marked the start of the Civil War.

Q: Which of the following can be inferred from the passage?

(a) People in Southern states were more affluent than those in northen states.
(b) The Republican Party was organized by anti-slavery activists.
(c) Confederate States of America was the name taken by Northern states.
(d) It was the North which started the American Civil War first.

해석

미국 독립전쟁은 1860년에 뽑힌 에이브러햄 링컨 대통령이 노예제도 문제로 인해서 위협을 받은 미합중국을 보존하기로 결심하면서 시작되었다. 북쪽은 부와 인구가 급격하게 증가하였고, 남쪽의 주들에게 있어서 북쪽이 결국 노예제도를 폐지하는 헌법 수정을 가져올 정도로 충분히 강해질 것이라는 것이 분명했다. 노예제도에 반대하기 위해서 1854년에 공화당이 결성되었다. 남쪽의 지도자들은 공화당 대통령이 선출이 될 때, 그들은 미합중국에서 탈퇴할 것이라고 결심했다. 그 결과로, 링컨이 대통령이 되자, 일곱 개의 주가 탈퇴하여, 미국 남부 연방을 결성하였고, Jefferson Davis를 대통령으로 선출하였다. 1861년 4월 12일, 남부 연합은 Sumter 항구를 포격하였고, 이것이 시민전쟁의 시작을 알렸다.

해설

미국 시민전쟁(남북전쟁)의 시작과 관련한 역사적 내용들을 담고 있는 지문이다. 중간에 'The Republican Party had~ oppose slavery'를 통해서, '공화당은 반노예제도 활동가들에 의해서 조직되었다'라는 (b)가 정답임을 알 수 있다. 나머지 보기들은 다 주어진 사실과 반대되는 내용이다.

어휘

Civil War 남북전쟁	amendment 수정, 개정	the Confederate States of America 남부 연방
elect 선거하다, 선임하다	abolish 폐지하다	bombard 포격하다
the Union 미국 합중국	oppose 반대하다	affluent 풍부한, 유복한
slavery 노예제도	secede 정식으로 탈퇴하다	

Mini-Test 5

Okinawa is the largest island of the Ryuku Islands between Taiwan and Japan. (a) The Americans intended to use it as a springboard for the invasion of Japan. (b) The invasion of Okinawa showed how high the cost of invading the Japanese mainland would be and may have influenced President Truman's decision to drop an atomic bomb on Hiroshima. (c) The Japanese had carefully prepared defensive lines, with deep dug-outs and well concealed artillery, so US progress was slow and costly. (d) The Japanese tried to destroy the invading fleet and American beachheads by air and sea suicide attacks.

 해석

오키나와는 대만과 일본 사이의 류쿠 열도 중 가장 큰 섬이다. 미국은 이 섬을 일본을 침략하기 위한 도약판으로 사용하려고 했다. 오키나와 침입은 일본의 본토를 침입하기 위한 대가가 얼마나 클 것인가를 보여줘, 트루먼 대통령이 히로시마에 원자폭탄을 떨어뜨리자고 한 결정에 영향을 주었을지도 모른다. 일본인들은 깊게 판 참호와 잘 숨겨놓은 포들과 함께 조심스럽게 방어선을 준비했고, 그래서 미국의 전진은 그 속도가 느렸다. 일본인들은 침략을 해오는 함대와 미국의 해안 교두보들을 공중과 바다의 자살 공격을 파괴하기 위해 노력했다.

 해설

첫 문장에서 오키나와가 무엇인지 설명을 해준 후 (a)에서 미국이 이 섬을 일본 침략의 도약판으로 사용하려 했음을 말하고 있다. (c)에서는 이와 관련해 일본인들의 대응준비와 관련한 내용을 얘기해주고 있고, (d)에서는 좀 더 구체적으로 이 대응방법에 대한 설명을 해주고 있다. 반면, (b)는 이 섬에서의 전투에 대한 결과와 이에 따른 히로시마의 원자폭탄 관련 이야기를 언급해 결론의 성격을 띠는 문장이므로 문맥의 흐름상 적절하지 못한 문장이라고 할 수 있다.

어휘

intend ~할 작정이다, 의도하다	atomic-bomb 원자폭탄	artillery 포, 대포
springboard 도약판	defensive 방어의	fleet 함대
invasion 침입, 침략	dug-out 참호	beachhead 해안교두보
mainland 대륙, 본토	conceal 숨기다	

Vocabulary 역사·인물

앞에서 학습한 지문들에 등장하는 TEPS 빈출 출제 어휘 및 표현들을 다시 한 번 확인하고 그 외 주제와 관련한 빈출 필수 어휘 및 표현들을 학습하고 넘어 갑시다.

- aborigine (호주의) 원주민
- convict 죄인, 죄수
- (1) _____ 이주민
- decade 10년
- compete 경쟁하다
- firearm 화기
- (2) _____ 부족
- estimate 평가, 견적
- (3) _____ 불러일으키다
- violent 폭력적인
- militancy 교전상태, 호전성
- one-sided 일방적인
- (4) _____ 손해를 끼치다
- puritan 청교도(의)
- self-righteous 독선적인
- overbearing 거만한
- secretary of state 국무장관
- (5) _____ 조약, 협정

- (6) _____ 양보하다, 인도하다
- come to an end 끝나다, 마치다
- appear ~로 보이다
- presidential candidate 대통령 후보
- election 선거
- mechanic 기계공
- concentrate 집중하다
- budget 남북전쟁
- (7) _____ 노예제도
- (8) _____ 수정, 개정
- (9) _____ : 폐지하다
- oppose 반대하다
- secede 정식으로 탈퇴하다
- bombard 포격하다
- affluent 풍부한, 유복한
- intend ~할 작정이다, 의도하다
- springboard 도약판
- (10) _____ 침입, 침략

Theme 07 역사·인물 독해 10가지 주제별 접근법

History · People

☐ atomic-bomb 원자폭탄	☐ factor 요인, 요소
☐ conceal 숨기다	☐ morale 사기, 의욕
☐ artillery 포, 대포	☐ ironic 얄궂은, 아이러니컬한
☐ fleet 함대	☐ descendent 후손
☐ colony 식민지	☐ inhabitant 주민, 거주자
☐ civilize 문명화하다, 교화하다	☐ found 설립하다, 창시하다
☐ aristocracy 귀족정치, 귀족계급	☐ sermon 설교
☐ contemporary 동시대의, 현대의	☐ originate 유래하다, 기원하다
☐ revolt 반란을 일으키다, 반항하다	☐ unearth 발굴하다, 파다
☐ religious 종교적인	☐ precede ~보다 앞서다
☐ benefit 혜택, 이득을 얻다	☐ covenant 규약
☐ well-known 잘 알려진	☐ poignant 매서운, 통렬한
☐ firm 확고한	☐ inherent 고유의, 본래의
☐ athletic 원기왕성한, 운동을 잘하는	☐ villain 악한, 악인
☐ portrayal 초상(화)	☐ ancient 고대의
☐ confront 직면하다	☐ engrave 새기다
☐ define A as B A를 B로 정의하다	☐ reflect 반영하다, 나타내다
☐ liberal 자유주의의	☐ marginal 가장자리의, 중요치 않은

Answers (1) settler (2) tribe (3) evoke (4) take one's toll (5) treaty (6) cede (7) slavery (8) amendment (9) abolish (10) invasion

30 DAYS TEPS 800 + Final Sum-up

Theme 08
환경 · 생물
Environment · life

1. 생물들의 멸종위기, 지구온난화와 같은 주제들은 환경, 생물과 관련해 대표적으로 다루어지는 주제들이다. 평소에 이러한 내용의 뉴스기사 내용들을 접하여 배경지식을 쌓는 것이 문제 해결에 도움을 준다.

2. Part 1, 2, 3 전반에 걸쳐서 출제가 되는 주제유형이다. 주제에 대한 한 가지 관점만 설명하기보다는, 두 가지 서로 다른 관점이 등장하는 경우가 있으니, Part 2 대의파악 유형의 경우, 전체를 아우를 수 있는 선택지를 고를 수 있도록 주의한다.

3. Part 2의 세부사항 유형 역시 주어진 선택지들을 하나하나 꼼꼼히 읽어, 본문의 내용과 비교, 대조하여 출제자의 오답 함정에 빠지지 않도록 세심한 주의를 기울여야 한다.

Theme 08
환경 · 생물

Mini-Test

Read the passage and choose the option that best fits the blank. (1~2)

1. Debates over the culling of crocodiles near tourist locations could become moot points as it seems that cane toads are _____.
Research by Dr. Letnic of the University of Sydney's School of Biological Sciences suggests that the toads pose a major threat to the iconic species. Dr. Letnic points out that in a one-year period as many as 77% of the crocodiles have died as a result of eating cane toads, with second-year data also showing evidence of high mortality. Populations can't really withstand that year-after-year of high mortality, particularly in these really long-lived species that take a long time to mature before they are reproductive.

    (a) a good source of nutrients for crocodiles
    (b) in a symbiotic relationship with crocodiles
    (c) being taken advantage of by men
    (d) doing the job without being hired

2. A study suggests that drastic declines in the number of bees and other pollinator species have not prevented global growth in pollinator-dependent crop yields. Colony collapse disorder, a phenomenon in which bees from a beehive abruptly disappear, is seeing honeybee hives, including many commercial pollination services, suddenly abandoned. Slower declines caused by mites and viruses have been occurring for a while, and wild populations of pollinating insects are also affected in many regions, possibly as a result of insecticide misuses. The research team scored crops on how much they depend on pollinators for maximum production, and they found that, depending on the crop, this dependence ranges from zero to 100%. _____, cereal crops like wheat don't need to be pollinated but, at the other end of the scale, unpollinated almond trees produce no nuts.

    (a) Meanwhile
    (b) For instance
    (c) After all
    (d) Instead

Choose the option that correctly answers the question. (3~5)

3. Some scientists argue that genetic modification is no more than a sophisticated form of cross-breeding. In the 19th century, pioneer geneticist Gregor Mendel experimented by cross-breeding pea plants to create variations in their flower colours. In the early 20th century scientists cross-bred plant relatives to create "hybrids". The hybrids were designed to produce higher crop yields, or to be more resistant to pests. But current methods of genetic manipulation take a radical new step. They cross the natural boundaries between species and entire biological "kingdoms". DNA from plants, animals and micro-organisms can now all be blended to create a new genetic mix.

    Q: What is the main topic of the passage?

    (a) The stagnant methods of crossbreeding
    (b) The development of genetic screening tests
    (c) The continuing evolution of genetic science
    (d) A new approach to human cloning

4. Tasmania is one of the world's most beautiful islands. It's amazing how many great attractions are squeezed into this Australia's smallest state. There are many places in the Island that are worth to visit. The Tasman Peninsula is where you will find wild coastal scenery and the island's premier attraction, the Port Arthur convict settlement. It's very hard to believe this beautiful, serene setting was once the scene of such dreadful acts. A number of historic towns are located in the midlands, with Richmond and Ross, the pick of the bunch. Along the north and east coasts are a string of small beach towns and the magnificent Freycinet National Park, famous for the beautiful Wineglass Bay.

    Q: Which of the following is correct according to the passage?

    (a) Tasmania is a peninsular country.
    (b) Many criminals dwelled in Tasmania.
    (c) Freycinet National park is famous for its winery.
    (d) Richmond is one of the small beach towns along the north coast.

5. Sunscreen lotions are under suspicion of causing environmental damage and as a possible health risk. Italian scientists have found the creams can cause rapid and total bleaching of corals in the sea. Fraser Island already has a no-sunscreen policy to preserve its freshwater lakes. Now there's additional concern about the use of the nano particles of titanium dioxide and zinc used to make sunscreen disappear into the skin. These have replaced the old white emulsion formulas that were harder to rub in. Although manufacturers are required to label all ingredients, they do not need to specify the form they are in. Therefore, nano particles in sunscreens remain largely undisclosed to buyers. Scientists believe there may be changes to the toxicity of the metal oxides as they are readily absorbed in the skin when reduced to nano particulate size.

Q: What can be inferred from the passage?

(a) Sunscreen lotions have an affirmative effect on coral preservation.
(b) Nano particles increase the absorption of new lotions into the skin.
(c) The form of ingredients are precisely detailed in the product label.
(d) All ingredients in lotions are not required to be specified on the label.

Theme 08
환경 · 생물

Mini-Test 1

Debates over the culling of crocodiles near tourist locations could become moot points as it seems that cane toads are _____.
Research by Dr. Letnic of the University of Sydney's School of Biological Sciences suggests that the toads pose a major threat to the iconic species. Dr. Letnic points out that in a one-year period as many as 77% of the crocodiles have died as a result of eating cane toads, with second-year data also showing evidence of high mortality. Populations can't really withstand that year-after-year of high mortality, particularly in these really long-lived species that take a long time to mature before they are reproductive.

(a) a good source of nutrients for crocodiles
(b) in a symbiotic relationship with crocodiles
(c) being taken advantage of by men
(d) doing the job without being hired

해석

관광지 근처의 악어들을 추려서 죽이자는 논쟁은 사탕수수 두꺼비들이 알아서 그 일을 수행하는 것으로 보이기에 별 소용없는 논쟁이 될 것으로 보인다. 시드니 대학교 생물과학부의 Letnic 박사의 연구조사는 두꺼비들이 이 상징적인 종들에게 중대한 위협을 가하고 있다는 것을 시사했다. Letnic 박사는 1년의 기간 동안 많게는 악어의 77%가 사탕수수 두꺼비를 먹은 결과로 죽었다는 것을 지적했고, 두 번째 해의 자료들 역시도 높은 사망률의 증거를 보여주고 있다. 특히나 번식이 되기 전 성숙해지기까지 오랜 시간이 걸리는 장수 종인 악어에게 있어서 이렇게 해마다의 높은 사망률은 견딜 수가 없을 것이다.

해설

빈칸이 포함된 문장은 전체 문장에서 종속절에 해당하는 내용으로 악어를 추려서 죽이자는 논쟁을 소용없이 만들어버린 이유에 해당된다. 뒤의 지문 내용을 통해 악어들이 사탕수수 두꺼비를 먹은 결과로 77% 가까이 죽었으며, 이로 인해 개체수가 유지되기 힘들다는 내용을 언급하고 있다. 그러므로 두꺼비들이 소위 말해 시키지도 않았는데 알아서 처리했다는 내용의 보기 (d)가 정답이 된다.

어휘

debate 토론, 논쟁
cull 추려서 죽이다
crocodile 악어
moot 미결의
toad 두꺼비
pose a threat to ~에게 위협을 가하다
mortality 사망률, 폐사율
withstand ~에 저항하다, 견디다
mature 성숙한, 성숙하다
reproductive 재생의, 다산의
nutrient 자양물, 음식
symbiotic relationship 공생관계
take advantage of ~을 이용하다
hire 고용하다

Mini-Test 2

A study suggests that drastic declines in the number of bees and other pollinator species have not prevented global growth in pollinator-dependent crop yields. Colony collapse disorder, a phenomenon in which bees from a beehive abruptly disappear, is seeing honeybee hives, including many commercial pollination services, suddenly abandoned. Slower declines caused by mites and viruses have been occurring for a while, and wild populations of pollinating insects are also affected in many regions, possibly as a result of insecticide misuses. The research team scored crops on how much they depend on pollinators for maximum production, and they found that, depending on the crop, this dependence ranges from zero to 100%. _____, cereal crops like wheat don't need to be pollinated but, at the other end of the scale, unpollinated almond trees produce no nuts.

(a) Meanwhile
(b) For instance
(c) After all
(d) Instead

해석

벌과 다른 꽃가루 매개자 종들의 숫자의 급격한 하락이 꽃가루 매개자에 의존하는 수확 농작물들의 세계적인 증가를 방해하지 못했다. 벌집으로부터 벌들이 갑작스럽게 사라져 버리는 현상인 벌떼폐사장애로 인해 수많은 상업용 꽃가루 매개 서비스들을 포함해서 꿀벌의 벌집들이 갑작스럽게 버려지고 있다. 진드기들과 바이러스들에 의해서 늦춰진 하락현상이 당분간 나타나기도 했다, 그리고 꽃가루 매개 역할을 하는 야생 벌레들의 수 또한 아마도 살충제의 잘못된 사용으로 여러 지역에서 영향을 받았다. 연구조사팀은 농작물들이 최대 수확량을 위해 얼마나 많이 꽃가루 매개자들에게 의지하는지 기록을 했고, 그들은 수확물의 종류에 따라서 이 의존도는 0에서 100%의 범위를 오간다는 것을 알아냈다. 예를 들어, 밀과 같은 곡물 수확물은 꽃가루 매개를 받을 필요가 없지만, 다른 쪽에서는 꽃가루 매개를 받지 못한 아몬드 나무가 아무런 견과도 생산해내지 못했다.

해설

벌들과 다른 꽃가루 매개자 벌레들이 사라지고 있다는 내용의 글이다. 빈칸이 포함된 문장의 앞에서 꽃가루 매개자들이 곡물의 생산량에 영향을 얼마나 영향을 미치는가에 대한 조사결과에서 의존도가 0에서 100%까지 다양한 것을 알려주고 있다. 빈칸 뒤에는 두 가지 수확물의 예를 들어 설명해주고 있다. 그러므로 가장 적절한 접속사는 (b)이다.

어휘

drastic 격렬한, 과감한
decline 감소, 쇠퇴
pollinator 꽃가루 매개자
crop 수확(물)
phenomenon 현상
abruptly 갑작스럽게
abandon 버리다
occur 일어나다, 생기다
mite 진드기
depending on ~에 따라서
insecticide 살충(제)
misuse 오용, 남용
cereal 곡물
pollinate ~에 수분하다

Environment · life

Mini-Test 3

Some scientists argue that genetic modification is no more than a sophisticated form of cross-breeding. In the 19th century, pioneer geneticist Gregor Mendel experimented by cross-breeding pea plants to create variations in their flower colours. In the early 20th century scientists cross-bred plant relatives to create "hybrids". The hybrids were designed to produce higher crop yields, or to be more resistant to pests. But current methods of genetic manipulation take a radical new step. They cross the natural boundaries between species and entire biological "kingdoms". DNA from plants, animals and micro-organisms can now all be blended to create a new genetic mix.

Q: What is the main topic of the passage?

(a) The stagnant methods of crossbreeding
(b) The development of genetic screening tests
(c) The continuing evolution of genetic science
(d) A new approach to human cloning

해석

몇몇 과학자들은 유전적 변형은 정교한 형태의 이종교배 이상의 것이 아니라고 주장한다. 19세기에 선구적 유전학자인 Gregor Mendel은 콩 식물들을 그들의 꽃의 색깔에 변화를 만들어내기 위해서 이종교배하는 실험을 했다. 20세기 초반에 과학자들은 "잡종"을 만들어내기 위해서 비슷한 종의 식물들을 이종교배했다. 이 잡종들은 더 높은 수확량을 생산하거나 혹은 해충들에 더 내성이 있도록 의도되었다. 하지만 유전적 조작의 현재 방법들은 급진적인 새 단계를 밟았다. 그것들은 종들 간의 그리고 전체 생물학적 왕국의 자연적 경계를 넘나든다. 식물, 동물 그리고 미생물들의 DNA는 이제 새로운 유전적 혼합을 탄생시키기 위해서 모두 혼합될 수가 있다.

해설

지문의 대의를 파악하는 문제다. 19세기 단순 이종교배에서 20세기 '잡종'의 설계, 그리고 현재의 종을 뛰어넘는 새로운 유전적 혼합방법에 이르기까지 지문은 시간의 흐름에 따른 유전학의 발전내용들을 간략히 설명하고 있다. 그러므로 정답은 '유전과학의 지속적인 혁명'인 (c)이다.

어휘

argue 주장하다	pioneer 선구자, 개척자, 초기의	radical 급진적인, 과격한
genetic 유전의	experiment 실험하다	boundary 경계선
modification 수정, 변형	variation 변화, 변이	micro-organism 미생물
sophisticated 정교한, 복잡한	hybrid 잡종, 혼성	stagnant 정체된
crossbreed 잡종, 잡종을 만들다	manipulation 조작	

Mini-Test 4

Tasmania is one of the world's most beautiful islands. It's amazing how many great attractions are squeezed into this Australia's smallest state. There are many places in the Island that are worth to visit. The Tasman Peninsula is where you will find wild coastal scenery and the island's premier attraction, the Port Arthur convict settlement. It's very hard to believe this beautiful, serene setting was once the scene of such dreadful acts. A number of historic towns are located in the midlands, with Richmond and Ross, the pick of the bunch. Along the north and east coasts are a string of small beach towns and the magnificent Freycinet National Park, famous for the beautiful Wineglass Bay.

Q: Which of the following is correct according to the passage?

(a) Tasmania is a peninsular country.
(b) Many criminals dwelled in Tasmania.
(c) Freycinet National park is famous for its winery.
(d) Richmond is one of the small beach towns along the north coast.

 해석

타즈메니아는 세계에서 가장 아름다운 섬들 중에 하나이다. 이 호주의 가장 작은 주에 그렇게나 많은 훌륭하고 매력적인 장소들이 모여 있다는 것은 정말 놀랍다. 이 섬에서는 방문할 가치가 있는 많은 장소들이 있다. 이 타즈메니아 반도는 여러분들이 야생 연안 풍경과 이 섬에서 첫째 인기장소인 Arthur 항구의 죄수유배지를 발견할 수 있는 곳이다. 이 아름답고 고요한 장소가 한때는 그렇게 무시무시한 행위의 장소였다는 것은 믿기 어려운 일이다. 내륙지방의 여러 개의 관광장소 중에 몇 개를 꼽자면 Richmond와 Ross와 같은 수많은 역사적인 마을들이 자리를 잡고 있다. 북쪽과 동쪽 연안을 따라서 자그마한 해변 마을들이 줄 지어 있고, 아름다운 와인 잔 모양의 만으로 유명한 Freycinet 국립공원이 있다.

 해설

지문을 자세히 읽으며 내용과 일치하지 않는 보기를 제거해 간다. 타즈메니아는 반도 국가가 아니라 호주의 한 주이며 국립공원은 양조장으로 유명한 것이 아니라 와인 모양의 만으로 유명한 것이다. Richmond는 내륙지방의 마을이지 북쪽 연안의 마을이 아니므로 (a), (c), (d)는 모두 오답이다. 타즈메니아의 Authur 항구에 유명한 죄수거주지(convict settlement)가 있다고 했으므로, '많은 죄수들이 타즈메니아에 거주했다'는 (b)가 정답이다.

어휘

attraction 인기거리, 매력
coastal 연안의, 근해의
premier 최초의, 첫째의
convict settlement 죄수 유배지
serene 고요한, 잔잔한
dreadful 무시무시한
the midlands 중부지방, 내륙지방
pick 선택, 고르다
magnificent 장엄한, 멋진
bay 만
peninsular country 반도 국가
dwell 살다, 거주하다
winery 포도주 양조장

Environment · life

Mini-Test 5

Sunscreen lotions are under suspicion of causing environmental damage and as a possible health risk. Italian scientists have found the creams can cause rapid and total bleaching of corals in the sea. Fraser Island already has a no-sunscreen policy to preserve its freshwater lakes. Now there's additional concern about the use of the nano particles of titanium dioxide and zinc used to make sunscreen disappear into the skin. These have replaced the old white emulsion formulas that were harder to rub in. Although manufacturers are required to label all ingredients, they do not need to specify the form they are in. Therefore, nano particles in sunscreens remain largely undisclosed to buyers. Scientists believe there may be changes to the toxicity of the metal oxides as they are readily absorbed in the skin when reduced to nano particulate size.

Q: What can be inferred from the passage?

(a) Sunscreen lotions have an affirmative effect on coral preservation.
(b) Nano particles increase the absorption of new lotions into the skin.
(c) The form of ingredients are precisely detailed in the product label.
(d) All ingredients in lotions are not required to be specified on the label.

해석

햇빛차단 로션들은 환경파괴를 일으키고, 건강에 위협을 가져올 가능성이 있다는 의심을 받고 있습니다. 이탈리아의 과학자들은 햇빛차단 크림이 바다 속 산호들의 빠르고 완전한 표백작용을 일으킬 수 있다는 것을 알아냈습니다. Fraser 섬은 이미 민물 호수들을 보호하기 위해서 햇빛차단 로션을 사용하지 말라는 정책을 가지고 있습니다. 이제는 햇빛차단 로션이 피부 속으로 사라질 수 있도록 하기 위한 용도의 티타늄 이산화물과 아연의 미세 입자들의 사용에 관한 추가적인 걱정이 있습니다. 이 미세입자들은 문질러서 스며들게 하기가 어렵던 과거의 하얀 유상액들을 대체하게 되었습니다. 제조업자들은 비록 모든 성분들의 명칭을 붙이도록 규정되어 있지만, 그들은 성분들이 어떤 형태로 있는지에 대해서는 명시할 필요가 없습니다. 햇빛차단제들의 미세 입자들은 대부분 구입자들에게 드러내어지지 않은 채 있게 되지요. 과학자들은 금속 산화물들이 미세 입자 크기로 줄어들 때, 쉽게 피부 속으로 스며들면서 독성의 변화가 있을 것이라 믿고 있습니다.

해설

'Now there's~disappear into the skin' 이란 문장을 통해서, 이제 로션을 피부 속으로 사라지게 하기 위해서 특정 성분들의 미세입자들이 사용되고 있음을 알 수 있다. 즉, '미세입자들은 새 로션의 피부로의 흡수력을 증가시킨다' 라는 (b)가 정답이다. 로션의 모든 성분들을 딱지에 적어야 할 필요는 있지만, 그 성분들의 형태에 대해서는 그럴 필요가 없다는 것이므로 (c)와 (d)는 정답이 될 수 없다.

어휘

under suspicion 의심을 받고	nano 10억 분의 1	oxide 산화물
environmental damage 환경파괴	dioxide 이산화물	readily 즉시, 쉽사리
bleaching 표백(법)	label 딱지를 붙이다	particulate 미립자(의)
coral 산호	specify 일일이 상술하다	affirmative 긍정의
preserve 보존하다, 유지하다	toxicity 독성	absorption 흡수(작용)

Vocabulary 환경 · 생물

앞에서 학습한 지문들에 등장하는 TEPS 빈출 출제 어휘 및 표현들을 다시 한 번 확인하고 그 외 주제와 관련한 빈출 필수 어휘 및 표현들을 학습하고 넘어 갑시다.

- debate 토론, 논쟁
- crocodile 악어
- (1) _____ ~에 위협을 가하다
- mortality 사망률, 폐사율
- mature 성숙한, 성숙하다
- reproductive 재생의, 다산의
- (2) _____ 자양물, 음식
- (3) _____ 공생관계
- take advantage of ~을 이용하다
- drastic 격렬한, 과감한
- crop 수확(물)
- (4) _____ 현상
- abruptly 갑작스럽게
- abandon 버리다
- occur 일어나다, 생기다
- (5) _____ 살충(제)
- misuse 오용, 남용
- pollinate ~에 수분하다

- (6) _____ 유전의
- modification 수정, 변형
- sophisticated 정교한, 복잡한
- crossbreed 잡종, 잡종을 만들다
- (7) _____ 선구자, 개척자, 초기의
- experiment 실험하다
- variation 변화, 변이
- hybrid 잡종, 혼성
- (8) _____ 조작
- (9) _____ 미생물
- coastal 연안의, 근해의
- serene 고요한, 잔잔한
- bay 만
- peninsular country 반도국가
- environmental damage 환경파괴
- in conjunction with ~와 관련하여
- bleaching 표백
- stagnant 정체된

Environment · life

- (10) _____ 독성
- absorption 흡수 (작용)
- pollution 환경파괴, 오염
- carbon dioxide 이산화탄소
- contaminate 오염시키다
- dispose 처리하다, 처분하다
- exhaust (자동차의) 배기가스
- exploit 개발하다, 착취하다
- fossil fuel 화석연료
- greenhouse effect 온실효과
- incinerator (쓰레기의) 소각로
- natural resources 천연자원
- ozone layer 오존층
- powerhouse 발전소
- acid rain 산성비
- offspring 자손
- ban 금지하다
- prey 먹이
- windmill 풍차
- come into use 이용되다
- generate (전기, 열 등을) 일으키다
- paleontologist 고생물 학자
- skeleton 골격, 뼈대
- loophole (법률 등의) 허점
- climate 기후
- electricity 전기
- atmosphere 대기
- release 배출하다
- temperature 온도
- global warming 지구온난화
- barren 불모의, 메마른
- carcass 시체
- shelf life 유효 기간
- readily 즉시, 쉽사리
- particulate 미립자(의)
- affirmative 긍정의

Answers (1) poses a threat to (2) nutrient (3) symbiotic relationship (4) phenomenon (5) insecticide (6) genetic (7) pioneer (8) manipulation (9) micro-organism (10) toxicity

30 DAYS TEPS 800+Final Sum-up

Theme 09
건강 · 의학
Health · Medical Science

1. 스트레스, 비만 등의 일반적으로 우리가 접할 수 있는 내용의 건강 및 의학과 관련한 지문들이 출제가 된다.

2. Part 1, 2에서 주로 출제가 되며, 지문에서 말하고자 하는 핵심내용 및 세부사항들이 무엇인가를 파악하는 것이 중요하다. 예를 들어, 어떤 조사 결과에 있어서 한 음식이 사람의 건강에 해를 끼친다고 한다면, 구체적으로 신체 어느 부위에 좋지 않고, 어떤 방식으로 해를 끼치는가에 대한 내용을 문제 출제 포인트로 잡는 경우가 많다.

3. 특정 약에 관한 설명을 다룬 지문에서 대의파악과 관련한 문제가 출제된 경우, 지문에서 언급된 장·단점들을 종합적으로 아우를 수 있는 선택지를 고르는 것이 중요하다. 세부내용 파악이나 추론 문제 역시 지문에서 언급된 내용과 선택지를 꼼꼼히 비교하여 문제를 풀도록 한다.

Theme 09
건강·의학

Mini-Test

Read the passage and choose the option that best fits the blank. (1~3)

1. Scientists found that popular mouthwashes can cause oral cancer and should be pulled from supermarket shelves immediately. Their warning accompanies the latest evidence _____.
Their review, published in the Dental Journal of England, concluded that there is sufficient evidence that such mouthwashes contribute to the increased risk of getting oral cancer. The ethanol in mouthwash is thought to allow cancer-causing substances to permeate the lining of the mouth more easily and cause harm. Acetaldehyde, a toxic byproduct of alcohol that may accumulate when swished around the mouth, is also believed to be carcinogenic.

    (a) showing how mouthwashes can cause various types of cancers in human beings
    (b) linking alcohol-containing mouthwashes to the deadly disease
    (c) proving that cancer can be deteriorated by using mouthwashes
    (d) showing a daily routine of brushing is enough to prevent tooth decay

2. Fish oil may protect people against potentially deadly liver cancer. Researchers have found that a high intake of omega-3 fatty acids ,which are found in oily fish such as salmon and sardines, could decrease the risk of developing the cancer by 40%. They have also found that it can _____ an inherited gene which is known to increase the risk of liver cancer. The study compared the diets of 500 people diagnosed with the disease and the same number of healthy people. It found the people who ate oily fish rich in omega-3 every day for a month, had a 30% lower risk of liver cancer than those who never ate it.

    (a) bolster the influence of
    (b) reverse the effect of
    (c) maintain the properties of
    (d) identify the structure of

3. Are you feeling stressed? Despite all the joys of motherhood there are times when the constant demands of caring for young children as well as doing chores can make you feel stressed. This is a normal reaction. Some mothers may also experience additional stress such as sleep deprivation, financial worries, a pressure to return to work, or they may have an un-supportive partner or intrusive family members. This can cause her to feel trapped and that she can't cope with everyday demands of life. This can have both physiological and psychological effects. Research shows that too much unwanted stress can be harmful to our health. It can contribute to medical conditions and is linked to chronic diseases such as coronary heart diseases. Psychologically, too much stress can reduce your ability to cope with daily tasks, effect your self-confidence and diminish your self-esteem. _____, it is important to reduce and manage the stress you have in your life.

(a) Nevertheless
(b) Besides
(c) Thus
(d) Similarly

Choose the option that correctly answers the question. (4~5)

4. A team at the Walter and Eliza Hall Institute (WEHI) found that a combination of the cell death drug ABT 737 and traditional cancer treatments dramatically improves the prospects of survival for mice with melanoma. ABT 737's discovery was announced by US health care company Abbott in 2005, but is being developed in conjunction with WEHI. ABT 737 causes cancer cells to undergo apoptosis, a form of cell death, with apparently minimal effects on healthy cells. It blocks proteins like BCL-2 that enable cancerous growth by preventing normal apoptosis from keeping cell growth and death in balance. Many cancer drugs rely on inhibitors to slow malignant growth but are unable to provide a knock-out blow. ABT 737 offers the promise that such knock-outs may be possible.

Q: What is the best title for this article?

(a) The combination therapy which lowers doses of cancer-killing drugs.
(b) A drug that helps cancer cells to multiply uncontrollably.
(c) How BCL-2 keeps cancer cells from undergoing apoptosis.
(d) The mighty effect of the new anti-cancer agent.

Health · Medical Science

5. A research suggests that although women think there may be a link between brain capacity and pregnancy and motherhood, there are certainly no permanent ones that could be found. A female researcher studied a group of young people in 1999. One of her earliest results was that pregnancy did not cause memory loss, even though many participants blamed forgetful episodes on their condition. Later, she conducted follow-up interviews in 2003 and 2007. Subjects completed tests of immediate and delayed memory, concentration and ability to translate codes. The result turned out that pregnancy and motherhood did not affect any of them. The only thing she was able to observe was that women who have children become marginally less well-educated than women who don't have children in their twenties. However, this is hardly surprising, as having children will interrupt education in most cases.

Q: What can be inferred from the passage?

(a) Children who think their parents are dumb should be disciplined harshly.
(b) Pregnancy brings the negative effect of low self-esteem.
(c) Neither pregnancy nor motherhood affect cognitive functioning.
(d) Early mothers usually regret not furthering their education.

Theme 09
건강 · 의학

30 DAYS TEPS 800+Final Sum-up

Mini-Test 1

Scientists found that popular mouthwashes can cause oral cancer and should be pulled from supermarket shelves immediately. Their warning accompanies the latest evidence _____.
Their review, published in the Dental Journal of England, concluded that there is sufficient evidence that such mouthwashes contribute to the increased risk of getting oral cancer. The ethanol in mouthwash is thought to allow cancer-causing substances to permeate the lining of the mouth more easily and cause harm. Acetaldehyde, a toxic byproduct of alcohol that may accumulate when swished around the mouth, is also believed to be carcinogenic.

(a) showing how mouthwashes can cause various types of cancers in human beings
(b) linking alcohol-containing mouthwashes to the deadly disease
(c) proving that cancer can be deteriorated by using mouthwashes
(d) showing a daily routine of brushing is enough to prevent tooth decay

 해석

과학자들은 유명한 양치질 물약들이 구강암을 일으킬 수 있고, 즉시 슈퍼마켓의 선반에서 밀어내져야 한다는 것을 발견했다. 그들의 경고는 알코올을 함유하고 있는 양치질 물약들이 이러한 치명적 병과 연관성이 있다는 최근의 증거와 함께 하는 것이다. 잉글랜드 치과의 간행물에 실린 그들의 조사내용은 이러한 양치질 물약들로 인해 구강암에 걸릴 수 있는 위험이 증가되는 원인으로 작용하는 충분한 증거가 있다고 결론을 내렸다. 양치질 물약에 있는 에탄올이 암을 유발하는 물질들이 좀 더 쉽게 입의 내면으로 스며들게 하고 손상을 미치게 한다고 여겨지고 있다. 입 안 주위를 돌 때 축적될 수 있는 알코올의 독성 부산물인 아세트알데히드 또한 발암성이라고 여겨지고 있다.

 해설

빈칸을 포함하는 문장의 앞에서는 과학자들이 구강암을 일으킬 수 있는 양치질 물약을 슈퍼마켓에서 끄집어내야 한다는 내용을 담고 있다. 즉, 이러한 경고와 함께 하는 증거의 내용은 (b)이다. 이는 빈칸 뒤의 문장의 내용에서도 다시 한 번 언급되고 있다. 양치질 물약에 의해서 구강암이 걸릴 수 있다는 것이지 (c)의 양치질 물약에 의해서 암이 더 악화된다는 것은 아니므로 (c)는 정답이 될 수 없다.

🔍 어휘

mouthwash 양치질 약
oral cancer 구강암
immediately 바로, 즉시
warning 경고

accompany ~에 동반하다
evidence 증거
review 평론, 논평
sufficient 충분한

contribute (to) ~의 원인이 되다
ethanol 에탄올
permeate 스며들다, 침투하다
lining 내층

Health · Medical Science

Mini-Test 2

Fish oil may protect people against potentially deadly liver cancer. Researchers have found that a high intake of omega-3 fatty acids, which are found in oily fish such as salmon and sardines, could decrease the risk of developing the cancer by 40%. They have also found that it can _____ an inherited gene which is known to increase the risk of liver cancer. The study compared the diets of 500 people diagnosed with the disease and the same number of healthy people. It found the people who ate oily fish rich in omega-3 every day for a month, had a 30% lower risk of liver cancer than those who never ate it.

(a) bolster the influence of
(b) reverse the effect of
(c) maintain the properties of
(d) identify the structure of

해석

생선 기름이 사람들을 잠재적이며 치명적인 간암으로부터 보호해줄지도 모릅니다. 연구원들은 연어와 정어리 같은 기름진 생선에서 발견되는 omega-3 지방성 산을 많이 섭취하면 40% 가까이 간암이 전개될 위험을 감소시킬 수 있다는 것을 발견했습니다. 그들은 또한 간암의 위험을 증가시킨다고 알려진 유전적 인자의 효과를 뒤집을 수 있다는 것도 발견했습니다. 본 연구는 이 병을 진단받은 500명의 사람들과 함께 이들과 동일한 숫자의 건강한 사람들을 비교했습니다. 이 연구는 omega-3가 풍부한 기름진 생선을 매일 한 달 동안 먹은 사람들이 절대 먹지 않은 사람들보다 간암의 위험이 30% 낮추어졌다는 것을 발견했습니다.

해설

기름진 생선에서 발견되는 Omega-3를 섭취하면 간암의 위험을 줄일 수 있다는 내용의 글이다. Omega-3의 긍정적인 효과를 고려할 때, 간암의 위험을 높이는 유전 인자는 Omega-3에 의해서 그 효과가 뒤집어진다는 (b)가 정답이다.

어휘

protect 보호하다
potentially 잠재적으로
deadly 치명적인
liver cancer 간암
intake 섭취량
salmon 연어
sardine 정어리
inherited 유전된
diet 식이요법, 식사내용
diagnose 진단하다
bolster 지지하다, 강화하다
influence 영향(력)
reverse 뒤집다
property 성질, 특성

Mini-Test 3

Are you feeling stressed? Despite all the joys of motherhood there are times when the constant demands of caring for young children as well as doing chores can make you feel stressed. This is a normal reaction. Some mothers may also experience additional stress such as sleep deprivation, financial worries, a pressure to return to work, or they may have an un-supportive partner or intrusive family members. This can cause her to feel trapped and that she can't cope with everyday demands of life. This can have both physiological and psychological effects. Research shows that too much unwanted stress can be harmful to our health. It can contribute to medical conditions and is linked to chronic diseases such as coronary heart diseases. Psychologically, too much stress can reduce your ability to cope with daily tasks, effect your self-confidence and diminish your self-esteem. _____, it is important to reduce and manage the stress you have in your life.

(a) Nevertheless
(b) Besides
(c) Thus
(d) Similarly

Health · Medical Science

Mini-Test 4

A team at the Walter and Eliza Hall Institute(WEHI) found that a combination of the cell death drug ABT 737 and traditional cancer treatments dramatically improves the prospects of survival for mice with melanoma. ABT 737's discovery was announced by US health care company Abbott in 2005, but is being developed in conjunction with WEHI. ABT 737 causes cancer cells to undergo apoptosis, a form of cell death, with apparently minimal effects on healthy cells. It blocks proteins like BCL-2 that enable cancerous growth by preventing normal apoptosis from keeping cell growth and death in balance. Many cancer drugs rely on inhibitors to slow malignant growth but are unable to provide a knock-out blow. ABT 737 offers the promise that such knock-outs may be possible.

Q: What is the best title for this article?

(a) The combination therapy which lowers doses of cancer-killing drugs.
(b) A drug that helps cancer cells to multiply uncontrollably.
(c) How BCL-2 keeps cancer cells from undergoing apoptosis.
(d) The mighty effect of the new anti-cancer agent.

해석

WEHI의 팀은 세포사 약물인 ABT 737과 암 치료의 결합이 극적으로 흑색 종양을 가진 쥐들의 생존율 가능성을 향상시킨다는 것을 발견했습니다. ABT 737의 발견은 미국 건강 관리 회사인 Abbott에 의해서 2005년에 발표되었지만, WEHI와 협력하여 개발이 진행중입니다. ABT 737은 건강한 세포들에 대해서는 분명히 최소한의 영향을 주고, 암세포들은 세포사의 일종인 아포토시스를 겪게 하는 원인이 됩니다. 이것은 정상 아포토시스가 세포의 성장과 죽음이 균형을 유지하는 것을 막음으로써 암의 성장을 가능케 하는 BCL-2 같은 단백질을 차단합니다. 많은 암 약물들은 악성 성장을 늦추는 억제제에 의존합니다. 하지만 압도적인 타격을 주지는 못하지요. ABT 737은 그러한 압도적인 타격이 가능하도록 기대를 제공합니다.

해설

암세포의 죽음을 유도하는 약물인 ABT 737에 대한 설명을 위주로, 이 약물이 다른 억제제는 하지 못했던 결정적인 한 방을 날릴 수 있을 것이라는 내용의 글이다. 이 지문이 강조하고자 하는 것은 바로 ABT 737의 강력한 효과다. 그러므로 ABT 737을 '새로운 암 배척 약품의 강력한 효과'라는 (d)가 정답이다.

어휘

cell 세포	in conjunction with ~와 함께	malignant 악성의
treatment 치료(법)	undergo 받다, 겪다	knock-out blow 결정적인 한 방
dramatically 극적으로, 눈부시게	apoptosis 세포자멸사	therapy 치료(요법)
prospect 예상, 기대	enable 가능하게 하다	dose (1회의) 복용량
survival 생존	rely on ~에 의지하다	agent 약품
melanoma 흑색종양	inhibit 방해하다, 억제하다	multiply 늘리다, 증가시키다

Mini-Test 5

A research suggests that although women think there may be a link between brain capacity and pregnancy and motherhood, there are certainly no permanent ones that could be found. A female researcher studied a group of young people in 1999. One of her earliest results was that pregnancy did not cause memory loss, even though many participants blamed forgetful episodes on their condition. Later, she conducted follow-up interviews in 2003 and 2007. Subjects completed tests of immediate and delayed memory, concentration and ability to translate codes. The result turned out that pregnancy and motherhood did not affect any of them. The only thing she was able to observe was that women who have children become marginally less well-educated than women who don't have children in their twenties. However, this is hardly surprising, as having children will interrupt education in most cases.

Q: What can be inferred from the passage?

(a) Children who think their parents are dumb should be disciplined harshly.
(b) Pregnancy brings the negative effect of low self-esteem.
(c) Neither pregnancy nor motherhood affect cognitive functioning.
(d) Early mothers usually regret not furthering their education.

해석

한 연구조사는 여성들이 그들의 두뇌 능력과 임신 그리고 엄마가 됨 사이에 연결점이 있을 것이라고 생각하지만, 분명 영구적인 그 어떤 것도 발견된 바가 없습니다. 한 여성 연구원은 1999년에 젊은 사람들의 그룹을 연구했습니다. 그녀의 초기 결과들 중 하나는 비록 실험참여자들의 그들의 상태에 무언가를 깜박 잊어버리는 일들의 책임을 돌렸지만, 임신이 기억력 손실의 원인이 되지 않는다는 것입니다. 후에, 2003년과 2007년도에 그녀는 후속 인터뷰를 실시했습니다. 조사대상자들은 즉각 기억력 그리고 연기 기억력, 집중력, 그리고 암호를 해석할 수 있는 능력 등의 시험을 완료했습니다. 결과는 임신과 어머니가 됨이 어느 것에도 영향을 주지 않았습니다. 그녀가 목격할 수 있었던 유일한 한 가지는 아이들을 가진 어머니들 20대에 여성을 가지지 않은 여성들보다 다소 교육을 덜 받았다는 것뿐입니다. 그러나 아이를 갖는다는 것이 대부분의 경우 교육을 방해하기에 이것은 놀라울 것이 없습니다.

해설

여성들이 생각하는 것과는 다르게 두뇌능력과 임신, 그리고 엄마가 됨 사이에는 아무런 연관성이 없다는 내용의 지문이다. 즉, '임신과 엄마가 됨 둘 다 인지 기능에 영향을 미치지 못한다'는 (c)가 정답입니다. 조사 결과 일찍 엄마가 된 사람들이 교육을 덜 받았다고는 했지만, 이를 여성들이 후회한다고는 한 적이 없기에 (d)는 정답이 될 수 없다.

어휘

capacity 수용량, 능력	subject 피 실험자, 실험 대상자	discipline 훈계하다, 징벌하다
pregnancy 임신	turn out ~로 들어나다	further 조장하다, 촉진하다
forgetful 잘 잊는	observe 관찰하다	
blame A on B A를 B의 책임으로 돌리다	cognitive 인식의	

Vocabulary 건강·의학

앞에서 학습한 지문들에 등장하는 TEPS 빈출 출제 어휘 및 표현들을 다시 한 번 확인하고 그 외 주제와 관련한 빈출 필수 어휘 및 표현들을 학습하고 넘어 갑시다.

- immediately 바로, 즉시
- warning 경고
- accompany ~에 동반하다
- (1) _____ 증거
- (2) _____ 충분한
- contribute (to) ~의 원인이 되다
- (3) _____ 발암성의
- deteriorate 악화하다, 저하하다
- oral cancer 구강암
- potentially 잠재적으로
- deadly 치명적인
- (4) _____ 섭취량
- inherited 유전된
- diet 식이요법, 식사내용
- (5) _____ 진단하다
- influence 영향력
- reverse 뒤집다
- property 성질, 특성

- feel stressed 스트레스를 느끼다
- constant 변치 않는, 일정한
- (6) _____ 결핍, 궁핍
- cope with ~을 극복하다
- demand 요구, 수요
- physiological 생리학적인
- harmful 해로운
- (7) _____ 만성의, 고질적인
- reduce 줄이다, 떨어뜨리다
- be linked to ~와 관련(연관) 되다
- cell 세포
- (8) _____ 치료(방법)
- dramatically 눈부시게, 극적으로
- prospect 예상, 기대
- survival 생존
- in conjunction with ~와 함께
- (9) _____ 받다, 겪다
- rely on ~에 의지하다

Health · Medical Science

- inhibit 방해하다, 억제하다
- (10) _____ 악성의
- therapy 치료(요법)
- dose (1회의) 복용량
- pregnancy 임신
- blame A on B A를 B의 책임으로 돌리다
- observe 관찰하다
- (11) _____ 인식의
- check-up (종합) 건강진단
- contraception 피임(법)
- digestion 소화(작용), 소화력
- epidemic 유행병, 전염병
- fatal 치명적인
- fitness 건강, 적합성
- germ 병원균, 세균
- assimilate 소화하다, 동화하다
- contagion 전염, 감염
- abortion 낙태

- addiction 중독, 탐닉
- antibiotic 항생제
- vigorous 원기 왕성한, 정력적인
- vaccinate 예방접종을 하다
- transplant 이식하다, 옮겨 심다
- susceptible 병에 걸리기 쉬운
- stroke 발작, 뇌졸중
- soothe (고통을) 덜어주다
- respire 호흡하다, 숨 쉬다
- plague 전염병, 역병
- hospitalization 입원
- immunization 면역
- infect 감염시키다
- miscarriage 유산
- nutritious 영양분이 풍부한
- operate 수술하다
- perspire 땀을 흘리다

Answers (1) evidence (2) sufficient (3) carcinogenic (4) intake (5) diagnose (6) deprivation (7) chronic (8) treatment (9) undergo (10) maliganant (11) cognitive

30 DAYS TEPS 800+ Final Sum-up

Theme 10
사회·문화
Society · Culture

1. 최근 현대사회의 사회적 현상이나 문화적 현상들과 관련한 글들이 본 주제에 해당한다. 평소에 영자신문이나 Newsweek 등의 시사 잡지를 통해서 특히 미국을 중심으로 이슈가 되는 기사들을 읽는 습관을 들인다면 어떤 지문이 등장해도 어렵지 않게 독해할 수 있는 능력을 기를 수 있을 것이다.

2. 보통 지문의 서두에서 주제와 관련한 문장이 등장하여 내용을 이끄는 경우가 많다. 그러므로 Part 2의 대의 찾기 문제는 지문의 앞부분을 집중해서 읽도록 한다.

3. 사회 및 문화와 관련한 지문의 경우, 지문 중에 however, but, nonetheless, therefore 등의 접속어가 자주 등장하는 편이다. 그러므로 접속어를 중심으로 앞뒤 문맥의 흐름을 출제 포인트로 삼아 문제가 출제되는 경우가 많으니 주의 깊게 살펴볼 수 있도록 한다.

Theme 10
사회 · 문화

30 DAYS TEPS 800+Final Sum-up

Mini-Test

Read the passage and choose the option that best fits the blank. (1~3)

1. Among young American married couples, there's a lot of cheating going on. Studies show that the number of unfaithful wives in their 20s rose 20% over the past 15 years, while the number of unfaithful husbands in that age group grew 45%. Perversely, all this is happening while_____. One survey shows that more than 90% of people consider that cheating on one's spouse is always wrong. So why so many people are doing it? Today, experts say, most people get married only after they've had multiple partners, and the most common way to leave these early relationships is by cheating on a current partner. It's a habit that's hard to break, especially when people hit a rough spot in their marriage. Another temptation arises from the fact that many people in their 20s maintain close, long-lasting friendships with members of the opposite sex.

   (a) a lot of people think cheating is not a bad idea
   (b) such behavior is still frowned upon
   (c) divorce rates are as high as they have always been
   (d) many people don't want to get married

2. "Transsexual children under 12 years old ought to be given drugs to delay puberty." That's the suggestion of controversial draft guidelines issued last week by the International Endocrine Society. The guidelines state that transsexual children who have begun early puberty ought to be given puberty-blockers to get away from inevitable changes to their bodies, which they perceive as out of line with their true gender. In the worst scenario, these changes might drive children to self-harm or even suicide. The purpose of the idea is to _____ so they can decide if they really want to begin a sex change using hormones when they get older.

   (a) help young people get used to the change
   (b) make them feel like a woman
   (c) help them find their true gender
   (d) buy thinking time for young people

Society · Culture

3. What is a hero? The heros of classical Greek mythology were self centered and flawed. But in serving others, they blundered their way into discovering something of their divine potential. The idea of a hero, though, sits awkwardly on the mantelpiece of an ordinary life. You think you're not a hero. Even those who have surely earned the title have the good sense to shrug it off. "I was just doing my job" says the reluctant heroes of our daily news events and dramas. _____, we continue to insist on the heroism of others. There's resonance in that timeless action, in the story told in different ways in every culture : something defeated, something gained, danger averted and a land redeemed.

 (a) Accordingly
 (b) Nonetheless
 (c) In other words
 (d) Similarly

Choose the option that correctly answers the question. (4~5)

4. Who Moved My Cheese?, the parable that could be understood by a sixth grader, has become the best-selling business book ever. It's now more popular than the bible and it sold more than 22 million copies worldwide in 37 languages so far. The book is the story of two little people and two little mice living in a maze where there is plenty of cheese. When the cheese disappears, the mice instinctively look for new cheese, while the people are more resistant to change. The apparent message of the book is to embrace change because it is inevitable.

 Q: What is the passage mainly about?

 (a) The diminishing popularity of the Bible.
 (b) The inspiring message people should remember.
 (c) The book that some age groups can relate to.
 (d) The book that has become the world best seller.

5. More than half of Australian motorists are risking disaster by using mobile phones while driving. More motorists than ever admit using their phone while behind the wheel, with women and the increasing number of tech-savvy elderly the fastest growing group of culprits. The results of a study, published by the Department of Transport and Infrastructure, have caused concern among road-safety experts and police, who said drivers were risking lives. The department's social research center interviewed 1592 motorists and found 61 percent of Australian drivers reported having used a mobile phone while driving, up from 55 percent in 2006, and 47 percent in 2005. And 28 percent read text messages, against 21 percent in 2006 and 16 percent in 2005. The spike in numbers has been attributed to more women, the middle-aged and the elderly admitting to offending. A third of people aged 60 and over who responded to the survey admitted they used a phone while driving while two-thirds of women admitted chatting on the phone.

Q: Which is correct according to the passage?

(a) More than 60% of Australian motorists drive under the influence.
(b) The number of older citizens using phones while driving is diminishing.
(c) More older people are using phones as they get familiar with new technology.
(d) Some people risk their lives by reading letters while driving.

Theme 10
사회·문화

Mini-Test 1

Among young American married couples, there's a lot of cheating going on. Studies show that the number of unfaithful wives in their 20s rose 20% over the past 15 years, while the number of unfaithful husbands in that age group grew 45%. Perversely, all this is happening while _____.

One survey shows that more than 90% of people consider that cheating on one's spouse is always wrong. So why so many people are doing it? Today, experts say, most people get married only after they've had multiple partners, and the most common way to leave these early relationships is by cheating on a current partner. It's a habit that's hard to break, especially when people hit a rough spot in their marriage. Another temptation arises from the fact that many people in their 20s maintain close, long-lasting friendships with members of the opposite sex.

(a) a lot of people think cheating is not a bad idea
(b) such behavior is still frowned upon
(c) divorce rates are as high as they have always been
(d) many people don't want to get married

해석

젊은 미국인 부부들 중에, 수많은 이들이 바람을 피우고 있습니다. 연구조사에 의하면 20대의 부정한 행위를 한 아내들의 수가 지난 15년간 20%가 증가했고, 같은 나이대의 부정한 남편들의 수는 45%가 증가했다고 합니다. 잘못된 것은, 그러한 행동들이 사람들의 눈살을 찌푸리게 하는 것임에도 이러한 일들이 벌어지고 있다는 겁니다. 한 조사는 90%가 넘는 사람들이 배우자 몰래 바람을 피우는 것은 언제나 잘못된 것이라고 생각하고 있다는 결과를 보여주었습니다. 그렇다면 왜 그렇게 많은 사람들이 바람을 피우는 것일까요? 전문가들은 오늘날 대부분의 사람들이 다수의 애인들과 사귀고 난 후에 결혼을 한다고 말합니다. 그리고 이전의 관계를 정리하는 가장 흔한 방법은 현재 사귀는 애인 몰래 바람을 피우는 것이라고 합니다. 이것은 특히, 결혼 생활 중 힘든 시련에 부딪히게 되었을 때, 굉장히 끊기가 어려운 습관이 되어버립니다. 20대의 많은 사람들은 이성들과 가깝고 오랜 기간 지속되는 우정을 유지한다는 사실에서부터 또 다른 유혹이 나타나게 되는 것이죠.

해설

빈칸이 포함된 문장의 앞에서 바람을 피우는 유부남, 유부녀들의 비율이 증가하고 있다고 설명하고 있다. 빈칸이 포함된 문장은 부사 perversely를 통해서 무언가 일치하지 않는 뒤틀어진 상황을 나타내는 문장이 나와야 한다. 그러므로 '이러한 행동들이 눈살을 찌푸리게 하는 것' 임에도 불구하고 지속된다는 의미로 (b)가 정답이다. 이는 뒤에서 이어지는 조사내용의 예를 통해서도 뒷받침되고 있다.

어휘

cheat 속이다, 바람피우다
n) cheating 바람피우는 것
survey 조사
go on 계속되다
unfaithful 부정한
perversely 뒤틀어진 것은, 잘못된 것은
consider 심사숙고하다, ~로 간주하다
spouse 배우자
break a habit 습관을 버리다
temptation 유혹
arise 일어나다, 발생하다
maintain 유지하다, 지속하다

Mini-Test 2

"Transsexual children under 12 years old ought to be given drugs to delay puberty." That's the suggestion of controversial draft guidelines issued last week by the International Endocrine Society. The guidelines state that transsexual children who have begun early puberty ought to be given puberty-blockers to get away from inevitable changes to their bodies, which they perceive as out of line with their true gender. In the worst scenario, these changes might drive children to self-harm or even suicide. The purpose of the idea is to _____ _____ so they can decide if they really want to begin a sex change using hormones when they get older.

(a) help young people get used to the change
(a) make them feel like a woman
(c) help them find their true gender
(d) buy thinking time for young people

 해석

"12살 이하의 성전환을 원하는 아이들은 사춘기를 늦추기 위해서 약물을 투여 받아야만 한다." 이것이 국제 내분비선 학회에 의해서 지난 주 발행되어 논란을 불러일으키고 있는 초안 지침서의 제안이다. 이 지침서는 사춘기가 일찍 시작된 성전환을 원하는 아이들은 그들이 생각할 때 그들의 진정한 성별과는 일치하지 않는 부득이한 신체적 변화를 피할 수 있도록 사춘기 차단제를 투여 받아야 한다고 언급하고 있다. 최악의 경우에는 이러한 변화들이 아이가 스스로를 상처내거나 자살에까지 이르게 할 수도 있다. 이러한 아이디어의 목적은 어린 친구들에게 그들이 나이가 들었을 때, 호르몬을 사용하여 성 변화를 시작하기를 진정 원하는지를 결정할 수 있도록 생각할 시간을 벌어 주자는 것이다.

 해설

성전환을 원하는 어린 아이들이 후에 나이가 들어서 제대로 된 결정을 할 수 있도록 사춘기를 억제하는 약물을 투여해야 한다는 제안에 대한 내용을 다루는 지문이다. 빈칸의 내용은 이러한 제안에 대한 목적을 설명하는 내용으로, 나이가 들어 최종 결정을 하기 전 어린 아이들에게 시간을 벌어주기 위해서라는 내용의 (d)가 정답이다. 사춘기를 억제하는 약물을 투여하자는 것이 진정한 성별을 찾는 것을 도와주는 것은 아니기에 (c)는 정답이 될 수 없다.

 어휘

transsexual 성전환을 한(원하는)
delay 미루다, ~을 늦추다
puberty 사춘기
endocrine 내분비선

controversial 논쟁의 여지가 있는
guideline 지침
inevitable 피할 수 없는, 부득이한
suicide 자살

discover 발견하다, 깨닫다
get used to ~에 익숙해지다

Society · Culture

Mini-Test 3

What is a hero? The heros of classical Greek mythology were self centered and flawed. But in serving others, they blundered their way into discovering something of their divine potential. The idea of a hero, though, sits awkwardly on the mantelpiece of an ordinary life. You think you're not a hero. Even those who have surely earned the title have the good sense to shrug it off. "I was just doing my job" says the reluctant heroes of our daily news events and dramas. _____, we continue to insist on the heroism of others. There's resonance in that timeless action, in the story told in different ways in every culture: something defeated, something gained, danger averted and a land redeemed.

(a) Accordingly
(b) Nonetheless
(c) In other words
(d) Similarly

Mini-Test 4

Who Moved My Cheese?, the parable that could be understood by a sixth grader, has become the best-selling business book ever. It's now more popular than the bible and it sold more than 22 million copies worldwide in 37 languages so far. The book is the story of two little people and two little mice living in a maze where there is plenty of cheese. When the cheese disappears, the mice instinctively look for new cheese, while the people are more resistant to change. The apparent message of the book is to embrace change because it is inevitable.

Q: What is the passage mainly about?

(a) The diminishing popularity of the Bible.
(b) The inspiring message people should remember.
(c) The book that some age groups can relate to.
(d) The book that has become the world best seller.

해석

누가 내 치즈를 옮겼을까?는 6학년 학생들도 이해가 될 법한 우화로 지금까지 최고로 많이 팔린 비즈니스 책이 되었습니다. 이 책은 이제 성경책보다도 더 인기가 있으며, 지금까지 37개의 언어로 전 세계에서 2천 2백만 부가 팔렸습니다. 이 책은 두 명의 작은 사람들과 치즈가 많이 있는 미로 속에서 살아가는 두 마리의 작은 생쥐의 이야기입니다. 치즈가 사라져 버렸을 때, 생쥐들은 본능적으로 새로운 치즈를 찾지만 사람들은 좀 더 저항을 합니다. 책의 명백한 메시지는 변화란 피할 수 없는 것이기 때문에 변화를 받아들여야 한다는 것입니다.

해설

세계에서 가장 많이 팔린 책인 'Who Moved My Cheese?' 에 대해서 소개하고 있다. 그러므로 정답은 (d)이다. 베스트셀러 자리를 빼앗겼다고 성경의 인기가 줄고 있다고 볼 수도 없고, 그것이 주제는 더더욱 아니다.

어휘

parable 우화
grader 학년 cf) a third grader 3학년
bible 성경
copy (책의) 부, 권
disappear 사라지다, 실종되다
instinctively 본능적으로, 직감적으로
resistant to ~에 저항하는
apparent 뚜렷한, 명백한
embrace 얼싸안다, 받아들이다
diminish 감소하다

Mini-Test 5

More than half of Australian motorists are risking disaster by using mobile phones while driving. More motorists than ever admit using their phone while behind the wheel, with women and the increasing number of tech-savvy elderly the fastest growing group of culprits. The results of a study, published by the Department of Transport and Infrastructure, have caused concern among road-safety experts and police, who said drivers were risking lives. The department's social research center interviewed 1592 motorists and found 61 percent of Australian drivers reported having used a mobile phone while driving, up from 55 percent in 2006, and 47 percent in 2005. And 28 percent read text messages, against 21 percent in 2006 and 16 percent in 2005. The spike in numbers has been attributed to more women, the middle-aged and the elderly admitting to offending. A third of people aged 60 and over who responded to the survey admitted they used a phone while driving while two-thirds of women admitted chatting on the phone.

Q: Which is correct according to the passage?

(a) More than 60% of Australian motorists drive under the influence.
(b) The number of older citizens using phones while driving is diminishing.
(c) More older people are using phones as they get familiar with new technology.
(d) Some people risk their lives by reading letters while driving.

Vocabulary 사회·문화

앞에서 학습한 지문들에 등장하는 TEPS 빈출 출제 어휘 및 표현들을 다시 한 번 확인하고 그 외 주제와 관련한 빈출 필수 어휘 및 표현들을 학습하고 넘어 갑시다.

- □ cheat 속이다, 바람을 피우다
- □ survey 조사
- □ consider 심사숙고 하다, ~로 간주하다
- □ (1) _____ 습관을 버리다
- □ maintain 지속하다, 유지하다
- □ (2) _____ 논쟁의 여지가 있는
- □ guideline 지침
- □ (3) _____ 피할 수 없는, 부득이한
- □ suicide 자살
- □ discover 발견하다, 깨닫다
- □ ordinary 보통의, 평범한
- □ (4) _____ 되찾다, 회복하다
- □ disappear 사라지다, 실종되다
- □ instinctively 본능적으로, 직감적으로
- □ be resistant to ~에 저항하는
- □ embrace 얼싸안다, 받아들이다
- □ (5) _____ 영감을 주다, 고무시키다
- □ risk 위험, 위험에 내맡기다

- □ admit 인정하다, 고백하다
- □ behind the wheel 운전 중에
- □ (6) _____ 죄인, 원인
- □ concern 걱정, 염려
- □ (7) _____ ~에 기인하다
- □ under the influence 술에 취하여
- □ (8) _____ 감소하다
- □ get familiar with ~와 친숙해지다
- □ (9) _____ 위반하다
- □ unfaithful 부정한
- □ puberty 사춘기
- □ temptation 유혹
- □ arise 일어나다, 발생하다
- □ delay 미루다, ~을 늦추다
- □ self-centered 이기적인, 자기중심적인
- □ defeat 쳐부수다
- □ (10) _____ 또렷한, 분명한
- □ disaster 재해, 참사

Society · Culture

- poll 여론조사
- upswing 상승, 향상
- definition 정의
- uncertainty 불확실(성)
- emerge 나오다, 출현하다
- deem ~으로 간주하다
- worthy of ~하기에 족한
- predict 예상하다, 예언하다
- long-term 장기간의
- name 명명하다, 이름을 짓다
- commemorate 기념하다, 축하하다
- society 사회
- persist 지속하다, 존속하다
- literature 문학
- distribute 분배하다, 배포하다
- anniversary 기념일
- revive 회복시키다, 부흥시키다
- sociologist 사회학자
- in terms of ~의 측면에서
- conceptualize 개념화하다
- sizable 상당한 크기의, 방대한
- mark 특징짓다, 기념하다
- culture 문화
- regardless of ~에 관계없이
- address 연설, ~에게 말을 걸다
- discussion 토론
- education 교육
- gender (사회적) 성
- praise 칭찬하다
- vary 변화하다
- favor 편애하다, 두둔하다
- sexual harrassment 성희롱
- refer to 언급하다, 관계하다
- compromise 타협, 타협하다
- ambiguous 애매모호한
- simultaneously 동시에

Answers (1) break a habit (2) controversial (3) inevitable (4) redeem (5) inspire (6) culprit
(7) be attributed to (8) diminish (9) offend (10) apparent

Section 03

30 DAYS TEPS 800+Final Sum-up

Actual Test

앞에서 우리는 TEPS 독해에서 출제 가능한 모든 유형과 주제들의 문제를 풀어보면서 TEPS 고득점을 위한 사전 준비 작업을 완료했다. 이제 총 3회분의 실전 독해 모의고사를 풀어 봄으로써 실전 TEPS 시험을 대비한 최종 점검을 해보도록 하자.

○━ 실제 시험, 이것만은 꼭 기억하자!!!

1. 총 40개의 독해 문항을 풀기 위해 주어지는 시간은 단 45분!! 최종적으로 모든 문제들에 대한 답안을 확인하는 시간까지 고려하면 한 문제당 60초 정도의 시간 내에 정답을 찾아내야 한다. 절대로 한 지문에 너무 많은 시간을 소비하지 않도록 하고, 정답을 못 찾겠으면 과감히 다음 문제로 넘어간다.

2. Part 1 빈칸 넣기 질문은 총 16문제가 출제되고 그 중, 15번과 16번 두 문제는 접속(부)사 유형이 나옴을 기억하자. 보통 빈칸이 전체 지문의 서두나 말미에 오는 경우 주제를 묻는 문제일 경우가 많다는 것을 기억하고, 빈칸이 중간에 위치하면 빈칸의 앞뒤 문장을 집중적으로 확인해 문맥에 어울리는 선택지 내용을 고르도록 한다.

3. Part 2 내용이해와 관련된 문제는 총 21문제가 출제 된다. 반드시 문제가 무엇인지 먼저 파악한 후, 지문을 읽으면서 그에 해당하는 정답을 찾을 수 있도록 한다. 지문을 읽으면서 빠르게 선택지들의 내용과 비교해보며 틀린 것은 x 표시를 해 놓는 습관을 들이도록 하자.

4. Part 3 내용의 흐름상 어색한 문장 찾기 유형은 총 3문제가 출제된다. 선택지에 포함되지 않는 첫 번째 문장의 내용을 명확히 이해하도록 한다. 바로 이 문장에 지문이 이야기하고자 하는 맥락이 숨어 있다. 이 맥락에 근거하여 글을 읽어가며 글의 논리가 갑자기 비약하거나 혹은 글의 주제와는 상관성이 떨어지는 내용이 언급되는 문장을 골라내도록 한다. 이 문장을 제외하고 나머지 문장들을 읽었을 때, 그 흐름이 자연스럽다면 선택한 문장이 분명 정답이다.

Reading Comprehension

Actual Test

1 • 2 • 3

Reading Comprehension

Actual Test • 1

Directions

This part of the exam tests your ability to comprehend reading passages.
You will have 45 minutes to complete the 40 questions.
Be sure to follow the directions given by the proctor.

Part 1 *Questions 1~16*

Read the passage. Then choose the option that best completes the passage.

1. Generally, the sustainability of a seafood harvest is judged on _____.
   High levels of regulation in the New Zealand industries mean that we can be confident the local seafood we buy is sustainably caught and grown, according to seafood consultant John Cage. "We follow world's best practice." he says, "We keep the three key points—diversity, quality, and sustainability." Experts say that fishing a species to 40~60 percent of its original numbers encourages breeding and maximizes the sustainable yield.

   (a) how fresh the fishes are
   (b) the ongoing levels of wild stocks
   (c) the variety of fish species in the sea
   (d) the environmental impact of fishing methods

2. Runners who buy expensive sneakers could be wasting their money. Researchers at the University of Canterbury found there is no scientific evidence to support claims that specially designed running shoes _____.
   Kevin Douglas, a general practitioner who is a runner, was inspired to conduct the research after sustaining a series of injuries in his own expensive set of sneakers. Douglas found there was some evidence that hi-tech running shoes actually contributed to injury by making athletes land on their heels. These shoes could impair balance and promote ankle strains. He concluded that if you're not experiencing problems, you should stick with the shoes you're wearing. Because that's obviously the ones working for you.

   (a) help run faster
   (b) make you stand out among the crowd
   (c) are lighter and more comfortable
   (d) help prevent physical damages

3. Perched near the top of Vietnam, Hanoi, which means "the hinterland between the rivers", isn't only the country's official capital, but also its heart. Its people are proud and friendly, its food is diverse and divine, and the incessant beeping of car horns and humming of Honda motorbikes is strangely exhilarating. A beautiful blend of ancient oriental traditions and European style, Hanoi was ruled by the Chinese until 1428 when Le Loi—a Vietnamese general—established the nation's independence. The Portuguese arrived in Vietnam in the 1500s, but it was the French, who invaded in the mid 1800s, who _____ _____. Among the Asian environs, you'll find French-style buildings, as well as baguettes and croissants on most cafe menus.

   (a) destroyed the country the most
   (b) handed down the French recipes
   (c) left the biggest European mark
   (d) massacred the Vietnamese people

4. Dear Jenny Smith,

   Welcome to FlyBuys!

   Now you can start earning reward points on your everyday shopping. Inside the enclosed brochure, you'll find some Bonus Point offers to get you started on your way to enjoying shopping coupons, fine dining, escapes to the leading hotels, movies coupons, chances to fly off to far away destinations and many more rewards. All you have to do is present your FlyBuys card every time you shop at participating FlyBuys businesses. You'll find all the details on points and how to redeem them for rewards inside the enclosed brochure. You can also register your email address to get regular updates on the latest program information. Put your new FlyBuys card in your wallet right away, so next time you shop you _____.

   Thank you.

   (a) can get a copy of a brochure
   (b) can redeem your gifts
   (c) can make it count
   (d) can receive discounts

5. "Reading the mid-sections of this book is like being thrown into a thriller," said Lucy Sussex in the Washington Post. In 1997, Israeli intelligence service Mossad tried to assassinate Palestinian activist Khalid Mishal. Their method was bizarre because the plan was to deliver poison via a fake camera. The Mossad agents succeeded in poisoning Mishal in Jordan but _____.
King Hussein of Jordan, incensed by the attack, ignited a row between Israel, the US and the Arab states by demanding an antidote to the poison in exchange for the release of the Israeli agents. This gripping, real-life intrigue threatened to blow the Middle East apart and makes for superb, informative reading.

   (a) were decapitated by the Jordan government
   (b) killed themselves after accomplishing their duty
   (c) were apprehended by his bodyguards
   (d) were captured later in the US

6. US president recently lifted the media ban on images of the coffins of American war dead arriving at Denver Air Force Base. Many suspect that the ban, in place since 1991, was imposed solely to hide the human cost of the war. The conventional wisdom is that rows of flag-draped coffins _____, especially if it is going badly. Yet US president has lifted the ban just as he is trying to drum up backing from people for an expansion of the Afghan war effort. Bad timing? Probably not. The American public's view appears to be based largely on a cost-benefit calculation. They tend to tolerate casualties if they believe going to war was the right decision and they will win. Although a majority of Americans hold the view that Afghanistan is a war worth fighting, most believe they aren't winning. That's why US president Obama should concentrate on devising a path to victory.

   (a) sap support for any conflict
   (b) raise patriotism among Americans
   (c) make Americans mourn and grieve
   (d) increase support for the government

7. The American with a generous girth and loud check shirt nabbed me outside the National Gallery of Victoria. He wanted advice. He had seen the gallery's collection of Australian landscapes and was stunned by Australian artist Fred Williams' bold canvases. "I will never forget those images of that vast burning ochre desert and the curve of that endless horizon dotted with stunted scrub," he enthused with a rolling Texan drawl. This man needed to find a travel agent, and soon. He was one of the typical overseas travellers who are inspired to tour Australia after seeing extraordinary photographs, paintings and films that _____.

   (a) portrait the journey of Australians
   (b) display urban Australian landscapes
   (c) showcase the scenery
   (d) inspire creative images

8. Soul, groove and disco music have _____ over the past few years. The hits that seeped into the consciousness of the music-loving public around the world have been given new life by a myriad of popular performers from boy bands to solo artists. That said though, it's hard to find a female performer in the current spectrum who embodies that soul energy quite like Lisa Hunt. This vibrant, enigmatic, diva has one of the biggest voices in the business, and the energy on-stage to match, resulting in an unforgettable live show. She skips through a variety of genres in her repertoire, turning her incredible vocals to not only soul, but also some R&B, pop and disco favourites.

   (a) lost their popularity among people
   (b) become popular for the first time
   (c) witnessed a massive resurgence
   (d) made many artists break through into the mainstream

9. Hindu ethics _____ the castes system in which fatalism and narrow role expectations are key elements. For instance, if a person is born into the warrior caste, that person is bound to kill enemy soldiers when it's necessary to defend their community. On the other hand, waging war in the sense of indiscriminate killing has been prohibited consistently for a long time. The Hindu warriors are not supposed to kill the weak, including the wounded, deserters or non-combatants out of a sense of fairness and chivalry. Considering what is expected of them, it was thought to be unprofessional to attack non-soldiers.

   (a) have contradicted the basic theory of
   (b) have been strongly influenced by
   (c) have been basically replaced by
   (d) have criticized the very essence of

10. Japan is in the midst of the biggest drugs-in-sport scandal the country has ever seen. But forget sprinters on steroids or blood-doping cyclists. This is far more serious: sumo wrestlers smoking pot. In the past six months, four wrestlers have been kicked out of the ancient sport for smoking marijuana. The revelations are big news because many Japanese believe that to stain the purity of sumo is to tarnish the heart of Japan itself. The Japan Sumo Association acted quickly, dismissing the wrestlers and stepping up its testing regime to head off the scandal. But many, including sports minister Ryu Shinoya, are calling for _____ to stem this shameful behavior.

   (a) a ban on smoking pot
   (b) more severe punishment
   (c) eviction of the involved players
   (d) abolition of the sport

11. Female suicide bombers are becoming more and more common in Iraq. The occurrence of girls serving as human bombs has more than tripled since 2007. In the past 18 months, 27 female suicide bombers have been reported in the province of Diyala. The increase has been attributed to improved security in Iraq over the past six months, which has made it more difficult for male suicide bombers to get past checkpoints. Men are _____, even at security checks in Iraq, so many conceal explosives beneath their abayas, black head-to-toe robes worn by Islamic women. Girls are often recruited from poor or unstable families who are told their only hope of salvation is to give up their daughters. Some reports suggest al-Qaeda have even established a group called Young people of Paradise, which recruits teens to train for suicide assignments.

    (a) not allowed to touch women
    (b) unwilling to do their jobs
    (c) unable to work as security guards
    (d) not conducting thorough inspections

12. Social skills are an essential part of our dog's etiquette. When these skills are not taught and put to practice, we often have bad experiences with our dogs in public. Whether it be with other dogs, people, cats or the vet clinic, the best way to improve our dogs' social skills is to give them regular exposure to these experiences. That's why dog training classes are ideal for _____. Pupstars is offering you two new, unique ways to keep your dog socialized—through monthly social days and specific breed days. The social days are a once a month gathering for dogs and owners, filled with fun, games and interactions for dogs of all shapes and sizes. The specific breed days are an opportunity for you and your dog to bond with other owners and dogs of the same breed.

    (a) teaching dogs how to behave
    (b) effectively making dogs do tricks
    (c) creating controlled situations for mingling
    (d) training dogs to very high levels of obedience

13. In 1939 scientists in the USA, England and Germany informed their governments that it _____ to make an atomic explosion. In 1940, two American physicists published an account of the process, so there was no secret about the principles behind the bomb: the problem was to apply them. It was in Britain that an atomic bomb was first seen as a weapon which could win the war. In March 1940, two Nazi refugees, wrote a memo to show how an atom bomb could be constructed from uranium-235 and outlined the lethal effects from its explosion and the accompanying radiation. The British gave a high priority to nuclear research, as did the Americans when the USA entered the war in December 1941. By 1945, the USA had produced an atom bomb which used uranium, and one which used a man-made material, plutonium.

   (a) was morally unacceptable
   (b) was feasible now
   (c) was out of the question
   (d) was theoretically possible

14. The origins of morality lie in the disgust that makes us avoid rotting food, says the Times. This discovery explains why injustice is said to leave a bad taste in the mouth. Psychologists from the University of Toronto found that the feeling of being cheated evokes the same revulsion response as foul-tasting food and drink. The involuntary emotional reaction that keeps us away from sources of infection also prompts us to uphold moral standards and to shun those who don't. These findings suggest that disgust was important to the evolution of morality and that our sense of what is ethical is based not only on reasoning but powerful gut reactions as well. While morality has been seen as the pinnacle of human development, disgust is an ancient, rather primitive emotion which _____.

   (a) aided evolutionary survival
   (b) caused racial discrimination towards others
   (c) promoted healthy diet
   (d) prevented epidemics

15. After more than a decade of prosperity, the wheels have fallen off the world economy with some likening the present downturn to the Great Depression 80 years ago. Interest rates were lowered to stimulate economic activity, and the government threw billions of dollars at the electorate to shore up the flatlining retail sector before Christmas. As the government again pushed forward a plan to splash tens of billions of dollars to keep the economy from going into recession, debate raged over whether the initial stimulus had, in fact, stimulated the economy. _____, questions should have been raised about the long-term benefits of the hand-outs. We should ask if it is good planning if the nation's tax revenue is spent in the shops on t-shirts, toys and chocolate cake, much of which would have found its way into sewers or landfill by New Year's Day?

(a) Indeed
(b) Therefore
(c) For example
(d) Instead

16. Women are now earning higher salaries, starting their own companies and influencing more buying decisions than ever before. _____ research has shown many women still don't feel confident when it comes to investing or protecting their income or assets. At Citibank we are committed to helping women learn more about growing and protecting their wealth as well as understanding the value of professional financial advice. Ask about our Pearls of Wisdom brochure series, covering investing, insurance, retirement and estate planning. There's also over 400 qualified Citibank financial Planners ready to give you the confidence to be better off. Whatever your age or circumstance, if you are a woman who wants more from life, see our financial planners. Make an appointment now at your local branch.

(a) In addition
(b) Consequently
(c) Yet
(d) Likewise

Part 2 Questions 17~37

Read the passage and the question. Then choose the option that best answers the question.

17. News has surfaced about the opening last December of an Italian restaurant in the North Korean capital. The Japanese-based newspaper Choson Sinbo, closely aligned with Pyoung-yang, reported that ingredients for pizza and pasta were flown in from Italy. The opening of the restaurant is the result of a long campaign by the North Korean leader Kim Jong-il to introduce Western food to the country, with delegations sent to Italy to learn the pizza craft, and Italian chefs brought to North Korea to train locals. The new restaurant caters for the country's elite while the mass of the population remains impoverished.

    Q: What is the best title for the news article?

    (a) The opening of a restaurant in Italy.
    (b) The friendly relations between Italy and North Korea.
    (c) The successful campaign to open a restaurant for the public.
    (d) North Korea's first foreign eatery for the upper classes.

18. A study in the US has found that people who live in smoggy cities are up to 50% more likely to die from lung disease than people living in the fresher air of the country. Scientists studied 500,000 Americans for 18 years and found that ground-level ozone was a key factor in respiratory deaths. Previous research linked increases in ground-level ozone levels to heart attacks and severe asthma. It also indicated that long-term exposure to tiny particles of soot and dust found in smog is a risk factor for heart and lung disease. This is the first study to look at the long-term health impacts of ozone, which is formed through the chemical reaction between sunlight and the nitrogen oxides released by vehicle exhaust and industrial emissions.

    Q: What is the main topic of the passage?

    (a) The pros of living in the country.
    (b) The impacts of ozone on heart-related diseases.
    (c) The effects of surface ozone on human health.
    (d) The mixture of chemicals that makes ozone.

19. Dear Tenant,

We value you as a tenant and every endeavor will be made by our property management staff to ensure that you are treated with respect and fairness. It is important that you understand the terms of the tenancy agreement. Please ask if you are unsure about any term or clause, and our Property Management staff will be happy to provide you with information on local services. We look forward to developing a friendly business relationship with you and if we can be of any further assistance, please contact our office.

Sincerely,

Q: What is the purpose of this letter?

(a) To arrange a meeting
(b) To welcome the leaseholder
(c) To warn the tenant of the lease
(d) To express gratitude

20. Teeth-whitening products and procedure are becoming increasingly popular, mainly due to the increase in society's value on whiter, brighter teeth. Smoking, coffee and red wine are common culprits of staining to the teeth and should be minimized if possible. However, often stains are just normal occurrences. There are many whitening products currently on the market, from the supermarket bought, less expensive options to in-chair dental procedures performed by a qualified dentist. Currently, and perhaps the most effective and popular is the take-home kits, which most dental professionals recommend as the best option in teeth whitening.

Q: What is the best title for the passage?

(a) The reasons why teeth get stained.
(b) The rising popularity of oral beauty products.
(c) The wise way to choose the best whitening product.
(d) The most widely used product for teeth whitening.

21. An airport baggage handlers' strike delayed flights and left thousands of passengers fuming at London Airport yesterday. The baggage handlers walked off the job during peak hours in London yesterday after their union claimed British Airways was outsourcing baggage handling to a company that was paying workers less to do the job. At the domestic airport, there were delays of up to three hours on arriving and departing British Airways flights, and crowds at check-in counters and baggage carousels.

   Q: What is the main idea of the passage?

   (a) Flights were cancelled due to late arrival of passengers.
   (b) The workout at airport hits passengers.
   (c) People should know how to handle missing baggage.
   (d) A greedy airline laid off thousands of employees.

22. If you're not too bright, blame your old man. Researchers have found that children with older fathers seem to perform worse in intelligence tests and score lower in a variety of cognitive tests than those born to younger fathers. While there's a general trend for men to have children later in life, a team led by John McGrath of the California Brain Institute believes this needs rethinking. He says that the offspring of older fathers show subtle impairments on tests of neurocognitive ability during infancy and childhood. Other research has also shown links between advanced paternal age, men over 35, and an increased risk of neurodevelopmental disorders such as autism and dyslexia.

   Q: What is the passage mainly about?

   (a) The difference in fitness level between younger and older fathers.
   (b) Teenagers' rude behavior towards their fathers.
   (c) The effect of fathers' age on the intelligence of offspring.
   (d) Children's brain damage risk due to fathers' low intelligence.

23. Dengue fever is caused by a virus passed on by some species of mosquitoes. The virus itself is not usually present in North Queensland, but needs to be introduced by someone infected with dengue overseas. There are four types of dengue virus that causes dengue fever. These types are Dengue 1, 2, 3 and 4 and they all cause the same symptoms. The two main illnesses caused by the dengue virus are: dengue fever and dengue hemorrhagic fever. As there are four types of dengue virus, a person can contract dengue up to four times. The risk of dengue hemorrhagic fever increases if you contract more than one type of dengue. That is why it is important to know if you have dengue and which type. The type of dengue virus can only be confirmed by a blood test.

   Q: Which of the following is correct according to the passage?

   (a) There are 4 different types of dengue fever.
   (b) Dengue hemorrhagic fever only occurs when catching the type 2 Dengue virus.
   (c) Different dengue virus types make people suffer different symptoms.
   (d) Dengue hemorrhagic fever can occur during primary dengue infection.

24. Make it easier to put the pen through resolutions about getting in shape with a 10-week belly dancing course. New courses start on February 2 at The Belly Dance Academy in Franklin Street, including evening classes. Director and founder Nayima Hassan opened the doors 14 years ago when belly dancing was considered a fringe exercise. Today the successful academy welcomes hundreds of women and children weekly at more than 30 classes. Nayima says students can choose from traditional Egyptian belly dancing to modern versions to hybrid gypsy forms. Class sizes are kept to a minimum and the academy is now famous for offering students the most enjoyable hour of achieving fitness through this exotic form of recreation. Nayima says people can come in and watch classes this month prior to booking. The academy is also holding a free, Arabic Drum class for men and women.

   Q: Which of the following is correct according to the advertisement?

   (a) Belly dancing prevailed when Nayima Hassan first started the academy.
   (b) People can book to learn how to belly dance for free this month.
   (c) The academy offers belly dancing mixed with new influences.
   (d) The classes are known to help people flex their muscles.

25. The Semaphore Palace, a remarkable building, whose opening is in 1922, reputedly attracted one-third of the population of Adelaide. It combines an eastern fantasy with the beach-side romance of the art nouveau and art deco eras and harks back to the British fascination with the coast. It has variously been a dance hall, tea rooms, a bather's pavilion, and an evacuative backdrop to a day at the beach. And even better, you can get a drink and a meal there! We are fortunate in 2009 to still have the Palace with us after it fell into dreadful disrepair in the 1980s, culminating in a fire which almost destroyed the palace in 1994. Today, it is back to its former glory as one of our great architectural landmarks and continue to attract people, if for no other reason, that it is there, looks amazing and serves delicious food after 12.

Q: Which of the following is correct about the Semaphore Palace?

(a) About 13 percent of the population in Adelaide visited the Semaphore Palace.
(b) People can enjoy tasty breakfast at the Semaphore Palace.
(c) The location of the palace is far from the shore.
(d) The Semaphore Palace was not intact during the 1980s.

26. Matching wine with food isn't a dark, mysterious art—it's actually quite straightforward. Put a steak with a reasonable glass of red wine and you've got it. But it's just as easy to get it wrong. Pair that same red wine with a piece of barbecued kingfish, and you might find it creating a strange metallic taste in your mouth. There are very good reasons why certain wines match certain foods and why they don't. By simply following a few easy color and taste rules you're guaranteed to get it right. The standard "red wine with red meat, white wine with white meat" rule is an old one but a good one. Generally, red meat has a lot of flavor and texture, which means it can cope with the more generous wine flavors in red wine as well as the texture that comes from the tannins. White meat, like white wine, is more delicately flavored and textured, making them more suited to each other

Q: Which of the following is correct according to the passage?

(a) Pairing the right wine with the right food is a matter of personal taste.
(b) It's a good combination to serve kingfish with red wine.
(c) It's an innovative idea to match meat with wine of the same color.
(d) Red meat needs more chewing than white meat does.

27. Many parents are worried about their kids eating peanuts because of possible food allergy. Food allergies are on the rise—currently about one in 20 children has a food allergy in England, so it pays to be careful. When your child turns two, introduce a tiny amount of peanut butter—about an eighth of a teaspoon. The best time to do this is on a weekday morning, so if there's a reaction there'll be plenty of staff at your local general practitioner, surgery or hospital. A mild reaction is defined as swelling around the mouth, vomiting, body hives or a stomachache immediately after eating or in the following few hours. If this happens, stay with your child so you can monitor any changes. If symptoms include swelling of the tongue, wheezing, difficulty breathing or a hoarse voice, call an ambulance as it could be anaphylactic shock. If your child has eczema, or if his siblings have allergies, he's at increased risk of food allergy, so talk to your doctor about skin-prick tests instead of food test.

   Q: Which of the following is correct according to the passage?

   (a) More and more parents are suffering from food allergies.
   (b) Parents should not try to identify their children's food allergies.
   (c) Allergists can perform skin-prick tests to check for allergic responses.
   (d) Throwing up is one of the symptoms from the anaphylactic shock.

28. Pity the future cyborg insect. Not only will humans control their movements, but these movements may power the electronics that hijack their bodies. Engineers have been attempting to gain control of insect bodies for some time, hoping to use them as spies, and to harness their sense of smell to detect chemicals and explosives. To do this, researchers implant electrical stimulators that zap certain nerves of brain cells, triggering an impulse that makes the insect move in a desired direction. This process can be driven by a programmed chip or external remote control. So far, powering these "stimulator chips" has been the limiting factor. Now, scientists such as Keisuke Morishima from the Tokyo University have shown that piezoelectric fibers can harness the energy of insect movements and power "slave-driving chips". This method could also be applied to larger animals such as rats.

   Q: What will the future cyborg insects be used for?

   (a) They will be used for supplying electric power to appliances.
   (b) They will be used for digging up intelligence.
   (c) They will be used for destroying buildings.
   (d) They will be used for controlling other larger animals.

29. The Haymarket Square riot took place in Chicago in 1886. A small anarchist movement there was led by German Immigrants, who called for violent revolution. On 3 May, police clashed with strikers at the McCormick Harvester plant, killing three strikers and wounding several more. Union leaders called for a mass rally the next day in Haymarket Square to protest at police brutality. During the rally someone threw a bomb which killed one policeman and six other people and injured sixty-seven. Police opened fire, killing four more. Eight anarchists were charged with conspiracy to murder. There was no evidence of their involvement in the bomb-throwing but all were convicted and seven were sentenced to death. In 1893, the liberal governor of Illinois pardoned the three anarchists who were still in prison, as he said that a miscarriage of justice had occurred.

Q: Which of the following is correct according to the passage?

(a) Several policemen got killed during the clash on May 3rd.
(b) A total of seven people died in Haymarket Square.
(c) Proofs of who had thrown the bomb were not found.
(d) All of those who received death sentences were later released from the jail.

30. The New Zealand government of Prime Minister John Key sparked a national debate with its decision to reintroduce royal honors. These had been abolished by the Labor government of Helen Clarke in 2000, replacing it with a Companion of the Order of New Zealand. Eighty-five people who received that honor will now have the option of an upgrade. The New Zealand Herald polled 5,000 readers with 74% endorsing the change. New Zealanders are watching to see who among the non-royal honors recipients put their hands up for a sir or a dame. In the meantime, knighthoods still have a place, but many people think the title is a quaint, antiquated system that has no relevance in 21st century New Zealand.

Q: Which of the following is correct according to the passage?

(a) Royal honors were reintroduced in 2000.
(b) Other honors were awarded instead of Knighthoods
(c) Many people take Knighthoods for granted.
(d) 85 people can choose to be addressed "Sir" or "Dame"

Actual Test · 1

31. Bedbugs which feed on the blood of human beings are putting the bite on tourists in the cheapest backpacker hostel beds, luxury hotel suites and even restaurant chairs. The hot and wet climate and growing number of international travellers in recent years has resulted in a steady infestation increase. Gilligans, the biggest backpacker hostel with a high turnover of international travellers through its 615 beds, plans to introduce a register for guests to fill in to help keep tabs on pests they may have inadvertently brought with them in shoes, baggage or other items. Keeping the bugs out completely is almost impossible but the hostel now has one of the lowest percentages of infestations in the local industry. Treatment involved stripping the room bare and heating them to more than 80 degrees celsius to kill the bugs.

    Q: Which of the following can be inferred from the passage?

    (a) Budbugs suck on the blood of other insects.
    (b) Humidity is one of the culprits of a growing infestation
    (c) Travellers may bring pests with them on purpose.
    (d) People should have the sun shine on beds to kill the bugs.

32. Children don't bring happiness. In fact, more often they seem to bring unhappiness. A study by the University of York in Britain concluded there was no difference between life satisfaction levels of parents and non-parents. Scholars even found some evidence that parents report statistically significant lower levels of happiness, life satisfaction, marital satisfaction and mental well-being compared with non parents. There's also evidence that the strains associated with parenthood continue after children become independent. So why do we have them in the first place? Does nature fit us with rose-colored glasses? One theory is that the belief that children bring happiness transmits itself much more successfully from generation to generation than the belief that children bring misery. Those who choose not to have children are unlikely to pass on the belief beyond their own generation.

    Q: What can be inferred from the passage?

    (a) In general, non-parents are more satisfied with their lives than parents.
    (b) Parents feel emancipated when their children become self-reliant.
    (c) Many believe that having children implies felicity in itself.
    (d) The negativity against having children is widespread among people now.

33. Jenny Kitson had several interviews and is in touch with several job agencies, but for now she has to be content with her part-time cafe work. The 18-year-old hoped to find work in tourism promotion or marketing after finishing high school last year, but found the job market a tough nut to crack. It is a situation becoming more and more common in Los Angeles, with the unemployment rate reaching 9.6 percent in February. That compares with a national average of 5.2 percent and is the highest figure since the early 1990s when the country was battling the effects of recession. "I guess I wanted to get my career going rather than study when I left school, but I've found with the tourism industry employers are really looking for people with experience, especially in the current market" Ms. Kitson said.

   Q: What can be inferred from the article?

   (a) Jenny Kitson is currently unemployed due to the tough job market.
   (b) Jenny Kiston left school to get a job before graduation.
   (c) Landing a job in Los Angeles is harder than other cities in the country.
   (d) Current tourism industry are looking for people with university degrees.

34. There is not always a cycle lane on the highway. Oncoming traffic doesn't slow down to pass safely and cyclists must stop and get off the road. Cycle lanes often have broken glass on them and cyclists have to use the road or get a puncture. Cyclists and motorists should be courteous to each other. There should be give way signs for motorists where there is danger to cyclists and cyclists should go single file in traffic. There should also be regular sweeping of cycle lanes to keep them in good condition. Treat cyclists as equal road users with mandatory driving courses for all motorists to be renewed by a short test every two years or a license will be withdrawn. There should also be traffic lights on intersections for cyclists.

   Q: What can be inferred from the passage?

   (a) Highway conditions are not safe for car drivers.
   (b) Motorists are not cautious with cyclists on the road.
   (c) There are too many cycle lanes on the road for cyclists.
   (d) A driver's license is withdrawn if a person fails the short test.

Actual Test · 1

35. When you hear the words "all you can eat", it conjures images of diners piling their plates high with food and coming back to the buffet table several times, all for the one fixed price. Now take that concept and apply it to digital music and you can understand what NewTech, the world's largest mobile manufacturer, has come up with in its new service. From March 20, customers can pay $ 979 for a 12-month subscription or $ 1109 for 18 months to receive the 5800-dollar-touchscreen handset and the right to legally download as much music as they want from more than four million tracks within the NewTech Music Store. This price will not include the monthly mobile plan costs. The only catch with this service is the downloaded music can be played only on the device or on one nominated PC. The PC can be changed once every three months during the subscription and two years after the subscription ends.

   Q: What is the passage advertising?

   (a) A fixed price buffet
   (b) Multi-functional automobiles
   (c) New concept cell phones
   (d) Flat rate for mobile music downloads

36. A recent report which made national headlines claims there is no safe level of alcohol consumption. In short, we are probably all at higher risk of cancer if we drink. While only women were tested in the study, the results were believed to be so conclusive after tracking a million females and their drinking habits that it was assumed that male drinkers are probably increasing their risk as well. Most of us will carry on regardless, cheerfully imbibing under the banner of excuses which could feasibly range from, "a guy/girl's got to have some pleasure in life", to "you're going to die of something, so might as well go happy". There is credence in both, especially in the current climate of financial doom. However, for those who may feel a twinge of guilt at the possibility of sending themselves to an early grave, here are some ways to counter-balance the effects of a drink or two.

   Q: What is the next paragraph likely to be about?

   (a) A list of ways to refuse alcohol.
   (b) The habits for long life.
   (c) Effective methods to alleviate guilty conscience.
   (d) The ways to offset the negative consequences of alcohol consumption.

37. Indigenous Australians use fresh water and salt water turtles as a food source throughout Australia. They are a great source of fresh meat for them. The turtles are not an endangered species so why should they not be harvested as they have been by Australia's indigenous people for thousands of years? Australia is not, and never will, be the exclusive domain of non-indigenous Australians and indigenous people are entitled to the practice of their cultures. Indigenous hunting is not the reason so many animals have become extinct in Australia in the last 221 years. Those extinctions have been caused through the destruction and the pollution of their habitats or all-out indiscriminate slaughter of that particular species by the European settlers.

   Q: What can be inferred from the passage?

   (a) There are not plenty of turtles in Australia anymore.
   (b) Few animals have become extinct in the last hundreds years.
   (c) Non-indigenous Australians have slaughtered turtles for their meat.
   (d) Debates over killing turtles are taking place in Australia.

Part 3 *Questions 38~40*

Read the passage. Then identify the option that does NOT belong.

38. Research by the Henry Ford Hospital Sleep Disorders Center found that even people who felt well rested after an eight-hour sleep performed better and were more alert when they slept another two hours. (a) It's because human beings are designed to doze. (b) Before the invention of the light bulb we averaged ten hours of slumber a night. (c) But artists, writers and computer coders typically perform better by crashing near dawn. (d) Another reason to stay in bed is that our stress hormone, cortisol, normally peaks in the bloodstream around 7 am.

39. In many ways a recession is like a cyclone. (a) It's going to be uncomfortable and it's coming whether you like it or not. (b) But we've leant that one of the best ways to face cyclones is to be prepared. (c) This recession may be deeply felt and take a few years to recover but it will eventually pass. (d) Building up reserves of money, skills, network contacts and strong family and community ties make you feel stronger and protects against future loss.

40. Just as the individual strings of a well-tuned violin each participate in the making of a symphony, your body is composed of many different players working in harmony to make you who you are. (a) From individual cells and organs to entire body, the crux of true health depends not just on how each piece works as a unit but how they perform as a cohesive whole. (b) It is important to let your inner conductor free to do its magic. (c) For example, the act of eating an apple requires a tremendous feat of organization and precision. (d) From the muscles of your jaw and salivary glands to the redirection of blood from limbs and head towards organs of digestion, it's a symphony of bodily functions.

Reading Comprehension

Actual Test • 2

Directions

This part of the exam tests your ability to comprehend reading passages.
You will have 45 minutes to complete the 40 questions.
Be sure to follow the directions given by the proctor.

Part 1 *Questions 1~16*

Read the passage. Then choose the option that best completes the passage.

1. A man reversed a four-wheel drive Ford truck into the entrance of a police station and set it on fire. The perpetrator fled on foot leaving a damage bill estimated at more than $500,000. The incident occurred in the suburb of Saint Thomas. More than ten officers were on duty at the station but, as it was the noon of night, the attacker _____.
He's believed to have ignited a fuel tank in the back of the vehicle before escaping. The reception area and neighbouring offices were extensively damaged, forcing the station to close temporarily.

   (a) was caught red-handed
   (b) could not be identified
   (c) managed to get away with a simple warning
   (d) surrendered himself to the police

2. Like the story of Billy Elliot itself, this production, recently at Sydney's Capitol Theater, is a triumph of the creative spirit. With music by Sir Elton John and lyrics from the film's screenwriter, Lee Hall, this musical might even be better than the original movie. As a boy who discovers a passion for ballet, Billy struggles to pursue his goal in a mining town during a strike in England. The cast of child actors is _____ incredible. Especially, Dayton Tavares, who played Billy on the opening night is a superstar, bestowed with preternatural physical grace, vocal and acting abilities.

   (a) far from
   (b) not completely
   (c) anything but
   (d) nothing short of

3. I was reading a newspaper whilst enjoying my favorite addiction at a coffee shop in the cozy, warm weather. In the paper, I learned of a new term called Butt Dialing (BD). This denotes a situation where one inadvertently dials a cell phone by the accidental pressing of the keyboard. Like when you sit down with your cell phone in your hip pocket while your cell phone unlocked, and some auto-dial button is pressed making a call. This kind of accidental phone-calls can happen not only via the engagement mechanism of your butt, but also by _____.

   (a) pressing a keyboard on purpose
   (b) mistakes caused by mobile phone manufacturers
   (c) receiving BDs from your close acquaintances
   (d) the other parts of your body

4. It is good to see that taxi drivers continue to be booked for not wearing their seat-belts at Washington Airport. A crackdown on this illegal activity is well overdue and the Federal Police should be commended. Do taxi drivers believe they are above the law? Well, they'd better not. Also, as part of the crackdown on safety and regulations at the airport, police should be issuing on-the-spot fines for the myriad jaywalkers as it is illegal to do so. Many pedestrians are at real risk of injury and nothing is being done to assist them. Fining aberrant pedestrians would certainly raise significant revenue and think what a marvelous souvenir an infringement notice would be as a memento of their visit to Washington. Obviously, there is _____.

   (a) a good remembrance item to buy in Washington
   (b) a law that needs fine-tuning
   (c) a need for common sense
   (d) no one who abides by the law

5. Agave is best known as the main ingredient in the feisty Mexican spirit tequila, but the drought-resistant succulent is now being touted as the next big thing in biofuels. Central Americans have distilled the sap of the agave into spirits for centuries, but now an Australian company wants to _____ _____ to make ethanol for energy. Sugar cane is already used in Australian ethanol production and 10% ethanol petrol is widely available. Proponents of agave say they are not trying to replace sugar as a source of ethanol but point out the plant is ideal for climates where cane cannot flourish. Australian company Ausagave has 10,000 agave plants in pots that are ready for a trial cultivation. They believe the crop could produce between 10,000 and 16,000 liters of ethanol per hectare every year.

(a) sell agave to gather enough money
(b) cultivate more sugar canes
(c) harness its high sugar content
(d) launch a responsible drinking campaign

6. Most of the time locusts are innocent grasshoppers, but under the right conditions they transform into swarming creatures that are a byword for pestilence. Prof. Steve Simpson of the University of Georgia has previously demonstrated that this transformation occurs when locust populations become crowded, and has even tricked them into changing to the swarming state by tickling their back legs with paintbrushes. This discovery prompted interest in the neurochemical transmitter that triggers the change. Dr. Michael Anstey investigated the relationship between 13 chemicals and the shift to a swarming state, and only serotonin showed a relationship. The finding is not surprising since the serotonin is widespread through the animal kingdom, and _____ _____ in crustaceans, rodents and humans.

(a) elucidates evolutional changes
(b) prompts social behaviors
(c) causes fatal diseases
(d) helps population control

Actual Test 2

7. Few cities have a more picturesque setting than Santiago. Chile's capital sits on a coastal plain with the snow-capped Andes as a backdrop. Founded in 1541, this city of wide boulevards and leafy parks is re-claiming its reputation as a tourist destination now that the turbulent years have faded to a distant memory. Santiago is a fabulous walking city. It's a great place to stroll and soak up the buzzing Latino atmosphere, but if you _____, head for the neighborhoods where the crush of people falls away and you find hip, bohemian districts that lean towards art and culture. The Parque Metropolitano is a huge urban park where there's funicular that climbs to the summit of San Cristobal Hill. There, you can gaze in tranquility upon a sprawling cityscape that melts into the haze.

   (a) want to have some time in a party-like atmosphere
   (b) desire to make some local friends
   (c) yearn for something quieter
   (d) want to enjoy new fashion trends

8. Thailand's Health Ministry has warned people suffering from allergies and asthma to avoid eating fried insects. Fried insects are very popular in Bangkok and other cities in Thailand. A recent study by the ministry found that fried grasshoppers, silk worms and other six-legged delicacies often contain high levels of histamine which can provoke allergic reactions or asthma attacks. Insects have been on the menu in rural Thailand for many centuries but only in the past two decades have bulk bug wholesaling networks made the creatures _____. Health officials warn the bugs can pick up high levels of bacterial contamination during storage and excessive reuse of cooking oil to fry the insects can lead to toxic build up.

   (a) become extinct in Thailand
   (b) more vulnerable to diseases
   (c) popular in other parts of the world
   (d) widely available in urban areas

9. For most people, borrowing money is _____. People will receive a multitude of offers for store cards, credit cards, and home loans from the day of your first permanent job to the day you retire. Although these can all offer benefits at various stages of your life, taking a haphazard approach to how you borrow money can mean your loans end up becoming more burden than benefit. It can drain your finances heavily and unnecessarily over time. If you have more than one credit card, store card or loan, you need to consider consolidating all the cards you have into fewer facilities, or even just one. This can save you some extra money because it's more efficient.

   (a) not as easy as it seems
   (b) just a fact of life
   (c) a natural tradition for financing businesses
   (d) something to avoid if possible

10. With vessel ownership also comes the responsibility for the safety of all your passengers and your equipment. Be sure you have the right vessel and the right safety equipment for what you plan to do, so that your boating will be safe and enjoyable. Once you have your ideal vessel and have made sure it meets all the requirements of the regulations, make yourself familiar with its layout and equipment before you go out on the water. Take short trips on calm waters first. Ask an experienced friend along for advice and learn how your vessel responds at different speeds and in different weather conditions. Remember, obtaining a Boat Operator's License means that you know the rules, but the knowledge and skills to operate a vessel in all types of conditions _____.

   (a) are obtained from specialists and experts
   (b) come from the boost of your self-esteem.
   (c) are gained from taking complete responsibility
   (d) come from a lifetime of experience.

Actual Test·2

11. Britain's chief medical officer recommended the British government set a minimum price of 50 penny per unit of alcohol to _____. The proposal could double prices for some beverages, particularly the discounted beer and wine sold in supermarkets. It follows a recent decision by the Scottish government to introduce a minimum alcohol price. The cost to British taxpayers of alcohol abuse is thought to be more than 20 billion dollars annually, with alcohol-related hospital admissions of more than 200,000 a year. Opposition to the proposal comes from the alcohol industry and critics, including Prim Minister Gordon Brown, who argue it will punish moderate drinkers while doing little to deal with alcohol problems.

    (a) levy additional tax
    (b) penalize moderate drinkers
    (c) curb excessive drinking
    (d) reduce the rate of hospitalization

12. What is the purpose of a budget surplus? I was led to believe that a surplus should be invested in the country in the form of infrastructure, health and education for the betterment of society and to keep the wheels of the economy rolling. If storm clouds appear on the horizon, as they have, the money then should be used to keep the recession wolves from the door or at least minimize the impact of a recession by spending initiatives that keep people employed and businesses solvent. It would appear, though, that certain sections of the community are _____ to the point that they would rather see the country collapse into a screaming heap than weather the storm.

    (a) trying to invest as much money as possible
    (b) extremely protective of the surplus
    (c) inclined to take money out of the surplus
    (d) spending a significant amount of money on education

13. Ku Klux Klan is an organization to preserve white supremacy in the South after the American Civil War. "Ku Klux" comes from the Greek word kuklos, drinking-bowl. The Klan began in Tennessee in 1866, as a secret society with an elaborate ritual, and soon spread throughout the South. Members dressed up in white hoods and sheets and rode out at night carrying burning crosses. Their aim was to intimidate blacks, drive them from their land and prevent them from voting. When intimidation did not work Klansmen turned to violence. Opponents were flogged, tarred and feathered, their homes burnt and many were lynched. However, the violence _____.
Congress passed a Force Act in 1870, which imposed heavy fines for using force or intimidation to prevent from people voting. In 1871, the Klan and similar organizations were outlawed.

   (a) caused such silence
   (b) produced a backlash
   (c) succeeded in preventing a fair election
   (d) was verbal, not physical

14. Education is touted as the key to stopping the carnage on our roads. However, our education is censored and provides a distorted reality of the consequences of drink-driving or speeding. Too often we see a mangled wreck of a car but the victims and their horrific injuries are not shown. Every licensed driver should be required to view a small number of photos of accident scenes. Having spoken to a tow-truck drivers unlucky enough to _____ _____, I believe once is enough to change your mind on road safety. I know it is a gruesome way to tackle the problem, but someone needs to take a drastic stand such as this or we will never address this problem.

   (a) be punished for traffic infringements
   (b) have a talk with paramedics and police officers
   (c) have gotten minor injuries from traffic accidents.
   (d) view these things on a regular basis

15. "Make the World a Better Place" Movie Nights are a good opportunity to watch documentary films and commercial movies that deal with social and environmental issues. A rich discussion will be followed after the movies and all the participants can voice their own opinions. These events are free and open to the public. _____, voluntary donations will be accepted and used to help underwrite our educational programs at local public schools. If you have any questions or suggestions to make this event a more meaningful night, please contact us via e-mail address below.

    (a) Therefore
    (b) Consequently
    (c) However
    (d) In other words

16. I was seven when I first developed complex regional pain syndrome. I was out with a friend one day and he accidentally pushed his bike handle into my arm. Suddenly it froze up and my arm felt like it was in a boiling hot bath. I was prescribed drugs, but nothing completely dulled the pain. After a few weeks, the pain mysteriously stopped. In the years that followed, I had several more episodes. Once I tripped through a door, and was crippled by a burning pain that left me on crutches for 10 weeks. _____, I missed a lot of school. Luckily, my teachers were sympathetic and I managed to keep up good grades despite all my time off.

    (a) For example
    (b) As a result
    (c) Nevertheless
    (d) Instead

Part 2 *Questions 17~37*

Read the passage and the question. Then choose the option that best answers the question.

17. Flushed with the success of its moon mission, India is now taking a shot at Google. The Indian Space Research Organization is producing a competitor for Google's free satellite imagery service. The Indian version is called Bhuvan and will provide images of 20 times higher resolution than those Google makes available on the net. Google Earth can home in on big apartment blocks whereas Bhuvan will bring a vehicle the size of a mini-van into view. However, will Buhvan be a worthy competitor for Google? The Indian version may be only playing catch-up for a long time, given Google's superior skills at translating images into usable forms. More basically, they must first convince the growing internet community in India to use it.

    Q: What is the best title for the passage?

    (a) India's first successful mission to the moon.
    (b) The superiority of Google over Buhvan.
    (c) The challenges that lie ahead of Bhuvan.
    (d) Indians' indifference towards Bhuvan.

18. Isolationism was the policy of the USA which aimed at avoiding alliances with other countries or becoming involved in the affairs of other continents. It went back to George Washington, who advised Americans in his Farewell Address to steer clear of permanent alliances with foreign nations. Thomas Jefferson endorsed this policy when he became President in 1801: "Peace, commerce and honest friendship with all nations; entangling alliances with none". America's entry into the First World War in 1917 saw the abandonment of isolationism for a brief period. After the war Americans again turned their backs on the outside world and rejected President Wilson's plea to join the League of Nations.

    Q: What is the passage about?

    (a) How Isolationism became the diplomatic policy of America.
    (b) How the term "Isolationism" was defined.
    (c) Why America temporarily abandoned Isolationism.
    (d) President Wilson's hope to join the League of Nations.

19. Lindy Simpson hopes to cut her family's energy use by just switching off lights and household appliances. She says that it's just simple things like turning off the television if she goes outside. The Simpsons are one of seven households participating in the city's Energy Sustainability Street Initiative. Mrs. Simpson says that she notices the difference especially early in the morning a lot. She now turns off the bedroom air-conditioners and before long her family is running on just 15 cents an hour. Apart from cutting the electricity bill, Mrs. Simpson is keen to push the sustainability message to her children so the next generation is even more environmentally aware than this one.

Q: What is the passage about?

(a) How hard it is to teach children energy-saving skills.
(b) The money saved by turning off air-conditioners.
(c) The importance of participating in the community.
(d) The effects of simple energy-saving actions

20. Barium Enema is an X-ray test which shows the large bowel by coating it with barium and inflating the bowel with air. The barium and air are introduced by a tube which is inserted into the rectum. The images taken can show tumors, inflammation and structural changes in the large bowel. To take the test, the bowel must be as empty as possible. To do this, you will need to obtain a bowel cleansing kit from your doctor. It is important to follow the instructions closely for the best results. You will need to change into a gown. Then, you will be asked to lie on your side of the X-ray table. A thin plastic tube will be placed into your rectum. This can be uncomfortable but should not be painful at all. The barium fluid will then pass via the tube into your large bowel. You may need to be moved into different positions to coat the bowel. Once enough barium is in the bowel this will be drained out via the same tube and then air introduced. This will be seen on a TV monitor, and X-ray images will also be taken at this time.

Q: What is the main topic of the passage?

(a) The definition of the term "Barium Enema"
(b) Why patients take Barium Enema
(c) How Barium Enema is performed.
(d) How tube is inserted into the rectum.

21. Angry shoppers are abusing supermarket checkout staff for refusing to pack groceries in plastic bags, as Australian retailers start banning the plastic bags from their stores. Check-out staff are reporting incidents of bag rage, with workers being verbally threatened for denying customers free bags despite new laws banning their use. Retailers have until May 1 to implement a total ban on all single use of plastic bags from their stores, but must provide customers with alternatives. Some stores such as Target already have banned plastic bags completely while others have begun trialing bag-free lanes in preparation for the complete ban. However, customers have been getting upset at the checkout operators when it has got nothing to do with them. Store owners said that people have raised their voice saying that it's rubbish and that it's going to cost them more money.

Q: What is the passage about?

(a) The main culprits of shoplifting in stores.
(b) The date when the ban of plastic bags will be in effect.
(c) Disputes caused by prohibiting the use of plastic bags.
(d) The seriousness of verbal abuse by customers.

22. Great flexibility has been introduced into our water regime which recognizes that some gardens may require a mid-week watering in the heat of summer. Households now have the option of spreading their current three-hour a week watering times across two days. This flexible arrangement will reduce the risk of over-watering on weekends and provide a better chance of our trees and gardens surviving yet another dry summer. Under the new arrangements, hand-held hoses or drippers will be permitted for a maximum of 3 hours for even numbered houses between 6 to 9 p.m. on Tuesday and Sunday and for odd numbered houses during the same time on Wednesday and Sunday. Buckets and watering cans can be used any time on any day of the week.

Q: What is the passage about?

(a) The negative effects of over-watering
(b) The introduction of a new water arrangement
(c) The items allowed to be used for watering gardens
(d) The way to survive the coming summer

23. For crystal clear skin, read the following three-step plan. There's no better feeling than splashing your face with water and lathering it clean at the end of the day. Using a cleanser is important to remove make-up, sweat, toxins and bacteria that, if left on the skin, can cause irritations and blemishes. It's also important to use a cleansing product that's made specifically for your skin type. The second step is to exfoliate. Exfoliating makes your face look and feel healthier by polishing away dead skin cells. Choosing the right product is especially important in this stage of your three-step routine because the skin on your face is so delicate. Don't use products with sand granules or ground walnut shells—they're too harsh for your face. For best results, exfoliate once a week with the right product for your skin. The third step is to moisturize. whether your skin is dry, sensitive, ageing or oily, don't skip this step.

Q: Which of the following is correct according to the passage?

(a) The first step for clear skin is to get rid of your dead skin cells.
(b) Make-up can cause inflammation on your skin if not washed properly.
(c) Choosing the right moisturizer is the most important for crystal clear skin.
(d) It is recommended to use cleansing products with sand granules in them.

24. A man allegedly caught with 84g of cocaine in his possession was yesterday denied bail in Court. Sebastien Daquin was remanded in custody until his case resumes on April 24 after police argued he was at risk of re-offending and not reappearing if he was granted bail. Police allege Mr. Daquin was found at a Manchester tavern carrying the drugs, which was described by the police as a significant quantity. The court heard Mr. Daquin denied he was a supplier but had the drugs for personal use. Police said they had earlier seen Mr. Daquin at the airport about the same time another man was intercepted about drugs there. Mr. Darquin's lawyer said there was no evidence his client's presence at the airport was related to the police intercept.

Q: Which of the following is correct according to the article?

(a) Mr. Daquin was arrested at the airport for possessing drugs.
(b) Mr. Daquin was spotted at the airport with another man by police.
(c) Mr. Daquin sold his drugs to the man at the airport.
(d) Mr. Daquin will be locked up in jail until he appears in court again.

25. Our new Internet Stick modem is so small and sleek you can carry it around in your pocket wherever you go. Simply plug the Internet Stick modem into your USB port, wait for the automatic software installation, and you're connected to the Internet within minutes. Move it from room to room, city to city; and always stay in touch. You're never out of the loop. What's more, the new Internet Stick modem doubles as a memory card allowing you to store up to 4GB of files, documents, music and more. Our 3 giga high-speed broadband coverage already covers metropolitan areas in San Diego, Florida, Miami, and Los Angeles plus all major international airports in America.

   Q: Which of the following is correct about the advertised product?

   (a) The stick-shaped modem is small, but not easy to take a grip on it.
   (b) A manual is not needed to operate the modem.
   (c) The new Internet stick modem doubles the price of the 4GB memory card.
   (d) The modem allows people to surf the net in any international airports worldwide.

26. A great pair of sunglasses is the ultimate fashion accessory. So what styles should you be looking out for in 2009? Over the past few years, "big" has been best, and the trend continues. Oversized sunglasses will still be one of the hottest styles around this year. However, Look out for the latest designs which are '70s-inspired, with thick plastic frames. Classic sunglasses are also popular and are a firm favorite with celebs. Frame colors this season range from black through to turquoise and hot pink. The ultra-cool aviator-style sunnies suit most men and women. These sunnies are a great unisex option and you can swap them with your partner when you feel like wearing something different. Wrap-style sunnies are yet another option to keep you looking fashionable, and offer more protection.

   Q: Which of the following is correct according to the passage?

   (a) The large-sized sunglasses once used to be in style.
   (b) Black frame sunglasses are the most popular among people.
   (c) Wrap-style sunglasses can keep your face from being bashed.
   (d) Actors and actresses fancy wearing Classic Sunglasses.

27. As well as the excitement and eagerness surrounding the first day at school, there are elements of stress, not only for the child, but for parents as well. When some mothers wave their children off, they find to their surprise that the joy of their new freedom is also tinged with sadness and a few regrets. Your precious baby is heading off into the big, wide world! It can be scary, handing your child over to another adult, who will have a parent-like role in his life and teach him new ways of understanding the world. You might have a few niggling doubts about child moving away from the security of his home and out into the wider community, becoming part of a "System". And there's the worry of the other children—their acceptance of your child and the potential influence they may have.

Q: Why are mothers worried about their children according to the passage?

(a) Because their children will be travelling around the world.
(b) Because it's the first time for their children to meet other grown-ups.
(c) Because their children don't know how to hang out with others.
(d) Because it's the first time for their children to experience the world outside home.

28. The chemicals in cigaretts affect how your body works, and how well it copes during and after surgery. When you have surgery, you usually have an anesthetic drug so the operation can be performed without pain. Anaesthetic drugs can put your body under stress. They may lower your resistance to infection, and if you are unconscious, your breathing and heart need monitoring to prevent problems. If you smoke, your body is less able to cope with the stress caused by anaesthesia. Also, the nicotine in cigarette smoke increases your heart rate and blood pressure every time you smoke. Your heart works harder, and so it needs more oxygen. The carbon monoxide in cigarette smoke competes with the oxygen in your blood. If you smoke, you can have up to three times more carbon monoxide in your blood than non-smokers. This makes it harder to get the oxygen you need for your heart and body.

Q: Which of the following is correct according to the passage?

(a) Smoking reduces the effect of anesthetics.
(b) Non-smokers easily become short of breath than smokers.
(c) Smokers need more time to recover from a medical operation.
(d) Smoking elevates the level of stress in your body.

29. Dating back more than 100 million years, Australia's Wet Tropics Rainforests are the oldest continually surviving tropical rainforests on earth. These rainsforests once covered the entire Australia continent. Today, through evolution and climate change, they cover a tiny 0.1% of Australia's total land mass. Despite their size, they are home to an amazing diversity of plant and animal life, including over 3,000 plant species and many rare and endangered animals found nowhere else on earth. These rainsforests are one of 15 natural World Heritage sites in Australia, and one of few in the world to satisfy all four of the criteria for World Heritage listing. These rainsforests: represent a major stage of the earth's evolutionary history; provide outstanding examples of ongoing environmental processes; and contain the most important natural areas for the conservation of a variety of life.

Q: Which of the following is correct about Australia's Wet Tropics Rainforests?

(a) They are the only continually surviving rainforests in the world.
(b) Climate change has not affected the size of the rainforests in Australia.
(c) Many animals found in the rainforests can only be seen in Australia
(d) There is a total of 15 rainforests in Australia.

30. Running a successful small business is a dream many women have. In 2006, according to the American Bureau of Statistics, nearly one in three small businesses was owned and operated by a women, the majority of them based in New York. While the motives behind women starting small businesses are endlessly varied, it is often in response to circumstances, according to Holly Kramer, American Business Women's Awards ambassador. "Many of the women I've met through the awards started their businesses in response to something that happened in their lives", she says. "Almost all of them had some kind of personal mission at the core: their primary motivation wasn't about making money." Consequently, the stories behind their business start-ups are always unique, and inspiring.

Q: Which of the following is correct according to the passage?

(a) Most of the female small business owners were born in New York.
(b) Many women start to run their own businesses to become rich.
(c) Many women are inspired to run their own businesses through events in their lives.
(d) The products sold by female business owners are very distinct from others.

Actual Test · 2

31. The obesity explosion in recent years continues to grow and is projected by the World Health Organization to reach 1.5 billion by 2015. These staggering numbers will overwhelm medical, social and economic care-givers, creating an unparalleled chronic disease burden for the world in the next 10~20 years. Weight excess and obesity are major risk factors for heart disease, stroke, Type 2 diabetes and severe psychological conditions including depression. While the approach to combat obesity must involve a multidisciplinary collection of experts from medical, educational, governmental and social disciplines, the obesity epidemic has rapidly driven scientific researchers to understand how the brain controls human feeding behaviour.

    Q: Which of the following is correct about obesity?

    (a) Heart disease can contribute to the risk of obesity.
    (b) Obesity is becoming a major health hazard worldwide.
    (c) The number of people with obesity is higher than the number of care-givers.
    (d) It requires one specialized doctor to cure obesity.

32. Influenza is a common virus which spreads rapidly and can prove fatal to a small number of very young and elderly people. Occasionally the flu virus mutates and in a very virulent form causes high mortality. This occurred in 1918 when three waves of influenza engulfed the world in a matter of a few months. The flu appears to have originated in the US Mid-West in the spring of 1918 and to have been carried by troop movement and trade to every part of the globe. The second wave was the most lethal, resulting in high levels of mortality. Unlike previously known strains of flu, the 1918 variant universally killed proportionately larger numbers of men aged 15-40; there is no satisfactory explanation for this. Total global mortality is unknown but was probably between 30 and 100 million. However inaccurate the figures, it is clear that many more people died in the pandemic than from the direct results of the First World War.

    Q: Which of the following is correct according to the passage?

    (a) The virus only spreads to children or old people.
    (b) Influenza sporadically turns into another life threatening ailment
    (c) The first wave of influenza was more fatal than the second one.
    (d) More people died in the First World War than from the pandemic.

33. One of the jobs of the noses is to warm the air we breathe up to body temperature. It does this by expanding the blood vessels in the nose so that more warm blood can warm the cold air. Those expanded blood vessels make your nose feel blocked. The blocked nose feeling causes more mucous to be produced to clear the blockage. Normally most of the mucous we produce is swept towards the back of the throat by cilia—tiny hairs on the cells in our noses—and we swallow it without noticing. But in cold weather, the cilla can't cope with the extra workload and some of the mucous runs down the nose. The drip factor is exacerbated by the effect of condensation when warm air is breathed out through the nose and comes into contact with cold air. The end result is a runny nose.

Q: What can be inferred from the passage?

(a) The air we breath up is normally warmer than our body temperature.
(b) Runny noses in cold weather show that cold weather causes colds.
(c) Runny noses in cold weather are caused by a domino effect.
(d) Running a temperature is just part of the way our body functions.

34. Dear Mr. Lee,

Thank you for shopping with Danoz Direct!

Our records indicate that payment on your order is now due and your product is ready and waiting to be dispatched. If the amount has already been paid, please disregard this notice. If you have not yet mailed your payment, why not make out your cheque and place it in the enclosed postage-paid envelope while this reminder has your full attention. If you use a credit card you can arrange easy monthly payments. Simply call toll free 1800 300 345 now. Thank you in advance for your anticipated cooperation in this matter.

Kind regards from Danoz Direct.

Q: What can be inferred from this letter?

(a) Mr. Lee has not paid for his order yet.
(b) The product has already been shipped to Mr. Lee.
(c) Mr. Lee can decide to pay on an installment plan.
(d) Mr. Lee should buy a reply envelope to send the payment.

Actual Test · 2

35. Having previously instructed us on "How to Survive a Robot Uprising", robotics engineer Dr. Daniel Wilson turns his eyes to different circumstances, where robots are our only defense against alien invaders or the undead. Having scoured the archives of B-grade movies for instruction, Wilson offers up such chapters as "How to Use a Pet Robot to Terrorize Your Enemies" and "How to Command Robot Minions in Battle". The book offers no money-back guarantees should its advice fail, but it does combine some of the funniest moments in sci-fi with genuine information about the current state of robotics well.

Q: What is this passage introducing?

(a) The lecture on the latest trends in robotics.
(b) The new publication written by Dr. Wilson.
(c) The most hilarious moments from sci-fi movies
(d) Dr. Wilson's view on future developments in robotics.

36. You have beautiful eyes. We all do. Up close, you'll see incredible shapes, textures and colors you've probably never noticed before. Of course your eyes aren't just aesthetically amazing, they allow you to navigate around your environment with ease. You can recognize the faces of loved ones. You can also experience the splendid beauty of our world. That is why your local Eyecare Plus is focused primarily on the health and wellbeing of your eyes. Every Eyecare Plus practice is held to the highest standards of excellence in optical health care, technical expertise and customer service. We're passionate about eyes because we understand their importance. Cleary your eyes deserve to be framed in a way that enhances their natural beauty, so our range of eyewear is both fashionable and affordable.

Q: What is this passage advertising?

(a) Contact lenses
(b) Eye surgery service
(c) Affordable lasik surgery
(d) Spectacles

37. Obesity might be a problem in the human world but a bit of extra paunch can be a godsend for corals seeking to stave off coral bleaching. With coral bleaching an increasing issue for the world's oceans, a team of international scientists claims to have shown how corals can survive world climate change. Bleaching is caused when warm water circulates over the reef, causing the corals to shed essential algae needed for energy. The corals starve if they cannot recover their algae in time. Therefore, it mostly comes down to how well-fed the corals are before the bleaching event strikes. If they have high levels of lipids or fats in their system, it gives them the energy to hang on until they can re-establish their symbiotic relationship.

Q: What can be inferred from the passage?

(a) Gaining weight is dangerous for coral's survival.
(b) Corals discard algae to get energy needed to survive bleaching.
(c) Global warming has a devastating effect on corals.
(d) Corals should be moved into cold water to avoid bleaching.

Part 3 *Questions 38~40*

Read the passage. Then identify the option that does NOT belong.

38. To. Ms. Johnson,

    Although the weather was not good with a bit of drizzling, We mostly had a great time at Fun Day. (a) To tell you more about the today's get together, I think the trophy presentations went a bit quickly. (b) I have to tell you that I have absolutely no problem with moving the day for the next event after Thanksgiving Day. (c) It would have given us more chance to take photos of our kids if only we could have our kids stand and pose for pictures in front of the table a bit longer. (d) After all, it would have been much better to see their faces rather than their backs.

    Best wishes,

39. It was once thought that the structure of our brain was incapable of further development after we reached adulthood. That's because, unlike other cells in the body, neurons do not regenerate. (a) A single thought, if repeated a few times, will build new synaptic docking points between those particular brain cells that can last indefinitely. (b) This seemed to support the view that what happens in childhood is our destiny—that the thought and behaviour that define our character are basically fixed by the age of twenty. (c) That view now seems to be a myth. (d) The cells are not like inert electrical wiring. because, while no new brain cells are born in adulthood, each cell is capable of establishing thousands of new connections with its neighbours, given the opportunities.

40. A hot cup of tea causes throat cancer. (a) Iranian researchers studying tea-drinking habits found that drinking very hot tea was associated with an eight-fold increase in the risk of throat cancer compared with sipping warm or lukewarm tea. (b) Both smoking rates and alcohol consumption are associated with the throat cancer. (c) People who regularly drank tea less than two minutes were five more times likely to develop the cancer compared with those who waited four or more minutes. (d) The research suggests people should let their drinks cold before consuming them.

Reading Comprehension

Actual Test • 3

Directions

This part of the exam tests your ability to comprehend reading passages.
You will have 45 minutes to complete the 40 questions.
Be sure to follow the directions given by the proctor.

Part 1 *Questions 1~16*

Read the passage. Then choose the option that best completes the passage.

1. We all know that stopping smoking is good for our health at any time of our life. Especially, it _____ before you have an operation. Why do you have to wait and increase your risks when you have surgery? You will not be able to smoke immediately after surgery, so you can make this a good opportunity for you to stop for good. Quitting completely is the only way to stop and reverse the damage done by cigarettes. You can cut down before stopping smoking completely, but the recovery of your body will only start from the time you stop completely.

    (a) is too late to stop smoking completely
    (b) can be too dangerous to stop smoking
    (c) might be the best time to quit smoking
    (d) might be considered inappropriate to quit smoking

2. Taking the boss hostage as a means of resolving an industrial dispute is popular in France. Earlier this month the head of Sony France was kidnapped by factory workers demanding a better severance deal. He was locked in a meeting room while the plant was barricaded with large tree trunks before being freed the following day after workers' demands were met. In January 2008 the British boss of an ice-cream factory was held hostage after announcing plans to fire more than half the workforce. Kidnapping the boss _____ in the next few months as more companies plan to lay off their workers.

    (a) is believed to diminish
    (b) will rarely happen
    (c) is expected to increase
    (d) might become an obsolete tactic

3. Adding dairy products to your diet is the easiest way to get your daily requirement of calcium, as well as plenty of other beneficial nutrients. But what if you're intolerant to lactose? The symptoms of lactose intolerance affect different people in different ways and can range from mild discomfort to abdominal pain. Lactose is the sugar found in milk. When we consume milk, an enzyme called lactase in the small intestine splits lactose into its two component sugars, called glucose and galactose, which the body uses for energy. Without sufficient quantities of lactase in the small intestine, lactose _____ and passes to the large intestine where it ferments and produces gases that may cause pain, bloating, and sometimes diarrhea. This is called lactose intolerance and almost all cases are permanent, usually because the production of lactase in the body has ceased.

(a) will remain as glucose and galactose
(b) can't be digested
(c) will be absorbed to the body
(d) can't produce enzyme

4. It's no secret that the hardest thing about a fitness regime is not the sit-ups, push-ups or even the long sessions on a bike. Anyone with an exercise routine knows _____ is the toughest part of all. Once summer is over, the motivation of getting into shape for the days on the beach disappears as the winter months loom. Suddenly, going out for a run or doing laps of the swimming pool doesn't seem so important. The exercise shoes are quietly packed away, with the promise to pull them out in October in time for next summer. "We see this happening every year, and it is a natural tendency for people to stop paying so much attention to not only their physical appearance but their fitness level as well." says Alicia Gibson of the American Fitness network.

(a) being on good terms with trainers
(b) resisting food temptations
(c) finding the right place to work out
(d) making exercise a part of your life

5. Malaysian police fired tear gas to disperse more than 2,000 protesters in the capital, Kuala Lumpur. The demonstrators attempted to present a petition to the Malaysian king, calling for the reinstatement of Bahasa Malay in the teaching of science and math. The government of former prime minister Mahathir Mohamad _____, concerned that poor English-language skills were undermining student performance. But activists and opposition politicians are concerned at the impact on the Malay language.

   (a) opposed to the idea of teaching the foreign language in classes
   (b) prohibited learning science and math in English
   (c) mandated teaching these subjects in English
   (d) supported the demonstrator's petition

6. When was the last time you truly got away from it all? With the ever-increasing demands of work, finances, and family, chances are the answer is "I can't remember". You need to be connected, every day, in more places, and that's where WestNet Wireless Broadband _____.
   Whether you're trapped in a corporate board room or holidaying up the coast, WestNet Wireless Broadband is as mobile as you are—and as flexible, reliable and accessible as you're expected to be. As well as having faster speeds in more places, America's greatest wireless broadband coverage and best value for money, WestNet Wireless Broadband has another great advantage: It is part of WestNet, so it's backed by the reliability and security of the country's largest internet service provider.

   (a) can help you take a rest at work
   (b) can give you the edge
   (c) can guarantee you the fastest speed
   (d) can prevent you from having a bill blow-out

Actual Test 3

7. Despite the recession, sales of guitars are booming, says Dominic White in The Canadian Financial Review. Imports of guitars and guitar amplifiers continue to grow and have almost doubled in the past five years. This increase in sales is partly due to a drop in the price of guitars as more are now made in China. Decent quality electric and acoustic guitars have collapsed in price from 1,000 dollars to 300 dollars. The surge in interest is being attributed to the "cocooning effect" which encourages people to stay at home and spend their spare cash on entertaining themselves. Manufacturers _____, offering starter packs and replicas of stars' instruments.

    (a) are struggling to survive the recession
    (b) have tried to export their guitars to China
    (c) raised the prices of guitars
    (d) have been quick to spot the trend

8. If your child has an allergy or food intolerance, there are plenty of food alternatives _____.
    Finding replacements for dairy and wheat products can be especially difficult when it seems to creep into the normal diet so readily. Children have special daily requirements for growth, brain function and energy, so it is important to encourage replacing healthy foods with those you are eliminating. If your child has lactose intolerance you can easily replace dairy milk with oat milk or rice milk. Here's the key. Don't tell them. Serve it differently, such as in a banana smoothie with honey and vanilla. They won't even notice the difference.

    (a) that can help cure their diseases
    (b) to be cultivated domestically
    (c) to make up for what they can't have
    (d) that add flavors to milk and wheat

9. When you have young children in your family, it's _____ _____ , both indoors and out. Just as we use a wide range of devices, such as safety latches and covers for electrical outlets, to help prevent accidents occurring inside the home, in the backyard, the right fence can provide peace of mind. Here is a smart and practical solution. Fencing made from COLORBOND steel gives you added protection against unwanted entry and unwelcome eyes. As it has no footholds, it's hard to climb and as the panels can't be loosened or removed, fencing made from COLORBOND steel turns your backyard into a secluded and safer space.

   (a) important to turn your home into the kids playground
   (b) significant to buy lots of safety home gadgets
   (c) vital to childproof your home
   (d) important to have child-friendly fencing

10. Most of us aren't perfectly symmetrical. For instance, one leg might be a tiny bit shorter than the other. Even this slight discrepancy adds pressure to the musculoskeletal system and impacts on how we use our muscles. Adding to the effect is the fact that _____, so we tend to use one side of our bodies much more than the other. For example, have you ever noticed that you always lead off with your right foot? Decades later it's not surprising that we end up with unbalanced bodies.

   (a) we can use both our right and left hands equally skillfully
   (b) most of our bodies are not proportionate
   (c) few of us are ambidextrous
   (d) most of us discriminate against people based on their looks

11. Dear editors,

Knowing that we were going to be facing two weeks of more than 40 degrees celsius weather this summer, I was at a loss for meals to make for my family in the heat. That was until I read your January issue, which was full of lots of fresh, filling and delicious recipes _____.
The meals are really quick to prepare, which means I've spent very little time at the stove on these hot days. Among the recipes, the Asian-Style Chicken Salad has become an instant favourite. Thank you Lovely Meals for helping me to survive the heat-wave with delicious meals!

Sincerely,

(a) that needed a good budget
(b) that required little or no cooking
(c) that needed meticulous accuracy
(d) that required melting, boiling and frying

12. A young woman was stripped naked, bound and gagged, tied to a log and set on fire by a band of villagers. she burnt to death in the blaze. Her crime was that she was suspected of being a witch. Belief in witchcraft is popular in rural Papua New Guinea, and _____ is a common practice. Last year alone some 50 people were victims of witchcraft-related murder in the Highlands provinces, and there were over 500 attacks linked to witchcraft throughout the entire country. However, these are only the deaths and attacks that are recorded. There is no precise figures as many incidents occur in remote areas and often go unreported. Furthermore, the locals often refuse to cooperate with the authorities when a death occurs. It is notoriously difficult to find eyewitnesses who are willing to talk. Therefore, it is difficult to apprehend the offenders and to solve these covert crimes.

(a) exorcism for the evil spirits
(b) extracting a confession of sorcery
(c) homicide against suspected sorcery
(d) using magic to slaughter people

13. The global financial crisis _____, especially in Asia, and women—as always—are the ones who suffer the most. The major reason is that female workers are concentrated in labor-intensive export industries. They are generally clustered at the lower levels in casual, temporary, sub-contracted and informal employment, The work is insecure, wages low and conditions poor. Women in the clothing, textiles and electronics industries will be the first to go. We know this from 1997 economic crisis: in Thailand 98% of those laid off from the garment sector were women and in the toys sector it was 88%. In Korea, 85% of those who lost jobs in financial services and banking were female. Failure to recognize this gender crisis could be worsening the working and living conditions of millions.

   (a) is gender blind
   (b) is adversely affecting every sector
   (c) is a man-made catastrophe
   (d) has a certain bias

14. An angry chimp has proved humans aren't the only ones _____ _____. When Santino, a chimpanzee at the Furuvik Zoo in Sweden, started pelting zoo visitors with stones and his keepers were puzzled. Chimps are often aggressive and this 31-year-old was a dominant male, so the behaviour was no surprise. But where was he finding his missiles? A search revealed that Santino had been stockpiling rocks. He'd fished stones from the land surrounding his enclosure and even shaped pieces of concrete into disc-shaped missiles. Fortunately for visitors he wasn't very good at throwing, so no one was badly hurt, but his behaviour has led scientists to conclude that planning ahead is not a uniquely human trait. It seems chimpanzees also have a sophisticated understanding of the past and future.

   (a) who can guess what others are thinking
   (b) capable of making an instrument
   (c) resorting to violence as a solution
   (d) who can premeditate

15. Skin cancer is caused by exposure to ultraviolet radiation from the sun. Experts say that ultraviolet radiation is strongest between 11 in the morning and 3 in the afternoon and is present all year. Boaters are particularly susceptible, as reflected radiation from the water gives an additional radiation effect. Preventive measures are very important and clothing provides the best protection. _____, They should cover areas of their bodies with a hat. A hat will cover their faces, ears and necks. They should wear a long-sleeved shirt. It is also essential to apply sunscreen to exposed areas with a maximum sun protector factor. It's important to apply the sunscreen 15 minutes before going out reapply every two and a half hours.

(a) Therefore
(b) In the end
(c) Moreover
(d) Unfortunately

16. Nocturnal cramps in the calf or foot are the most common in both pregnant women and the elderly, suggesting there's a connection with reduced blood circulation. However, research hasn't uncovered any underlying medical problem or sleep disorder that can account for the cramping. Dehydration can be a risk factor for cramps because it plays havoc with your electrolyte levels. _____, a diet lacking in essential minerals, especially potassium, which is found in fruits and vegetables, fish, meet, dairy and whole-grain foods, may make cramps more likely.

(a) On the contrary
(b) For instance
(c) Thus
(d) Likewise

Part 2 *Questions 17~37*

Read the passage and the question. Then choose the option that best answers the question.

17. Argentina's farmers' organizations halted sales of grains and livestock in a week-long strike against the government's export tax on soybean. They argue they're being penalized at a time when the country is in the grip of drought. The government said it could not forgo the revenue in the current economic crisis. But on the eve of the strike it announced that 30% of the export tax revenue would go to regional governments for infrastructure.

    Q: What is the main topic of the passage?

    (a) How unfair it is to tax the farmers.
    (b) Difficult economic conditions in Argentina.
    (c) A new duty imposed on an agricultural product.
    (d) The government's long-term plan to build infrastructure.

18. As Easter approaches, we need to be aware that chocolate is not suitable for dogs and cats; it results in a serious risk to their health. The problem is that the body systems of dogs and cats cannot handle the key ingredient in chocolate, theobromine, as well as humans can. Theobromine can cause a range of problems in domestic animals because it triggers the release of adrenaline and can lead to a greatly accelerated and irregular heart rate. In high dosage situations, pets can begin to vomit, suffer diarrhea and excessive urination. This can be followed by depression, coma, seizure and death.

    Q: What is the main idea of the passage?

    (a) People eat chocolate on Easter day.
    (b) Theobromine can bring negative effects to both humans and pets.
    (c) Chocolate poses a great threat to pets.
    (d) There are diseases that pets can transmit to humans.

19. Dear Max,

You've received this email from Amazon.com because your email address was used to register on our website. If you did not register at our site, please disregard this email. You do not need to unsubscribe or take any further action. Otherwise, You need to "validate" your registration to ensure that the email address you entered was correct. This protects against unwanted spam and malicious abuse. To activate your account, simply click on the link provided or depending on your email client you may need to cut and paste the link into your web browser. Thank you for registering and we hope you enjoy the site!

Kind Regards,

Q: What is the purpose of this letter?

(a) To confirm the email address change.
(b) To notify of safety concerns to its members.
(c) To help its members finish singing up for the website.
(d) To thank its members for their support.

20. A strong muscle jerk just after you've fallen asleep is called a hypnagogic jerk. It's thought to be caused by the brain misinterpreting sensations from your muscles. As you fall asleep your muscles relax and go slack, and sometimes the brain interprets this as falling. An actual sensation of falling may accompany the jerking as the muscles try to get you upright again, or you may simply experience the jerk of the muscles. Hypnagogic jerks are most likely to occur when you're trying to fight off sleep or when you haven't slept for more than 24 hours. Stress, intense physical exercise or a high intake of caffeine or other stimulants can also increase your chances of experiencing a hypnagogic jerk.

Q: What is the best title for the article?

(a) How muscle jerks affect people's health.
(b) How brain malfunctions occur.
(c) A reminder of how powerful our brain is.
(d) Why our bodies twitch during slumbering hours.

21. China's leaders are touchy about Tibet, and in scrapping a major summit with the EU they have let their anger boil over. A team of 150 political and business leaders was to meet in Lyon on 1 December, an annual fixture of ten years' standing. But the Chinese are furious that France's President agreed to meet the Dalai Lama during a trip to Poland. In response, they pulled out of the summit at the last moment, saying that the bad atmosphere meant nothing could come of it. After Dalai Lama said China's lack of moral authority made it unfit to be a super power, they are even threatening to cut trade with France. However, the Chinese didn't go overboard when England's prime minister gave the Dalai Lama the red carpet treatment this year. Nor did they do more than complain when President Bush awarded him the Congressional Medal of Honour. So, why are they picking on the France's president?

  Q: What is the main topic of the passage?

  (a) China's meticulously planned withdrawal from the summit.
  (b) The imprudent decision made by French President.
  (c) Dalai Lama's popularity among many Western countries.
  (d) China's inconsistent reactions toward matters concerning Tibet.

22. MRI is a form of imaging which uses a large magnet and radio waves. There is no X-ray radiation. A radiographer will perform the examination. They will position you on a MRI table. The Radiologist will supervise and report on the images. Depending on the body part scanned a separate "coil" maybe placed on the region to be imaged before you are moved into the open tunnel. The MRI scanner makes a loud knocking sound while the imaging occurs and you will be given earplug or earphones. You may feel quite warm as a normal response to the scan.

  Q: What is the best title of the passage?

  (a) How MRI helps in diagnosis.
  (b) Possible risks when taking a MRI scan.
  (c) How the MRI examination is performed.
  (d) Different roles between radiographers and radiologists.

23. Sir Andrew Lloyd Webber has announced that the button is pushed on a sequel to The Phantom of the Opera. The new musical, entitled Phantom: Love Never dies, hopes to make theatrical history by opening in three cities simultaneously at the end of 2009. Theaters in New York's Broadway and London's West End will be joined by a venue in a yet undecided Asian city, possibly Shanghai. The Phantom sequel will be set in Coney Island, Brooklyn, and fast-forwarded a decade after the events at the Paris Opera described in Gaston Leroux's original novel. The most likely candidates for the lead role are Australian Hugh Jackman and Scotsman Gerad Butler. The original Phantom of the Opera has been seen by more than 80 million theatergoers in 124 cities, and has taken more than US$ 5 billion at the box office.

Q: Which of the following is correct according to the article?

(a) The sequel to The Phantom of the Opera has finished filming.
(b) Phantom: Love never dies will be opening exclusively in London.
(c) One of the three venues for the musical's opening is yet to be decided.
(d) The lead role for the sequel will be played by two different actors.

24. Sharia is the Islamic system of law. Sharia derives from the teaching of the Koran and from the Prophet Mohammed's precepts and example. Unlike Western systems of law, sharia is regarded as the expression of the divine will. Some commentators believe that since much of the process of interpreting the divine word had, in theory, been concluded by the end of the tenth century, it is a static system. Rather than change with society. However, there are many modern developments in sharia which demonstrate otherwise, for example Islamic banking and finance principles to accommodate the prohibition on charging and earning interest. Its other main distinction is the way it regulates every area of life—not just the criminal and civil law, but ritual and custom from prayer to dress, and personal hygiene. And unlike Western law, it isn't confined to man's relationship with his neighbours and the state, but also covers his relationship with God. It not only categorizes acts according to whether they're permissible or forbidden, but also whether they are praiseworthy or blameworthy.

Q: Which of the following is correct about Sharia?

(a) It has never been changed since the end of the 10th century.
(b) It also deals with matters concerning business.
(c) It has always been a cause of major controversy in Islamic countries.
(d) It has a lot in common with Western systems of law.

25. You might look back and laugh at the outdated outfits and hairdos in old photos. But it does make you realize how quickly time passes. Just as life changes, so do your savings needs. And if you haven't reassessed these in a while, perhaps it's time to bring them up to date. We offer a range of savings and investment options to suit you, no matter what type of saver you are. Are you the type who needs access to your money at anytime? Or are you prepared to pop your money away for a while? Do you prefer to manage your financial affairs online? Or do you simply need to be more disciplined? The answer to all these questions and more is simple. To find the savings product that's right for you, go to our website. Alternatively, visit your local branch or call 1800 384 345.

   Q: What is being promoted in the advertisement?

   (a) Personalized fashion and style advice.
   (b) A confidential stock tip.
   (c) A newly introduced savings option.
   (d) Financial consultation services.

26. In Manchester, England, the final of the street soccer competition saw the Zambian women's team beat Liberia 7-1. In the men's round, Afghanistan beat Russia 5-4. The Cup began in Graz, Austria, in 2003, with 18 nations taking part. It has since grown to 56 teams. The tournament is credited with raising the esteem of the homeless while helping many to get off drugs and alcohol and find housing and jobs. At the end of the games, 15 Zimbabwean and Afghani players sought asylum and the entire Liberian women's team, as well as a Kenyan player, went missing.

   Q: Which of the following is correct according to the article?

   (a) The woman's Cup was won by Liberia.
   (b) Afghanistan beat Russia by one goal.
   (c) The street soccer competition was first launched in England.
   (d) A number of players disappeared after they returned to their countries.

27. Acclaimed director Clint Eastwood focuses on the plight of a woman in this true story of single mother Christine Collins taking on the Los Angeles police force as she tries to find out what happened to her missing son. Set in 1928, when police corruption was rife, a police captain tries to foist another nine-year-old boy on Christine, claiming he's her son when she knows he's not. Malkovich co-stars as a Protestant minister who decides to support Christine in her cause. The discovery of a serial killer of young boys may hold the answer to Christine's agony. It's a fine film, beautifully realized by a Hollywood legend.

Q: Which of the following is correct about the movie?

(a) The story of the movie is fictional.
(b) The heroine of the movie is a police officer in Los Angeles.
(c) The level of depravity was high among police officers in the late 1920's.
(d) The main character in the movie was acted by a Hollywood legend.

28. For over 50 years, Biotherm has studied the skin's natural mechanisms to deliver innovative and effective skincare solutions. Biotherm's biologists have discovered Pure Thermal Plankton, a natural agent located deep in the thermal springs of the French Pyrenees. Pure Thermal Plankton rejuvenates the appearance of the skin, leaving it radiant and glowing with health. Plus, it helps stimulate the skin's natural self-renewal process, improving your skin's natural defence mechanisms against the signs of ageing and helping control skin sensitivity.

Q: What can Pure Thermal Plankton do to skin?

(a) It warms up skin to prevent itching.
(b) It stimulates breaking out under skin on face.
(c) It makes skin visibly younger on the outside.
(d) It protects skin from sun damage.

29. Sleepwalking is a misnomer because it often involves more than walking. The sleeper may also talk, cook, rearrange the furniture or even drive. Sleepwalking occurs during the deep stages of sleep so it can be hard to wake sleepwalkers, and when you do they will feel groggy and disoriented. If you find your kids sleepwalking at home, the best thing to do is to gently guide them back to bed. The condition is most common in primary school aged children, and usually gets better as the child ages. It's usually associated with overtiredness or a full bladder, so good sleep hygiene, which means going to bed at the same time every night in a dark quiet room and a comfortable bed, helps reduce the risk. Adult sleepwalking may be caused by fever, illness, stress or alcohol intake. It also seems to be hereditary.

Q: Which of the following is correct according to the passage?

(a) Sleepwalking is common in teenagers.
(b) Sleepwalkers will feel exuberant if they're woken up.
(c) A quiet bedroom would not be good for sleepwalkers.
(d) Sleepwalking can run in the family.

30. Teaching about long-term water efficiency and educating children on the value of water is the main aim of Seqwater's dedicated water education program for primary and secondary school students. Seqwater is the single treated and bulk water service provider for the southeast Queensland region. It has responsibility for managing physical assets worth $ 1.8 billion comprising 24 dams and 49 weirs across the southeast. Seqwater currently operates 46 water treatment plant facilities. Schools can now enroll to take conducted tours and learn valuable insights about dam operations, links between catchment areas and the treatment of water. Education programs can also be customized for each school.

Q: Which of the following is correct about Seqwater?

(a) It manages personal assets and provides consulting assistance.
(b) It is an education institute that instructs students on water management.
(c) It offers programs that help students learn more about water supplies.
(d) It is a personalized tour agency based in Queensland.

Actual Test 2

31. A research, carried out on people who'd attended business conferences in the last three months, found that 71% of respondents rated the general standard of business presentations to be below average or poor. Only 9% said they had seen a presentation they rated as excellent. The standard bullet-point presentation was ineffective, especially when the speaker read each bullet point aloud. Other things to avoid when giving a presentation include delivering too much information, overuse of industry jargon and acronyms, hiding behind the lectern, avoiding eye contact with the audience, and using a monotone voice. Also, more than half said they preferred to receive the PowerPoint material via email prior to the presentation.

    Q: Which of the following is correct according to the passage?

    (a) Most of people think the general level of presentation skills is high.
    (b) Many people prefer receiving presentation materials in advance.
    (c) Speakers should speak with a constant, loud voice during presentations.
    (d) The common response to a boring presentation is checking their e-mails.

32. Many new cars have onboard sensors that indicate when you're at risk of getting a flat tyre. Wouldn't it be good if your body had the same level of tech support? Proteus Biomedical, a Californian company, is working on "smart pills"—internal sensors that monitor health. The plan is for these sensors to be linked to a computer hub that wirelessly broadcasts a stream of diagnostic data. The company likens the benefits of the systems to telling you to get a tune-up before you have an expensive breakdown. For the moment, the smart pills are being designed to help monitor mechanical and electrical devices rather than vital body parts, but its developers believe the market for smart "pharmacy technology" is already large enough to create a whole new industry.

    Q: Which of the following is correct according to the article?

    (a) Smart pills can examine people's health by their looks.
    (b) Smart pills will transmit gathered data through landline to the hub.
    (c) Car sensors were designed after the mechanisms behind how the smart pills work.
    (d) Smart pills are not being produced for the purpose of pharmaceutical use yet.

33. A car billed as the world's cheapest was launched by Tata Motors in India's financial capital, Mumbai. The launch has been delayed when protests by farmers over land seizures for the Tata factory in West Bengal forced the company to relocate to other region. The car, which will sell for 2,800 dollars, is seen as an affordable people's car and an alternative to unsafe motorcycle use. But critics argue it will contribute to increased pollution and road congestion. A version of the car may eventually be marketed in Europe and the US.

   Q: What can be inferred from the passage?

   (a) Tata Motors has cancelled its plan to build a new factory.
   (b) The launch of the car was scrapped due to protests by farmers.
   (c) The car's safety features are better than those of motorbikes.
   (d) The car has been launched in the US.

34. Indicting Omar al-Bahir for war crimes is a big step for international justice. An arrest warrant has been issued for Sudan's president by the International Criminal Court in The Hague accusing him of orchestrating the violence in Darfur, where an estimated 300,000 have died and nearly three million left homeless in an orgy of government-sponsored rapes and killings. Chief prosecutor Luis Moreno-Ocampo says more than 30 witnesses will testify against Bashir, although the genocide charge has been dropped because it was judged too hard to prove. But there is little prospect of anyone arresting Bashir, who has significant support from other African countries as well as China and Russia. He dismissed the warrant as a colonialist plot. Barshir also expelled eleven international aid agencies.

   Q: What can be inferred from the passage?

   (a) Sudan's president is under arrest for criminal offences.
   (b) There is enough evidence to prove the charges of mass murder against Bashir.
   (c) Sudan's neighboring countries are looking after Bashir's back.
   (d) It's only a matter of time before the Court brings him to trial.

35. Analysis of more than 1,500 coprolites, or fossilized dung, has revealed the diet of several moa species, throwing light on the ecology of New Zealand prior to human settlement. Moa dominated New Zealand prior to human arrivals, with almost a dozen species making up virtually the entire local mega-fauna. The females of the largest moa species were 3 meters tall and weighed 250 kg. Some of the droppings studied were 15 cm long. Surprisingly for such large birds, over half the plants that were detected in the feces were under 30 cm in height. This suggests that some moa grazed on tiny herbs, in contrast to the current view of them as mainly shrub and tree browsers. There is no satisfactory answer as to why these species with few predators would need to grow so big if they were largely living off low-growing herbs.

Q: Which of the following can be inferred from the passage?

(a) The dissection of Moa revealed their dietary intake.
(b) Moa became extinct due to indiscriminate hunting by humans.
(c) The reasons to why Moa was so small in size were finally uncovered.
(d) Moa was rarely attacked by other species of animals.

36. In Denmark, the family farm has traditionally passed from one generation to the next. Each successive heir would try to expand upon the work already put in by their parents, their grandparents, sometimes even their great-grandparents. As agriculture and animal husbandry have become more scientific over the past 50 years, sons and daughters have gone off to college and brought home new methods to cut costs and increase output, and the family farm has evolved into a business like any other, requiring accountants and financial planners. For many, this was a blessing that helped reduce overheads, increase profits and maximize return. However, these days, the youngsters going off to further their education often don't come back—at least not to work. They find careers in the city and build lives for themselves that are different to that of their forefathers.

Q: What is the next paragraph likely to be about?

(a) How Danish family farms prospered over the past 50 years.
(b) The difficulties Danish family farms are currently going through.
(c) The merits and demerits of further education.
(d) The increasing rate of family collapse in Denmark.

37. Most of us have our own precious memories growing up climbing trees, walking pet or playing on swings. Kids are naturally energetic and their parents should take advantage of their youngsters' inbuilt need for fun and activity. Some parents may even find it's contagious and start moving about more themselves. South African families are some of the luckiest in the world because their splendid climate lets them spend much of the year outside. Not only does outdoor play encourage activity that strengthens and helps young bodies to grow, it also gets them off the sofa, away from computers and television screens, into fresh air and sunshine. Initially, some kids may complain this simpler playtime is a bit boring, but there's so much to do out there that most kids quickly embrace a change of scene. Planting a herb or vegetable patch, weeding, watering and picking the produce is a great way to involve young children with nature and reap the rewards with some health-giving goodies as well.

Q: What can be inferred from the passage?

(a) The weather in South Africa is very sunny but stormy.
(b) Children can receive manufactured goods by doing outdoor activities.
(c) It's healthy for kids to venture out into the great outdoors.
(d) Many people have memories of either watching television or playing computer games.

Part 3 *Questions 38~40*

Read the passage. Then identify the option that does NOT belong.

38. Like most experiences with your first child, our first trip overseas with our 18 month old daughter was a major learning curve. (a) Both of us have globe-trotted many times but nothing could prepare us for the trepidation of taking our daughter with us on a trip to France. (b) It started really well. (c) She handled the two flights there with no difficulty and received compliments from all the flight crew for being so well behaved. (d) It was a major clean up operation and throughout it all we awkwardly smiled at our fretful baby.

39. Whooping cough is a highly contagious respiratory infection that is particularly dangerous for young babies. (a) The symptoms are similar to a cold but they quickly progress to a severe cough which includes the characteristic whooping sound and vomiting at the end of a bout of coughing. (b) Babies under 6 months are more at risk because they are more seriously affected by the disease than older children or adults. (c) One in every 200 babies who contract whooping cough will die and it is most often spread to babies from family members who are not immunized. (d) It was the first death in America from this disease since the early 1990's.

40. The right of women to vote had been demanded by feminist movements in Europe and the USA in the nineteenth century but made little headway before the first world war, as most males were hostile or indifferent. (a) New Zealand was the first country to give the vote to women in 1893, followed by the states of Australia between 1893 and 1909. (b) Israeli women serve two years of mandatory military service. (c) In Europe the only countries to enfranchise women before 1914 were Finland and Norway. (d) The important role played by women during the war, far more than the activities of the suffragettes, helped to persuade the British Parliament to give the vote to women over thirty in 1918 and women over twenty-one in 1928.

J&L English Lab

정기 TOEIC 시험 만점자이며 TEPS 1+ 등급의 소유자들이 뭉쳐서 만든 전문 컨텐츠 개발팀이다. 에듀조선 출판사의 TEPS 문항 개발 작업을 담당하기도 했던 이들은 해외유학생활의 경험과 학원 강의, 영어연구원 등의 경력을 바탕으로 현재 호주에 거주하며 다양한 수험서들의 집필과 문제개발을 진행하고 있다.

텝스한달만 제대로 공부 해보자 Perfect TEPS Series

| Reading | Listening | Grammar & Vocabulary |

 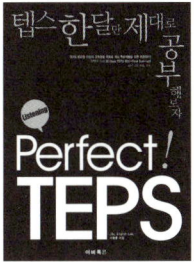 

- 이충훈 & J&L English Lab 지음
- 304쪽 / 18,000원

- 이충훈 & J&L English Lab 지음
- 320쪽 / 20,000원

- 이충훈 & J&L English Lab 지음
- 288쪽 / 18,000원

텝스 한달만 제대로 공부해 보자

Reading 정답편

Perfect! TEPS

이충훈 &
J&L English Lab 지음

이비톡

Perfect TEPS

텝스 한달만 제대로 공부해보자

Reading

정답편

Pre-Test 1 · 2 · 3
Actual Test 1 · 2 · 3

Pre-Test · 1 Answers

Type 01 (b)　Type 02 (d)　Type 03 (c)　Type 04 (b)
Type 05 (c)　Type 06 (d)　Type 07 (c)　Type 08 (c)

Type 01 초반 빈칸 유형

Have you noticed how tricky it is for American women to _____? American women talk about anything and everything, from our husbands' bald spots spreading, to the price of petrol rising, to the fungal infection we got from a pedicure. And that's what we discuss with the man who comes to fix the fridge. However, we simply don't feel feminine having a conversation about money. We can question the cost of a coffee and talk about the prices of supermarkets. We also enthuse about a bargain but we do it for the indignation or the envy, those vital ingredients for a satisfying life. Come to think of it, women seem to be perfectly happy to talk about money going out, but not about the money coming in.

(a) backbite other people
(b) talk about money
(c) maintain friendly relationships with others
(d) discuss daily routines

🔒 해설

빈칸을 포함한 문장은 이 글의 주제문으로 미국 여성들에게 있어서 굉장히 다루기 힘든(tricky) 것이 무엇인지 글을 통해 찾아내야 한다. 빈칸 뒤의 문장들에서 미국 여성들은 무엇이든 다 이야기를 나눌 수 있지만, 돈에 관련한 대화를 나누는 것은 여성스럽지 못하다고 생각한다고 언급하고 있다. 좀 더 자세히는, 나가는 돈은 자연스럽게 이야기하지만, 들어오는 돈에 대해서는 그렇지 않다는 것으로 보아, 미국 여성들에게 다루기 힘든 일은 '돈과 관련한 이야기를 하는 것'일 것이다. 그러므로 정답은 (b)다.

🔒 해석

당신은 미국 여자들에게 있어 돈에 관한 이야기를 나눈다는 것이 얼마나 힘든 일인지 알아차리신 적 있나요? 미국 여성들은 남편들의 머리가 빈 부분이 넓어지는 것에서부터, 기름 값 상승, 발톱 관리 중에 얻은 곰팡이 감염에 이르기까지 그 어떤 것이든 그리고 모든 것에 대해서 이야기를 나눕니다. 그리고 이러한 것들을 냉장고를 고치러 방문하는 남자와도 이야기를 나누지요. 하지만 우리는 간단히 돈에 관해서 이야기하는 것은 여성스럽지 못하다고 느낍니다. 우리는 커피 값에 대해서 질문을 던지고, 슈퍼마켓의 값에 대해서 이야기를 나눕니다. 우리는 또한 떨이에 대해서 열광을 하지요. 하지만, 우리는 이러한 이야기들을 만족스러운 삶을 위한 필수 요소인 분노 또는 질투심에서 합니다. 생각해보면, 여자들은 돈이 나가는 것과 관련해 이야기를 나누는 것은 완벽히 행복해 보이지만, 들어오는 돈에 대해서 이야기하는 것은 그렇지 않아 보이네요.

🔍 어휘

tricky 다루기 힘든, 교묘한
fungal infection 곰팡이 감염
tradesman 점원, 소매상인
indignation 분노
envy 질투심
vital 필수의
fridge 냉장고
enthuse 열광하다
backbite 뒤에서 험담하다, 중상하다
routine 일상, 판에 박힌 일

 정답 (b)

Type 02 중반 빈칸 유형

The Subaru Forester combines functionality and beauty to produce an outstanding driving experience. Premium styling and sweeping contemporary lines set a new standard in style. Intelligent use of interior space _____, functionality and flexibility to handle anything your weekday routine or weekend adventures can throw at it. Across the range, from the fully equipped Forester X through to the luxurious Forester XS, the engineering and superior safety philosophy for which Subaru is renowned is very evident.

(a) delivers exceptional car-like handling
(b) offers unbeatable speed and versatility
(c) provides electronic stability control
(d) offers greater seating comfort

🔒 해설

자동차 광고에 관한 지문으로 빈칸 바로 앞의 내용만 파악하면 정답을 금방 알 수 있는 난이도가 낮은 문제이다. 자동차의 내부 공간을 현명하게 사용한 것이 탑승자들에게 더 훌륭한 좌석의 편안함을 제공한다는 (d)가 정답이 된다. (a)의 핸들링, (b)의 스피드, (c)의 전자안정성 통제능력은 모두 내부 공간의 현명한 사용의 결과로 보기 힘든 내용이다.

🔒 해석

Subaru Forester는 뛰어난 운전 경험을 제공하기 위해서 기능성과 미를 혼합하였습니다. 뛰어나게 우수한 스타일과 큰 곡선을 그리며 뻗는 현대적인 라인은 스타일에 있어서 새로운 기준을 제시합니다. 내부공간의 지적인 사용은 더 훌륭한 좌석의 편안함과 기능성, 그리고 당신의 주중 일상과 주말의 모험이 던져줄 수 있는 어떤 것이라도 처리할 수 있는 융통성을 제공합니다. 상품라인의 모든 것을 갖춘 Forester X에서부터 호화스러운 Forester XS에 이르기까지, Subaru가 명성을 얻고 있는 기술과 우수한 안전 철학은 너무나 명백합니다.

🔍 어휘

combine ~을 결합시키다
functionality 기능성
outstanding 걸출한, 눈에 띄는
premium 뛰어나게 우수한
contemporary 동시대의, 현대의
comfort 안락, 편안함
equipped 장비가 갖춰진
renowned 유명한, 명성 있는
evident 분명한, 명백한

 정답 (d)

Type 03 후반 빈칸 유형

Archaeologists and forensic experts believe they have identified the skeleton of Cleopatra's younger sister who was murdered more than 2000 years ago, says The Washington Post. Princess Arsinoe was put to death in 41 BC on the orders of Cleopatra and her Roman lover, Mark Antony, to eliminate her as a rival to the Egyptian throne. Arsinoe and Cleopatra were both descendants of Ptolemy, the Macedonian general who ruled Egypt after Alexander the Great, but they had different mothers. The remains were found in Turkey and, if genuine, indicate that Arsinoe's mother had African origins. The discovery challenges long-held beliefs about Cleopatra's family and suggests she, too, _____.

(a) lost her mother when she was young
(b) was a Turkish
(c) was probably of mixed race
(d) was put to death

해설

클레오파트라의 여동생의 해골을 확인하면서 나타난 사실을 다루고 있는 지문이다. 빈칸 앞의 문장에서는 아버지는 같고 어머니가 다르던 두 자매 중 여동생의 해골을 검시한 결과, 엄마가 아프리카의 혈통을 가지고 있다는 것을 발견했다는 것이다. 즉, 사람들이 놀란 사실은 클레오파트라의 여동생에게 흑인의 피가 있었다는 것이다. 그러므로 빈칸에 적합한 내용은 비록 둘이 어머니는 다르더라도 클레오파트라 본인도 다른 인종의 피가 흐르지 않을까라는 점이다 그러므로 '아마도 혼혈 인종일 것이다' 라는 (c)가 정답이다.

해석

고고학자들과 법의학 전문가들은 그들이 2000년 전 보다 더 오래 전 살해당한 클레오파트라 여동생의 해골을 확인했음을 믿고 있다고 워싱턴 포스트 지가 말했다. Arisnoe 공주는 기원전 41년에 이집트 왕좌의 경쟁자로, 그녀를 제거하기 위한 클레오파트라와 그의 로마인 애인인 Mark Antony의 명령에 의해서 사형을 당했다. Arisone와 클레오파트라는 둘 다 마케도니아의 장군으로 알렉산더 대왕 이후에 이집트를 통치했던 프톨레마이오스의 자손이지만 어머니는 서로 달랐다. 터키에서 발견된 잔해가 만약 진짜라면 이는 Arisone의 엄마가 아프리카 혈통을 가졌음을 나타낸다. 이 발견은 클레오파트라의 가족에 관해서 오랫동안 이어져 왔던 믿음에 도전하는 것이고, 클레오파트라 그녀 역시도 아마 혼혈이었을 것이라는 사실을 시사한다.

어휘

archaeologist 고고학자
forensic 법의학의
skeleton 골격, 해골
throne 왕좌
descendant 자손, 후예
remain 유골, 유물
origin 태생, 혈통
mixed race 혼혈

정답 (c)

Type 04 접속(부)사 빈칸 유형

Sugar is totally devoid of the protein, vitamins, minerals, essential fats, dietary fiber or any of the essential nutrients we need each day. It provides nothing except calories, making it the ultimate junk food. If you eat all the goodies the body needs and are active enough to also burn off the calories from sugar, the main problem it causes is its adverse effects on teeth. _____, for the two-thirds of American men, half of the women and a quarter of our children who are overweight or obese, sugar simply adds calories that are likely to contribute to weight problems.

(a) Likewise
(b) However
(c) For example
(d) As a result

해설

빈칸이 포함된 문장에서 언급되는 과체중 및 비만의 사람들은 빈칸 앞 문장에서 등장하는 활동적인 사람들과는 서로 반대되는 대상이다. 즉, 활동적인 사람들에게 설탕은 단순히 이를 상하게 하는 역할만 하지만, 그렇지 않은 사람들에게 설탕은 체중문제를 일으키는 요인이 된다는 내용이다. 그러므로 역접의 연결사인 (b)가 정답이다.

해석

설탕은 단백질, 비타민, 미네랄, 필수지방, 식이섬유 혹은 우리가 매일 필요로 하는 그 어떤 필수의 영양분들도 완전히 결여되어 있다. 그것은 칼로리를 제외하고는 아무것도 제공하지 않는 궁극의 정크 푸드라고 할 수 있다. 만약 당신이 신체가 필요로 하는 모든 단 음식들을 먹고, 설탕으로부터 섭취한 칼로리들을 대체버릴 만큼 활동적이라면, 설탕이 일으키는 유일한 문제는 이에 끼치는 악영향뿐이다. 하지만 과체중이거나 비만인 미국의 남성의 2/3, 여성의 1/2 그리고 아이들의 1/4에게 있어서 설탕은 단순히 체중문제에 공헌할 가능성이 있는 칼로리를 더할 뿐이다.

어휘

devoid of ~이 결여된
essential 필수의
fiber 섬유
adverse 거스르는, 해로운
obese 살찐, 뚱뚱한
overweight 과체중인
contribute (to) ~에 공헌하다

정답 (b)

Type 05 대의 파악 유형

A research shows that Americans collectively throw away more than three million tones of food each year, which means that one in every five bags of shopping is going straight in the bin. According to the American Institute, an independent public research center, food waste costs us more than 5 billion dollars annually, and the main food group going to waste is fresh fruit and vegetables. This means the billions of liters of water, fuel and other resources used to produce and deliver this food are also being wasted. Therefore, to start reducing your food waste, be mindful of how much you're throwing away and the impact that it's having on the environment, not to mention your wallet.

Q: What is the main idea of the passage?
(a) Americans are intentionally wasting lots of money by throwing away food.
(b) Americans are not eating recommended amount of fruit and vegetables.
(c) Americans should be aware of the consequences of food waste.
(d) Americans should save money by buying less food.

해설
한 연구조사 결과를 들어 미국인들이 엄청난 양의 음식물 쓰레기를 버림으로 인해서 생기는 여러 가지 결과들을 예를 들어 설명하고 있다. 이를 통해, 글의 후반부에 이러한 낭비를 줄이기 위해서 유념해야 할 사항들을 언급해 주고 있다. 이 글의 주제를 묻는 질문이므로, '미국인들은 음식물 쓰레기의 결과를 인지하고 있어야 한다'라고 한 (c)가 정답이다. 음식물을 버림으로써 발생하는 문제는 돈에만 국한된 것도 아니고, 의도적으로 버리는 것은 더욱 아니기에 보기 (a), (d)는 오답이다.

해석
한 연구조사는 미국인들이 총괄하여 매년 3백만 톤이 넘는 음식을 버린다는 것을 보여주고 있다. 이는 쇼핑 시 다섯 개의 봉지 중에 매번 하나는 곧바로 쓰레기통으로 향한다는 것을 의미한다. 독립적인 공공 연구 센터인 American Institute에 따르면, 음식물 쓰레기로 인해 매년 50억 달러 이상의 비용이 든다고 한다. 그리고 쓰레기가 되어버리는 주요 음식군은 신선한 과일과 야채들이라고 한다. 이는 본 음식들을 생산하고 배달하기 위해 사용되는 수십억 리터에 해당하는 물, 연료 그리고 다른 자원들도 역시 낭비가 되고 있다는 것을 뜻한다. 그러므로 음식물 쓰레기를 줄이기 시작하기 위해서는 당신이 얼마나 많은 양을 버리고 있는지 그리고 그것이 당신의 지갑은 말할 것도 없고, 환경에 미치는 영향을 유념해야 한다.

어휘
collectively 집합적으로, 총괄하여
mindful 유념하는, 염두에 두는
intentionally 의도적으로
waste 낭비, 쓰레기 v. 낭비하다
annually 매년
throw away 버리다
not to mention ~은 말할 것도 없고
recommend 추천하다
consequence 결과

정답 (c)

Type 06 세부 내용 파악 유형

If you are a first home buyer you may be eligible for additional support from the Australian Government through the "First Home Owners Boost". To be eligible for up to $21,000, you must enter into a contract to purchase or construct a home between 12 November 2008 and 29 May 2009. If you are a first home buyer who purchases an existing home, you may receive an extra $7,000, taking the total payment to $14,000. If you are a first home buyer who constructs or purchases a new home, you may receive an extra $14,000, taking the total payment to $21,000. The Boost can be used to buy a property of any value. To be eligible for the Boost, you must be at least 18 years of age and be an Australian citizen, or permanent resident.

Q: Which of the following is correct according to the passage?
(a) Anyone who lives in Australia is eligible for the Boost.
(b) A person who entered into a contract in March 2009 is not eligible for the support.
(c) The maximum amount of money a person can get from the Boost is $28,000.
(d) The price of houses doesn't affect the eligibility of successful candidates.

해설
끝에서 세 번째 줄의 문장에서 본 후원 프로그램은 어떤 가격의 부동산의 구매에도 사용이 가능하다고 이야기하고 있으므로, 집 가격은 지원자의 적합성에 영향을 주지 않는다는 (d)가 정답이다. 호주에서 산다고 모두 호주 시민 또는 영주권자는 아니므로 (a)는 정답이 될 수 없고, 지원받을 수 있는 최고 금액은 21,000달러라고 얘기하고 있으므로 (c) 역시 오답이다.

해석
만약 당신이 처음으로 집을 구매하는 거라면, 당신은 "첫 번째 집소유자 후원"을 통해서 호주 정부로부터 추가적인 지원을 받을 자격이 될 수도 있습니다. 21,000달러에 달하는 금액에 자격이 되기 위해서는, 당신은 2008년 11월 12일부터 2009년 5월 29일 사이에 집을 구매 또는 건축을 하기 위한 계약을 반드시 맺어야만 합니다. 만약 당신이 이미 지어진 집을 구매하는 생애 처음 주택 구입자라면, 당신은 추가로 7,000달러를 받아 총금액 14,000달러를 받으실 수 있습니다. 만약 당신이 새로운 집을 건축하거나 구입하는 생애 처음 주택 구입자라면, 당신은 추가로 14,000달러를 받아 총금액 21,000달러를 받을 수 있습니다. 본 후원은 어떠한 가격의 부동산에도 사용될 수가 있습니다. 본 후원을 받을 자격이 되려면, 당신은 최소한 18세이어야 하고 호주 시민 또는 영주권 소유자이어야 합니다.

어휘
eligible 적합한, 자격이 있는
additional 부가적인, 추가의
construct 건설하다, 세우다
existing 현존하는, 현재의
permanent 영구적인, 오래가는
cf)permanent resident 영주권자
boost 후원, 격려
temporary visa 임시비자
affect ~에 영향을 미치다
candidate 후보

정답 (d)

Type 07 추론 유형

Often referred to as "Little Madrid", Buenos Aires is the vibrant, cosmopolitan capital of Argentina. European in flavor, it retains a South American swagger, where cobbled streets and old-time cafes compete with modern architecture. It all comes together to produce one fascinating city. Visitors will find fantastic shopping, an energetic nightlife, incredible antique markets, arguably the best steaks in the world, and cake shops and ice-creameries on every corner. The locals are mostly Italian and Spanish descent, which makes for good wine, great food and fiery people!

Q: What can be inferred from the passage?
(a) The city is located close to Madrid.
(b) Old coffee shops are strongly competing with new coffee chains.
(c) Visitors can enjoy dancing and drinking all night long.
(d) The local people are mixed bloods of Spanish and Italian.

해설
정답인 보기가 명확하지만, 오답들이 다소 헷갈릴 수 있는 문제이다. 방문객들은 활기찬 밤의 유흥을 발견할 수 있다고 했으므로, '밤새 춤과 술을 즐길 수 있다' 는 (c)가 정답이다. 오래된 카페와 거리들이 현대적인 건축물과 경쟁을 한다는 것이지, 새로운 커피체인점들과 경쟁을 한다는 얘기는 연관성이 적으므로 (b)는 정답이 될 수 없고, 지역민들은 이탈리아와 스페인 각각의 혈통들이지, 두 민족의 혼혈이라고 하는 것은 지나친 비약이다.

해석
종종 "작은 마드리드"라고 언급되는, 부에노스 아이레스는 아르헨티나의 힘찬 국제적인 수도이다. 유럽의 운치가 느껴지고, 자갈이 깔린 거리들과 오래된 카페들이 현대적인 건축물과 경쟁하는 이곳은 남미의 자랑스러움을 보유하고 있다. 그 모든 것들은 함께 모여 하나의 매혹적인 도시를 만들어낸다. 방문자들은 환상적인 쇼핑, 활기 넘치는 밤의 유흥, 놀라운 골동품 시장, 논의의 여지가 있지만 세계에서 최고의 스테이크와 케이크 상점 그리고 아이스크림 판매점을 각 코너마다 찾을 수 있을 것이다. 현지인들은 대부분 이탈리아와 스페인 혈통들로, 이는 좋은 와인과 훌륭한 음식 그리고 열정적인 사람들을 이루어낸다.

어휘
refer 언급하다
vibrant 진동하는, 힘찬
cosmopolitan 전 세계적인
cobbled (도로에) 자갈을 깐
compete 경쟁하다
fascinating 매혹적인, 황홀한
antique 골동품
arguably 이론의 여지는 있지만, 거의 틀림없이
descent 출신, 혈통
fiery 불같은, 정열적인

정답 (c)

Type 08 문맥 파악 유형

A new stem-cell technique can enlarge breasts while reducing the waistline. (a) The treatment for breast enlargement involves taking stem cells from excess fat on the butt, thigh or stomach, and then growing them in the breasts. (b) Doctors say that breasts treated with stem cells would feel more natural because the tissue has the same softness as the rest of the breast. (c) Implants are associated with long-term complications and require replacement. (d) Currently, the process can only make breasts one cup size bigger, but it is expected larger augmentations will be possible as the technique develops.

해설
새로운 줄기세포 기술로 신체의 다른 부위의 지방을 이용해 가슴을 키울 수 있다는 내용을 담고 있다. (a)는 신체의 어느 다른 부위를 이용하는지에 대한 설명, (b)는 수술을 했을 때의 장점을 이야기해주고 있다. (d)에서는 현 수술의 한계와 그 한계마저도 곧 극복될 것이라는 기대를 언급하고 있다. 반면, (c)는 수술의 합병증과 교체라는 부정적 이야기를 언급하고 있으므로, 전체 문맥의 흐름과 어울리지 않는다.

해석
새로운 줄기세포 기술은 허리 굵기는 줄이면서 가슴 크기는 확대시킬 수 있다. (a) 치료방법은 엉덩이, 허벅지, 배의 과도한 지방으로부터 줄기세포를 떼어낸 후, 이를 가슴속에서 성장시키는 것이다. (b) 의사들은 줄기세포로 치료된 가슴은 그 조직이 나머지 가슴들과 같은 정도의 부드러움을 가지고 있기 때문에 더 자연스럽게 느껴질 것이라고 말한다. (c) 이식은 장기간의 합병증과 관련이 있고, 교체가 요구되어진다. (d) 현재, 이 과정은 가슴은 오직 한 컵 사이즈 정도만 크게 할 수 있지만, 기술이 발전함에 따라 더 큰 확대수술이 가능할 것으로 기대되어진다.

어휘
stem-cell 줄기세포
enlarge 확대하다, 크게 하다
waistline 허리 굵기
implant 이식
tissue 조직
be associated with ~와 관련되다
complication 합병증
augmentation 증가, 증대

정답 (c)

Pre-Test·2 Answers

Type 01 (d) Type 02 (d) Type 03 (c) Type 04 (a)
Type 05 (c) Type 06 (b) Type 07 (d) Type 08 (c)

Type 01 초반 빈칸 유형

Network your home with Sky Home Broadband, and then _____ from anywhere in your home without messy wires. While you're downloading a movie in the study or researching holidays in the garden, the kids can be playing games in the family room or surfing the internet in the kitchen. Plus day or night helps is available on a wide range of queries, simply by phoning our award-winning 24/7 technical support center. All of which makes for a much happier household, and it costs less than you might think.

(a) you can give your friends a call
(b) everyone can watch their favorite programs on television
(c) you can remote control all electric appliances
(d) everyone can be online at the same time

해설
공유인터넷과 관련한 광고문이다. 빈칸이 포함된 문장은 Sky Home Broadband와 함께 통신망을 형성하면 이것을 할 수 있다는 내용의 글이 들어가야 한다. 빈칸 뒤에 이어지는 글의 내용은 정원, 거실, 부엌 할 것 없이 어느 곳에서나 인터넷을 할 수 있다는 내용이 이어진다. 그러므로 빈칸에 가장 적절한 것은 '모든 이들이 같은 시간대에 인터넷에 접속할 수 있다'는 (d)가 가장 적절하다.

해석
Sky Home Broadband로 통신망을 형성하세요. 그리고 나면, 모든 사람들이 지저분한 선들 없이 당신의 집의 어디에서나 같은 시간에 온라인에 접속할 수 있습니다. 당신이 서재에서 영화를 다운 받거나 또는 정원에서 휴가계획을 조사하는 동안, 아이들은 거실에서 게임을 하거나 부엌에서 인터넷 검색을 할 수 있습니다. 게다가, 넓은 범위의 질문들은 간단하게 저희의 연중 내내 운영되는 기술 지원 센터에 전화를 하시면 밤낮을 가리지 않고 도움을 받으실 수 있습니다. 이 모든 것들은 더 행복한 가정을 만들어 드리고 당신이 생각하는 것보다 더 적은 비용이 든답니다.

어휘
network 통신망을 형성하다
be online 온라인에 접속하다
messy 지저분한
surf the internet 인터넷을 검색하다
query 질문
phone 전화하다
24/7(=24 days and 7 nights) 하루 종일(의)
household 가족, 세대

✓ 정답 (d)

Type 02 중반 빈칸 유형

Dog lovers often claim their dogs can communicate complex emotions and this idea lies at the heart of the novel Dog Boy. The dog boy of the title is Romochka, a four-year-old child abandoned by his parents in a Moscow flat. Starving and distressed, the child wanders onto the street and follows a large yellow dog to her hiding place. There he is adopted into a litter of suckling puppies, and _____. Through Romochka's perspective, we catch a glimpse of what it might be like to switch species. The events of Dog Boy are rich in interest and ideas, and set down in strong, plain language.

(a) learns how to love other creatures
(b) trains them to follow people's commands
(c) leaves on a journey to find his parents
(d) begins to forget his human habits

해설
Dog Boy라는 소설의 내용에 대해서 설명해 주고 있는 글이다. 빈칸이 포함된 문장은 부모에 의해서 버림을 받은 주인공 소년이 거리를 헤매다 개를 쫓아가고 거기서 강아지 무리들에 의해서 받아들여진 것과 문맥을 같이 해야 한다. 빈칸 뒤의 문장 중 'what it might be like to switch species'를 통해 소년이 인간의 습성을 버리고 개의 습성을 따랐다는 걸 예상해 볼 수 있다. 그러므로 빈칸은 '인간의 습관을 잊어버리기 시작했다'라는 (d)가 가장 적절하다.

해석
애견가들은 종종 개들이 복잡한 감정을 의사소통할 수 있다고 주장합니다. 그리고 이러한 생각은 "Dog Boy"란 소설의 중심에 놓여있습니다. 제목의 강아지 소년은 모스크바의 플랫주택에서 부모에 의해서 버려진 4살짜리 소년 Romochka입니다. 배고픔과 고뇌에 지쳐, 이 소년은 거리로 나와 헤매고 큰 노란색 강아지를 쫓아 강아지의 은신처로 따라갑니다. 거기서 그는 젖을 빠는 새끼강아지들의 무리들 속으로 받아들여져, 그의 인간 습성을 잊어버리기 시작합니다. Romochka의 시점을 통해서, 우리는 종을 전환하는 것이 어떤 것일지에 대해서 살짝이나마 살펴볼 수 있습니다. Dog Boy의 사건들은 흥미와 아이디어가 풍부하고, 강력하고 솔직한 언어로 쓰여 있습니다.

어휘
claim 주장하다
communicate 의사소통을 하다
lie ~에 있다, 존재하다
abandon 버리다, 버리고 떠나다
wander 헤매다, 방랑하다
adopt 입양하다, (일원으로) 받아들이다
litter (동물의) 한배 새끼
perspective 시각, 견지
switch 바꾸다
plain 분명한, 꾸밈없는

✓ 정답 (d)

Type 03 후반 빈칸 유형

A slump is never good news, whether it's happening to the global economy, or to your own body. Yet slumping, both seated and standing versions, has become so much a part of our postural habits that a recent study by The George Institute for International Health found more than 10 million Americans have recurrent back and neck problems. When your posture is all wrong, the disc of your vertebrae are strained and squashed, which can cause them to deteriorate. You also engage the wrong muscles, putting unnecessary stress on your neck, chest and shoulders, and even your jaw and throat. Slouching and slumping also compresses your rib cage, making it more difficult to take in deep breaths. The resulting shallow breathing _____ by not supplying enough oxygen through your entire body. No wonder you feel tired!

(a) affects your clear thinking
(b) makes you feel edgy
(c) makes you fatigued and sluggish
(d) completely paralyzes you

해설

잘못된 자세 습관이 건강에 미치게 되는 여러 가지 부작용들을 서술하고 있는 글이다. 빈칸 앞의 문장에서 잘못된 자세가 깊은 숨을 들이 마시는 것을 더욱 어렵게 한다고 설명하고 있다. 그리고 그 결과로 몸 전체에 충분한 산소가 공급되지 않으면서 나타난 현상이 빈칸의 정답으로 들어가야 한다. 마지막 문장 'No wonder you feel tired'를 통해서 이 현상이 몸의 피로와 관련이 있음을 알 수 있다. 그러므로 정답은 (c)이다.

해석

슬럼프(경제의 폭락)는 그것이 세계 경제에 일어나고 있든 아니든, 혹은 당신의 신체에 일어나고 있든 결코 좋은 소식이 아닙니다. 그런데도 슬럼프(구부정한 자세)는 그것이 앉아 있을 때든 아니면 서 있을 때든 모두 우리의 자세 버릇의 큰 일부가 되어버렸고, "국제 건강 George 협회"의 최근 조사는 천만 명 이상의 미국인들이 재발되는 등과 목 문제를 가지고 있다는 것을 발견했습니다. 당신의 자세가 전혀 올바르지 않을 때, 당신의 척추 디스크는 뒤틀리고 으그러지며 이러한 자세는 결국 이들의 상태를 더 악화시키는 원인이 될 수 있지요. 또한 잘못된 근육을 사용하게 되면서 목, 가슴과 어깨, 그리고 턱과 목에까지도 불필요한 압박을 주게 됩니다. 축 늘어져서 걷고 구부정하게 걷는 것은 또한 흉곽을 압박하여 깊은 숨을 들이 마시는 것을 더욱 어렵게 합니다. 그 결과로 인한 얕은 호흡은 몸 전체를 통해 충분한 공기를 공급하지 않으면서 당신을 더욱 피로하고 굼뜨게 합니다. 이러니 당신이 피곤을 느끼는 것이 놀라울 게 없는 것입니다.

어휘

postural 체위
slump 경제의 폭락, 자세의 꾸부정함
vertebral 척추의
slouch 축 늘어지다, 몸을 굽히다
rib cage 흉곽
fatigued 피로한, 지친
sluggish 나태한, 게으른
edgy 날카로운, 안절부절 못하는
paralyze 마비시키다, 불수가 되게 하다

정답 (c)

Type 04 접속(부)사 찾기 유형

Internet is a remarkable invention. It is a valuable tool that provides people with opportunities for learning, getting in touch with friends by email, finding information, shopping and for chatting to other people with similar interests. _____, it is safe to say that the Internet is an adult environment, with few limits on what is posted on it, and where the information may not always be sound and reliable. As such, it is obvious that it can often be a very dangerous place for children to play. Most of young boys and girls at some stage will have some sort of contact with the Internet. That is why parents should understand the influence of the technology and monitor the Internet access of your children.

(a) However
(b) Furthermore
(c) For example
(d) In other words

해설

빈칸 앞의 내용은 놀라운 발명인 인터넷의 여러 가지 장점들을 설명하고 있는 반면, 빈칸 뒤에서는 성인 환경으로서의 인터넷의 위험성을 말하고 있다. 이 두 내용은 서로 상반되는 것이므로 (a)가 정답이다.

해석

인터넷은 놀라운 발명품이다. 이것은 사람들에게 배움의 기회와 이메일을 통해서 친구들과 연락을 하고, 정보를 찾고 쇼핑을 하고, 같은 관심사를 가진 사람들과 채팅을 할 수 있게끔 해주는 소중한 도구이다. 하지만, 인터넷은 인터넷상에 등록되는 내용들에 거의 제한이 없는 성인 환경이라고 말한다 해도 과언은 아니다. 그리고 그 정보들은 항상 건전하고 믿을 만한 것도 아니다. 그 자체로, 인터넷은 종종 아이들이 놀기에는 매우 위험한 장소일 수 있다는 것은 명백하다. 대부분의 어린 소년들과 소녀들은 언젠가는 인터넷과 어떤 식으로든 접촉을 하게 될 것이다. 그것이 바로 부모들이 이 기술의 영향력을 이해하고 아이들의 인터넷 접근을 감시해야 하는 이유이다.

어휘

remarkable 주목할 만한, 놀라운
invention 발명품
It is safe to say ~라 말해도 과언이 아니다
adult 성인(의)
sound 건전한
reliable 믿음직한, 신뢰성 있는
as such 그 자체로, 그것만으로도
monitor 감시하다, 관찰하다

정답 (a)

Type 05 대의 파악 유형

A substance similar to hippopotamus sweat could one day protect us from sunburn. Hippos can stand in the hot sun all day without getting burnt thanks to a glandular secretion that contains microscopic particles to scatter light, protecting the animals from burns. Scientists hope to create a sunscreen product inspired by hippo sweat. Researcher Christopher Viney from the University of California is also attempting to replicate the antiseptic and insect repellent characteristics of the sweat. This would form the basis of a four-in-one product: sunscreen, sunblock, antiseptic and insect repellent. It would be an advertiser's dream as long as the product doesn't smell like a hippo.

Q: What is the passage mainly about?
(a) The importance of using sun protection.
(b) Scientists' effort to understand hippos.
(c) Positive properties of hippo sweat.
(d) The newly invented cosmetics made from hippo sweat.

해설
지문의 대의를 찾는 문제이다. 하마 땀의 여러 가지 긍정적인 성질들을 언급하며 이를 이용해서 꿈의 상품을 만들 수 있기를 바란다는 것이 글의 내용이다. 그러므로 '하마 땀의 긍정적인 성질들'란 (c)가 정답이다.

해석
하마의 땀과 비슷한 물질은 언젠가 우리를 햇볕에 타는 것으로부터 보호해 줄 수도 있을 것이다. 하마들은 하루 종일 태양에 있어도 몸이 타지 않는데, 이는 극히 작은 입자들을 가지고 있어 빛을 산란시키는 체액 분비액 덕분이다. 과학자들은 이 하마 땀에서 영감을 얻어 햇볕타기 방지제 상품을 만들기를 희망하고 있다. 캘리포니아 대학교의 Christopher Viney 연구원은 또한 하마 땀의 살균제와 벌레를 쫓는 특징을 모사하기 위해서 노력 중에 있다. 이는 네 가지 특징을 하나에 담은 상품의 기반을 형성할 수 있을 것이다. 그것들은 바로 햇볕타기 방지제, 자외선 방지, 살균제, 그리고 벌레퇴치이다. 그 상품이 하마와 같은 냄새만 나지 않는 한 이는 광고자들의 꿈의 상품이 될 것이다.

어휘
substance 물질, 재료
hippopotamus 하마
sweat 땀, 땀을 흘리다
sunburn 햇볕에 탐
microscopic 극히 작은
glandular secretion 체액 분비
antiseptic 방부제, 살균제
repellent 퇴치하는
antiseptic 살균의, 소독된

✓ 정답 (c)

Type 06 세부 내용 파악 유형

It is recommended that you sleep aboard the vessel the night before the voyage in order to let your body get used to the boat's motion. However, this may not be possible in small boats. Otherwise, you can take seasickness tablets, but be cautious as some may make you drowsy. If you feel seasick, you need to keep yourself busy and stay in the fresh air. You should avoid the head down position, as this aggravates illness. It is also helpful to nibble on a dry biscuit, chew gums or dried fruit. Ginger is also considered a good anti-seasickness remedy. Don't forget to stay out of enclosed areas where fumes from fuel and food odors may temporarily collect. Experienced sailors keep their diet free of greasy foods and alcohol both before going to sea and while aboard.

Q: Which of the following is correct according to the passage?
(a) Seasickness occurs due to the small size of vessels.
(b) Some of the seasickness pills may cause sleepiness.
(c) Dried fruit is considered to be an effective medicine for seasickness.
(d) Sailors supply refreshments for the people on board.

해설
뱃멀미를 예방할 수 있는 다양한 방법들을 알려주고 있는 내용의 글이다. 지문 중 'Otherwise, you can ~ make you drowsy'를 통해서 멀미를 막기 위해 먹은 약으로 인해 졸음이 생길 수 있음을 확인할 수 있다. 그러므로 정답은 (b)이다. 지문 중, (c)에서 마른 과일을 씹는 것이 도움이 된다는 것이지 마른 과일 자체가 뱃멀미에 좋은 약으로 여겨진다는 것은 정답으로 볼 수 없다.

해석
배의 이동에 여러분의 신체를 적응시키기 위해서 항해 전날 밤에 배에서 수면을 취하는 것을 추천합니다. 하지만, 이는 작은 보트의 경우는 가능하지 않을 수도 있지요. 딴 방법으로, 여러분은 뱃멀미 정제약을 복용하실 수도 있습니다만, 몇몇 종류는 여러분을 졸음이 오게 할 수도 있으니 조심할 필요가 있습니다. 만약 여러분이 뱃멀미를 느끼신다면, 여러분은 바쁘게 움직이시거나, 시원한 바람과 함께 머무시면 됩니다. 머리를 아래로 숙이는 자세는 피하셔야 하는데 이는 멀미를 더 악화시키기 때문입니다. 또한 마른 과자를 조금씩 씹어 먹거나, 껌 또는 마른 과일을 씹는 것도 도움이 됩니다. 연료에서부터 생기는 증기와 음식의 악취가 일시적으로 고일 수 있는 닫힌 공간은 피하는 것을 잊지 마세요. 경험이 많은 항해사들은 항해를 나가거나 또는 항해 중에 술과 기름진 음식의 섭취를 하지 않는 답니다.

어휘
recommend 추천하다
vessel (큰) 배
seasickness 뱃멀미
cautious 신중한, 조심하는
avoid 피하다
aggravate 악화시키다
remedy 치료, 치료약
voyage 항해
nibble 조금씩 먹다
free of ~이 없는

✓ 정답 (b)

Type 07 추론 유형

Twenty-nine-year old Iranian blogger Omid Mirsayafi died in Iran's notorious Evin prison after taking an overdose of medication. Omid was suffering from depression. Another political prisoner, Dr. Hessam Firouzi, leaked news of the death and accused prison authorities of not taking Omid's illness seriously. The young blogger had been jailed for 30 months in February due to the post insulting the country's Supreme Leader, and the Islamic Republic's founder. Another political prisoner, Amir Saran, suffered a stroke and died earlier this month. His family also accused prison authorities of negligence.

Q: What can be inferred from the passage?
(a) Omid Mirsayafi died due to the misprescription of drugs.
(b) Amir Saran died from a stroke despite treatment attempts.
(c) Officials in prison are not responsible for the death of the two people.
(d) Iranian internet users have no freedom of expression on the net

해설
감옥에서 사망한 이란의 블로거와 관련한 기사 내용이다. 지문에서 'The young blogger had been jailed~insulting the country's Supreme Leader, and the Islamic Republic's founder'를 통해서 이란은 인터넷 상에 표현의 자유가 없음을 유추할 수 있다. 그러므로 정답은 (d)이다. 과다복용과 잘못된 처방은 서로 동일한 것이 아니기에 (a)는 정답이 될 수 없다.

해석
29살의 이란 블로거인 Omid Mirsayfi가 이란의 악명 높은 Evin 감옥에서 약물 과다복용으로 숨졌다. Omid는 우울증으로 시달리고 있었다. 또 다른 정치범인 Hessam Firouzi 박사는 이 죽음에 관한 소식을 누설했고, 그는 교정당국이 Omid의 병을 심각하게 받아들이지 않았다고 비난했다. 이 젊은 블로거는 2월 달에 이란의 최고 지도자와 회교공화국 설립자를 비난한 등록 글 때문에 30개월 동안 감옥에 갇혀 있던 중이었다. 또 다른 정치범인 Amir Saran은 뇌졸중으로 고생했는데 이번 달 초에 숨졌다. 그의 가족들 또한 교정당국을 임무태만으로 비난했다.

어휘
notorious 악명 높은
overdose 지나친 투여, 과량
leak 새다, 누설하다
prison authorities 교정 당국
insult 모욕하다
accuse ~을 비난하다, 고소하다
negligence 태만, 부주의

✓ 정답 (d)

Type 08 문맥 파악 유형

Early food experiences can set a life time of eating pattern and influence health status later in life. (a) The use of food as a reward can send inappropriate messages to our children that can adversely affect both their short and long term health. (b) Frequently, quick and easy rewards such as sweets and soft drinks given to our children encourages them to believe that these low nutritional foods and drinks are a more desirable choice than other healthier options. (c) The best time for sweets is prior to exercise or after a main meal. (d) Also, they begin to associate achievement and reward for good behavior with sweets when it should be understood that there is no connection between behavior and food.

해설
어린 시절 올바른 식습관 형성의 중요성을 이야기하고 있는 글이다. (a)에서는 올바른 식습관의 형성을 방해하는 예로 아이들에게 포상으로 사탕과 청량음료를 제공하는 것을 언급하고 있고, (b)에서는 이러한 행위의 결과가 어떠한 부정적인 상황을 조장하는지 말해주고 있다. (d)에서는 (b)에서 언급한 부정적인 상황을 다시 한 번 구체화 시켜주고 있다. 하지만 (c)는 단순히 사탕거리를 먹을 가장 최고의 시간이 언제인지를 말하고 있으므로 아이들의 올바른 식습관 형성과는 연관성이 떨어지는 내용이다. 그러므로 정답은 (c)이다.

해석
어린 시절 음식에 대한 경험은 평생의 식습관 패턴을 결정하고 후에 삶에 있어서의 건강에 영향을 미칩니다. (a) 음식을 포상으로서 사용하는 것은 우리의 아이들에게 부적절한 메시지를 보내 역으로 단기간 그리고 장기간의 아이들 건강에 안 좋게 영향을 미칠 수 있습니다. (b) 빈번하게, 우리의 아이들에게 사탕이나 청량음료와 같은 빠르고 쉬운 포상거리를 주는 것은 그들이 이러한 영양분이 낮은 음식과 음료수가 다른 건강한 식품들에 비해서 더 바람직한 것이라고 믿게 되도록 조장합니다. (c) 사탕거리를 먹을 최고의 시간은 운동이 끝나거나 주요 식사를 먹고 난 후입니다. (d) 또한, 아이들은 그들의 행동과 음식 사이에는 아무런 관련이 없다고 이해해야 하는 것에도 불구하고, 성취와 좋은 행동에 대한 포상을 사탕과 연관시키기 시작합니다.

어휘
health status 건강 상태
reward 보상, 포상
inappropriate 적절치 못한
adversely 역의, 거슬러, 반대하여
sweets 캔디
desirable 바람직한
associate A with B A를 B와 연상시키다
achievement 성취, 업적
behavior 행동

✓ 정답 (c)

Pre-Test • 3 Answers

Type 01 (d) Type 02 (d) Type 03 (c) Type 04 (d)
Type 05 (c) Type 06 (d) Type 07 (c) Type 08 (c)

Type 01 초반 빈칸 유형

The Iowa Supreme Court unanimously upheld a lower court decision overturning as unconstitutional a state law that defined marriage as _____. In doing so, the court made Iowa the third state in the US, with Massachusetts and Connecticut, in which gay and lesbian marriage will be legal. On the other hand, California legalized gay marriage in 2008 only to have it overturned by a referendum. A challenge to that result is now before the California Supreme Court. Meanwhile, votes in the New Hampshire and Vermont legislatures are moving those states closer to approving same-sex unions.

(a) a union between persons of the same race
(b) open to both opposite and same-gender couples
(c) a contract for the production of children
(d) exclusive to heterosexual partners

해설
빈칸의 문장은 결혼을 이것으로 정의해 위헌 결정이 된 아이오와 주의 법에 대한 설명이 들어가야 한다. 빈칸 뒤의 문장에서는 이를 통해 아이와 주가 동성 간의 결혼이 합법화가 되었다는 내용이 나오고 있다. 그러므로 빈칸은 이와는 반대의 내용 즉, '이성애자들 간에만 한정된'이라는 (d)가 정답으로 와야 한다.

해석
아이오와 주의 대법원은 만장일치로 결혼은 이성애자들 간에만 한정된 것으로 정의한 주 법을 위헌으로서 뒤집어엎은 하급법원의 결정을 확정했다. 이렇게 함으로써, 법원은 아이오와가 미국에서 매사추세츠와 코네티컷과 함께 게이와 레즈비언 간의 결혼이 합법화가 된 세 번째 주가 되도록 했다. 이와는 반대로, 캘리포니아는 2007년에 동성애자들 간에 결혼을 합법화시켰지만, 일반 투표에 의해서 이 결정은 뒤집히고 말았다. 이 결과에 대한 도전은 현재 캘리포니아 대법원 앞에 놓여 있다. 그러는 동안, 뉴햄프셔와 버몬트 입법부에서의 투표로 이 주들은 동성 간의 혼인을 승인하는 주가 될 가능성이 높아지고 있다.

어휘
Supreme Court (주의) 대법원
unanimously 만장일치로
uphold 지지하다, 확정하다
overturn 뒤집어엎다
unconstitutional 위헌의, 비헌법적인
exclusive 배타적인, 한정적인
heterosexual 이성애자
legalize 합법화하다
referendum 일반 투표
legislature 입법부, 입법기관
move closer to ~에 가까이 다가가다

정답 (d)

Type 02 중간 빈칸 유형

Helicobacter pylori is the bacteria that sometimes causes gastritis and stomach ulcers. They survive in the acidic environment of the stomach, and symptoms can include bloating, reflux, belching, nausea and abdominal pain. Medical treatment is two types of antibiotics and a stomach acid suppressor over one to two weeks. But, there's concern the bacteria are becoming resistant to antibiotics and treatment may cause bad side effects. On the other hand, _____ treating the bug with probiotics, unartificial alkalisers to reduce stomach acid, and other nutrients to improve stomach function.

(a) Synthetic drug treatment includes
(b) The faster way to cure stomach ulcers includes
(c) The most efficient treatment to eliminate the bug involves
(d) The natural approach involves

해설
위염과 위궤양의 원인이 되는 병원균을 치료하는 방법에 대한 지문이다. 빈칸 앞에 연결사 On the other hand가 위치한 것으로 보아 빈칸 앞의 문장과 빈칸 뒤의 문장은 서로 상반되는 내용이 될 것임을 예측할 수 있다. 앞에서는 항생제를 사용한 치료방법을 언급했고 이것이 부작용을 일으킬 수도 있다고 언급하고 있다. 반면, 뒤에서는 비인공성 약품과 음식의 영양분에 의한 치료를 언급하고 있기에 빈칸은 '자연 그대로의 접근 방법'을 얘기한 (d)가 가장 적절하다

해석
Helicobacter pylori는 때때로 위염과 위궤양의 원인이 되는 박테리아이다. 이들은 위의 산성인 환경에서 살아가고, 증상들은 복부팽창, 음식물 역류, 트림, 메스꺼움, 복부 통증을 포함한다. 의학적 치료방법에는 한 주에서 두 주에 걸친 두 가지 종류의 항생물질과 위산 억제제가 있다. 하지만, 이 박테리아가 항생제에 대한 저항성이 커지고 있다는 것과 이 치료방법이 나쁜 부작용을 불러 올 수 있다는 걱정이 있다. 이와는 반대로, 자연스러운 접근방법은 위산을 줄이기 위해서 이 병원균을 유산균 처방약과 비인공성 산성중화제로 치료하는 것과 위 기능을 향상시키기 위한 다른 영양분들이 포함된다.

어휘
gastritis 위염
ulcer 궤양
acidic 산성의
abdominal 복부의
antibiotic 항생물질
unartificial 인공이 아닌
naturopathy 자연요법
synthetic 합성의, 인조의

정답 (d)

Type 03 후반 빈칸 유형

More renowned for smoothing the furrowed foreheads of stars, Botox can now be used to help people recover from a stroke. The treatment, which relaxes face muscles for cosmetic reasons, can also reduce upper limb spasticity, a stiffening of the muscles that can immobilize the arms and cause a victim's hands to clench permanently. Botox is now used for the treatment of moderate to severe cases of upper-limb spasticity, a common effect of stroke. Doctors can now offer the treatment when alternative muscle-relaxant drugs fail, or in conjunction with physiotherapy to help restore _____ .

(a) brain damage due to stroke
(b) the ability to walk erect
(c) the use of stroke-affected limbs
(d) healthy and radiant skin

해설
미용의 목적으로 사용되는 보톡스가 이제 뇌졸중 환자들의 상체 사지가 움직일 수 있도록 하는 치료에 사용될 수 있다는 내용의 글이다. 빈칸이 포함된 문장은 의사들이 이것의 회복을 돕기 위해 본 치료방법을 제공할 수 있다는 문장으로, 빈칸에는 '뇌졸중으로 영향을 받은 사지의 사용'인 (c)가 정답으로 가장 적절하다. Botox를 활용한 치료방법은 상체 사지의 회복과 관련이 있기에 척추와 관련을 지은 (b)의 '서서 걸을 수 있는 능력'과는 상관이 없다.

해석
스타들의 주름이 진 이마를 매끄럽게 하는 것으로 더 유명한 보톡스는 이제 뇌졸중으로부터 사람들이 회복하는 것을 돕기 위해 사용되어 질 수 있습니다. 미용의 이유로 얼굴 근육을 완화시켜주는 이 치료법은 팔을 움직이지 못하게 할 수 있는 근육의 경직과 피해자가 영원히 손을 움켜지고 있게끔 야기하는 상체 사지의 경직을 줄여 줄 수 있습니다. 보톡스는 이제 뇌졸중의 가장 흔한 결과인 보통에서부터 심각한 경우까지의 상체 사지 경직을 치료하기 위해서 사용되어집니다. 의사들은 이제 대체 근육 이완제가 실패했을 시, 물리요법과 함께 뇌졸중으로 인해 영향을 받은 사지의 사용을 복구시켜 주기 위한 치료법을 제공할 수 있게 되었습니다.

어휘
furrow 고랑이 지다, 주름이 지다
stroke 뇌졸중
cosmetic 화장의, 미용의
limb 수족, 사지
spasticity 경직
stiffen 뻣뻣하게 하다, 경직시키다
clench 꽉 지다
in conjunction with ~와 협력하여
restore 복원하다, 회복시키다
immobilize 움직이지 않게 하다, 고정하다
physiotherapy 물리요법

정답 (c)

Type 04 접속(부)사 찾기 유형

The majority of pedestrian fatalities last year were elderly, young or intoxicated. Many pedestrian deaths are on roads signposted at 50-60 km/h. The 50 km/h limit will work if only drivers stick to it. _____, some drivers think pedestrian safety is not their concern. At 50 km/h, a pedestrian will probably still be killed, but an alert driver who brakes could save their life. If the suburban limit was dropped to 40 km/h, and the limit was policed, the death toll might drop. If you wait that extra five seconds rather than play chicken with traffic, it might drop. Develop one of your own action plan. Then, the life saved might be yours.

(a) In consequence
(b) For all that
(c) Similarly
(d) Unfortunately

해설
빈칸 앞의 문장은 50km/h의 속도제한을 지킬 경우 그 역할을 할 것이라고 얘기하고 있다. 그리고 빈칸 뒤의 문장에서는 몇몇 운전자들이 보행자의 안전을 자기들의 관심이 아니라고 생각한다는 얘기를 하고 있다. 지켜져야 할 사항이 지켜지지 않아 사고가 벌어지고 있는 것임으로 이 두 문장 사이에 가장 적절한 것은 보기 (d)이다.

해석
작년 보행자 사망수의 대다수가 나이가 많으신 분들, 어리거나 술에 취했던 사람들이었다. 많은 보행자들의 죽음이 50~60km/h 푯말이 세워진 도로에서 발생했다. 50km/h라는 속도제한은 운전자들이 그것을 고수하기만 한다면 그 역할을 할 것이다. 유감스럽게도, 몇몇 운전자들은 보행자의 안전은 그들의 관심이 아니라고 생각한다. 50km/h의 속도에서는, 보행자가 사고 시 사망할 가능성이 있지만, 방심하지 않고 브레이크를 밟는 운전자라면 보행자의 삶을 구할 수도 있다. 만약 도시 주변의 제한속도가 40km/h로 낮춰지고, 이 속도가 경찰에 의해서 단속되어진다면, 사망자수는 낮아질 것이다. 만약 당신이 사람들과 누가 물러서냐라는 식의 도전을 하기보다 5초 정도를 더 기다려 준다면, 사망률은 낮춰질 것이다. 당신만의 행동 계획을 세워라. 그러면 당신에 의해서 누군가의 목숨이 구해질 수도 있다.

어휘
signpost 푯말을 세우다
alert 정신을 바짝 차린, 빈틈없는 방심하지 않는
suburban 도시 주변의
police 단속하다 n. 경찰
play chicken 상대가 물러서기를 기대하면서 서로 도전하다
traffic (사람, 차의) 왕래, 통행

정답 (d)

Type 05 대의 파악 유형

A new kind of Automatic Teller Machine is being launched in America that can vary its transaction charges depending on the time of day, says The New York Times. The CashOut is being promoted as a way for pub owners to raise transaction fees at times when clients are more likely to be intoxicated. The company has suggested that on Saturday nights the charge to draw cash could go from $1.50 to $2 after 11 pm. "Most people will start not to care about the charge after that time", said the company. They are expecting to have 50 CashOut operating in pubs across New York by the end of the month.

Q: What is the best title for the passage?
(a) A rise in transaction fees of Automatic Teller Machines.
(b) How intoxication causes reckless behavior.
(c) An introduction of an innovative Automatic Teller Machine.
(d) A prospering future for pub owners.

해설
이미 첫 문장에서 주제가 드러나고 있다. 기존의 것과는 다른 새로운 종류의 ATM의 출시가 이 글의 주제이다. 그러므로 정답은 '혁신적인 ATM의 소개' 라는 (c)가 정답이다. 새로운 종류(a new kind of)를 혁신적인(innovative)이란 단어로 대체하였다.

해석
하루의 시간대에 따라서 수수료가 달라지는 새로운 종류의 ATM 기계가 미국에서 등장할 것이라고 뉴욕타임즈가 말합니다. CashOut은 고객들이 취했을 가능성이 더 높은 시간대에 술집 주인들이 수수료를 올릴 수 있는 수단으로 선전되고 있습니다. 이 회사는 토요일 밤에는 현금을 뽑기 위한 수수료가 11시 이후에 $1.50에서 $2로 올라갈 수 있다고 넌지시 말했습니다. "대부분의 사람들은 그 시간 이후에는 수수료에 대해서는 상관하지 않기 시작할겁니다" 라고 회사는 말합니다. 그들은 이번 달 말까지 뉴욕을 걸쳐 여러 술집에서 50개의 CashOut이 운영될 것으로 기대하고 있습니다.

어휘
Automatic Teller Machine(=ATM) 자동 현금 출납기
transaction charges 거래 수수료
pub 술집
intoxicate 취하게 하다
draw cash 현금을 뽑다
operate 작동하다, 운영하다
reckless 분별없는, 무모한
prosper 번영하다, 성공하다

정답 (c)

Type 06 세부 내용 파악 유형

A meeting of more than 2,000 scientists and economists has warned that the 2007 worst-case predictions of the Intergovernmental Panel on Climate Change have been realized and that the continued failure of governments to act on global warming could see abrupt or irreversible climate shifts. They warned of consequent social and economic catastrophe. On the bright side, the meeting, in preparation for the United Nations Climate Change Conference in Copenhagen in December this year, emphasized that governments now had the technology to control climate change if they chose to act. Meanwhile, more than 600 climate change skeptics met in New York, challenging the view that global warming is linked to human activity.

Q: Which of the following is correct according to the passage?
(a) Economists and scientists fight against each other for different reasons.
(b) The UN Climate Change Conference will be held in December next year.
(c) Nations do not have the technology to control environmental change.
(d) People gathered in New York think humans do not affect global warming.

해설
지구온난화와 이를 통제할 정부의 행동을 촉구하는 경제학자들과 과학자들에 대한 내용이 지문에서 다뤄지고 있다. 지문의 마지막 문장 'more than 600 climate change skeptics met in New York, challenging the view that global warning is linked to human activity'를 통해서 뉴욕에 모인 사람들은 지구온난화와 인간의 활동 간에는 관련이 없다고 생각함을 알 수 있다. 그러므로 정답은 (d)이다.

해석
2000명 이상의 과학자들과 경제학자들의 모임은 2007에 정부 간 위원단의 환경변화의 최악의 경우를 고려한 예상이 현실화되었고, 지구온난화에 대해 정부가 지속적으로 행동을 취하지 않음으로써 갑작스럽고 되돌릴 수 없는 환경 변화가 일어날 수 있다고 경고했다. 그들은 결과로서 일어날 수 있는 사회적 그리고 경제적 재앙을 경고했다. 긍정적인 면에서는, 내년 12월 코펜하겐에서의 국가연합 기후 변화 회담을 대비하여 열린 회의에서 이제는 정부가 행동하기로 결정만 한다면 기후변화를 통제할 수 있는 기술을 보유하고 있다는 점을 강조한 것이다. 한편, 600명 이상의 기후변화 회의론자들은 지구온난화가 인간의 활동과 연관이 있다는 관점에 도전하기 위해서 뉴욕에서 만났다.

어휘
economist 경제학자
warn 경고하다
realize 실현하다, 현실화하다
global warming 지구온난화
irreversible 돌이킬 수 없는
shift 변화
catastrophe 큰 재해, 파국
meanwhile 한편, 그동안에
skeptic 회의론자
challenge ~에 도전하다

정답 (d)

Type 07 추론 유형

It is hard to believe that biting into a peanut butter sandwich almost proved fatal for a young boy. The two-year-old toddler has since been diagnosed with a life threatening allergy to peanuts and tree nuts. It was one year ago when he took a bit of his sister's peanut butter sandwich and suffered anaphylaxis. His family have made significant lifestyle changes as a result of his allergy. Wherever the boy goes, there is an adrenaline auto-injector close by, ready to be administered should the toddler suffer an anaphylactic reaction. Then, there is grocery shopping and reading labels carefully to ensure products carry no traces of peanuts or tree nuts. And when the family dines out, it means verifying whether peanuts or tree nuts are part of any of the dishes.

Q: What can be inferred from the passage?
(a) Kids are more likely to develop peanut allergy.
(b) The boy inherited the allergy from his father.
(c) The boy is the only one who has the peanut allergy in his family.
(d) The boy is taken to the hospital when he needs to get an injection.

해설
땅콩 알레르기를 갖고 있는 한 소년과 그의 가족들에 대한 이야기를 다룬 지문이다. 중간에 'His family~as a result of his allergy'를 통해서, 소년이 그의 가족들 중 땅콩 알레르기를 갖고 있는 유일한 사람이라는 것을 알 수 있다. 그러므로 정답은 (c)이다. (a)는 내용에서 언급된 바 없다.

해석
땅콩버터 샌드위치를 베어 먹었다는 것으로 한 어린 소년이 거의 생명을 잃을 뻔했다는 것은 믿기 어려운 일입니다. 이 두 살짜리 유아는 그 이후로 땅콩과 나무 견과에 대해 목숨을 위협할 수 있는 치명적인 알레르기가 있다고 진단받았습니다. 그가 그의 누나의 땅콩버터 샌드위치를 한 입 먹고 과민성 반응을 겪게 된 것은 1년 전입니다. 그의 가족들은 그의 알레르기로 인해 크게 생활양식에 변화를 주게 됩니다. 아이가 가는 곳은 어디든, 아이가 과민 반응을 일으키게 되면 바로 투약할 수 있도록 가까운 곳에 아드레날린 자동 주사기가 있습니다. 그 다음에는, 식료품 쇼핑 시에는 상품들이 어떠한 땅콩이나 나무 견과들이 없도록 확실히 하기 위해서 딱지를 주의 깊게 읽습니다. 그리고 가족들이 식사를 하러 나가면, 땅콩이나 나무 견과가 요리에 들어있는지 없는지를 확인해야 한다는 것을 의미하지요.

어휘
fatal 치명적인, 생명에 관계되는
toddler 유아
anaphylaxis 과민성 반응
significant 중대한, 의미심장한
injector 주사기
administer 복용시키다, 집행하다
trace 자취, 흔적
contract (병에) 걸리다
inherit 물려받다, 상속하다

정답 (c)

Type 08 문맥 파악 유형

Traditionally here in the UK, Sunday has always been the day of the week to enjoy a really good and hearty lunch. (a) With that in mind, this month's recipes are all about comforting, delicious food. (b) I've used one of my favourite birds-duck-and a roasted lamb shoulder in my arrosto misto recipe. (c) In some respects, slow cooking is quick cooking. (d) Arrost misto means 'mixed roast' and is a simple but wonderful Italian dish that includes different joints of meat roasted together.

해설
일요일을 맞이하여 준비할 음식에 관한 글이다. (a)에서는 준비할 요리의 성격을 얘기하고, (b)에서는 구체적으로 무엇을 요리할지 설명해 주고 있다. (d)에서는 (b)에서 언급한 단어의 의미를 설명해주며, 준비할 요리에 대해서 다시 한 번 구체적으로 말해준다. 반면 (c)는 요리의 속도와 관련된 내용으로 전체 맥락과 어울리지 않는 내용이다.

해석
전통적으로 이곳 영국에서는, 일요일은 한 주 중 항상 정말 맛있고 영양가 있는 음식을 즐기는 날이었습니다. (a) 사실을 기억하면서 이번 달의 조리법들은 기운을 돋우는 맛있는 음식들에 관한 것들입니다. (b) 전 제가 가장 좋아하는 조류 중의 하나인 오리와 양의 어깨살을 제 arrosto misto 요리법에 사용했습니다. (c) 어떤 면에서는 천천히 요리하는 것이 빠르게 요리하는 것과 같습니다. (d) Arrost misto는 "혼합된 구운 고기"란 뜻이고 간단하지만 환상적인 이탈리아 요리로 서로 다른 고기 덩어리들을 함께 구운 것을 포함합니다.

어휘
traditionally 전통적으로
hearty 영양가 있는
recipe 조리법
comforting 기운을 돋우는
in some respects 어떤 점에서는
dish 요리
joint 잘라놓은 큰 고기 덩어리

정답 (c)

Actual Test 1 Answers

1. (b)	2. (d)	3. (c)	4. (c)
5. (c)	6. (a)	7. (c)	8. (c)
9. (b)	10. (b)	11. (a)	12. (c)
13. (d)	14. (a)	15. (d)	16. (c)
17. (d)	18. (c)	19. (b)	20. (b)
21. (b)	22. (c)	23. (d)	24. (c)
25. (d)	26. (d)	27. (c)	28. (b)
29. (c)	30. (d)	31. (b)	32. (c)
33. (c)	34. (b)	35. (d)	36. (d)
37. (d)	38. (c)	39. (c)	40. (b)

1 Generally, the sustainability of a seafood harvest is judged on _____. High levels of regulation in the New Zealand industries mean that we can be confident the local seafood we buy is sustainably caught and grown, according to seafood consultant John Cage. "We follow world's best practice." he says, "We keep the three key points – diversity, quality, and sustainability." Experts say that fishing a species to 40~60 percent of its original numbers encourages breeding and maximizes the sustainable yield.

(a) how fresh the fishes are
(b) the ongoing levels of wild stocks
(c) the variety of fish species in the sea
(d) the environmental impact of fishing methods

해설
해산물 수확의 유지 가능성이 무엇에 의해 판단되는지 찾아야 한다. 빈칸 다음 문장에서 규제(regulation)에 관한 언급이 되고, 마지막 문장에서 최초 수의 40~60% 정도를 잡는 것이 유지 가능한 수확량을 최대화 할 수 있다는 내용으로 보아, '지금 야생축적량의 수준' 인 (b)가 정답임을 알 수 있다.

해석
일반적으로, 해산물 수확의 유지 가능성은 현재의 야생축적량의 수준에 의해서 판단됩니다. 해산물 컨설턴트인 John Cage에 따르면, 뉴질랜드 산업의 높은 수준의 규제는 우리가 구입하는 지역 해산물들이 고갈됨 없이 수확되고 길러진 것들이라는 것에 확신을 해도 괜찮다는 것을 의미합니다. "저희는 세계에서 최고라고 할 수 있는 실행방법을 따릅니다." 라고 그는 말합니다.' 저희는 세 가지 키 포인트를 지킵니다. 바로 다양성, 질, 그리고 유지 가능성이지요." 전문가들은 종의 최초 수의 40~60%를 수확하는 것이 번식을 장려하고 고갈됨 없이 유지 가능한 수확량을 최대화 할 수 있다고 말합니다.

어휘
sustainability (자원의) 고갈됨 없이 이용할 수 있는 정도
harvest 수확(량)
judge 판단하다
regulation 규정, 단속
diversity 다양성
fish 고기잡이를 하다
species 종류
breeding 번식, 양식
yield 산출, 수확(량)

✓ **정답** (b)

2 Runners who buy expensive sneakers could be wasting their money. Researchers at the University of Canterbury found there is no scientific evidence to support claims that specially designed running shoes _____. Kevin Douglas, a general practitioner who is a runner, was inspired to conduct the research after sustaining a series of injuries in his own expensive set of sneakers. Douglas found there was some evidence that hi-tech running shoes actually contributed to injury by making athletes land on their heels. These shoes could impair balance and promote ankle strains. He concluded that if you're not experiencing problems, you should stick with the shoes you're wearing. Because that's obviously the ones working for you.

(a) help run faster
(b) make you stand out among the crowd
(c) are lighter and more comfortable
(d) help prevent physical damages

해설
지문의 맨 앞에서 비싼 신발을 사는 것은 돈 낭비일 수도 있다고 언급하고, 빈칸의 뒤에서는 연구 결과, 비싼 신발이 오히려 부상을 더 일으킬 수 있다고 말하고 있다. 그러므로 빈칸에 들어갈 내용은 비싼 신발 즉, 특별히 설계된 신발이라고 '부상의 예방을 도와준다는 증거는 없다' 라는 (d)가 정답임을 알 수 있다.

해석
비싼 운동화를 사는 달리기 선수들은 돈을 낭비하는 것일 수도 있다. 캔터베리 대학교의 연구원들은 특별히 제작된 달리기 신발이 부상의 방지를 도와준다는 주장을 뒷받침하는 과학적인 증거는 없다는 것을 발견했다. 달리기 선수이자 일반의인 Kevin Douglas 씨는 그 자신이 비싼 운동화들을 신고 연이어 부상을 입은 후 이 연구를 해보자는 영감을 받았다. Douglas 씨는 첨단기술의 달리기 신발들이 실상 육상선수들이 그들의 뒤꿈치로 땅을 딛게 함으로써 부상을 일으킨다는 몇 가지 증거를 발견했다. 이 신발들은 균형을 무너뜨리고, 발목 접질림을 조장할 수 있다. 그는 특별히 문제가 없다면, 지금 신고 있는 신발을 고수해야 한다는 결론을 내렸다. 왜냐하면 그것이 당신에게 적합한 신발이라는 것이 분명하기 때문이다.

어휘
sneaker 운동화
scientific evidence 과학적인 증거
claim 주장, 주장하다
specially designed 특별히 설계된
general practitioner 일반의
inspire 고무시키다, 영감을 주다
sustain 받다, 입다
impair 손상시키다
promote 조장하다
conclude 결론을 내리다
stick with ~을 고수하다

✓ **정답** (d)

3 Perched near the top of Vietnam, Hanoi, which means "the hinterland between the rivers", isn't only the country's official capital, but also its heart. Its people are proud and friendly, its food is diverse and divine, and the incessant beeping of car horns and humming of Honda motorbikes is strangely exhilarating. A beautiful blend of ancient oriental traditions and European style, Hanoi was ruled by the Chinese until 1428 when Le Loi-a Vietnamese general-established the nation's independence. The Portuguese arrived in Vietnam in the 1500s, but it was the French, who invaded in the mid 1800s, who _____
_____. Among the Asian environs, you'll find French-style buildings, as well as baguettes and croissants on most cafe menus.

(a) destroyed the country the most
(b) handed down the French recipes
(c) left the biggest European mark
(d) massacred the Vietnamese people

해설

베트남의 수도인 하노이를 설명하면서, 도시가 고대 동양의 전통과 유럽의 스타일이 섞인 아름다운 도시라고 말하고 있다. 빈칸 뒤에 위치한 문장에서 아시아적인 주변 환경 가운데서, 프랑스 스타일의 빌딩들을 발견할 수 있다는 내용을 통해, 베트남의 영향을 미친 유럽 국가는 프랑스임을 알 수 있다. 그러므로 프랑스인들이 '가장 큰 유럽의 흔적을 남겼다'는 (c)가 정답이다.

해석

베트남 꼭대기에 자리를 차지하고 있는 하노이는 "강 사이의 후배지"라는 뜻으로 베트남의 공식 수도일 뿐만이 아니라, 베트남의 심장이기도 하다. 그곳의 사람들은 자존심이 있고 친근하며, 음식은 다양하고 신성하며, 자동차 경적의 끊임없는 빵빵거림과 혼다 오토바이의 윙윙대는 소리는 이상하게도 유쾌하다. 고대 동양의 전통과 유럽의 스타일을 아름답게 혼합한 하노이는 베트남 장군인 Le Loi가 국가의 독립을 확립한 1428년까지 중국에 의해서 통치되었다. 포르투갈 인들은 1500년대에 베트남에 도착했다. 하지만, 1800년 중순에 침략을 한 것은 프랑스 인들이었고, 그들은 가장 큰 유럽의 흔적을 남겼다. 아시아적인 주변 모습 사이에서 여러분은 프랑스 스타일의 빌딩들과 대부분의 카페들의 메뉴에 적혀 있는 바게트와 크로상을 발견하게 될 것이다.

어휘

perch 자리를 차지하다
hinterland 후배지, 시골
divine 신성한, 성스러운
incessant 끊임없는
exhilarating 유쾌한, 상쾌한
blend 혼합
rule 통치하다
invade 침략하다
environs 주변, 근교
hand down 전수하다
recipe 조리법
massacre 학살하다

정답 (c)

4 Dear Jenny Smith,

Welcome to FlyBuys!

Now you can start earning reward points on your everyday shopping. Inside the enclosed brochure, you'll find some Bonus Point offers to get you started on your way to enjoying shopping coupons, fine dining, escapes to the leading hotels, movies coupons, chances to fly off to far away destinations and many more rewards. All you have to do is present your FlyBuys card every time you shop at participating FlyBuys businesses. You'll find all the details on points and how to redeem them for rewards inside the enclosed brochure. You can also register your email address to get regular updates on the latest program information. Put your new FlyBuys card in your wallet right away, so next time you shop you _____.

Thank you.

(a) can get a copy of a brochure
(b) can redeem your gifts
(c) can make it count
(d) can receive discounts

해설

편지 내용은 FlyBuys 포인트 카드를 통해서 쇼핑 때마다 적립점수를 얻고 이를 모아서 상품을 받으라는 내용의 편지이다. 빈칸이 포함된 문장은 FlyBuys 카드를 지갑에 넣어 다음 쇼핑 때는 이것을 하라는 내용으로 문맥상 가장 적절한 것은 적립점수를 쌓으라(count)는 의미의 (c)가 정답이다.

해석

제니 스미스 씨에게

FlyBuys에 가입하신 것을 환영합니다.

이제 당신은 매일 매일의 쇼핑에서 적립 포인트를 얻으실 수 있습니다. 동봉된 소책자 안에는 쇼핑 쿠폰, 멋진 식사, 주요 호텔로의 탈출, 영화 쿠폰, 저 멀리 있는 목적지로 비행기 타고 떠나실 수 있는 기회와 함께 더 많은 보상들을 즐기실 수 있도록 약간의 보너스 포인트를 받으실 수 있는 제안을 찾으실 수 있으실 겁니다. 고객님께서 하실 일은 FluyBuys 사업체들이 참여하고 있는 곳에서 매번 쇼핑을 하실 때마다, 갖고 계신 FlyBuys 카드를 제시하는 것뿐입니다. 여러분은 동봉된 소책자 안에서 포인트에 대한 세부사항들과 상품을 위해서 포인트를 되찾는 방법을 찾으실 수 있습니다. 여러분은 또한 본인의 이메일 주소를 등록하여 최신 프로그램 정보에 대한 정기적인 소식을 받으실 수 있습니다. 지금 당장 FlyBuys 카드를 지갑에 넣으십시오. 그래서 다음 번 쇼핑을 하실 때는 포인트를 받도록 하세요.
감사합니다.

어휘

reward point 적립 포인트
enclosed 동봉된
get started 시작하다, 착수하다
redeem 되찾다, 회수하다
register 등록하다
update 최신정보

정답 (c)

5 "Reading the mid-sections of this book is like being thrown into a thriller," said Lucy Sussex in the Washington Post. In 1997, Israeli intelligence service Mossad tried to assassinate Palestinian activist Khalid Mishal. Their method was bizarre because the plan was to deliver poison via a fake camera. The Mossad agents succeeded in poisoning Mishal in Jordan but _____. King Hussein of Jordan, incensed by the attack, ignited a row between Israel, the US and the Arab states by demanding an antidote to the poison in exchange for the release of the Israeli agents. This gripping, real-life intrigue threatened to blow the Middle East apart and makes for superb, informative reading.

(a) were decapitated by the Jordan government
(b) killed themselves after accomplishing their duty
(c) were apprehended by his bodyguards
(d) were captured later in the US

해설
빈칸 앞의 but 뒤에 이어지는 문장이기에 앞서 언급된 임무에 성공했다는 긍정적인 내용과는 상반되는 내용이 나와야 한다. 뒤의 문장에서 격분한 후세인 왕이 이스라엘 요원들의 석방과 교환하여 해독제를 요구했다고 했으므로 요원들이 붙잡혔음을 알 수 있다. 그러므로 정답은 (c)이다. 석방을 언급한 것은 요르단 국왕이므로 (d)의 미국에서 잡혔다는 것은 정답이 될 수 없다.

해석
"이 책의 중간부를 읽는 것은 마치 전율 속으로 던져지는 것과 같다"라고 Washington Post지의 Lucy Sussex가 말했다. 1997년에 이스라엘의 정보기관인 모사드는 팔레스타인의 활동가인 Khalid Mishal의 암살을 시도했다. 그들의 방법은 기묘했는데 왜냐하면 그 계획은 가짜 카메라를 통해서 독물을 전달하는 것이었기 때문이다. 모사드 요원들은 Mishal을 요르단에서 독을 먹이는 데 성공하지만 그의 보디가드들에 의해서 붙잡힌다. 이 공격에 몹시 화가 난 후세인 왕은 이스라엘 요원들의 석방과 독극물에 대한 해독제의 교환을 요구하며 이스라엘, 미국 그리고 아랍 국가들 간의 싸움에 불을 붙인다. 중동을 날려버릴 정도로 위협을 했던 흥미를 끄는 실화인 이 음모는 훌륭하고 유익한 독서가 될 것이다.

어휘
intelligence service 정보기관
assassinate 암살하다
deliver 전달하다
via ~을 거쳐
poison 독, 독살하다
incense 성나게 하다
antidote 해독제
gripping 흥미를 끄는
informative 유익한
decapitate 참수하다
accomplish 성취하다, 이루다
apprehend 체포하다

정답 (c)

6 US president recently lifted the media ban on images of the coffins of American war dead arriving at Denver Air Force Base. Many suspect that the ban, in place since 1991, was imposed solely to hide the human cost of the war. The conventional wisdom is that rows of flag-draped coffins _____, especially if it is going badly. Yet US president has lifted the ban just as he is trying to drum backing from people support for an expansion of the Afghan war effort. Bad timing? Probably not. The American public's view appears to be based largely on a cost-benefit calculation. They tend to tolerate casualties if they believe going to war was the right decision and they will win. Although a majority of Americans hold the view that Afghanistan is a war worth fighting, most believe they aren't winning. That's why US president Obama should concentrate on devising a path to victory.

(a) sap support for any conflict
(b) raise patriotism among Americans
(c) make Americans mourn and grieve
(d) increase support for the government

해설
빈칸을 포함하는 문장과 그 뒤의 문장은 역접의 접속사 Yet으로 연결되고 있으므로, 이 두 내용은 서로 상반되어야 한다는 것을 알 수 있다. Yet 이하의 내용은 미 대통령이 지지를 모으려고 하는 시기에 전사자들의 관을 대중에게 보여주지 말라던 금지령을 해지했다는 것이고, 이것이 시기가 좋지 않은 것인가라는 질문을 던지고 있다. 이는, 곧, 지지를 모으려고 한다면 금지령을 해지하지 않는 것이 낫다는 뜻이므로, 전사자들의 관이 '전투에 대한 지지도를 약화시킨다'라는 (a)가 빈칸의 정답으로 와야 한다.

해석
미국 대통령은 최근에 덴버 공군 기지에 도착하는 미국 전사자들의 관 사진들에 대해 매스컴에 내린 금지조항을 해지했다. 많은 사람들은 1991년도에 내려진 이 금지령이 오로지 전쟁에 의한 인명의 희생을 감추기 위해 내려진 것이라고 의심해왔다. 기존의 생각은 깃발이 드리워진 관들이 줄 이어 있는 것은 그것이 어떠한 전투일지라도 그에 대한 지지도를 약화시킨다는 것이고, 전투가 좋지 못한 방향으로 흐를 땐 더욱 그렇다. 그럼에도, 미국 대통령은 아프가니스탄의 전쟁 노력의 확장과 관련한 지지를 모으기 위한 노력을 하는 와중에 이 금지령을 해지한 것이다. 타이밍이 좋지 않다고? 아마도 그렇지는 않을 것이다. 미국 대중의 관점은 크게 비용대비 이득에 대한 계산을 기반으로 하는 것으로 보인다. 그들은 전쟁을 하는 것이 옳은 결정이고 그들이 이길 수 있다면 사상자들을 묵인하는 경향이 있다. 대다수의 미국인들은 아프가니스탄은 싸울만한 가치가 있는 전쟁이라는 견해를 가지고 있지만, 대부분은 그들이 승리하고 있지 않다고 생각하고 있다. 그것이 바로 미국 대통령인 오바마가 전쟁을 승리로 이끄는 방법을 궁리하는 데 집중해야 하는 이유이다.

어휘
lift 해제하다
ban 금지령
coffin 관
impose (의무, 법령 따위를) 부과하다
row 소동, 싸움
flag-draped 국기가 드리워진
sap 약화시키다
conflict 투쟁, 전투, 충돌
drum up ~을 모으다
cost-benefit 비용 대비 효과
tend to ~하는 경향이 있다
tolerate 묵인하다
mourn 슬퍼하다, 한탄하다

정답 (a)

7 The American with a generous girth and loud check shirt nabbed me outside the National Gallery of Victoria. He wanted advice. He had seen the gallery's collection of Australian landscapes and was stunned by Australian artist Fred Williams' bold canvases. "I will never forget those images of that vast burning ochre desert and the curve of that endless horizon dotted with stunted scrub," he enthused with a rolling Texan drawl. This man needed to find a travel agent, and soon. He was one of the typical overseas travellers who are inspired to tour Australia after seeing extraordinary photographs, paintings and films that _____.

(a) portrait the journey of Australians
(b) display urban Australian landscapes
(c) showcase the scenery
(d) inspire creative images

해설
에세이 형태의 글이다. 한 미국 방문객이 호주의 멋진 풍경에 대해 자신에게 감탄을 쏟아내었던 내용을 말하고 있다. 이 미국인이 감탄한 것은 사막과 덤불들을 포함한 호주의 시골적 풍경이었다는 것을 기억하자. 그러므로 이처럼 여행객들이 호주를 여행하고 싶게끔 하는 사진, 그림, 영화들은 (호주의) 풍경을 소개하는 것이라는 (c)가 빈칸의 정답이 된다.

해석
헐렁한 허리띠와 요란한 셔츠를 입은 미국인이 Victoria 주 국립미술관 밖에서 나를 붙잡았다. 그는 조언을 구하고 있었다. 그는 호주 경치의 미술관 작품들을 보았고, 호주 예술가인 Fred Williams의 거친 그림들을 보고 충격을 받았던 것이다. "전 그 광대하게 불타는 황토색 사막의 이미지들과 왜소한 덤불들로 점점이 흩어져 있던 끝없는 수평선의 곡선을 결코 잊을 수가 없을 겁니다." 그는 굴러가는 듯한 텍사스 사람의 느린 말투로 열변을 쏟아냈다. 이 남자는 여행사 직원을 찾을 필요가 있다, 그것도 급하게 말이다. 그는 경관을 보여주는 비범한 사진들, 그림들, 그리고 영화를 본 후 호주를 방문하기로 영감을 받는 전형적인 해외 여행객 중 하나였던 것이다.

어휘
girth 끈, 허리띠
loud (색깔, 의복이) 화려한, 야한
nab 붙잡다, 거머쥐다
ocher 황토색의
drawl 느린 말투
portrait 그리다, 묘사하다
showcase 전시하다, 두드러지게 나타내다
urban 현대의, 도시의
creative 창조적인

정답 (c)

8 Soul, groove and disco music have _____ _____ over the past few years. The hits that seeped into the consciousness of the music-loving public around the world have been given new life by a myriad of popular performers from boy bands to solo artists. That said though, it's hard to find a female performer in the current spectrum who embodies that soul energy quite like Lisa Hunt. This vibrant, enigmatic, diva has one of the biggest voices in the business, and the energy on-stage to match, resulting in an unforgettable live show. She skips through a variety of genres in her repertoire, turning her incredible vocals to not only soul, but also some R&B, pop and disco favorites.

(a) lost their popularity among people
(b) become popular for the first time
(c) witnessed a massive resurgence
(d) made many artists break through into the mainstream

해설
빈칸 뒤의 문장에서 '전 세계 사람들의 의식 속으로 스며들었던 히트곡들이 수많은 인기가수들에 의해서 새로운 삶을 얻었다'라는 문장이 문제 해결의 핵심이다. 즉, 과거의 음악이라고 할 수 있는 소울, 그루브, 디스코 음악들이 지난 몇 년간 엄청난 재유행을 했다는 (c)가 정답이 된다. 지난 몇 년간 많은 인기 가수들이 언급된 장르들의 노래를 다시 부른 것이지 이 장르들이 이 가수들을 주류에 편입시킨 것은 아니므로 (d)는 오답이다.

해석
소울, 그루브, 그리고 디스코 음악들은 지난 몇 년간 엄청난 재유행을 목격했다. 전 세계 음악을 사랑하는 대중들의 의식 속으로 스며들었던 히트곡들은 남성아이돌 그룹에서부터 솔로 가수들까지 인기 있는 수많은 가수들에 의해서 새 생명을 얻었다. 그럼에도 불구하고, 현재 범위에서는 Lisa Hunt 만큼이나 소울 음악의 에너지를 구체적으로 표현하는 여성가수를 찾는 것은 어렵다. 이 힘차고, 수수께끼 같은 디바는 음악업계에서 가장 파워풀한 목소리를 갖고 있고 무대 위에서의 에너지에 부합하는 목소리를 가지고 있어, 잊혀지지 않을 라이브 공연을 보여준다. 그녀는 그녀의 뛰어난 목소리로 소울뿐만이 아니라 R&B, 팝, 그리고 디스코 인기곡까지 다양한 장르들을 넘나들고 있다.

어휘
seep (into) 침투하다, 서서히 스며들다
spectrum 범위
consciousness 자각, 의식
embody 구체화하다, 구체적으로 표현하다
diva 탁월한 여가수
repertoire 연주곡목
witness 목격하다
resurgence 재유행
mainstream 주류

정답 (c)

9 Hindu ethics _____ the castes system in which fatalism and narrow role expectations are key elements. For instance, if a person is born into the warrior caste, that person is bound to kill enemy soldiers when it's necessary to defend their community. On the other hand, waging war in the sense of indiscriminate killing has been prohibited consistently for a long time. The Hindu warriors are not supposed to kill the weak, including the wounded, deserters or non-combatants out of a sense of fairness and chivalry. Considering what is expected of them, it was thought to be unprofessional to attack non-soldiers.

(a) have contradicted the basic theory of
(b) have been strongly influenced by
(c) have been basically replaced by
(d) have criticized the very essence of

해설
단락의 첫 문장이 주제문으로 빈칸에 들어갈 말은 (b)이다. 힌두교는 카스트 제도에 의해 강하게 영향 받았다고 해야 한다. 빈칸 뒤에서는 자신이 태어나면서 그렇게 살아야 한다고 믿고 받아들이는 숙명론의 영향에 의해, 운명을 받아들인다는 전체적인 내용과 그 예를 들고 있으므로 (b)가 정답이다.

해석
힌두교의 윤리는 카스트 제도에 의해 강하게 영향을 받아 왔는데, 이 윤리에 의하면 숙명론과 제한된 역할에 대한 기대가 핵심적인 요소가 된다. 예를 들어, 어떤 사람이 전사 카스트(계급)로 태어난다면, 그 사람은 적의 군사를 죽이는 숙명을 타고 났으며 필요하다면 자신들의 지역을 방어하는 임무를 타고 났다. 다른 한편으로는 무차별적인 살상을 의미하는 전쟁을 일으키는 것은 오랜 시간동안 일관적으로 금지되어 왔다. 힌두교의 전사들은 약자들, 부상자, 탈영병 혹은 전사가 아닌 자들을, 공정함과 기사도 정신이라는 점에서 죽일 수 없다. 그들에게 기대하는 것을 고려해볼 때, 전사가 아닌 자를 공격하는 것은 프로가 아닌 것으로 생각되어졌다.

어휘
fatalism 숙명론
caste (인도의) 카스트 제도
indiscriminate 무차별의
inhibit 억제하다
chivalry 기사도
deserter 탈영병
replace 대신하다

정답 (b)

---

10 Japan is in the midst of the biggest drugs-in-sport scandal the country has ever seen. But forget sprinters on steroids or blood-doping cyclists. This is far more serious: sumo wrestlers smoking pot. In the past six months, four wrestlers have been kicked out of the ancient sport for smoking marijuana. The revelations are big news because many Japanese believe that to stain the purity of sumo is to tarnish the heart of Japan itself. The Japan Sumo Association acted quickly, dismissing the wrestlers and stepping up its testing regime to head off the scandal. But many, including sports minister Ryu Shinoya, are calling for _____ to stem this shameful behavior.

(a) a ban on smoking pot
(b) more severe punishment
(c) eviction of the involved players
(d) abolition of the sport

해설
일본에서 벌어진 스모선수들의 마리화나 사건으로 관련자들이 쫓겨나고, 사건의 재발을 막기 위한 관계자들의 노력을 내용에 담고 있다. 빈칸에 들어갈 내용은 많은 사람이 이 수치스러운 행동을 저지하기 위해 요구하고 있는 추가적인 내용을 담고 있어야 한다. 이미 앞에서 레슬러들이 쫓겨나고 테스트 절차의 강화가 언급되었음에도 좀 더 가혹한 처벌이 필요하다는 (b)가 정답이다. (d)의 이 사건을 뿌리 뽑기 위해 스모를 폐지하자는 것은 내용의 흐름을 보아 지나친 비약이며, 선수들이 마약을 피는 것은 이미 금지사항이므로 (a) 역시 오답이다.

해석
일본은 지금까지 목격한 것 중 가장 큰 스포츠 마약 스캔들의 한 가운데에 있다. 하지만 스테로이드를 맞은 육상선수라든지 혈액도핑에 걸린 사이클 선수들은 잊어버려라. 이것은 훨씬 더 심각한 것인데 바로 네 명의 스모레슬링 선수가 마약을 핀 사건이다. 지난 6개월 간, 네 명의 레슬러가 마약을 피운 이유로 이 고대의 운동에서부터 추방당했다. 이러한 내용의 폭로가 큰 뉴스인 것은 많은 일본인들이 스모의 순수성을 더럽히는 것은 곧 일본의 심장을 더럽히는 것과 같다고 믿고 있기 때문이다. 일본 스모 협회는 이 레슬러들을 면직시키고 이 스캔들을 저지하기 위해서 자체 테스팅 방식을 강화시키는 등 재빠르게 행동했다. 하지만, 스포츠장관인 Ryu Shinoya를 포함한 많은 사람들은 이러한 수치스러운 행동을 저지하기 위해서 좀 더 가혹한 처벌을 요청하고 있는 중이다.

어휘
in the midst of ~의 한 가운데에
drug 마약
blood doping 혈액 도핑
smoke pot 마약을 피다
kick out of ~에서 쫓아내다
revelation 폭로, 누설
stain 더럽히다
tarnish 더럽히다, 손상시키다
head off 뿌리 뽑다
stem 저지하다

정답 (b)

11 Female suicide bombers are becoming more and more common in Iraq. The occurrence of girls serving as human bombs has more than tripled since 2007. In the past 18 months, 27 female suicide bombers have been reported in the province of Diyala. The increase has been attributed to improved security in Iraq over the past six months, which has made it more difficult for male suicide bombers to get past checkpoints. Men are _____, even at security checks in Iraq, so many conceal explosives beneath their abayas, black head-to-toe robes worn by Islamic women. Girls are often recruited from poor or unstable families who are told their only hope of salvation is to give up their daughters. Some reports suggest al-Qaeda have even established a group called Young people of Paradise, which recruits teens to train for suicide assignments.

(a) not allowed to touch women
(b) unwilling to do their jobs
(c) unable to work as security guards
(d) not conducting thorough inspections

12 Social skills are an essential part of our dog's etiquette. When these skills are not taught and put to practice, we often have bad experiences with our dogs in public. Whether it be with other dogs, people, cats or the vet clinic, the best way to improve our dogs' social skills is to give them regular exposure to these experiences. That's why dog training classes are ideal for _____. Pupstars is offering you two new, unique ways to keep your dog socialized – through monthly social days and specific breed days. The social days are a once a month gathering for dogs and owners, filled with fun, games and interactions for dogs of all shapes and sizes. The specific breed days are an opportunity for you and your dog to bond with other owners and dogs of the same breed.

(a) teaching dogs how to behave
(b) effectively making dogs do tricks
(c) creating controlled situations for mingling
(d) training dogs to very high levels of obedience

해설

빈칸 앞의 문장을 통해서 검문소의 강화된 경비 때문에 남성 자살폭탄범들이 검문소를 통과하기가 어렵게 되었고, 빈칸 뒤에서는 그래서 여성들이 옷에 폭탄을 숨긴다는 내용이 전개되고 있다. 강화된 경비에도 여성들이 폭탄을 숨겨서 갈 수 있다는 것을 통해서 검문소에서조차 남자들이 여성을 만지지 못하게 되어 있다는 (a)가 정답임을 알 수 있다.

해석

여성 자살폭탄테러범들이 이라크에서 점점 더 공공연해지고 있다. 소녀들이 인간 폭탄 역할을 하는 경우가 2007년 이후로 세배 이상 증가했다. 과거 18개월 간, Diyala 지방서 27건에 달하는 여성 자살폭탄 건이 보고되었다. 이러한 증가는 지난 6개월간 이라크 내의 강화된 보안으로 남성 폭탄테러범들이 검문소를 통과하기 더 어렵게 되는데 그 원인이 있다고 할 수 있다. 이라크에서는 검문소에서조차 남성들이 여성을 만지는 것이 허락이 되지 않는다. 그로 인해 많은 이들이 폭발물들을 이슬람 여성들이 머리에서 발끝까지 걸치는 검은색 망토인 abays 아래에 숨긴다. 소녀들은 종종 딸을 바치는 것이 구원에 이르는 길이라는 말에 가난하고 안정적이지 못한 가정에서부터 모집된다. 몇몇 기사들은 알카에다가 "젊은이들의 파라다이스"라는 그룹을 만들었고 이는 자살임무를 수행하기 위해 10대들을 모으고 있다고 보고되고 있다.

어휘

suicide bomber 자살 폭탄범
occurrence 사건, 발생
triple 3배 증가하다
be attributed to ~에 기인하다, ~가 책임이 있다
checkpoint 검문소
conceal 숨기다
explosive 폭탄
recruit 모집하다, 보충하다
assignment 임무

정답 (a)

해설

빈칸이 들어간 문장은 앞에서 언급된 내용에 대한 이유(That's why ~)가 되는 문장이다. 빈칸 앞의 내용은 강아지들의 사회력을 키우기 위해서 지속적으로 공공장소에서 어울리는 것과 같은 경험들을 강아지들에게 노출시켜야 한다고 말하고 있다. 즉, 강아지 훈련 수업이 이상적인 이유는 '교제를 위한 통제된 상황을 만든다' 라는 (c)가 정답이 된다. 이는 뒤에서 언급되는 구체적인 예를 통해서도 알 수 있다. (a), (d)의 보기처럼 강아지를 얌전하게 있도록 가르치고, 복종의 수준을 높이는 것은 사회력, 즉 서로 교제하는 방법을 가르쳐 주는 것과는 다른 내용의 이야기다.

해석

사회성은 우리가 기르는 개들의 에티켓 중 중요한 부분이다. 이러한 습성이 가르쳐지지 않고 연습이 되지 않으면, 우리는 종종 공공장소에서 다른 개들과의 안 좋은 경험을 하게 된다. 그것이 다른 개들과든, 사람, 고양이 혹은 동물병원에서든 간에, 우리가 기르는 개들의 사회성을 개선할 최고의 방법은 그들을 정기적으로 이러한 경험들에 노출시켜 주는 것이다. 이것이 바로 강아지 훈련 교실들이 교제를 위한 통제된 상황을 만들기 위해서 이상적인 이유이다. Pupstars는 여러분의 개들의 사회성을 키워주기 위해 두 가지 새롭고 독특한 방법을 제안하고 있다. 월 1회의 "사교일"과 "특수혈통일"을 통해서 말이다. 사교일은 강아지들과 주인들이 한 달에 한 번 모이는 날로 재미와 게임 그리고 모든 종류와 크기의 강아지들이 교감을 나누는 날이다. "특수혈통일"은 여러분과 여러분의 강아지가 다른 주인들과 같은 혈통의 강아지들과 유대관계를 맺을 수 있는 기회이다

어휘

social skill 사회성
put to practice 실행에 옮기다
exposure 노출
controlled situation 통제된 상황
mingle 어울리다
socialize 사회화하다
breed 품종, 혈통
behave 얌전히 굴다
do tricks 묘기를 부리다
obedience 복종

정답

13 In 1939 scientists in the USA, England and Germany informed their governments that it _____ _____ to make an atomic explosion. In 1940, two American physicists published an account of the process, so there was no secret about the principles behind the bomb: the problem was to apply them. It was in Britain that an atomic bomb was first seen as a weapon which could win the war. In March 1940, two Nazi refugees, wrote a memo to show how an atom bomb could be constructed from uranium-235 and outlined the lethal effects from its explosion and the accompanying radiation. The British gave a high priority to nuclear research, as did the Americans when the USA entered the war in December 1941. By 1945, the USA had produced an atom bomb which used uranium, and one which used a man-made material, plutonium.

(a) was morally unacceptable
(b) was feasible now
(c) was out of the question
(d) was theoretically possible

해설
지문은 원자력 폭탄이 완성되기까지의 사건들을 연도 순서대로 설명해주고 있다. 빈칸이 포함된 문장은 원자력 폭탄의 설계 과정의 첫 번째 사건으로, 빈칸 뒤의 문장에서 언급되는 두 번째 사건이 원자폭탄 설계의 원리가 대중에 공개되었다는 내용인 것과 관련지었을 때, 그 이전의 단계는 (d)의 '이론적으로 가능하다'가 가장 적절하다.

해석
1939년에, 미국, 영국 그리고 독일의 과학자들은 그들의 정부에 원자력에 의한 폭발을 일으키는 것이 이론적으로 가능하다는 것을 알렸다. 1940년에, 두 명의 미국인 물리학자들은 그 과정에 대한 이야기를 출판하였고, 이로 인해 더 이상 원자폭탄 뒤의 원리에 대한 비밀은 없게 되었다. 하지만, 문제는 그것을 적용하는 것이었다. 1940년 3월에, 두 명의 나치 망명자들은 우라늄-235로부터 원자폭탄이 조립될 수 있는 방법을 보여주는 메모를 작성하였고, 폭발의 치명적인 효력과 그로 인해 수반되는 방사선의 개요를 작성하였다. 영국인들은 원자력 연구에 높은 우선권을 두었고, 미국 역시 1941년 12월에 전쟁에 참여하면서 그랬다. 1945년이 되어, 미국은 우라늄을 사용한 원자폭탄과 인공 물질인 플루토늄을 사용한 폭탄도 생산해냈다.

어휘
theoretically 이론적으로
atomic explosion 원자 폭발
apply 적용하다
refugee 망명자
outline 초안을 쓰다, 윤곽을 그리다
accompanying 수반하는, 동반하는
give priority to ~에 우선권을 주다
physicist 물리학자
feasible 실행할 수 있는
out of the question 말도 안 되는, 절대 불가능한

✓ 정답 (d)

---

14 The origins of morality lie in the disgust that makes us avoid rotting food, says the Times. This discovery explains why injustice is said to leave a bad taste in the mouth. Psychologists from the University of Toronto found that the feeling of being cheated evokes the same revulsion response as foul-tasting food and drink. The involuntary emotional reaction that keeps us away from sources of infection also prompts us to uphold moral standards and to shun those who don't. These findings suggest that disgust was important to the evolution of morality and that our sense of what is ethical is based not only on reasoning but powerful gut reactions as well. While morality has been seen as the pinnacle of human development, disgust is an ancient, rather primitive emotion which _____.

(a) aided evolutionary survival
(b) caused racial discrimination towards others
(c) promoted healthy diet
(d) prevented epidemics

해설
도덕성은 이성에 의한 판단뿐만 아니라, 썩은 음식을 피하게 하는 역겨움이란 본능적 반응에도 그 기원이 있다는 내용의 글이다. 본문의 중간에 'The involuntary emotional ~ those won don't.'에서 이러한 무의식적인 감정의 반응은 감염으로부터 우리를 보호해주고, 도덕적 규정을 유지하면서 그렇지 않은 사람들을 피할 수 있도록 해준다고 언급하고 있다. 이를 포괄적으로 생각해봤을 때, 역겨움이란 다소 원시적이지만 우리의 진화적 생존에 도움을 주는 감정이라고 보는 것이 적절하다. 정답은 (a)이다.

해석
도덕성의 유래는 우리가 썩어가는 음식을 피하도록 하는 역겨움에서 찾을 수 있다고 타임지는 말한다. 이러한 발견은 왜 부정행위가 입에 개운치 않은 맛을 남긴다고 말해지는지에 대한 설명을 해준다. 토론토 대학의 심리학자들은 속았을 때의 기분은 더러운 음식 또는 음료수에 대한 것과 같은 혐오 반응을 일으킨다는 것을 발견했다. 우리를 감염의 원천으로부터 멀리 떨어져 있게 해주는 무의식적인 감정의 반응은 우리가 도덕적인 기준을 떠받치도록 촉구하고, 그렇지 않은 사람들을 피하도록 해준다. 이러한 발견들은 역겨움이 도덕성의 진화에 있어서 중요했다는 것과 그리고 무엇이 윤리적인가에 대한 우리의 판단은 이성에 기초한 것만이 아니라 강력한 본능의 반응에 기초한 것이기도 하다는 것을 암시한다. 도덕성이 인간의 발달에 있어서의 정점으로 보여졌던 한편, 역겨움은 진화적 생존에 도움을 준 오래되고 다소 원시적인 감정이다.

어휘
morality 도덕성
disgust 역겨움
avoid 피하다
rot 썩다
evoke 불러일으키다
revulsion 극도의 불쾌감, 혐오감
prompt (행동을) 촉구하다, 유발하다
reasoning 추론, 이론
gut reaction 본능적 반응
evolutionary 진화적인
racial discrimination 인종차별
epidemic 전염병, 유행병

 정답 (a)

15 After more than a decade of prosperity, the wheels have fallen off the world economy with some likening the present downturn to the Great Depression 80 years ago. Interest rates were lowered to stimulate economic activity, and the government threw billions of dollars at the electorate to shore up the flatlining retail sector before Christmas. As the government again pushed forward a plan to splash tens of billions of dollars to keep the economy from going into recession, debate raged over whether the initial stimulus had, in fact, stimulated the economy. _____, questions should have been raised about the long-term benefits of the hand-outs. We should ask if it is good planning if the nation's tax revenue is spent in the shops on t-shirts, toys and chocolate cake, much of which would have found its way into sewers or landfill by New Year's Day?

(a) Indeed
(b) Therefore
(c) For example
(d) Instead

16 Women are now earning higher salaries, starting their own companies and influencing more buying decisions than ever before. _____ research has shown many women still don't feel confident when it comes to investing or protecting their income or assets. At Citibank we are committed to helping women learn more about growing and protecting their wealth as well as understanding the value of professional financial advice. Ask about our Pearls of Wisdom brochure series, covering investing, insurance, retirement and estate planning. There's also over 400 qualified Citibank financial Planners ready to give you the confidence to be better off. Whatever your age or circumstance, if you are a woman who wants more from life, see our financial planners. Make an appointment now at your local branch.

(a) In addition
(b) Consequently
(c) Yet
(d) Likewise

해설

세계 경제가 사상 유례가 없는 침체에 빠지게 되자, 정부는 수십억 달러를 경기부양을 위해 국민들에게 뿌렸고, 다시 또 수백억 달러를 뿌리려는 계획을 진행하고 있다는 내용을 이야기 하며, 이로 인해 과연 최초의 촉진 정책이 경제를 부흥시키는 데 효과가 있었느냐에 대한 논쟁이 붙고 있다고 말하고 있다. 하지만 빈칸 뒤의 내용은 뿌려진 돈이 경제를 부흥시켰냐는 논쟁이 아닌, 돈의 배포가 가져올 장기적인 효과에 대한 질문들이 나왔어야 했다며 다른 관점으로 이야기를 돌리고 있다. 그러므로 정답은 (d)의 instead(그 대신에, 그 보다도) 이다.

해석

십년 이상의 호황 이후에, 현재의 침체가 80년 전 대공황에 비유가 될 정도로 세계 경제의 바퀴들이 떨어져 나갔습니다. 이자율들은 경제활동을 촉진시키기 위해서 낮추어졌고, 정부는 크리스마스 전 죽어가는 소매 부분을 강화하기 위해서 유권자들에게 수십억 달러를 던졌습니다. 정부가 또다시 경제가 침체로 가는 것을 막기 위해 수백억 달러를 뿌리려는 계획을 진행하려고 하면서, 최초의 촉진정책이 실제로 경제를 활기 띠게 하였는가 그렇지 않은가에 대한 논쟁에 불이 붙었습니다. 그 보다도, 이렇게 돈을 나눠주는 것의 장기적 관점에서의 이득에 관한 질문이 나왔었어야 합니다. 국가의 세금 수익이 티셔츠, 장난감, 초콜릿 케이크, 그리고 늦어도 새해 전에 하수구나 쓰레기 매립지로 가게 될 다른 상품들에 사용되는 것이 좋은 계획인지 우리는 질문을 해야만 합니다.

어휘

prosperity 번영, 호황
liken to ~에 비유되다
electorate 유권자
shore up 강화하다
flatline 죽어가다
recession 경기 침체
long-term 장기간의
tax 세금
sewer 하수구
landfill 매립지

정답 (d)

해설

빈칸의 앞부분에서는 더 높은 연봉과 구매력을 가진 지금의 여성들에 대해서 언급하고 있고, 빈칸의 뒷부분에서는 아직 돈과 자산을 투자하고 보호하는 것에는 여성들이 자신 없어 한다는 조사내용을 언급하고 있다. 이 두 문장에서 언급된 오늘날 여성의 모습은 서로 상반되는 내용이므로 (c)의 Yet(그럼에도 불구하고)이 정답이 된다.

해석

여성들은 이제 그들의 사업을 시작하고 그 어느 때보다도 더 구매결정에 영향력을 미치며 더 높은 연봉을 벌고 있습니다. 그럼에도 불구하고, 어느 조사는 많은 여성들이 아직 투자를 한다거나 혹은 그들의 소득이나 자산을 보호하는 것에 대해서는 자신감이 없어한다는 것을 밝혀내었습니다. Citibank는 여성들이 그들의 부를 키우고 보호하는 것과 함께 전문적인 재정과 관련한 조언의 가치를 이해하도록 하는 데 전념하고 있습니다. 투자, 보험, 은퇴, 그리고 부동산계획을 포괄하는 저희의 '지혜의 진주목걸이' 책자 시리즈에 대해서 물어봐주세요. 또한 400여 명이 넘는 자격을 갖춘 Citibank의 재정 관리사들이 여러분에게 더 잘 살 수 있는 자신감을 드리기 위해 준비되어 있습니다. 당신의 나이와 상황이 무엇이든, 만약 당신이 삶으로부터 더 많은 것을 원하는 여성이시라면, 저희의 재정 관리사를 만나보십시오. 당신의 지역 지점에서 약속날짜를 잡으십시오.

어휘

influence ~에 영향을 미치다
buying decision 구매결정력
when it comes to ~에 관해서는
invest 투자하다
asset 자산
be committed to ~에 전념하다
retirement 은퇴
financial planner 자산 관리사
be better off 전보다 살림살이가 나아지다
branch 지점

정답 (c)

17 News has surfaced about the opening last December of an Italian restaurant in the North Korean capital. The Japanese-based newspaper Choson Sinbo, closely aligned with Pyoung-yang, reported that ingredients for pizza and pasta were flown in from Italy. The opening of the restaurant is the result of a long campaign by the North Korean leader Kim Jong-il to introduce Western food to the country, with delegations sent to Italy to learn the pizza craft, and Italian chefs brought to North Korea to train locals. The new restaurant caters for the country's elite while the mass of the population remains impoverished.

Q: What is the best title for the news article?
(a) The opening of a restaurant in Italy.
(b) The friendly relations between Italy and North Korea.
(c) The successful campaign to open a restaurant for the public.
(d) North Korea's first foreign eatery for the upper classes.

해설

북한에서 지도자 김정일의 오랜 기간 동안의 캠페인을 통해서 이탈리안 식당이 오픈을 했다는 내용의 뉴스이며, 마지막 부분에 이 식당이 오직 나라의 엘리트들만을 위해 운영될 것이라는 짧은 언급이 추가되어 있다. 기사의 제목으로 가장 적절한 것은 '북한의 첫 번째 상류층을 위한 외국식당'인 (d)가 정답이다.

해석

지난 12월에 북한의 수도에서 이탈리아 식당이 개업했다는 소식이 떠올랐다. 평양과 긴밀한 관계를 갖고 있는 일본에 근거를 둔 신문사인 Choson Shinbo는 피자와 파스타를 위한 재료들이 이탈리아에서 배송되었다고 보도했다. 이 식당의 개업은 북한 지도자인 김정일이 서양음식을 자국에 소개하고자 대표단을 이탈리아에 보내 피자 기술을 배우게 하고 이탈리아 주방장을 북한으로 불러 주민들을 훈련시키는 등의 오랜 시간의 캠페인의 결과이다. 이 새로운 식당은 북한 인구의 대부분이 가난에 찌들어 있는 동안 엘리트들을 위해 음식을 제공하게 된다.

어휘

surface 떠오르다
align 제휴하다
campaign (선거, 사회) 운동
delegation 대표단, 파견 위원단
craft 기능, 솜씨
be impoverished 가난에 찌들다
public 국민, 대중
upper class 상류층

정답 (d)

18 A study in the US has found that people who live in smoggy cities are up to 50% more likely to die from lung disease than people living in the fresher air of the country. Scientists studied 500,000 Americans for 18 years and found that ground-level ozone was a key factor in respiratory deaths. Previous research linked increases in ground-level ozone levels to heart attacks and severe asthma. It also indicated that long-term exposure to tiny particles of soot and dust found in smog is a risk factor for heart and lung disease. This is the first study to look at the long-term health impacts of ozone, which is formed through the chemical reaction between sunlight and the nitrogen oxides released by vehicle exhaust and industrial emissions.

Q: What is the main topic of the passage?
(a) The pros of living in the country.
(b) The impacts of ozone on heart-related diseases.
(c) The effects of surface ozone on human health.
(d) The mixture of chemicals that makes ozone.

해설

오존층이 폐암과 같은 호흡기 질환으로 인한 사망에 가장 주요 원인이라고 말하며, 그 외에도 심장발작, 천식 등의 질환도 오존과 관련이 있음을 말하며, 끝에서 이러한 오존의 구성요소에 대해서 살짝 언급해 주고 있다. 이 모든 것을 아우를 수 있는 것은 (c) '지상 오존이 인간의 건강에 미치는 결과'이다.

해석

미국에서의 한 연구조사는 스모그가 자욱한 도시에서 살아가는 사람들이 시골의 더욱 신선한 공기에서 살아가는 사람들보다 폐질환으로 사망할 가능성이 50% 가량 높다고 밝혔다. 과학자들은 500,000명의 미국인들을 18년 동안 연구했고, 호흡성 사망의 주요 원인이 지상의 오존이라는 것을 알아냈다. 이전 연구조사는 지상의 오존 수준을 심장발작과 극심한 천식과 연관지었었다. 또한 연기에서 발견되는 매연과 먼지의 작은 입자에 오랜 시간 동안 노출되는 것은 심장과 폐질환의 위험요소라는 것을 지적했다. 이는 일광과 차량의 배기가스 그리고 공업 배출물에 의해서 방출되는 질소산화물 간의 화학 작용에 의해서 형성이 되는 오존이 장기간 건강에 미치는 영향을 살펴본 최초의 연구조사이다.

어휘

smoggy 스모그가 자욱한
respiratory 호흡성의
nitrogen oxides 질소산화물

정답 (c)

19 Dear Tenant,

We value you as a tenant and every endeavor will be made by our property management staff to ensure that you are treated with respect and fairness. It is important that you understand the terms of the tenancy agreement. Please ask if you are unsure about any term or clause, and our Property Management staff will be happy to provide you with information on local services. We look forward to developing a friendly business relationship with you and if we can be of any further assistance, please contact our office.

Sincerely,

Q: What is the purpose of this letter?
(a) To arrange a meeting
(b) To welcome the leaseholder
(c) To warn the tenant of the lease
(d) To express gratitude

해설
부동산 관리회사에서 세입자에게 보내는 편지로, 자신들의 역할을 충실히 하겠다는 다짐과 이를 위해 성심성의껏 도움을 주겠다는 내용, 그리고 앞으로의 관계가 잘 발전되기를 기대한다는 내용을 담고 있다. 즉, 새로 들어온 세입자에게 보내는 환영의 편지임으로 정답은 (b)이다.

해석
세입자 분께,

저희는 귀하를 세입자로서 존중하며, 저희 부동산 관리 직원들에 의해서 당신이 존중과 공평함으로 대접받을 수 있도록 보장하기 위해 모든 노력을 할 것입니다. 귀하가 세입자 계약서의 약정들을 이해하는 것은 중요합니다. 만약 귀하가 약정이나 조항들 중에 확실치 않은 것이 있다면 물어 봐 주세요, 그리고 저희의 부동산 관리 직원들은 지역 서비스들과 관련한 정보들을 여러분에게 기꺼이 제공해 드리겠습니다. 저희는 귀하와 우호적인 사무관계를 발전시키기를 기대하고 있으며, 만약 저희가 좀 더 도움이 되어 드릴 수 있는 것이 있다면 저희 사무실로 연락주시기 바랍니다.

어휘
value 존중하다, 소중히 하다
tenant 차지인, 세입자
endeavor 노력
property 재산, 동산
be treated 대접받다
term 약정
clause 조항
local 지역의
warn 경고하다
lease 임대, 임차
gratitude 감사

정답 (b)

---

20 Teeth-whitening products and procedure are becoming increasingly popular, mainly due to the increase in society's value on whiter, brighter teeth. Smoking, coffee and red wine are common culprits of staining to the teeth and should be minimized if possible. However, often stains are just normal occurrences. There are many whitening products currently on the market, from the supermarket bought, less expensive options to in-chair dental procedures performed by a qualified dentist. Currently, and perhaps the most effective and popular is the take-home kits, which most dental professionals recommend as the best option in teeth whitening.

Q: What is the best title for the passage?
(a) The reasons why teeth get stained.
(b) The rising popularity of oral beauty products.
(c) The wise way to choose the best whitening product.
(d) The most widely used product for teeth whitening.

해설
지문은 치아 미백 제품의 인기가 증가함에 따라, 다양한 관련 상품들이 있다는 내용을 담고 있다. 끝에서, 그 중 가장 인기 있고 효과적인 상품이 무엇인지 짧게 언급해 주고 있다. 지문 전체의 대의는 (b)의 '구강미 제품들의 증가하고 있는 인기'가 정답이고, 본문에서 언급되지 않은 (c)를 제외한 나머지 보기들은 전체 대의에 대한 세부적인 사항이다.

해석
치아를 하얗게 해주는 물품들과 절차가 주로 하얗고 더 빛나는 치아에 대한 사회적 가치가 증가함으로 인해서 점점 더 인기 있어지고 있다. 담배, 커피, 적색 와인은 치아를 얼룩지게 하는 주요 원인으로 가능하면 이들의 섭취는 최소화 하여야 한다. 하지만, 종종 (치아의) 얼룩은 단지 정상적으로 발생하는 일이기도 하다. 슈퍼마켓 구매에서부터, 가격이 덜 저렴한 선택제품들, 그리고 의자에서 전문 치과의사에 의해 행해지는 치과 절차에 이르기까지 현재 시장에는 많은 미백 상품들이 있다. 현재, 그리고 아마도 가장 효과적이고 인기 있는 것은 대부분의 치과 전문의들이 미백을 위한 최고의 선택으로 추천하는 take-home kits(집으로 가져갈 수 있는 용구통)일 것이다.

어휘
teeth-whitening 치아 미백
procedure 절차, 과정
due to ~ 때문에
culprit 죄인, 피의자
minimize 최소화하다
qualified 면허가 있는, 검증된
effective 효과적인
recommend 추천하다

정답 (b)

21. An airport baggage handlers' strike delayed flights and left thousands of passengers fuming at London Airport yesterday. The baggage handlers walked off the job during peak hours in London yesterday after their union claimed British Airways was outsourcing baggage handling to a company that was paying workers less to do the job. At the domestic airport, there were delays of up to three hours on arriving and departing British Airways flights, and crowds at check-in counters and baggage carousels.

Q: What is the main idea of the passage?
(a) Flights were cancelled due to late arrival of passengers.
(b) The workout at airport hits passengers.
(c) People should know how to handle missing baggage.
(d) A greedy airline laid off thousands of employees.

해설
글의 대의를 파악하는 문제이다. 보통 주제는 글의 첫 문단에 나타나는 경우가 많다. 이 글은 '공항 수화물 관리인들의 파업으로 인해 승객이 불편을 입었다'라는 것이 핵심 내용이다. 그러므로 정답은 (b)이다.

해석
어제 런던 공항의 수화물 관리인들의 파업이 비행기들을 연착시키고 수천 명의 승객들을 노발대발하게 만들었습니다. 수화물 관리인들은 영국 항공사가 수화물 관리업무를 하는 것에 있어서 더 낮은 임금을 지불하는 한 회사에 하청을 주고 있다고 관리인 조합이 주장한 이후에 어제 런던의 가장 혼잡한 시간에 일터를 떠났습니다. 이 국내 공항에서, 영국 항공사 비행기들의 착륙과 출발이 3시간 가까이 지연되었고 체크인 카운터와 수화물 찾는 곳은 사람들로 붐비었습니다.

어휘
strike 파업
delay 연기하다, 늦추다
fume 노발대발하다
walk off 떠나가다
peak hour 가장 혼잡한 시간
outsource 하청하다
domestic 국내의
carousel (둥근 원형의) 수화물 찾는 컨베이어 벨트

정답 (b)

22. If you're not too bright, blame your old man. Researchers have found that children with older fathers seem to perform worse in intelligence tests and score lower in a variety of cognitive tests than those born to younger fathers. While there's a general trend for men to have children later in life, a team led by John McGrath of the California Brain Institute believes this needs rethinking. He says that the offspring of older fathers show subtle impairments on tests of neurocognitive ability during infancy and childhood. Other research has also shown links between advanced paternal age, men over 35, and an increased risk of neurodevelopmental disorders such as autism and dyslexia.

Q: What is the passage mainly about?
(a) The difference in fitness level between younger and older fathers.
(b) Teenagers' rude behavior towards their fathers.
(c) The effect of fathers' age on the intelligence of offspring.
(d) Children's brain damage risk due to fathers' low intelligence.

해설
똑똑하지 않다면 늙은 아버지를 원망하라는 첫 문장에서 이미 주제가 드러나 있다. 뒤에 이어지는 'Researchers have found~to younger fathers'가 이 글이 말하고자 하는 핵심내용이다. 그러므로 '아빠의 나이가 자식의 지능에 미치는 영향'이란 의미의 (c)가 정답이다.

해석
만약 당신이 너무 똑똑하지 않다면, 당신의 아버지에게 책임을 돌리세요. 연구원들은 나이가 많은 아버지를 둔 아이들이 젊은 아버지를 둔 아이들보다 지능검사에서 수행력이 떨어지고, 다양한 인지능력 검사에서 낮은 성적을 받는 것으로 보인다는 내용을 알아냈습니다. 남자들이 늦게 아이들을 가지려고 하는 일반적인 경향이 있다고는 하나, 캘리포니아 두뇌협회의 John McGrath가 이끄는 팀은 이런 경향을 다시 생각해 볼 필요가 있다고 믿고 있습니다. 그는 나이가 많은 아버지를 둔 자녀들은 유아기와 유년기 동안의 신경인지능력 테스트에서 미묘한 장애를 보인다고 말합니다. 다른 연구결과는 35세가 넘는 늙은 아버지의 나이와 아이들의 자폐증과 난독증과 같은 신경발달 장애의 증가된 위험 간에 고리를 보여주기도 했습니다.

어휘
perform 실행하다, 수행하다
intelligence 지능
cognitive 인식(의)
offspring 자녀, 자손
subtle 미묘한, 희미한
impairment 장애
infancy 유년기
disorder 장애, 질환
autism 자폐증
dyslexia 난독증

정답 (c)

23 Dengue fever is caused by a virus passed on by some species of mosquitoes. The virus itself is not usually present in North Queensland, but needs to be introduced by someone infected with dengue overseas. There are four types of dengue virus that causes dengue fever. These types are Dengue 1, 2, 3 and 4 and they all cause the same symptoms. The two main illnesses caused by the dengue virus are: dengue fever and dengue hemorrhagic fever. As there are four types of dengue virus, a person can contract dengue up to four times. The risk of dengue hemorrhagic fever increases if you contract more than one type of dengue. That is why it is important to know if you have dengue and which type. The type of dengue virus can only be confirmed by a blood test.

Q: Which of the following is correct according to the passage?
(a) There are 4 different types of dengue fever.
(b) Dengue hemorrhagic fever only occurs when catching the type 2 Dengue virus.
(c) Different dengue virus types make people suffer different symptoms.
(d) Dengue hemorrhagic fever can occur during primary dengue infection.

해설
11번째 줄 문장에서 뎅기 출혈열 위험이 한 개 이상의 뎅기 바이러스에 감염될 경우 증가한다고 설명하고 있다. 이는 단 한 개의 뎅기 바이러스에 감염이 되었을 때도 출혈열이 나타날 위험은 있다는 것으로 해석할 수 있다. 그러므로 정답은 (d)이다. 뎅기 바이러스가 4종류가 있는 것이지 뎅기열이 4종류가 있는 것이 아니므로 (a)는 오답이다.

해석
뎅기열은 몇몇 모기 종들에 의해서 전달되는 바이러스에 의해 발생한다. 본 바이러스 보통 North Queensland에는 존재하고 있지 않지만, 해외에서 뎅기에 감염된 누군가에 의해서 이입되어질 수 있다. 뎅기열의 원인이 되는 뎅기열 바이러스는 네 가지 유형이 있다. 이 종류들은 뎅기 1, 2, 3 그리고 4이다. 그리고 이들은 모두 같은 증상의 원인이 된다. 뎅기열 바이러스에 의해 원인이 되는 두 가지 주요 병은 뎅기열과 뎅기 출혈열이 있다. 네 가지 유형의 뎅기 바이러스가 있기 때문에, 한 사람은 총 네 번에 걸쳐서 뎅기에 접촉될 수 있다. 뎅기 출혈열의 위험은 만약 당신이 하나의 종류 이상의 뎅기에 걸리게 된다면 증가한다. 그것이 당신이 뎅기를 가지고 있는지 그리고 그것이 어떤 종류인지를 아는 것이 중요한 이유이다. 뎅기 바이러스의 유형은 혈액 테스트만을 통해서 확인될 수 있다.

어휘
Dengue fever 뎅기열병 hemorrhagic 출혈의
mosquito 모기 contract (병에) 걸리다
infect ~에 감염시키다 confirm 확인하다
symptom (병의) 증상 primary 최초의, 처음의

정답 (d)

---

24 Make it easier to put the pen through resolutions about getting in shape with a 10-week belly dancing course. New courses start on February 2 at The Belly Dance Academy in Franklin Street, including evening classes. Director and founder Nayima Hassan opened the doors 14 years ago when belly dancing was considered a fringe exercise. Today the successful academy welcomes hundreds of women and children weekly at more than 30 classes. Nayima says students can choose from traditional Egyptian belly dancing to modern versions to hybrid gypsy forms. Class sizes are kept to a minimum and the academy is now famous for offering students the most enjoyable hour of achieving fitness through this exotic form of recreation. Nayima says people can come in and watch classes this month prior to booking. The academy is also holding a free, Arabic Drum class for men and women.

Q: Which of the following is correct according to the advertisement?
(a) Belly dancing prevailed when Nayima Hassan first started the academy.
(b) People can book to learn how to belly dance for free this month.
(c) The academy offers belly dancing mixed with new influences.
(d) The classes are known to help people flex their muscles.

해설
지문 중간에서 학생들이 선택할 수 있는 벨리 댄싱의 여러 종류 중에 현대화된 혼성 버전이 언급되고 있다. 보기 중 학원은 새로운 영향력을 혼합한 벨리 댄싱을 제공하고 있다는 (c)가 정답이 된다. Nayima Hassan 씨가 학원을 열었을 때 벨리 댄싱은 주변 운동으로 여겨졌고, 이번 달 무료로 제공되는 것은 드럼 수업이며, 수업은 학생들이 건강을 가꾸도록 도와주는 것이지 힘자랑을 하게끔 하도록 알려진 것이 아니므로 (a), (b), (d) 모두 정답이 될 수 없다.

해석
10주 벨리 댄스 과정과 함께 건강을 가꾸겠다는 새해 결심을 이루는 것을 더 쉽게 만드세요. 새로운 코스들이 저녁 수업을 포함해서 프랭클린 거리에 있는 벨리 댄스 아카데미에서 2월 2일에 시작합니다. 책임자이자 설립자인 Nayima Hassan 씨는 벨리 댄싱이 여전히 주변 운동으로 여겨지던 14년 전에 학원 문을 열었습니다. 이제 성공적인 이 학원은 수백 명의 여성들과 아이들에게 매주 30개가 넘는 수업을 제공하고 있습니다. Nayima 씨는 학생들이 전통 이집트 벨리 댄싱에서부터 현대화된 버전의 집시 형태 혼성에 이르기까지 선택을 할 수 있다고 말합니다. 수업 인원은 최소한으로 유지되고 있고, 이제 학원은 이 이국적인 오락 활동을 통해서 건강을 이룰 수 있는 가장 즐거운 시간을 학생들에게 제공하는 것으로 유명해졌습니다. Nayima 씨는 예약에 앞서서 이번 달 수업을 참관하러 사람들이 와도 된다고 말합니다. 이 학원은 남성과 여성을 위한 무료 드럼 수업도 열고 있습니다.

어휘
resolution 결심, 결의 prior to ~이전에
in shape 건강한 booking 예약
founder 설립자 prevail 만연하다
fringe 가장자리, 주변 flex one's muscles (근육을 보이며) 힘을 과시하다
traditional 전통의

정답 (c)

25 The Semaphore Palace, a remarkable building, whose opening is in 1922, reputedly attracted one-third of the population of Adelaide. It combines an eastern fantasy with the beach-side romance of the art nouveau and art deco eras and harks back to the British fascination with the coast. It has variously been a dance hall, tea rooms, a bather's pavilion, and an evacuative backdrop to a day at the beach. And even better, you can get a drink and a meal there! We are fortunate in 2009 to still have the Palace with us after it fell into dreadful disrepair in the 1980s, culminating in a fire which almost destroyed the palace in 1994. Today, it is back to its former glory as one of our great architectural landmarks and continue to attract people, if for no other reason, that it is there, looks amazing and serves delicious food after 12.

Q: Which of the following is correct about the Semaphore Palace?
(a) About 13 percent of the population in Adelaide visited the Semaphore Palace.
(b) People can enjoy tasty breakfast at the Semaphore Palace.
(c) The location of the palace is far from the shore.
(d) The Semaphore Palace was not intact during the 1980s.

해설
Semaphore Palace의 역사와 그 역할에 대해서 설명하고 있는 지문이다. 본문 중에 건물이 1994년도 화재로 거의 파괴되는 정점에 이르기 전 1980년대에 지독한 파손상태에 빠졌다고 말하고 있으므로 80년도 기간 동안 건물이 완전치 못했다는 (d)가 정답이다. 본문에서 본 건물의 위치가 바다 근처이고 식사는 12시 이후부터 제공하고 있다고 했으므로 (b), (c)는 정답이 될 수 없다.

해석
Semaphore Palace는 1922년에 문을 연 놀라운 건물로 좋은 평판과 함께 Adelaide 인구의 1/3을 끌어들였다. 이곳은 동쪽의 환상을 아르누보와 아트데코 시대의 해변가 로맨스와 함께 결합시키고, 연안에 대한 영국인들의 매혹을 상기시켜준다. 이곳은 춤 강당, 다실, 입욕자들의 별관으로 다양하게 사용되었고, 해변에서 보내는 도피적 하루의 배경막 역할을 했다. 더 좋은 것은, 여러분들이 이곳에서 식사와 음료도 할 수 있다는 것이다. 이 건물이 1980년대에 지독한 파손상태에 빠져 1994년에 화재로 인해 거의 파괴되었던 후인 2009년에 우리가 아직도 이 Palace를 보유하고 있는 것은 매우 행운이라고 할 수 있다. 이제, 이 건물은 우리의 가장 훌륭한 건축적 경계표로서 과거의 영광을 되찾았고 특별한 이유가 없다면 그 위치에 있으면서 맛있는 점심과 저녁을 제공하며 계속해서 멋진 모습으로 사람들을 끌어들일 것이다.

어휘
remarkable 주목할 만한, 놀라운
reputedly 평판으로
attract 끌어들이다
hark back (to) ~을 상기하다
fascination 매혹, 매력
pavilion 큰 천막, 별관
backdrop 배경막
dreadful 지독한, 무시무시한
disrepair 파손, 황폐
culminate 정점에 이르다
landmark 경계표
intact 완전한

정답 (d)

---

26 Matching wine with food isn't a dark, mysterious art – it's actually quite straightforward. Put a steak with a reasonable glass of red wine and you've got it. But it's just as easy to get it wrong. Pair that same red wine with a piece of barbecued kingfish, and you might find it creating a strange metallic taste in your mouth. There are very good reasons why certain wines match certain foods and why they don't. By simply following a few easy color and taste rules you're guaranteed to get it right. The standard "red wine with red meat, white wine with white meat" rule is an old one but a good one. Generally, red meat has a lot of flavor and texture, which means it can cope with the more generous wine flavors in red wine as well as the texture that comes from the tannins. White meat, like white wine, is more delicately flavored and textured, making them more suited to each other

Q: Which of the following is correct according to the passage?
(a) Pairing the right wine with the right food is a matter of personal taste.
(b) It's a good combination to serve kingfish with red wine.
(c) It's an innovative idea to match meat with wine of the same color.
(d) Red meat needs more chewing than white meat does.

해설
와인의 색깔과 고기의 색깔을 똑같이 맞추는 것이 가장 좋은 조합이라는 내용을 다루고 있는 지문이다. 붉은 색 고기의 경우 맛과 씹히는 느낌이 많이 있고, 흰색 고기의 경우 은은하게 씹히는 느낌이 있다고 했으므로, '붉은 색 고기가 흰색 고기보다 더 많이 씹을 필요가 있다'고 한 (d)가 정답이다. 같은 색깔로 와인과 고기를 맞추는 것은 예전부터 있던 조합법이기에 혁신적이라는 (c)는 정답이 될 수 없다.

해석
와인을 음식과 매치시키는 것은 어둡고 불가사의한 예술이 아닙니다. 사실 꽤 간단한 일이죠. 적당한 양의 붉은 와인과 함께 스테이크를 놓으세요, 그러면 다 된 겁니다. 하지만 쉬운 만큼 잘못되기도 쉽습니다. 동일한 붉은 와인을 바비큐된 kingfish와 함께 드셔보세요. 그러면 여러분은 입 안에서 금속과 같은 이상한 맛이 만들어진다는 것을 발견하실 겁니다. 특정한 와인이 특정한 음식과 잘 어울리거나 그렇지 않게 되는 데에는 매우 합당한 이유들이 있습니다. 간단한 몇 가지의 색깔과 맛의 규칙을 따르신다면, 여러분은 이들을 제대로 조화시킬 수 있음을 보장받으실 수 있습니다. "붉은 색 고기에는 붉은 색 와인을, 흰색 고기에는 흰색 와인을"이란 기본 규칙은 오래된 것이지만 좋은 것이기도 합니다. 일반적으로, 붉은 색 고기는 더 진한 맛과 씹히는 느낌을 가지고 있어서, 이는 붉은 색 와인의 좀 더 일반적인 와인 맛과 함께 타닌산에서 오는 느낌에 대처할 수 있다는 것을 의미합니다. 흰색 고기는 흰색 와인과 같이 좀 더 부드러운 맛과 은은하게 씹히는 느낌을 가지고 있어 서로에게 좀 더 적합하도록 만들어 주지요.

어휘

straightforward 솔직한, 간단한
pair 짝짓다
kingfish 북아메리카 산의 큰 물고기
guarantee 보증하다
generally 일반적으로
texture 결, 씹히는 느낌
cope with ~을 극복(대처)하다
tannin 타닌산
elicately 섬세한, 부드러운

정답 (d)

27 Many parents are worried about their kids eating peanuts because of possible food allergy. Food allergies are on the rise – currently about one in 20 children has a food allergy in England, so it pays to be careful. When your child turns two, introduce a tiny amount of peanut butter – about an eighth of a teaspoon. The best time to do this is on a weekday morning, so if there's a reaction there'll be plenty of staff at your local general practitioner, surgery or hospital. A mild reaction is defined as swelling around the mouth, vomiting, body hives or a stomachache immediately after eating or in the following few hours. If this happens, stay with your child so you can monitor any changes. If symptoms include swelling of the tongue, wheezing, difficulty breathing or a hoarse voice, call an ambulance as it could be anaphylactic shock. If your child has eczema, or if his siblings have allergies, he's at increased risk of food allergy, so talk to your doctor about skin-prick tests instead of food test.

Q: Which of the following is correct according to the passage?
(a) More and more parents are suffering from food allergies.
(b) Parents should not try to identify their children's food allergies.
(c) Allergists can perform skin-prick tests to check for allergic responses.
(d) Throwing up is one of the symptoms from the anaphylactic shock.

해설

점점 더 많은 아이들이 음식 알레르기의 가능성이 있으므로, 부모들이 집에서 간단히 해 볼 수 있는 음식 테스트를 설명해주고 있다. 끝부분에서는 아이에게 습진이나 친척들 중에 알레르기가 있을 경우, 음식 테스트 대신에 의사에게 피부 단자검사를 요청하라고 권하고 있다. 그러므로 '알레르기 전문의는 알레르기 반응을 확인하기 위해 피부단자검사를 할 수 있다' 는 (c)가 정답이다.

해석

많은 부모님들이 음식 알레르기의 가능성 때문에 아이들이 땅콩을 먹는 것에 대해서 걱정을 합니다. 음식 알레르기는 늘고 있고, 영국에서는 현재 약 20명의 아이들 중 한 명이 음식 알레르기를 갖고 있습니다. 그러므로 조심해서 나쁜 건 없겠죠. 아이가 두 살이 될 때, 아주 작은 양의 땅콩버터를 먹여보세요. 약 찻숟가락의 1/8 정도만요. 이것을 해볼 최고의 시간은 주중 아침입니다. 그래서 만약 반응이 있을 경우, 지역의 일반의가 있는 작은 내과의원, 외과의원, 그리고 혹은 병원에 충분한 스태프가 있을 수 있도록 말이죠. 가벼운 반응으로는 먹고 난 후 바로 혹은 몇 시간이 지난 후에 입 주위가 부풀어 오른다거나 토를 한다거나, 몸에 두드러기가 난다거나, 복통과 같은 것들이 있습니다. 이러한 증상이 발생한다면, 변화를 감시할 수 있도록 아이와 함께 머물러 주세요. 만약 증상이 혀의 부풀어 오름, 천명증상, 호흡곤란, 혹은 쉰 목소리를 포함한다면, 과민성 쇼크일 수도 있으니 앰뷸런스를 부르세요. 만약 아이가 습진이 있거나 혹은 친척들 중에 알레르기가 있으면 아이는 음식 알레르기가 있을 가능성이 더 커지니, 의사에게 음식 테스트 대신에 피부단자검사에 관해서 말해보십시오.

어휘

general practitioner 일반의, 일반의가 있는 작은 내과의원
swell 부풀어 오르다
vomit 토하다
hives 두드러기
monitor 감시하다
wheeze 천명증상
anaphylactic shock 과민성 쇼크
skin-prick test 피부단자검사
eczema 습진
prick 찌르다, 쑤시다
throw up 토하다

정답 (c)

28. Pity the future cyborg insect. Not only will humans control their movements, but these movements may power the electronics that hijack their bodies. Engineers have been attempting to gain control of insect bodies for some time, hoping to use them as spies, and to harness their sense of smell to detect chemicals and explosives. To do this, researchers implant electrical stimulators that zap certain nerves of brain cells, triggering an impulse that makes the insect move in a desired direction. This process can be driven by a programmed chip or external remote control. So far, powering these "stimulator chips" has been the limiting factor. Now, scientists such as Keisuke Morishima from the Tokyo University have shown that piezoelectric fibers can harness the energy of insect movements and power "slave-driving chips". This method could also be applied to larger animals such as rats.

Q: What will the future cyborg insects be used for?
(a) They will be used for supplying electric power to appliances.
(b) They will be used for digging up intelligence.
(c) They will be used for destroying buildings.
(d) They will be used for controlling other larger animals.

해설
본문 초반에 나온 'Engineers have been attempting to gain control of insect bodies for some time, hoping to use them as spies'란 문장을 통해, 스파이로 사용될 것임을 알 수 있다. 그러므로 '정보를 캐내기 사용될 것이다' 라는 (b)가 정답이다.

해석
미래의 사이보그 벌레를 불쌍히 여기세요. 인간이 그들의 움직임을 통제할 뿐만 아니라, 이러한 움직임이 그들의 몸을 강탈한 전자부품에 동력을 전달해 줄지도 모릅니다. 기술자들은 상당 기간 동안 벌레들을 스파이로서 사용하고 화학제품이나 폭발물을 감지하기 위한 목적으로 그들의 후각 감각을 이용하기 위해 이들의 몸에 대한 통제를 얻기 위한 시도를 해왔습니다. 이를 위해서, 연구원들은 뇌세포의 특정 신경을 공격하여 벌레들이 요구되는 방향으로 움직이게끔 하는 추진력을 유발하는 전기 자극기를 이식했습니다. 이 과정은 프로그램화된 칩 혹은 외부의 원격 조종기에 의해서 가동될 수 있습니다. 지금까지는 이 자극기 칩들에 동력을 전달하는 부분에 있어서 제한요소가 있었습니다. 이제, 도쿄 대학의 Keisuke Morishima와 같은 과학자들은 압전 섬유를 사용하여 벌레가 움직일 때의 에너지를 이용하고 이 "노예를 부리는 칩들"에 동력을 가할 수 있음을 보여주었습니다. 이 방법은 쥐와 같이 더 큰 동물들에게도 적용이 될 수 있습니다.

어휘
control 통제하다
power ~에 동력을 공급하다
hijack 강탈하다
harness 이용하다
detect 탐지하다
explosive 폭약, 폭발성 물질
implant 심다, 이식하다
stimulator 자극기
zap 공격하다
impulse 추진(력), 충격
piezoelectric 압전
apply 적용하다
dig up 캐내다

정답 (b)

---

29. The Haymarket Square riot took place in Chicago in 1886. A small anarchist movement there was led by German Immigrants, who called for violent revolution. On 3 May, police clashed with strikers at the McCormick Harvester plant, killing three strikers and wounding several more. Union leaders called for a mass rally the next day in Haymarket Square to protest at police brutality. During the rally someone threw a bomb which killed one policeman and six other people and injured sixty-seven. Police opened fire, killing four more. Eight anarchists were charged with conspiracy to murder. There was no evidence of their involvement in the bomb-throwing but all were convicted and seven were sentenced to death. In 1893, the liberal governor of Illinois pardoned the three anarchists who were still in prison, as he said that a miscarriage of justice had occurred.

Q: Which of the following is correct according to the passage?
(a) Several policemen got killed during the clash on May 3rd.
(b) A total of seven people died in Haymarket Square.
(c) Proofs of who had thrown the bomb were not found.
(d) All of those who received death sentences were later released from the jail.

해설
본문 중에 'There was no evidence of ~ in the bomb-throwing' 을 통해서 폭탄을 던진 것에 대한 어떠한 증거도 없었다고 했으므로 '폭탄은 던진 것이 누구인가에 대한 증거가 발견되지 않았다' 는 (c)가 답이다.

해석
헤이마켓 광장의 폭동은 1886년 시카고에서 발생했다. 한 소규모의 무정부 시위가 그곳의 일부 독일 이민자들에 의해 발생되었는데 그들은 폭력을 수반한 혁명을 요구했다. 5월 3일에 경찰은 시위자들을 맥코믹 하베스트 공장에서 진압했으며 그로 인해 3명의 시위자들이 죽고 여러 명이 부상을 당했다. 노조 간부들은 다음 날 헤이마켓 광장에서 경찰의 잔인성에 대해 항의하고자 대규모 집회를 열 것을 촉구했다. 집회 기간 동안 누군가가 폭탄을 던져 한 명의 경찰과 6명의 다른 사람들이 죽고 67명이 부상당했다. 경찰은 발포를 했으며 이로 인해 4명이 더 죽게 되었다. 8명의 무정부주의자들은 살인 음모 혐의로 기소되었다. 그들이 폭탄을 던졌다는 어떠한 증거도 없었지만 이들 모두 기소되어 7명은 사형선고를 받았다. 1893년, 진보를 표방하는 일리노이 주지사는 감옥에 수감 중인 3명의 무정부주의자를 가석방시켰는데, 그때 그는 정의에 있어서 착오가 발생했다고 말했다.

어휘
riot 폭동
insurgent 반란군
anarchist 무정부주의자
brutality 잔인성
open fire 발포하다
conspiracy 음모
pardon 가석방하다, 용서하다
hostility 적의, 적대
be released 석방되다

정답 (c)

30 The New Zealand government of Prime Minister John Key sparked a national debate with its decision to reintroduce royal honors. These had been abolished by the Labor government of Helen Clarke in 2000, replacing it with a Companion of the Order of New Zealand. Eighty-five people who received that honor will now have the option of an upgrade. The New Zealand Herald polled 5,000 readers with 74% endorsing the change. New Zealanders are watching to see who among the non-royal honors recipients put their hands up for a sir or a dame. In the meantime, knighthoods still have a place, but many people think the title is a quaint, antiquated system that has no relevance in 21st century New Zealand.

Q: Which of the following is correct according to the passage?
(a) Royal honors were reintroduced in 2000.
(b) Other honors were awarded instead of Knighthoods
(c) Many people take Knighthoods for granted.
(d) 85 people can choose to be addressed "Sir" or "Dame"

해설
지문 중간에 85명이 과거 폐지되었던 왕실훈장 대신에 뉴질랜드 명예훈장을 받았고, 지문의 마지막에 이들(non-royal honors recipients)이 '경' 또는 '귀부인' 호칭을 신청할 수 있다고 언급하고 있다. 그러므로 '85명의 사람들이 경 또는 귀부인으로 불리길 선택할 수 있다'고 한 (d)가 정답이다.

해석
John Key 수상이 이끄는 뉴질랜드 정부의 왕실훈장을 재도입하기로 한 결정은 국가적 토론에 불을 붙였습니다. 이 훈장들은 2000년에 Helen Clarke이 이끄는 노동당 정부에 의해서 폐지되었고, 이를 뉴질랜드 명예훈장으로 대신하였습니다. 85명의 본 훈장을 받은 사람들은 이를 한 단계 높일 선택권을 가지게 될 것입니다. New Zealand Herald 지는 5,000명의 독자들을 상대로 여론조사를 했고 이중 74%가 이 변화를 찬성했습니다. 뉴질랜드 인들이 비 왕실훈장의 수령자들 중에 누가 "경(sir)" 또는 "귀부인(dame)"이란 호칭을 신청할지 지켜보고 있습니다. 한편, 기사작위는 여전히 남아있지만, 많은 사람들이 이 직함은 이상하고 21세기 뉴질랜드와는 관련성이 없는 너무 구식의 제도라고 생각하고 있습니다.

어휘
prime minister 국무총리, 수상
spark 발화시키다, 불러일으키다
royal honors 왕실훈장
abolish 폐지하다
poll 여론조사하다
endorse 승인하다, 찬성하다
antiquate 구식이 되게 하다, 낡게 하다
recipient 수령인, 수상자
in effect 실시되어, 효력이 있는

정답 (d)

---

31 Bedbugs which feed on the blood of human beings are putting the bite on tourists in the cheapest backpacker hostel beds, luxury hotel suites and even restaurant chairs. The hot and wet climate and growing number of international travellers in recent years has resulted in a steady infestation increase. Gilligans, the biggest backpacker hostel with a high turnover of international travellers through its 615 beds, plans to introduce a register for guests to fill in to help keep tabs on pests they may have inadvertently brought with them in shoes, baggage or other items. Keeping the bugs out completely is almost impossible but the hostel now has one of the lowest percentages of infestations in the local industry. Treatment involved stripping the room bare and heating them to more than 80 degrees celsius to kill the bugs.

Q: Which of the following can be inferred from the passage?
(a) Bedbugs suck on the blood of other insects.
(b) Humidity is one of the culprits of a growing infestation
(c) Travellers may bring pests with them on purpose.
(d) People should have the sun shine on beds to kill the bugs.

해설
따뜻하고 축축한 날씨, 그리고 증가하는 국제 관광객들에 의해서 숙박업소의 침대 위 빈대가 증가하고 있다는 내용이다. 축축한 날씨는 곧 습도를 의미하므로 '습도가 증가하는 벌레의 기생의 원인 중 하나이다'라는 (b)가 정답이다.

해석
사람의 피를 빨아먹고 사는 빈대들이 싸구려 배낭여행 호스텔 침대와 고급 호텔 방, 그리고 식당 의자에서조차 여행객들을 물고 있다. 뜨겁고 축축한 기후와 최근에 점점 더 증가하는 국제 관광객들의 수가 기생충들의 견고한 증가라는 결과를 낳았다. 615개의 침대들을 통해서 가장 높은 국제 관광객들의 이동률을 보유한 제일 큰 배낭여행 호스텔인 Gillgans는 방문객들이 무심코 그들의 신발, 가방 또는 다른 물품을 통해서 가지고 들어 올 해충들을 감시하기 위해서 방문객들이 작성해야 할 기록부를 도입할 계획이다. 벌레들을 완벽하게 안에 들이지 않는 것은 거의 불가능하지만, 이 호스텔은 이제 지역 산업에서 가장 낮은 퍼센테이지의 벌레 기생률을 가지고 있다. 치료방법은 방의 이불들을 완전히 벗긴 후, 그것들을 80도 이상의 온도로 가열하여 벌레들을 죽이는 방법이 포함되었다.

어휘
bedbug 빈대
steady 견고한, 끊임없는
infestation (기생충 따위의) 출몰, 만연
turnover 회전(율)
register 등록부, 기록부
keep tabs on ~에 주의하다, ~을 감시하다
pest 해충
suck 빨아들이다
culprit 죄인, 원인제공자
on purpose 고의로

정답 (b)

32 Children don't bring happiness. In fact, more often they seem to bring unhappiness. A study by the University of York in Britain concluded there was no difference between life satisfaction levels of parents and non-parents. Scholars even found some evidence that parents report statistically significant lower levels of happiness, life satisfaction, marital satisfaction and mental well-being compared with non parents. There's also evidence that the strains associated with parenthood continue after children become independent. So why do we have them in the first place? Does nature fit us with rose-colored glasses? One theory is that the belief that children bring happiness transmits itself much more successfully from generation to generation than the belief that children bring misery. Those who choose not to have children are unlikely to pass on the belief beyond their own generation.

Q: What can be inferred from the passage?
(a) In general, non-parents are more satisfied with their lives than parents.
(b) Parents feel emancipated when their children become self-reliant.
(c) Many believe that having children implies felicity in itself.
(d) The negativity against having children is widespread among people now.

해설

'아이들은 행복을 가져다준다'는 일반적인 믿음을 반박하는 내용의 글이다. 지문 후반부의 'One theory is that ~ than the belief that children bring misery'를 통해서 많은 사람들이 아이들이 그들의 삶에 행복을 가져다준다고 믿고 있다는 것을 추측할 수 있다. 그러므로 정답은 (c)이다. 삶에 대한 만족도는 결론적으로(일반적으로) 부모나 부모가 아닌 사람이나 차이가 없다고 했으므로 (a)는 정답이 될 수 없다.

해석

아이들은 행복을 가져다주지 않습니다. 실상 더 많은 경우, 아이들은 불행을 가져다 줍니다. 영국의 York 대학교의 연구조사는 부모와 부모가 아닌 사람들의 삶의 만족도 수준은 차이가 없다는 결론을 내렸습니다. 학자들은 몇몇 증거들은 부모인 사람들이 통계학적으로 더 낮은 수준의 행복을 보이고 있다는 증거를 찾아내기도 했습니다. 아이들이 독립한 후에 부모 역할과 연상되는 피로가 지속된다는 증거 또한 있습니다. 그렇다면 왜 우리들은 애초에 아이들을 갖게 되는 걸까요? 자연이 우리에게 장밋빛 안경을 씌우는 것일까요? 한 이론은 아이들이 행복을 가져준다는 믿음이 아이들은 불행을 가져다준다는 믿음보다 세대에서 세대를 걸쳐서 더 성공적으로 전달해지는데 있다고 합니다. 아이들을 가지지 않는 사람들이 그들의 믿음을 그들 자식세대에까지 전달할 가능성은 희박하니까요.

어휘

satisfaction 만족(감)
statistically 통계적으로
mental 정신의
strain 긴장, 피로
be associated with ~와 연상되다(관련되다)
parenthood 부모 역할
rose-colored 장밋빛의
transmit 후세에 전하다
generation 세대
in general 일반적으로
feel emancipated 해방감을 느끼다
felicity 큰 행복감, 경사

 정답 (c)

33 Jenny Kitson had several interviews and is in touch with several job agencies, but for now she has to be content with her part-time cafe work. The 18-year-old hoped to find work in tourism promotion or marketing after finishing high school last year, but found the job market a tough nut to crack. It is a situation becoming more and more common in Los Angeles, with the unemployment rate reaching 9.6 percent in February. That compares with a national average of 5.2 percent and is the highest figure since the early 1990s when the country was battling the effects of recession. "I guess I wanted to get my career going rather than study when I left school, but I've found with the tourism industry employers are really looking for people with experience, especially in the current market" Ms. Kitson said.

Q: What can be inferred from the article?
(a) Jenny Kitson is currently unemployed due to the tough job market.
(b) Jenny Kiston left school to get a job before graduation.
(c) Landing a job in Los Angeles is harder than other cities in the country.
(d) Current tourism industry are looking for people with university degrees.

해설

지문에서 Los Angeles의 실업률이 나라 전체 평균보다 높고, 1990년 이후 최고 수치라는 사실을 언급하고 있다. 이를 통해 Los Angeles에서 직업을 구하는 것이 나라의 다른 도시보다 더 어렵다는 (c)가 정답임을 알 수 있다. Jenny Kitson은 고등학교를 마치고 학교를 떠난 것이지 졸업을 하지 않은 것은 아니므로 (b)는 정답이 될 수 없다.

해석

Jenny Kitson 씨는 몇 개의 인터뷰를 보았고, 몇 군데 직업소개소와 연락을 취하고 있다. 하지만, 당분간 그녀는 아르바이트로 카페 일에 만족해야만 한다. 18살의 그녀는 작년에 고등학교를 졸업한 후에 관광사업 홍보 및 마케팅 분야에서 일자리를 찾기를 희망했지만, 고용시장이 만만치 않다는 것을 알았다. 이는 2월달 실업률이 9.6%에 달하고 있는 것과 함께, 점점 더 일반화되어가고 있는 Los Angeles에서의 상황이다. 이는 국가 평균인 5.2%와 비교가 되고, 나라가 경기후퇴의 영향과 싸우던 1990년대 초반 이후 가장 높은 수치이다. "전 고등학교를 졸업했을 때, 공부를 하기보다는 경력을 쌓기를 원했던 것 같아요. 하지만 관광산업에서 특히 요즘과 같은 시장상황에서는 고용주들이 정말 경험을 가진 사람들을 찾고 있는 것 같아요."라고 Kitson 씨는 말했다.

어휘

be in touch with ~와 접촉(교제)하고 있다
be content with ~에 만족하다
a tough nut to crack 어려운(만만치 않은) 문제
unemployment rate 실업률
average 평균
battle ~와 싸우다, 투쟁하다
tourism 관광사업
university degree 대학 졸업장

 정답 (c)

34 There is not always a cycle lane on the highway. Oncoming traffic doesn't slow down to pass safely and cyclists must stop and get off the road. Cycle lanes often have broken glass on them and cyclists have to use the road or get a puncture. Cyclists and motorists should be courteous to each other. There should be give way signs for motorists where there is danger to cyclists and cyclists should go single file in traffic. There should also be regular sweeping of cycle lanes to keep them in good condition. Treat cyclists as equal road users with mandatory driving courses for all motorists to be renewed by a short test every two years or a license will be withdrawn. There should also be traffic lights on intersections for cyclists.

Q: What can be inferred from the passage?
(a) Highway conditions are not safe for car drivers.
(b) Motorists are not cautious with cyclists on the road.
(c) There are too many cycle lanes on the road for cyclists.
(d) A driver's license is withdrawn if a person fails the short test.

35 When you hear the words "all you can eat", it conjures images of diners piling their plates high with food and coming back to the buffet table several times, all for the one fixed price. Now take that concept and apply it to digital music and you can understand what NewTech, the world's largest mobile manufacturer, has come up with in its new service. From March 20, customers can pay $ 979 for a 12-month subscription or $ 1109 for 18 months to receive the 5800-dollar-touchscreen handset and the right to legally download as much music as they want from more than four million tracks within the NewTech Music Store. This price will not include the monthly mobile plan costs. The only catch with this service is the downloaded music can be played only on the device or on one nominated PC. The PC can be changed once every three months during the subscription and two years after the subscription ends.

Q: What is the passage advertising?
(a) A fixed price buffet
(b) Multi-functional automobiles
(c) New concept cell phones
(d) Flat rate for mobile music downloads

해설
고속도로에서 자전거 운전자와 자동차 운전자가 서로를 존중하고, 자전거 운전자를 위한 여러 가지 조치들을 통해서 안전을 도모하자는 내용의 글이다. 첫 줄의 'Oncoming traffic ~ to pass safely'에서 자동차 운전자들이 자전거 운전자들에게 주의를 기울이지 않음을 알 수 있다. 그러므로 정답은 (b)이다. 고속도로 상태는 자동차 운전자가 아닌 자전거 운전자들에게 위험하다는 글이고, 시험을 통한 운전면허증의 박탈은 글이 제안하는 내용이지 현재 그렇게 시행되고 있는 것은 아니므로 (a)와 (d) 모두 정답이 될 수 없다.

해석
고속도로에 항상 자전거 길이 있는 것은 아닙니다. 다가오는 차들은 자전거 운전자 옆을 안전하게 지나기 위해서 속도를 줄이지 않고 있으므로, 자전거 운전자들은 멈춰서 도로에서 벗어나야만 합니다. 자전거 길은 종종 그 위에 깨진 유리들이 있어서, 자전거 운전자들이 도로를 이용하게 되면 자전거 바퀴에 펑크를 얻게 됩니다. 자전거 운전자들과 자동차 운전자들은 서로를 존중해야만 합니다. 자전거 운전자들에게 위험이나 자전거 운전자들이 교통 속에서 일렬로 가야 하는 곳에는 양보 표지판이 있어야 합니다. 또한, 자전거 도로들을 좋은 상태로 유지하기 위한 정기적인 청소작업이 있어야 합니다. 2년마다 한 번씩 짧은 시험에 의해서 도로 운전자들의 의무 운전 코스가 갱신되도록 하거나 그렇지 않다면 면허증이 박탈되도록 해, 자전거 운전자들을 동등한 도로 사용자들로서 대해야 합니다. 자전거 운전자들을 위해 교차로마다 신호등 또한 있어야만 합니다.

어휘
oncoming 접근하는, 다가오는
slow down 속도를 늦추다
puncture 구멍, 펑크
courteous 예의 바른, 정중한
give way signs 양보 표지판
single file 일렬
mandatory 의무적인, 강제적인
renew 갱신하다
withdraw 취소하다, 박탈하다

 정답 (b)

해설
지문이 광고하고 있는 상품이 무엇인지 알아내야 한다. 정해진 가격에 뭐든지 먹을 수 있는 뷔페와 비교하여, 정해진 가격에 듣고 싶은 음악을 마음껏 들을 수 있는 정액제요금제를 광고하고 있는 지문이다. 그러므로 정답은 (d)이다.

해석
"뭐든지 먹을 수 있다"란 말을 듣게 되면, 그것은 식사를 하는 사람들이 음식으로 그들의 접시를 높게 쌓고, 수차례에 걸쳐서 뷔페 테이블로 돌아가는 이미지를 불러일으킵니다. 모든 음식을 고정된 하나의 가격만으로 말이죠. 이제 이 개념을 가져와서 디지털 음악에 적용에 보세요. 그리고 여러분은 세계에서 가장 큰 휴대전화 제조사인 NewTech가 새로운 서비스와 함께 무엇을 떠올려냈는지 이해하실 수 있을 겁니다. 3월 20일부터, 고객들은 12개월의 계약기간 동안 979달러를 지불하거나 혹은 18개월간 1109달러를 지불하고, 5800달러 터치스크린 휴대폰과 NewTech 뮤직스토어에서 4백만 개가 넘는 음악들을 적법하게 원하시는 만큼 다운로드 받으실 수 있습니다. 이 가격은 다달의 휴대전화 계약 요금은 포함하고 있지 않습니다. 이 서비스를 통한 유일한 조건은 다운로드된 음악은 오직 휴대폰과 지정된 하나의 개인용 컴퓨터에서만 플레이가 가능하다는 것입니다. 지정된 개인용 컴퓨터는 신청기간 동안은 3개월마다 한 번씩, 계약 기간이 끝난 후에는 2년 뒤에 바꿀 수 있습니다.

어휘
conjure 불러내다, 생각해내다
pile 쌓아올리다
fixed price 고정된 가격
come up with ~을 생각해내다
subscription 가입
catch 조건
device 장치
nominate 지명하다
flat rate 정액제
mobile 휴대전화

 정답 (d)

36 A recent report which made national headlines claims there is no safe level of alcohol consumption. In short, we are probably all at higher risk of cancer if we drink. While only women were tested in the study, the results were believed to be so conclusive after tracking a million females and their drinking habits that it was assumed that male drinkers are probably increasing their risk as well. Most of us will carry on regardless, cheerfully imbibing under the banner of excuses which could feasibly range from, "a guy/girl's got to have some pleasure in life", to "you're going to die of something, so might as well go happy". There is credence in both, especially in the current climate of financial doom. However, for those who may feel a twinge of guilt at the possibility of sending themselves to an early grave, here are some ways to counter-balance the effects of a drink or two.

Q: What is the next paragraph likely to be about?
(a) A list of ways to refuse alcohol.
(b) The habits for long life.
(c) Effective methods to alleviate guilty conscience
(d) The ways to offset the negative consequences of alcohol consumption.

해설
술이 건강에 미치는 위험에 대해 언급하며, 이를 알면서도 계속해서 술을 마실 사람들에게 한두 잔의 술이 가져올 결과를 상쇄할 수 있는 방법이 여기 있다며 글을 마무리 짓고 있다. 그러므로 다음에 이어질 내용을 가장 적절한 것은 '술 섭취의 부정적 결과를 상쇄할 방법들'인 (d)가 정답이다. 술을 마셨을 때 취할 수 있는 방법이지 술 자체를 거부하는 방법이 아니므로 (a)는 정답이 될 수 없다.

해석
전국의 헤드라인을 장식한 최근의 보고서는 알코올 섭취에 있어서 안전한 수준은 없다고 주장하고 있습니다. 요약하자면, 만약 우리가 술을 마신다면 우리는 아마도 모두가 높은 암 발생의 위험에 있다고 할 수 있습니다. 본 연구에서 오직 여자들만이 테스트되었지만, 백만 명의 여성들과 그들의 음주 습관을 추적해 본 결과들은 너무나 확실해서 남성 음주자들에게 있어서도 아마 그들의 (암 발생) 위험 정도를 증가시키고 있다고 추측됩니다. 그럼에도 불구하고, "남성과 여성은 살면서 인생을 즐기기도 해야 한다"에서부터 "어차피 무언가에 의해 죽는 거 행복하게 죽자"에 이르는 변명의 구호 아래서 흥겹게 술을 계속 마실 겁니다. 현재의 어두운 경제의 기후 속에서 이 두 가지 구호는 일리가 있습니다. 하지만, 본인들을 일찍 무덤에 보내버릴 수 있다는 가능성에 죄책감을 느끼시는 분들을 위해, 여기 몇 가지 술 한잔 또는 두 잔의 효과를 상쇄시킬 수 있는 방법들을 알려드리겠습니다.

어휘
headline 방송뉴스의 주요 제목
consumption 소비
conclusive 결정적인, 확실한
assume 추정하다, 추측하다
carry on 계속하다
imbibe (술 등을) 마시다
might as well ~하는 편이 낫다, ~하는 것이나 같다
credence 신용, 믿음
doom 어두운 운명
twinge 쑤시는 듯한 아픔, 양심의 가책
counterbalance 균형을 맞추다
alleviate 완화하다
offset 상쇄하다

정답 (d)

37 Indigenous Australians use fresh water and salt water turtles as a food source throughout Australia. They are a great source of fresh meat for them. The turtles are not an endangered species so why should they not be harvested as they have been by Australia's indigenous people for thousands of years? Australia is not, and never will, be the exclusive domain of non-indigenous Australians and indigenous people are entitled to the practice of their cultures. Indigenous hunting is not the reason so many animals have become extinct in Australia in the last 221 years. Those extinctions have been caused through the destruction and the pollution of their habitats or all-out indiscriminate slaughter of that particular species by the European settlers.

Q: What can be inferred from the passage?
(a) There are not plenty of turtles in Australia anymore.
(b) Few animals have become extinct in the last hundreds years.
(c) Non-indigenous Australians have slaughtered turtles for their meat.
(d) Debates over killing turtles are taking place in Australia.

해설
호주 원주민들이 거북이를 음식공급원으로 죽이는 식문화와 관련해서 호주에 온 이주민(비원주민)들이 이를 금지할 권리는 없다고 주장하는 글이다. 이 글을 통해서, 현재 호주에 거북이를 죽이는 것과 관련한 논쟁이 벌어지고 있음을 추측해 볼 수 있다. 그러므로 정답은 (d)이다. 비원주민 호주인들이 학살한 것은 거북이가 아니라 다른 특정 동물들이라고 언급되어 있으므로 (c)는 정답이 될 수 없다.

해석
호주 원주민들은 호주 전역에 걸쳐서 민물과 바닷물 거북이를 음식공급원으로 사용한다. 이 거북이들은 그들에게 있어서 훌륭한 신선한 고기 공급원이다. 거북이들은 멸종위기의 종이 아니다. 그러므로 왜 수천 년 동안 호주 원주민들에 의해서 그래왔던 것처럼, 왜 거북이들이 수확이 되면 안 되는 건가? 호주는 현재도 그렇고 미래에도 절대로 비 원주민 호주인들의 독점적인 영토가 아니다. 그리고 원주민들은 그들의 문화를 실행할 권리가 있다. 원주민들의 사냥이 지난 221년간 호주에서 수많은 동물들이 멸종되게 한 이유가 아니다. 이 멸종들은 유럽에서 온 정착주민들에 의해 특정 종에 대한 전면적인 무차별적인 도살 혹은 그들의 서식지에 대한 파괴와 오염에 의해 원인이 되어 왔다.

어휘
indigenous 토착의
endangered species 멸종위기의 종
harvest 수확하다
exclusive 독점적인
domain 영토, 영역
be entitled to ~할 권리가 있다
slaughter 도살, 살인
become extinct 멸종하다
all-out 전면적인
indiscriminate 무차별적인
settler 이주민
take place (사건이) 일어나다, 생기다

정답 (d)

38 Research by the Henry Ford Hospital Sleep Disorders Center found that even people who felt well rested after an eight-hour sleep performed better and were more alert when they slept another two hours. (a) It's because human beings are designed to doze. (b) Before the invention of the light bulb we averaged ten hours of slumber a night. (c) But artists, writers and computer coders typically perform better by crashing near dawn. (d) Another reason to stay in bed is that our stress hormone, cortisol, normally peaks in the bloodstream around 7 am.

해설
사람이 충분한 수면을 취해야 하는 이유에 대해서 설명하고 있는 글이다. (a)에서는 인간들이 낮잠을 졸도록 설계되었고, (b)는 전구가 발견되기 전 인간은 평균 10시간이나 잤다고 말하고 있다. (d) 역시 우리가 늦잠을 자야 하는 이유를 건강상의 문제를 들어 설명해주고 있다. (c)는 새벽까지 밤을 새며 일하는 직업군의 사람들의 업무 능률과 관련한 이야기를 하고 있으므로 전체 맥락에 맞지 않는다.

해석
헨리 포드 병원 불면 센터의 연구는 8시간 동안의 수면을 통해 잘 쉬었다고 느끼는 사람들조차도 두 시간을 더 잤을 때, 더 일을 잘했고, 더 정신을 바짝 차리고 있었다는 것을 알아냈습니다. 그것은 인간들이 낮에는 꾸벅꾸벅 졸도록 신체가 설계되어 있기 때문입니다. 전등이 발명되기 전에, 우리는 평균 밤에 10시간의 잠을 잤습니다. 그래서 예술가, 작가 그리고 컴퓨터 코딩작업자들은 새벽에 다 되어서 수면을 취함으로써 전형적으로 더 일을 잘합니다. 잠을 자야 하는 또 다른 이유는 우리의 스트레스 호르몬인 cortisol이 보통 아침 7시에 혈류에서 최고점에 도달한다는 것입니다.

어휘
sleep disorder 수면 장애
rest 쉬다, 휴식하다
alert 정신을 바짝 차린
human being 인간
be designed to ~하도록 설계되어지다
doze 꾸벅꾸벅 졸다
light bulb 백열전구
average 평균하다
slumber 잠
crash 잠을 자다
peak 최고치에 이르다

정답 (c)

39 In many ways a recession is like a cyclone. (a) It's going to be uncomfortable and it's coming whether you like it or not. (b) But we've leant that one of the best ways to face cyclones is to be prepared. (c) This recession may be deeply felt and take a few years to recover but it will eventually pass. (d) Building up reserves of money, skills, network contacts and strong family and community ties make you feel stronger and protects against future loss.

해설
경기후퇴를 사이클론과 비교하여 쓴 글이다. (a)에서는 둘이 비교되는 이유를 언급해주고, (b)에서는 사이클론에 대한 대비 방법으로서의 준비의 중요성, 마지막으로 (d)에서는 이를 통해서 경기후퇴시에 준비해 두어야 할 다양한 요소들을 언급해 주고 있습니다. (c)는 현재의 경기후퇴를 언급하며 시간이 걸리더라도 결국에는 지나갈 것이라는 말로, 준비를 강조하는 전체 글의 맥락과 어울리지 않습니다. 그러므로 정답은 (c)이다.

해석
여러 가지 면에서, 경기후퇴는 사이클론과 비슷합니다. 그것은 불편하고 당신이 좋던 싫던 다가오기 때문이지요. 하지만 우리는 사이클론을 맞이하는 최선의 방법은 준비를 해 두는 것임을 배웠습니다. 이번 경기후퇴는 매우 깊숙이 느껴지고 있고, 회복하는 데 몇 년이 걸리겠지만 결국에는 지나갈 것입니다. 여분의 돈과 숙련도, 인맥연락 그리고 강력한 가족과 공동체간의 끈을 쌓아 놓는 것은 여러분을 강하게 느끼도록 해주고 미래의 손실에서부터 보호해 줄 것입니다.

어휘
recession 경기후퇴
cyclone 폭풍우 바람, 사이클론
face 맞이하다, 직면하다
prepare 준비하다
recover 회복하다
eventually 최종적으로
reserve 비축, 예비

정답 (c)

40 Just as the individual strings of a well-tuned violin each participate in the making of a symphony, your body is composed of many different players working in harmony to make you who you are. (a) From individual cells and organs to entire body, the crux of true health depends not just on how each piece works as a unit but how they perform as a cohesive whole. (b) It is important to let your inner conductor free to do its magic. (c) For example, the act of eating an apple requires a tremendous feat of organization and precision. (d) From the muscles of your jaw and salivary glands to the redirection of blood from limbs and head towards organs of digestion, it's a symphony of bodily functions.

해설
바이올린의 각각의 줄들이 화음을 만들어 내듯이 신체도 각각의 기관과 세포들이 단합되어 화음을 만들어 낸다는 요지의 글이다. (a)에서는 건강의 핵심은 개개 조직이 아닌, 전체의 단결되어 만들어내는 조화라고 얘기하고, (c)에서는 이에 대한 예를 언급하고, (d)에서는 (c)에서 언급한 예가 어떻게 수행되는지 구체적으로 말해주고 있다. 반면, (b)는 내부의 지휘자라는 독립된 개체에 대해서 언급하고 있으므로 전체 맥락과 어울리지 않는다.

해석
잘 조율된 바이올린의 개개의 줄들이 화음을 만드는 데 있어서 참여하듯이, 당신의 신체는 당신을 당신이란 사람으로 만들기 위해서 조화를 이루어 굴러가는 여러 가지 다른 역할자들에 의해서 구성됩니다. 개개의 세포들 그리고 신체기관들에서부터 전체 몸까지 진정한 건강의 핵심은 개개의 조각들이 어떻게 작동하는 가에 따른 것이 아니라 그들이 단결된 전체로서 어떻게 수행하느냐에 따라 달려 있습니다. 내부의 지휘자가 그 마법을 수행할 수 있도록 자유롭게 하는 것이 중요합니다. 예를 들어, 사과를 먹는 행동은 놀라울 정도의 조직력과 정확도의 위업을 필요로 합니다. 턱 근육과 침샘 그리고 팔다리와 머리에서부터 소화기관들로 향하는 피의 흐름에 이르기까지 이는 신체 기능의 화음으로 만들어집니다.

어휘
participate 참여하다
symphony 심포니, 화음
be composed of ~로 구성되어 있다
cell 세포
organ 기관
crux 핵심
cohesive 응집력이 있는, 단결된
feat 위업, 공
salivary gland 침샘
limb 수족, 손발
bodily 신체의

정답 (b)

Actual Test 2 Answers

1. (b)	2. (d)	3. (d)	4. (c)
5. (c)	6. (b)	7. (c)	8. (d)
9. (b)	10. (d)	11. (c)	12. (b)
13. (b)	14. (d)	15. (c)	16. (b)
17. (c)	18. (a)	19. (d)	20. (c)
21. (c)	22. (b)	23. (b)	24. (d)
25. (b)	26. (d)	27. (d)	28. (c)
29. (c)	30. (c)	31. (b)	32. (c)
33. (a)	34. (c)	35. (b)	36. (d)
37. (c)	38. (b)	39. (a)	40. (b)

1 A man reversed a four-wheel drive Ford truck into the entrance of a police station and set it on fire. The perpetrator fled on foot leaving a damage bill estimated at more than $500,000. The incident occurred in the suburb of Saint Thomas. More than ten officers were on duty at the station but, as it was the noon of night, the attacker _____ _____. He's believed to have ignited a fuel tank in the back of the vehicle before escaping. The reception area and neighbouring offices were extensively damaged, forcing the station to close temporarily.

(a) was caught red-handed
(b) could not be identified
(c) managed to get away with a simple warning
(d) surrendered himself to the police

해설
지문 초반에 이미 한 남자가 차로 경찰서를 들이받고 걸어서 도망갔다는 내용이 언급된 바 있다. 빈칸의 앞에서 사고가 일어났을 때, 10명의 근무 인원이 있었지만, 한밤중이었던 사실이 언급되고 있으므로, 공격자의 얼굴이 확인되지 않았다고 하는 것이 문맥상 적절하다. 그러므로 정답은 (b)이다.

해석
한 남자가 4륜구동 포드 트럭을 후진하여 경찰서 출입구를 들이받고 차에 불을 붙였다. 범죄자는 500,000달러가 넘게 예상되는 피해금액을 남겨둔 채 걸어서 현장을 도망쳤다. 본 사고는 Saint Thomas의 교외 부근에서 발생했다. 10명이 넘는 경찰관들이 해당 경찰서에 근무 중이었지만 한밤중이었기 때문에, 그의 신원은 밝혀지지 않았다. 그는 도망치기 전 차량의 뒤에 있는 연료 탱크를 점화시킨 걸로 여겨지고 있다. 응접실 부분과 인접해 있던 사무실들이 광범위 하게 피해를 입어 경찰서는 일시적으로 폐쇄되었다.

어휘
reverse 후진하다
set something on fire ~에 불을 지르다

perpetrator 범죄자
flee 달아나다
the noon of night 한밤중에
ignite ~에 불을 붙이다
extensively 넓게, 광범위하게
be caught red-handed 현행범

으로 체포되다
identify (신원을) 확인하다
surrender oneself 자수하다

정답 (b)

2. Like the story of Billy Elliot itself, this production, recently at Sydney's Capitol Theater, is a triumph of the creative spirit. With music by Sir Elton John and lyrics from the film's screenwriter, Lee Hall, this musical might even be better than the original movie. As a boy who discovers a passion for ballet, Billy struggles to pursue his goal in a mining town during a strike in England. The cast of child actors is _____ incredible. Especially, Dayton Tavares, who played Billy on the opening night is a superstar, bestowed with preternatural physical grace, vocal and acting abilities.

(a) far from
(b) not completely
(c) anything but
(d) nothing short of

해설
영화로도 개봉되었던 Billy Elliot의 뮤지컬 공연과 관련한 기사이다. 빈칸이 포함된 문장은 아이들 배우의 캐스팅과 관련해 언급된 내용이다. 뒤의 문장에서 특히, 주인공인 소년을 슈퍼스타로 표현하며 극찬하는 것으로 보아 '아주 훌륭하다'는 (d)가 정답이다.

해석
Billy Elliot의 이야기처럼, 시드니 국회의사당 극장에서 최근 개봉된 이 작품은 창조적인 정신의 승리이다. 엘튼 존 경에 의해서 작곡되고 영화의 시나리오 작가인 Lee Hall이 가사를 붙인 노래들과 함께 본 뮤지컬은 원작인 영화보다도 더 나을지 모르겠다. 발레에 대한 열정을 발견하는 한 소년인 Billy는 영국의 파업기간 중인 광산마을에서 그의 꿈을 좇기 위해 고군분투한다. 아이들 연기자들의 캐스팅은 아주 훌륭하다. 개봉 일에 빌리를 연기한 Dayton Tavares는 초자연적인 육체적 우아함과 음성 그리고 연기 능력을 부여받은 슈퍼스타이다.

어휘
production 작품
triumph 승리, 대성공
original 원작
pursue 추구하다
mining town 광산 마을
bestow 주다, 수여하다

far from ~와는 거리가 먼
anything but A A를 제외하고 아무거나
nothing short of 아주 ~ 한

정답 (d)

3. I was reading a newspaper whilst enjoying my favorite addiction at a coffee shop in the cozy, warm weather. In the paper, I learned of a new term called Butt Dialing (BD). This denotes a situation where one inadvertently dials a cell phone by the accidental pressing of the keyboard. Like when you sit down with your cell phone in your hip pocket while your cell phone unlocked, and some auto-dial button is pressed making a call. This kind of accidental phone-calls can happen not only via the engagement mechanism of your butt, but also by _____
_____.

(a) pressing a keyboard on purpose
(b) mistakes caused by mobile phone manufacturers
(c) receiving BDs from your close acquaintances
(d) the other parts of your body

해설
새로운 용어에 대한 설명을 하고 있다. BD(Butt Dialing)라는 용어를 예를 들어 설명하고 있다. 이 용어는 우연히 신체 일부를 통해 자동적으로 전화를 하게 되는 내용인데, 대표적으로 엉덩이로 다이얼을 누르는 것이지만 엉덩이뿐만 아니라 다른 신체부위를 통해서도 얼마든지 전화를 걸 수 있다. 따라서 (d)가 답이다.

해석
나는 커피숍에서 내가 가장 좋아하는 커피를 음미하면서 푸근한 날씨 속에 편안하게 신문을 읽고 있었다. 신문에서, 새로운 용어인 BD(Butt Dialing)를 알게 되었다. 이것은 한 상황을 묘사하는 표현인데 어떤 사람이 누군가의 핸드폰으로 우연하게 전화를 걸게 되는 것이다. 당신의 핸드폰이 잠기지 않은 상태에서 엉덩이 뒷주머니에 넣어 둔 핸드폰을 엉덩이로 누르는 것과 같은 상황을 예를 들 수 있다. 그래서 자동으로 일부 전화 버튼을 눌러 전화를 하게 되는 것이다. 이런 종류의 우연히 걸게 되는 전화는 당신의 엉덩이와 관련된 메커니즘을 통해 일어날 뿐만 아니라 당신 신체의 다른 부위를 통해서도 일어날 수 있다.

어휘
addiction 탐닉, 몰두
cozy 아늑한, 편안한
term 용어, 조건
butt 엉덩이
denote 표시하다, 나타내다, 의미하다

inadvertently 우연하게
make a call 전화를 걸다
unlock 잠그지 않다
on purpose 고의로
acquaintance 아는 사람(사이)

정답 (d)

4 It is good to see that taxi drivers continue to be booked for not wearing their seat-belts at Washington Airport. A crackdown on this illegal activity is well overdue and the Federal Police should be commended. Do taxi drivers believe they are above the law? Well, they'd better not. Also, as part of the crackdown on safety and regulations at the airport, police should be issuing on-the-spot fines for the myriad jaywalkers as it is illegal to do so. Many pedestrians are at real risk of injury and nothing is being done to assist them. Fining aberrant pedestrians would certainly raise significant revenue and think what a marvelous souvenir an infringement notice would be as a memento of their visit to Washington. Obviously, there is _____.

(a) a good remembrance item to buy in Washington
(b) a law that needs fine-tuning
(c) a need for common sense
(d) no one who abides by the law

5 Agave is best known as the main ingredient in the feisty Mexican spirit tequila, but the drought-resistant succulent is now being touted as the next big thing in biofuels. Central Americans have distilled the sap of the agave into spirits for centuries, but now an Australian company wants to _____ to make ethanol for energy. Sugar cane is already used in Australian ethanol production and 10% ethanol petrol is widely available. Proponents of agave say they are not trying to replace sugar as a source of ethanol but point out the plant is ideal for climates where cane cannot flourish. Australian company Ausagave has 10,000 agave plants in pots that are ready for a trial cultivation. They believe the crop could produce between 10,000 and 16,000 liters of ethanol per hectare every year.

(a) sell agave to gather enough money
(b) cultivate more sugar canes
(c) harness its high sugar content
(d) launch a responsible drinking campaign

해설
공항에서 안전벨트를 하지 않는 운전자들이 경찰에 적발되고 있는 것을 긍정적으로 평가하며, 이와 함께, 불법임에도 공항에서 아무렇지 않게 무단횡단을 하는 사람들도 단속을 해서 벌금을 물게 해야 한다고 얘기하고 있다. 이 두 가지 내용은 모두 불법임에도 사람들이 자행하는 행위로 (c)의 '상식에 대한 필요성'이 정답이 되어야 한다.

해석
워싱턴 공항에서 택시 운전기사들이 안전벨트를 매고 있지 않아 계속 경찰에 의해 적발되고 있는 것은 보기 좋다. 이러한 불법적 행위에 대한 단속은 다소 늦은 감이 있지만, 연방경찰은 (이로 인해서) 칭찬받아야 한다. 택시 운전사들은 그들이 법 위에 있다고 믿고 있는 건가? 글쎄, 그들은 그렇게 생각하지 않는 것이 좋을 것이다. 또한, 공항에서의 안전과 규제에 대한 단속의 일환으로, 경찰들은 수많은 무단횡단자들에 대해서 그것이 불법이기에 즉석에서 벌금을 물려야 한다. 많은 도보자들이 진정한 부상의 위험에 있지만 아무것도 그들을 돕기 위해서 진행되고 있지 않다. 상식을 벗어난 도보자들에게 벌금을 물리는 것은 확실히 중대한 수익을 올려줄 수도 있고, 무단횡단 통지서가 그들의 워싱턴 방문의 기억에 있어서 얼마나 훌륭한 기념품이 될지 생각해보라. 분명히, 상식에 대한 필요성이 있다.

어휘
book 경찰 기록에 올리다
crackdown 단속
illegal 불법의
overdue 기한이 지난, 늦은
commend 칭찬하다
had better ~하는 것이 낫다
issue 발급하다
fine 벌금, 벌금을 물리다
myriad 무수히 많은
jaywalker 무단횡단자
aberrant 정도(상식)을 벗어난
souvenir 기념품
infringement 법규위반
memento 기념물
fine-tune 조정하다
common sense 상식

✓ 정답 (c)

해설
중앙 아메리카인들은 agave의 수액을 술로 증류시켜 왔지만, 호주인들이 에너지를 위한 에탄올을 만들기 위해 무엇을 하려는지 알아내야 한다. 빈칸 뒤를 통해서, 사탕수수가 이미 에탄올을 만들기 위해 사용되어지고 있고, agave는 사탕수수가 나지 않는 곳에서는 에탄올을 만들기 위한 이상적인 식물이라고 얘기하는 것으로 보아, 호주 회사는 agave에 있는 당분함유량을 이용해 에탄올을 만들려고 한다는 (c)가 정답이다.

해석
Agave는 톡 쏘는 멕시코산 데킬라 술에 들어가는 주요 성분으로 가장 잘 알려져 있다. 하지만, 이 가뭄에 저항력이 있는 즙이 많은 식물은 차세대 바이오 연료에 있어서 중요한 원료로 선전되고 있다. 중앙 아메리카인들은 수세기 동안 agave의 수액을 술로 증류시켜 왔다. 하지만 이제 한 호주 회사가 에너지를 위한 에탄올을 만들기 위해서 이 식물의 높은 당분 함유량을 이용하기를 원하고 있다. 사탕수수는 이미 호주의 에탄올 생산에 사용되고 있고, 10%의 에탄올 석유가 널리 이용가능하다. agave의 지지자들은 그들이 (사탕수수의) 설탕을 에탄올의 공급원으로 대체하려고 하는 것이 아니라, 사탕수수가 번성할 수 없는 기후를 가진 곳에서 이 식물이 이상적일 수 있다는 점을 지적한다. 호주 회사인 Ausagave는 시험재배를 위해 준비가 된 화분에 담은 10,000개의 agave 식물을 갖고 있다. 그들은 수확물이 매년 매 헥타르 당 10,000에서 16,000리터의 에탄올을 생산할 수 있을 것이라 믿고 있다.

어휘
feisty 기운찬, 혈기 왕성한
spirit 알코올, 독한 술
succulent 다즙의, 즙이 많은
be touted ~라고 말해진다, ~라고 선전되어진다.
distill 증류하다
harness 이용하다
proponent 제안자, 지지자

✓ 정답 (c)

6 Most of the time locusts are innocent grasshoppers, but under the right conditions they transform into swarming creatures that are a byword for pestilence. Prof. Steve Simpson of the University of Georgia has previously demonstrated that this transformation occurs when locust populations become crowded, and has even tricked them into changing to the swarming state by tickling their back legs with paintbrushes. This discovery prompted interest in the neurochemical transmitter that triggers the change. Dr. Michael Anstey investigated the relationship between 13 chemicals and the shift to a swarming state, and only serotonin showed a relationship. The finding is not surprising since the serotonin is widespread through the animal kingdom, and _____ in crustaceans, rodents and humans.

(a) elucidates evolutionary changes
(b) prompts social behaviors
(c) causes fatal diseases
(d) helps population control

7 Few cities have a more picturesque setting than Santiago. Chile's capital sits on a coastal plain with the snow-capped Andes as a backdrop. Founded in 1541, this city of wide boulevards and leafy parks is re-claiming its reputation as a tourist destination now that the turbulent years have faded to a distant memory. Santiago is a fabulous walking city. It's a great place to stroll and soak up the buzzing Latino atmosphere, but if you _____, head for the neighborhoods where the crush of people falls away and you find hip, bohemian districts that lean towards art and culture. The Parque Metropolitano is a huge urban park where there's funicular that climbs to the summit of San Cristobal Hill. There, you can gaze in tranquility upon a sprawling cityscape that melts into the haze.

(a) want to have some time in a party-like atmosphere
(b) desire to make some local friends
(c) yearn for something quieter
(d) want to enjoy new fashion trends

해설
Serotonin이 메뚜기들이 몰려다니는 상태로 변화시키는 유일한 신경화학물질이고, 그것이 모든 동물계에서 널리 퍼져있다는 빈칸 앞의 내용들을 통해서, serotonin이 갑각류, 설치류, 그리고 인간의 사회적 행동을 유발한다는 (b)가 정답임을 알 수 있다. 메뚜기가 몰려다니는 행동을 (a)의 진화적 변화, (d)의 인구통제와 연관지어 생각할 수는 없다.

해설
칠레의 수도인 그림 같은 도시 Santiago에 대해 설명하는 글이다. 만약 빈칸의 것을 원한다면, 붐비는 사람들이 멀어져가는 세련된 보헤미안 지역으로 가라고 권하고 있다. 특히 마지막 'you can gaze in tranquility ~ haze'의 문장을 통해 빈칸은 (c) 의 '더 조용한 곳을 갈망한다면'이 문맥상 가장 적절함을 알 수 있다.

해석
대부분 경우, 메뚜기 떼는 죄 없는 메뚜기들일 뿐입니다. 하지만 적절한 조건에서 그들은 페스트란 별명의 몰려다니는 생물체로 변형됩니다. 조지아 대학교의 Steve Simpson 교수는 이 변형이 메뚜기 수가 꽉 차게 될 때 발생한다는 것을 이전에 증명해보였고, 메뚜기들의 뒷다리를 페인트 솔로 간질여서 그들을 떼를 짓는 상태로 변화하도록 속이기도 했습니다. 이러한 발견은 변화를 일으키는 신경화학 송신기에 대한 관심을 유발했습니다. Michael Anstey 박사는 13개의 화학물질들과 무리를 짓는 상태로의 전환 간의 관계를 조사했고, 세로토닌만이 관계가 있음을 밝혀냈습니다. 이러한 결과는 놀라울 것도 없는 것이 세로토닌은 동물계에서 널리 퍼져 있고, 갑각류, 설치류 그리고 인간의 사회적 행동들을 유발시킵니다.

해석
산티아고보다 더 그림 같은 환경을 가진 도시는 드뭅니다. 이 칠레의 수도는 눈이 봉우리에 덮인 안데스 산맥을 배경으로 연안의 대지에 놓여 있습니다. 1541년도에 세워진 넓은 가로수 길과 잎이 무성한 공원들을 가진 이 도시는 이제 격동의 세월이 저 먼 기억 속으로 희미해졌기에 여행객의 목적지로서의 명성을 되찾으려는 중입니다. 산티아고는 환상적인 산책의 도시입니다. 이곳은 산책을 하고 와글거리는 라틴아메리카의 분위기에 스며들 수 있는 멋진 장소입니다. 하지만, 만약 무언가 더 조용한 것을 갈망하신다면, 붐비는 사람들이 멀어지는 근교로 향하십시오. 그리고 당신은 예술과 문화에 기댄 세련된 보헤미안 지역을 발견하실 겁니다. Parque Metropolitano은 거대한 현대적 공원으로 San Cristobal 언덕의 정상으로 오르는 케이블카가 있습니다. 그곳에서 당신은 안개 속으로 녹아들어 가는 쭉 뻗은 도시풍경 위의 고요함을 응시할 수 있습니다.

어휘
locust 메뚜기
grasshopper 메뚜기
swarm 떼를 짓다, 떼를 지어 몰려다니다
byword 속담, 별명
pestilence 페스트
paintbrush 페인트 솔
widespread 널리 퍼진, 만연한
prompt 자극하다, 유발하다
elucidate 명료하게 밝히다
crustacean 갑각류의 동물

정답 (b)

어휘
picturesque 그림과 같은
coastal 연안의, 근해의
boulevard 가로수 길
leafy 잎이 우거진
turbulent 몹시 거친, 사나운
fade 희미해져가다
stroll 산책하다
buzzing 와글거리는
hip 세련된
tranquility 고요함, 평화로움
yearn 그리워하다, 동경하다

정답 (c)

8 Thailand's Health Ministry has warned people suffering from allergies and asthma to avoid eating fried insects. Fried insects are very popular in Bangkok and other cities in Thailand. A recent study by the ministry found that fried grasshoppers, silk worms and other six-legged delicacies often contain high levels of histamine which can provoke allergic reactions or asthma attacks. Insects have been on the menu in rural Thailand for many centuries but only in the past two decades have bulk bug wholesaling networks made the creatures _____. Health officials warn the bugs can pick up high levels of bacterial contamination during storage and excessive reuse of cooking oil to fry the insects can lead to toxic build up.

(a) become extinct in Thailand
(b) more vulnerable to diseases
(c) popular in other parts of the world
(d) widely available in urban areas

9 For most people, borrowing money is_____ _____. People will receive a multitude of offers for store cards, credit cards, and home loans from the day of your first permanent job to the day you retire. Although these can all offer benefits at various stages of your life, taking a haphazard approach to how you borrow money can mean your loans end up becoming more burden than benefit. It can drain your finances heavily and unnecessarily over time. If you have more than one credit card, store card or loan, you need to consider consolidating all the cards you have into fewer facilities, or even just one. This can save you some extra money because it's more efficient.

(a) not as easy as it seems
(b) just a fact of life
(c) a natural tradition for financing businesses
(d) something to avoid if possible

10 With vessel ownership also comes the responsibility for the safety of all your passengers and your equipment. Be sure you have the right vessel and the right safety equipment for what you plan to do, so that your boating will be safe and enjoyable. Once you have your ideal vessel and have made sure it meets all the requirements of the regulations, make yourself familiar with its layout and equipment before you go out on the water. Take short trips on calm waters first. Ask an experienced friend along for advice and learn how your vessel responds at different speeds and in different weather conditions. Remember, obtaining a Boat Operator's License means that you know the rules, but the knowledge and skills to operate a vessel in all types of conditions _____.

(a) are obtained from specialists and experts
(b) come from the boost of your self-esteem.
(c) are gained from taking complete responsibility
(d) come from a lifetime of experience.

해설
배 소유권을 얻고 운행을 시작하기 전 안전을 위해 필요한 사항들을 알려주고 있는 글이다. 면허증을 딴 후, 스스로 사전 점검을 하고, 경험이 많은 친구들을 통해서 조언을 구하고, 직접 운행을 하는 것 등을 언급하고 있다. 그러므로 자격증과 별도로 배를 운전하기 위한 지식과 숙련도는 '일생을 걸쳐서 얻는 경험에서 나온다'라는 (d)가 정답이다.

해석
배 소유권을 갖게 되면 당신의 승객들 그리고 당신의 장비들의 안전에 대한 책임도 함께 따라오게 됩니다. 당신이 계획하는 것들을 하기 위해서 정상적인 배와 정상적인 안전 장비들을 갖추고 있음을 확실히 하시고 당신의 뱃놀이가 안전하고 유쾌할 수 있도록 하십시오. 당신이 바라던 배를 일단 소유하게 되고, 그것이 모든 규제의 요구사항들을 충족시킴을 확실히 확인하면 해역으로 나가기 전에 배의 배치도와 장비들에 익숙해지도록 하십시오. 우선 물결이 잔잔한 곳으로 짧게 항해를 나가보십시오. 경험이 많은 친구에게 조언을 구하고 배가 다른 속도와 다른 날씨환경에서 어떻게 반응하는지에 대해서 배우십시오. 기억하십시오. 보트운전사 면허증을 따는 것은 당신이 규칙에 대해서 안다는 것을 의미하는 것뿐이지, 모든 종류의 상황에서 배를 작동할 수 있는 지식 그리고 숙련도는 오직 경험에서 나온다는 것을요.

어휘
vessel 배
ownership 소유권
responsibility 책임, 의무
make sure 확실히 하다
requirement 요구(사항)
regulation 규칙, 규정
layout 배치, 설계
experienced 경험이 많은
obtain 획득하다
boost 증가, 증진
self-esteem 자존심, 자부심

정답 (d)

---

11 Britain's chief medical officer recommended the British government set a minimum price of 50 penny per unit of alcohol to _____.
The proposal could double prices for some beverages, particularly the discounted beer and wine sold in supermarkets. It follows a recent decision by the Scottish government to introduce a minimum alcohol price. The cost to British taxpayers of alcohol abuse is thought to be more than 20 billion dollars annually, with alcohol-related hospital admissions of more than 200,000 a year. Opposition to the proposal comes from the alcohol industry and critics, including Prim Minister Gordon Brown, who argue it will punish moderate drinkers while doing little to deal with alcohol problems.

(a) levy additional tax
(b) penalize moderate drinkers
(c) curb excessive drinking
(d) reduce the rate of hospitalization

해설
빈칸의 내용은 영국의 수석 주치의가 정부에 알코올 단위 당 최소 가격을 설정하자고 제안한 이유가 들어가야 한다. 'The cost to British taxpayers ~ admissions of more than 200,000 a year'를 통해 음주남용으로 인해 벌어지는 사회적 폐해를 알 수 있다. 그러므로 본 제안의 이유는 '과도한 음주를 억제하다'라는 (c)가 정답이다. 병원 입원율의 감소는 과도한 음주를 억제하면 따라올 긍정적 결과 중 하나일 뿐이므로 (d)는 정답이 될 수 없다.

해석
영국의 수석 주치의는 영국 정부가 과도한 음주를 억제하기 위해서 알코올 매 단위마다 50페니로 최소 가격을 정하자고 제안했습니다. 이 제안은 특히 슈퍼마켓에서 팔리는 할인된 맥주와 와인을 포함하여 몇몇 음료들에게 있어서는 가격을 두 배나 오르게 할 수 있는 것입니다. 이는 스코틀랜드 정부가 최소 주류 가격을 도입하기로 한 최근 결정을 뒤따르는 것입니다. 술 남용으로 인해 영국 세납자들이 입는 손실비용은 술과 관련한 병원 입원 건이 연간 200,000건이 넘는 것과 함께 연간 200억 달러가 넘는 것으로 여겨지고 있습니다. 이 제안에 대한 반대 의견은 주류 업계 및 본 제안이 술과 관련한 문제는 거의 해결 못하는 반면 적당히 술을 마시는 사람들만 피해를 보게 될 것이라고 주장하는 영국 수상 고든 브라운을 포함한 비평가들로부터 나오고 있습니다.

어휘
chief medical officer 수석 주치의
recommend 제안하다
double 두 배로 하다
annually 해마다, 연간
admission 입원
moderate 절제하는, 온건한
deal with ~을 다루다, 처리하다
levy 징수하다
penalize 벌하다
curb 억제하다
hospitalization 입원

 **정답** (c)

12 What is the purpose of a budget surplus? I was led to believe that a surplus should be invested in the country in the form of infrastructure, health and education for the betterment of society and to keep the wheels of the economy rolling. If storm clouds appear on the horizon, as they have, the money then should be used to keep the recession wolves from the door or at least minimize the impact of a recession by spending initiatives that keep people employed and businesses solvent. It would appear, though, that certain sections of the community are _____ to the point that they would rather see the country collapse into a screaming heap than weather the storm.

(a) trying to invest as much money as possible
(b) extremely protective of the surplus
(c) inclined to take money out of the surplus
(d) spending a significant amount of money on education

해설
경기가 어려울 때는 예산의 흑자 분을 기간시설, 건강, 교육 등 사회의 발전을 위해 사용하고, 이를 통해 경제가 계속 굴러갈 수 있도록 해야 한다는 것이 글쓴이의 주장이다. 반면, 빈칸을 포함하고 있는 문장은 'It would appear, though, ~'에서 보듯 앞의 주장과는 상반되는 의견이 되어야 하므로 '극도로 흑자금액에 보호적인' 이라는 (b)가 정답이다.

해석
예산 흑자의 목표는 무엇일까요? 저는 흑자는 기간 시설, 사회의 개선을 위해 건강과 교육의 형태로 나라에 투자되어야 하고, 경제의 바퀴가 계속 굴러갈 수 있게끔 유지하기 위해서 투자되어야 한다고 믿고 있습니다. 만약 이미 현재 나타난 것처럼, 수평선에 폭풍우 구름이 나타난다면, 돈은 경기후퇴라는 늑대들을 문에서 막아내거나, 혹은 사람들이 계속 고용이 되도록 하고 사업의 지급능력이 유지될 수 있게끔 하도록 사용하고 또한 최소한 경기후퇴의 충격을 극소화하기 위해서 사용되어야만 합니다. 하지만, 사회의 몇몇 단체들은 이 폭풍우를 견디는 것보다는 차라리 나라가 고통스러운 퇴적더미에 내려앉는 것을 보는 게 낫다고 할 만큼 극도로 흑자금액에 보호적인 것으로 생각됩니다.

어휘
surplus 잔여, 흑자
infrastructure 기간 시설
solvent 지급능력이 있는
weather (비, 바람에) 견디다
appear ~로 보이다, ~로 생각되다
be inclined to ~하는 경향이 있다
screaming 야단스러운, 고통스러운
protective 보호하는

정답 (b)

13 Ku Klux Klan is an organization to preserve white supremacy in the South after the American Civil War. "Ku Klux" comes from the Greek word kuklos, drinking-bowl. The Klan began in Tennessee in 1866, as a secret society with an elaborate ritual, and soon spread throughout the South. Members dressed up in white hoods and sheets and rode out at night carrying burning crosses. Their aim was to intimidate blacks, drive them from their land and prevent them from voting. When intimidation did not work Klansmen turned to violence. Opponents were flogged, tarred and feathered, their homes burnt and many were lynched. However, the violence _____. Congress passed a Force Act in 1870, which imposed heavy fines for using force or intimidation to prevent people from voting. In 1871, the Klan and similar organizations were outlawed.

(a) caused such silence
(b) produced a backlash
(c) succeeded in preventing a fair election
(d) was verbal, not physical

해설
백인 우월 집단인 KKK단에 대한 글이다. 빈칸 앞에서 KKK단의 위협이 폭력적으로 변질되었음을 말하고 있다. 반면, 빈칸 뒤에서는 의회가 이러한 폭력에 대한 벌금을 부과하고, 비슷한 조직들을 법으로 금지했다는 내용이 나오는 것으로 보아 '폭력이 반발을 불렀다' 라는 (b)가 정답이다.

해석
Ku Klux Klan은 미국 시민전쟁 이후에 남부에서 백인의 우월성을 지키기 위한 단체이다. "Ku Klux"는 그리스 어로 술잔이란 의미의 kuklos에서 왔다. 이 단체는 1866년도 테네시에서 정교한 의식을 가진 비밀 사회로서 시작되었고, 곧 남부로 퍼져나갔다. 구성원들은 하얀 모자가 달린 천을 뒤집어쓰고, 밤에 불타는 십자가를 들고 말을 타고 나갔다. 그들의 목표는 흑인들을 위협하는 것과 그들을 땅에서 내쫓고 그들이 투표하는 것을 막는 것이었다. 위협이 통하지 않자, 이들은 폭력적으로 변했다. 반대하는 자들은 채찍질과, 온몸에 타르 칠을 당하고 그 위에 깃털이 뿌려졌으며, 그들의 집은 불타고 많은 사람들이 집단 린치를 당했다 이러한 폭력은 반발을 불러일으켰다. 의회는 1870년에 강제 법령을 통과시켜, 사람들이 투표를 하는 것을 막기 위해 힘이나 협박을 사용할 경우 과한 벌금을 부과하게끔 했다. 1871년에는 Klan과 비슷한 단체들이 모두 법으로 금지 당했다.

어휘
Ku Klux Klan 3K단(백인 인종차별 집단)
preserve 보존하다, 유지하다
supremacy 우위, 우월
elaborate 공들인, 정교한
ritual 의식, 제식
intimidate 위협하다
vote 투표하다
flog 매질하다, 채찍질하다
tar and feather a person ~의 온몸에 타르를 바른 후 새 털을 씌우다[일종의 사형(私刑)]
outlaw 금지하다

정답 (b)

14 Education is touted as the key to stopping the carnage on our roads. However, our education is censored and provides a distorted reality of the consequences of drink-driving or speeding. Too often we see a mangled wreck of a car but the victims and their horrific injuries are not shown. Every licensed driver should be required to view a small number of photos of accident scenes. Having spoken to a tow-truck drivers unlucky enough to _____, I believe once is enough to change your mind on road safety. I know it is a gruesome way to tackle the problem, but someone needs to take a drastic stand such as this or we will never address this problem.

(a) be punished for traffic infringements
(b) have a talk with paramedics and police officers
(c) have gotten minor injuries from traffic accidents.
(d) view these things on a regular basis

해설
교통사고를 줄이기 위해서 실제 피해자들의 사고 장면 사진을 모든 운전자들에게 보여주어야 한다는 요지의 글이다. 빈칸은 필자가 대화를 나눈 구조차 운전사에 대한 설명이 들어가야 한다. 빈칸 뒤에서 그와 이야기한 후 단 한 장의 사고 사진이라도 큰 효과를 누릴 것이라는 내용으로 보아 그 만큼 사고를 직접 보았을 때의 충격을 간접적으로 설명해 주고 있음을 알 수 있다. 구조차 운전사는 '정기적으로 사고를 목격하는' 이라는 (d)가 가장 적절하다.

해석
교육은 도로에서의 살육을 멈출 수 있는 열쇠라고 말해진다. 하지만, 우리의 교육은 검열되어지고, 음주운전과 과속운전의 결과의 왜곡된 실상을 제공한다. 너무 자주 우리는 자동차의 난도질당한 잔해를 보지만, 피해자들과 그들의 끔찍한 부상들은 보여지지 않는다. 모든 면허증을 소유한 운전자들은 적은 수의 사고 장면 사진들을 보도록 규정되어야 한다. 이러한 것들은 정기적으로 봐야 하는 운이 없는 구조차 운전사와 이야기를 하고 난 후, 나는 이러한 장면을 한 번만 봐도 도로 안전에 대한 생각을 바꿀 수 있을 만큼 충분하다고 믿는다. 이것이 이 문제와 싸우기 위한 소름끼치는 방법이라는 것을 안다. 하지만 누군가는 이와 같은 과감한 입장을 취할 필요가 있고, 그렇지 않을 경우, 우리는 결코 이 문제를 해결할 수 없을 것이다.

어휘
be touted as ~로 말해진다
carnage 살육, 대량학살
censor 검열하다
distort 왜곡하다
mangle 난도질하다
gruesome 무시무시한, 소름끼치는
drastic 과감한
tackle 싸우다, 달려들다
on a regular basis 규칙적으로

정답 (d)

15 "Make the World a Better Place" Movie Nights are a good opportunity to watch documentary films and commercial movies that deal with social and environmental issues. A rich discussion will be followed after the movies and all the participants can voice their own opinions. These events are free and open to the public. _____, voluntary donations will be accepted and used to help underwrite our educational programs at local public schools. If you have any questions or suggestions to make this event a more meaningful night, please contact us via e-mail address below.

(a) Therefore
(b) Consequently
(c) However
(d) In other words

해설
다소 어려운 문제유형이라 할 수 있다. 빈칸 뒤에 이어지는 자발적인 기부에 관한 내용은 앞부분의 전반적인 흐름과 맥을 달리한다. 앞은 자유로운 토론과 의견을 말할 수 있는 데 반해 뒤는 모임을 의미있도록 하는 제안을 줄 수 있다는 것과 공립학교 발전을 위한 기부금에 관한 내용이 이어지고 있다. 보기 중에서는 (c)를 답으로 선택할 수 있다.

해석
"더 나은 세계를 만들자"는 제목의 영화의 밤(Movie Nights)은 사회와 환경 문제를 다루는 다큐멘터리 영화와 상업 영화를 볼 수 있는 좋은 기회입니다. 영화가 끝난 뒤에 값진 토의가 있을 것이며 토의를 통해 참석자들은 자신들의 의견을 말할 수 있습니다. 이 이벤트는 자유롭게 진행되며 대중에게 열려있습니다. (무료로 진행되지만) 자발적인 기부는 받아들이며 지역 공립학교들에 대한 저희의 교육 프로그램에 대한 비용을 부담하도록 동의하는 데 사용될 것입니다. 이 행사를 좀 더 의미있도록 하는데 질의 혹은 제안이 있는 사람이면 누구나, 우리의 아래 이메일 주소로 연락하기를 바랍니다.

어휘
commercial 상업의
voice one's opinion 의견을 내세우다
underwrite 지불을 보증하다
local public school 지역 공립학교
meaningful 의미 있는

정답 (c)

16 I was seven when I first developed complex regional pain syndrome. I was out with a friend one day and he accidentally pushed his bike handle into my arm. Suddenly it froze up and my arm felt like it was in a boiling hot bath. I was prescribed drugs, but nothing completely dulled the pain. After a few weeks, the pain mysteriously stopped. In the years that followed, I had several more episodes. Once I tripped through a door, and was crippled by a burning pain that left me on crutches for 10 weeks. _____, I missed a lot of school. Luckily, my teachers were sympathetic and I managed to keep up good grades despite all my time off.

(a) For example
(b) As a result
(c) Nevertheless
(d) Instead

해설
문에 걸려 넘어지면서 생긴 타는 듯한 아픔으로 절름발이가 되어 목발을 집고 다녔다고 한다. 빈칸 뒤에 내용은 학교를 많이 빠졌다는 것인데, 이는 곧 다리를 다침으로써 생긴 결과라고 볼 수 있다. 그러므로 정답은 (b)가 된다.

해석
내가 처음으로 복합부위통증 증후군에 걸렸을 때 나는 7살이었다. 나는 어느 날 한 친구와 밖에 있었고, 그가 우연히 그의 자전거 핸들을 내 팔쪽으로 밀었다. 갑자기 몸이 얼어붙었고, 내 팔은 마치 끓고 있는 뜨거운 욕조 속에 있는 것처럼 느껴졌다. 나는 약 처방받았지만, 아무것도 완전히 그 아픔을 가라앉히지는 못했다. 몇 주가 지난 후에 신비롭게도 고통이 멈췄다. 그 다음 해에 나는 몇 개의 사건을 더 겪었다. 한번은 문에 걸려 넘어졌고, 타는 듯한 아픔으로 인해 목발을 집게 되어 10주 동안 절름발이가 되어야 했다. 그 사건의 결과로 나는 학교를 많이 가지 못하게 되었다. 다행히도, 선생님께서 동정을 느끼셨고, 나는 빠진 시간들에도 불구하고 좋은 성적을 유지할 수 있었다.

어휘
develop (병에) 걸리다
accidentally 우연히
dull 완화하다
trip 걸려 넘어지다
cripple 불구가 되게 하다, 다리를 절다
sympathetic 동정적인

정답 (b)

---

17 Flushed with the success of its moon mission, India is now taking a shot at Google. The Indian Space Research Organization is producing a competitor for Google's free satellite imagery service. The Indian version is called Bhuvan and will provide images of 20 times higher resolution than those Google makes available on the net. Google Earth can home in on big apartment blocks whereas Bhuvan will bring a vehicle the size of a mini-van into view. However, will Buhvan be a worthy competitor for Google? The Indian version may be only playing catch-up for a long time, given Google's superior skills at translating images into usable forms. More basically, they must first convince the growing internet community in India to use it.

Q: What is the best title for the passage?
(a) India's first successful mission to the moon.
(b) The superiority of Google over Buhvan.
(c) The challenges that lie ahead of Bhuvan.
(d) Indians' indifference towards Bhuvan.

해설
글의 주제를 파악해야 하는 문제유형이다. 지문은 인도에서 Google Earth의 이미지 해상도를 능가하는 Bhuvan을 만들었지만, Google에 버금가는 경쟁자로서 크기 위해서는 몇 가지 해결해야 할 것들이 있음이 본 글의 핵심주제이다. 그러므로 가장 적절한 제목은 'Bhuvan 앞에 높인 도전들'인 (c)가 정답이다.

해석
달 임무의 성공으로 우쭐해진 인도는 이제 구글에 도전을 하려는 중이다. 인도의 우주 연구 기관은 구글의 무료 위성 이미지 서비스의 경쟁상대를 제작하려고 한다. 이 인도식 버전은 Bhuvan이라고 불릴 것이고, 구글이 온라인상에 가능하게끔 만들어내는 것보다 20배나 더 높은 해상도를 가진 이미지를 제공할 것이다. 구글 어쓰는 큰 아파트 단지들을 추적할 수 있는 반면, Bhuvan은 미니밴 정도 크기의 차량을 시야에 가져올 것이다. 하지만, Buhvan이 구글의 훌륭한 경쟁자가 될 수 있을까? 이 인도 버전은 구글의 이미지들을 사용가능한 형식의 이미지로 바꾸는 뛰어난 능력을 봤을 때, 오랜 기간 동안 후발주자로서의 역할만을 할지도 모르겠다. 좀 더 근본적으로, 그들은 인도의 증가하는 인터넷 사회가 자신들의 제품을 사용하도록 우선 설득부터 시켜야만 한다.

어휘
be flushed with 의기양양해지다, 우쭐해지다
competitor 경쟁자
satellite 인공위성
resolution 해상도
home in on 표적물을 향하다
whereas ~임에 반하여
catch-up 후발주자
challenge 도전
indifference 무관심

정답 (c)

18. Isolationism was the policy of the USA which aimed at avoiding alliances with other countries or becoming involved in the affairs of other continents. It went back to George Washington, who advised Americans in his Farewell Address to steer clear of permanent alliances with foreign nations. Thomas Jefferson endorsed this policy when he became President in 1801 : "Peace, commerce and honest friendship with all nations; entangling alliances with none". America's entry into the First World War in 1917 saw the abandonment of isolationism for a brief period. After the war Americans again turned their backs on the outside world and rejected President Wilson's plea to join the League of Nations.

Q: What is the passage about?
(a) How Isolationism became the diplomatic policy of America.
(b) How the term "Isolationism" was defined.
(c) Why America temporarily abandoned Isolationism.
(d) President Wilson's hope to join the League of Nations.

19. Lindy Simpson hopes to cut her family's energy use by just switching off lights and household appliances. She says that it's just simple things like turning off the television if she goes outside. The Simpsons are one of seven households participating in the city's Energy Sustainability Street Initiative. Mrs. Simpson says that she notices the difference especially early in the morning a lot. She now turns off the bedroom air-conditioners and before long her family is running on just 15 cents an hour. Apart from cutting the electricity bill, Mrs. Simpson is keen to push the sustainability message to her children so the next generation is even more environmentally aware than this one.

Q: What is the passage about?
(a) How hard it is to teach children energy-saving skills.
(b) The money saved by turning off air-conditioners.
(c) The importance of participating in the community.
(d) The effects of simple energy-saving actions

해설

과거 미국의 외교정책이었던 '쇄국주의(Isolationism)'가 어떻게 시작되었고, 진행되어 왔는지를 설명하고 있는 글이다. 조지 워싱턴에 의해서 쇄국주의가 권고되었고, 그 후 제퍼슨 대통령에 의해 승인되어 시간이 흐르면서 1차 세계대전을 제외하고 계속 유지되어 왔음을 알 수 있다. 그러므로 쇄국주의가 어떻게 미국의 외교정책이 되었는가인 (a)가 정답이다. 내용과 전혀 관련이 없는 (b)를 제외한 나머지 선택지들은 모두 지엽적이다.

해석

쇄국주의는 다른 국가들과의 동맹을 피하고 다른 대륙들과의 일에 엮이는 것을 피하는 것에 목표를 둔 미국의 정책이었다. 이는 조지 워싱턴 때로 돌아가는데, 그는 퇴임연설에서 해외 국가들 하고의 영구적인 동맹을 피할 것을 미국인들에게 충고하였다. 토마스 제퍼슨은 그가 대통령이 된 1801년에 이 정책을 승인하였다. 즉, 모든 국가들과 평화, 통상 그리고 정직한 우정을 유지하되 그 누구와도 얽히는 동맹을 하지 않겠다는 것이었다. 1917년 1차 세계대전에의 미국의 참전은 짧은 기간 동안 쇄국주의의 포기로 보였다. 전쟁이 끝난 후, 미국인들은 다시 외부 세계에 대해서 그들의 등을 돌렸고, 국제연맹에 가입하자는 윌슨 대통령의 청원을 거부하였다.

어휘

Isolationism 쇄국주의
aim (at) ~을 겨냥하다
steer clear of ~을 피하다
endorse 승인하다, 찬성하다
policy 정책
reject 거절하다, 사절하다
diplomatic 외교의
temporarily 일시의, 잠깐 동안의

정답 (a)

해설

지문 전체의 대의는 집에서 할 수 있는 간단한 행동들을 통해 얻을 수 있는 에너지 절약 효과를 말하고 있다. 따라서 정답은 (d)이다. (a)와 관련한 내용은 지문 상에 언급된 바 없고, 보기 (b)의 절약된 돈은 에너지 절약 행동을 통해 얻은 결과 중 하나일 뿐이다.

해석

Lindy Simpson 씨는 전등과 가정용 전자제품의 스위치를 끄는 것만으로 그녀의 가족의 에너지 사용을 줄일 수 있기를 바랍니다. 그녀는 그녀가 밖에 나가게 되면 텔레비전을 끄는 것과 같이 간단한 것들일 뿐이라고 말합니다. Simpson 가족은 시의 에너지 유지 거리 발의에 참여하고 있는 일곱 가정 중의 한 가정입니다. Simpson 씨는 특히 그녀가 이른 아침에 큰 차이를 보게 된다고 말합니다. 이제 그녀는 방의 에어컨을 끄는 데, 그로부터 오래지 않아서, 그녀의 가족은 시간당 15센트의 에너지 요금만 내고 있다고 합니다. 전기 요금비를 줄이는 것을 떠나서, Simpson 씨는 이 자원유지 메시지를 그녀의 아이들에게 전달하여 다음 세대들이 이것보다도 더 환경문제를 많이 의식하게 하도록 하는데 열정을 쏟고 있습니다.

어휘

switch off 스위치를 끄다
household 가정(의)
sustainability 유지성, (자원의) 비고갈성
apart from ~은 별개로
be keen to + V ~하는데 열심이다
environmentally 환경적으로
aware 깨닫고, 의식하고 있는

정답 (d)

20 Barium Enema is an X-ray test which shows the large bowel by coating it with barium and inflating the bowel with air. The barium and air are introduced by a tube which is inserted into the rectum. The images taken can show tumors, inflammation and structural changes in the large bowel. To take the test, the bowel must be as empty as possible. To do this, you will need to obtain a bowel cleansing kit from your doctor. It is important to follow the instructions closely for the best results. You will need to change into a gown. Then, you will be asked to lie on your side of the X-ray table. A thin plastic tube will be placed into your rectum. This can be uncomfortable but should not be painful at all. The barium fluid will then pass via the tube into your large bowel. You may need to be moved into different positions to coat the bowel. Once enough barium is in the bowel this will be drained out via the same tube and then air introduced. This will be seen on a TV monitor, and X-ray images will also be taken at this time.

Q: What is the main topic of the passage?
(a) The definition of the term "Barium Enema"
(b) Why patients take Barium Enema
(c) How Barium Enema is performed.
(d) How tube is inserted into the rectum.

21 Angry shoppers are abusing supermarket checkout staff for refusing to pack groceries in plastic bags, as Australian retailers start banning the plastic bags from their stores. Check-out staff are reporting incidents of bag rage, with workers being verbally threatened for denying customers free bags despite new laws banning their use. Retailers have until May 1 to implement a total ban on all single use of plastic bags from their stores, but must provide customers with alternatives. Some stores such as Target already have banned plastic bags completely while others have begun trialing bag-free lanes in preparation for the complete ban. However, customers have been getting upset at the checkout operators when it has got nothing to do with them. Store owners said that people have raised their voice saying that it's rubbish and that it's going to cost them more money.

Q: What is the passage about?
(a) The main culprits of shoplifting in stores.
(b) The date when the ban of plastic bags will be in effect.
(c) Disputes caused by prohibiting the use of plastic bags.
(d) The seriousness of verbal abuse by customers.

해설
바륨 관장의 테스트가 어떤 식의 절차로 이루어지는지를 자세하게 설명해 주고 있다. 그러므로 정답은 (c)이다. 나머지 보기들은 세부사항으로 언급되는 내용들일 뿐이다.

해석
바륨 관장은 대장을 공기로 부풀리고 바륨으로 코팅함으로써 대장을 보여주는 x-ray 테스트이다. 바륨과 공기는 직장으로 삽입된 관을 통해서 들어간다. 이렇게 해서 촬영된 사진들은 대장안의 종양, 염증, 구조적 변화를 보여줄 수 있다. 테스트를 받기 위해서는, 대장은 가능한 많이 비워져 있어야만 한다. 이를 위해서, 당신은 의사로부터 대장 청소도구를 받을 필요가 있다. 최고의 결과를 위해서 세심하게 지시사항을 따르는 것은 중요하다. 당신은 가운으로 갈아입고, 그러고 나서 x-ray 탁자 위에 옆으로 누우라는 요청을 받을 것이다. 얇은 플라스틱 관이 당신의 직장 안으로 놓일 것이다. 이것은 불편할 수 있으나, 전혀 고통이 따르지는 않는다. 바륨액은 그 후 당신의 대장 안으로 관을 통해서 통과할 것이다. 대장을 바륨으로 입히기 위해서 당신은 다른 자세들로 이동할 필요가 있을 수 있다. 충분한 바륨이 대장 안에 들어가게 되면, 이들은 같은 관을 통해서 밖으로 빠지고, 이제는 공기가 삽입될 것이다. 이는 텔레비전 모니터를 통해서 보여지며, 동시에 X-ray 사진들도 촬영이 될 것이다.

어휘
barium 바륨
enema 관장
large bowel 대장
rectum 직장
tube 관
coat 칠하다, ~에 씌우다
drain 배수하다, 물을 빼내다

정답 (c)

해설
지문의 주제를 파악해야 하는 문제이다. 지문의 주된 내용은 새로운 법으로 인해 상점에서 비닐봉지를 제공해 주지 않자 이로 인해 점원들과 고객들 간의 논쟁과 다툼이 발생하고 있다는 것이다. 그러므로 정답은 '비닐봉지 사용 금지로 인해 일어난 논쟁들' 이라는 (c)가 정답이다.

해석
호주의 소매점들이 상점에서의 비닐봉지를 금지하는 것을 시작함에 따라 화가 난 쇼핑객들이 비닐봉지에 식료품을 담는 것을 거부하는 슈퍼마켓 계산대의 직원들에게 욕을 하고 있다. 계산대 직원들은 새로운 법이 비닐봉지의 사용을 금지함에 따라 손님에게 공짜 비닐봉지를 주는 것을 거부한 것에 대해 언어적으로 위협을 당하는 등의 봉지와 관련한 (손님들의) 분노 사건들이 보고되고 있다. 소매점들은 5월 1일까지 가게에서 비닐봉지를 한 장이라도 사용하는 것에 있어서 전면 금지를 실행해야 한다. 하지만, 대부분은 고객들에게 대체 포장지를 제공하고 있다. Target과 같은 몇몇 가게들은 비닐봉지의 사용을 완전히 금지했고, 다른 곳들은 완전한 금지를 위한 준비과정으로 봉지가 없는 계산 줄을 시험적으로 운영해 보기 시작했다. 하지만, 고객들은 이러한 일들이 계산대 직원들과는 아무런 관계가 없음에도 그들에게 화를 내고 있는 상황이다. 가게 주인들은 사람들이 이러한 방침은 쓰레기이고, 이로 인해 그들에게 더 많은 돈이 들 것이라고 목소리를 높이고 있다고 말했다.

어휘
abuse ~에게 욕을 하다, 매도하다
refuse 거부하다
retailer 소매상인
rage 격노, 분노
verbally 말로, 구두로
trial 시도해보다
bag-free 가방을 주지 않는
in preparation for ~을 대비하여
has nothing to do with ~와는 아무런 상관이 없다

정답 (c)

22. Great flexibility has been introduced into our water regime which recognizes that some gardens may require a mid-week watering in the heat of summer. Households now have the option of spreading their current three-hour a week watering times across two days. This flexible arrangement will reduce the risk of over-watering on weekends and provide a better chance of our trees and gardens surviving yet another dry summer. Under the new arrangements, hand-held hoses or drippers will be permitted for a maximum of 3 hours for even numbered houses between 6 to 9 p.m. on Tuesday and Sunday and for odd numbered houses during the same time on Wednesday and Sunday. Buckets and watering cans can be used any time on any day of the week.

Q: What is the passage about?
(a) The negative effects of over-watering
(b) The introduction of a new water arrangement
(c) The items allowed to be used for watering gardens
(d) The way to survive the coming summer

해설
새로운 물 공급 체계의 도입에 대해 소개하고 있다. 짝수 혹은 홀수 주소에 따라 그리고 날짜에 따라 물 공급을 다르게 해 과잉 물 공급 등의 부정적인 측면을 줄이는 새로운 물 공급 체계를 설명하므로 (b)가 답이다.

해석
우리의 물 공급체계에 있어서 상당한 융통성을 도입했는데, 그것은 일부 정원은 여름철 더위 때에 일주일의 반 정도만 물을 필요로 한다는 것을 인정하는 것이다. 가계에서는 이제 그들이 현재 일주일에 3시간 동안 이틀 간격으로 물주는 시간을 가질 수 있는 선택권을 갖게 되었다. 이 유연성 있는 조정은 주말 동안, 물을 과하게 공급하는 위험을 줄이며 우리의 나무나 정원이 건조한 여름 동안 살아남을 수 있는 더 나은 가능성을 제공합니다. 새로운 조정으로 휴대용 물 호스나 물뿌리개는 짝수 번호 주소를 갖는 가정들에 있어서, 화요일과 일요일 오후 6시부터 9시까지 최대 3시간 동안 사용이 허가됩니다. 그리고 홀수 주소의 가정들은 같은 시간대, 수요일과 일요일에 사용이 가능합니다. 양동이와 물통은 주간 어느 때건 사용이 가능합니다.

어휘
flexibility 유연성
introduce 도입하다, 소개하다
regime 제도, 체계
household 가정
arrangement 조정, 조열
permit 허락하다, 허가하다
even number 짝수
odd number 홀수

정답 (b)

23. For crystal clear skin, read the following three-step plan. There's no better feeling than splashing your face with water and lathering it clean at the end of the day. Using a cleanser is important to remove make-up, sweat, toxins and bacteria that, if left on the skin, can cause irritations and blemishes. It's also important to use a cleansing product that's made specifically for your skin type. The second step is to exfoliate. Exfoliating makes your face look and feel healthier by polishing away dead skin cells. Choosing the right product is especially important in this stage of your three-step routine because the skin on your face is so delicate. Don't use products with sand granules or ground walnut shells – they're too harsh for your face. For best results, exfoliate once a week with the right product for your skin. The third step is to moisturize. whether your skin is dry, sensitive, ageing or oily, don't skip this step.

Q: Which of the following is correct according to the passage?
(a) The first step for clear skin is to get rid of your dead skin cells.
(b) Make-up can cause inflammation on your skin if not washed properly.
(c) Choosing the right moisturizer is the most important for crystal clear skin.
(d) It is recommended to use cleansing products with sand granules in them.

해설
지문 초반 'Using a cleanser is ~ cause irritations and blemishes'를 통해서 화장을 잘 씻지 않으면 피부에 염증을 일으킬 수 있다는 것을 알 수 있다. 그러므로 정답은 (b)이다.

해석
수정처럼 깨끗한 피부를 위해서 다음 3단계 계획을 읽어보세요. 하루가 끝나고 깨끗하게 얼굴에 비누 거품을 칠하고 물로 튀기는 것보다 더 기분 좋은 느낌은 없을 겁니다. 세척제를 사용하는 것은 피부에 남아 염증과 흠을 남기는 원인이 되는 화장, 땀, 독소, 그리고 박테리아를 제거하기 위해서 중요합니다. 또한 여러분의 피부 타입에 명확하게 맞는 세척제 상품을 사용한 것도 중요하죠. 두 번째 단계는 박피입니다. 박피를 하는 것은 죽은 피부 세포를 닦아 냄으로써 여러분의 얼굴이 더 건강하게 보이고 느껴지게끔 합니다. 세 단계 중에서 이번 단계가 특히 더 중요한데 왜냐면 여러분의 얼굴 피부는 굉장히 섬세하기 때문입니다. 모래 입자 또는 호두껍질이 들어간 상품은 사용하지 마세요. 그것들은 여러분의 얼굴에 너무 거칠습니다. 최고의 결과를 위해선 여러분의 피부에 맞는 상품으로 일주일에 한 번 박피를 하세요. 마지막 단계는 수분을 주는 것입니다. 여러분의 피부가 건조하던, 민감하던, 노화가 되었던, 기름이 많던 이 단계를 건너뛰지 마세요.

어휘
lather 비누거품을 칠하다
toxin 독소
irritation 염증
blemish 흠, 오점
specifically 본질적으로, 명확하게
exfoliate 박피하다
polish away 닦아내다
granule 작은 알갱이
moisturize 수분을 공급하다

정답 (b)

24. A man allegedly caught with 84g of cocaine in his possession was yesterday denied bail in Court. Sebastien Daquin was remanded in custody until his case resumes on April 24 after police argued he was at risk of re-offending and not reappearing if he was granted bail. Police allege Mr. Daquin was found at a Manchester tavern carrying the drugs, which was described by the police as a significant quantity. The court heard Mr. Daquin denied he was a supplier but had the drugs for personal use. Police said they had earlier seen Mr. Daquin at the airport about the same time another man was intercepted about drugs there. Mr. Darquin's lawyer said there was no evidence his client's presence at the airport was related to the police intercept.

Q: Which of the following is correct according to the article?
(a) Mr. Daquin was arrested at the airport for possessing drugs.
(b) Mr. Daquin was spotted at the airport with another man by police.
(c) Mr. Daquin sold his drugs to the man at the airport.
(d) Mr. Daquin will be locked up in jail until he appears in court again.

해설
Mr. Daquin 씨는 법원에 의해 보석이 거부되었고, 감옥에 재유치되었다고 밝히고 있으므로 '다음 법정에 나타날 때까지 감옥에 갇혀 있을 것이다' 라는 (d)가 정답이다. Mr. Daquin 씨가 공항에서 남자와 함께 있는 것이 목격된 것은 아니며, 그 남자에게 마약을 팔았다는 증거 또한 없으므로 (b)와 (c)는 정답이 될 수 없다.

해석
소식에 의하면 84g의 코카인을 소지하다 붙잡힌 남자가 어제 법정에서 보석신청이 거부되었다고 합니다. 경찰은 Sebastien Daquin에게 보석신청을 허가할 경우, 재범의 위험과 법원에 다시 출두하지 않을 위험이 있다고 주장하여 법원은 공판이 4월 24일에 재개되기 전까지 그가 구금 재유치되도록 되었습니다. 경찰에 따르면 Darquin 씨는 한 선술집에서 마약을 소지 중에 체포되었는데, 그 양이 상당했다고 전해지고 있습니다. 법원에서 Darquin 씨는 자신이 (마약의) 공급책이 아니며 단지 개인 용도로 마약을 소지하고 있었다고 주장했습니다. 경찰은 다른 남성이 공항에서 마약으로 인해 저지되던 거의 같은 시간대에 Darquin 씨를 공항에서 보았다고 말했습니다. Darquin 씨의 변호사는 그의 고객이 공항에 있었던 것이 경찰이 다른 남자를 차단했던 것과 연관이 있다는 증거는 없다고 말했습니다.

어휘
allegedly 전해지는 바에 의하며, 주장에 따르면
possession 소유
deny 거부하다
bail 보석, 보석금
resume 재개하다
be granted bail 보석이 허가되다
tavern 선술집, 여인숙
intercept 가로채기, 차단
remand (형이 확정될 때까지) 재유치(구속)하다

정답 (d)

25. Our new Internet Stick modem is so small and sleek you can carry it around in your pocket wherever you go. Simply plug the Internet Stick modem into your USB port, wait for the automatic software installation, and you're connected to the Internet within minutes. Move it from room to room, city to city; and always stay in touch. You're never out of the loop. What's more, the new Internet Stick modem doubles as a memory card allowing you to store up to 4GB of files, documents, music and more. Our 3 giga high-speed broadband coverage already covers metropolitan areas in San Diego, Florida, Miami, and Los Angeles plus all major international airports in America.

Q: Which of the following is correct about the advertised product?
(a) The stick-shaped modem is small, but not easy to take a grip on it.
(b) A manual is not needed to operate the modem.
(c) The new Internet stick modem doubles the price of the 4GB memory card.
(d) The modem allows people to surf the net in any international airports worldwide.

해설
언급되는 인터넷 스틱 모뎀의 특징을 하나하나 보기와 비교하며 정답을 골라내야 한다. 세 번째 문장에서 자동 소프트웨어 설치를 기다리라고 했으므로, '모뎀의 작동을 위해 설명서는 필요하지 않다' 는 (b)가 정답임을 알 수 있다. 모뎀이 매끈하다는 것은 디자인이 그렇다는 것이지 잡기가 힘들다는 것은 아니고, 모뎀이 메모리카드로의 두 가지 역할이 가능하다는 것이지 가격이 두 배라는 것은 아니므로 (a), (c)는 모두 오답이다.

해석
저희의 새로운 인터넷 스틱 모뎀은 너무 작고 매끄러워서 여러분은 어디를 가시던지 주머니에 넣은 채로 이동하실 수 있습니다. 간단히 인터넷 스틱 모뎀을 여러분의 USB 포트에 끼워 넣으시고, 자동 소프트웨어 설치가 될 때까지 기다리시면 여러분은 몇 분 내에 인터넷에 연결이 되실 겁니다. 방에서 방으로, 도시에서 도시로 이동해도 항상 인터넷에 연결되어 있습니다. 절대로 연결이 끊어지지 않습니다. 게다가, 새로운 인터넷 스틱 모뎀은 여러분이 4GB에 해당하는 파일과 문서, 음악 그리고 더 많은 것을 저장할 수 있도록 해주는 메모리 카드로서의 역할도 겸합니다. 저희의 3기가 고속도 무선 적용범위는 이미 미국의 모든 주요 국제공항을 포함하여 샌디에이고, 플로리다, 마이애미, 그리고 로스앤젤레스에 이르는 대도시 지역을 포함하고 있습니다.

어휘
sleek 매끄러운, 맵시가 좋은
installation 설치
be connected to ~에 연결되다
out of the loophole 의사결정에 관여하지 못하는
double (as) ~로서의 역할도 겸하다
metropolitan 대도시의

정답 (b)

26 A great pair of sunglasses is the ultimate fashion accessory. So what styles should you be looking out for in 2009? Over the past few years, "big" has been best, and the trend continues. Oversized sunglasses will still be one of the hottest styles around this year. However, Look out for the latest designs which are '70s-inspired, with thick plastic frames. Classic sunglasses are also popular and are a firm favorite with celebs. Frame colors this season range from black through to turquoise and hot pink. The ultra-cool aviator-style sunnies suit most men and women. These sunnies are a great unisex option and you can swap them with your partner when you feel like wearing something different. Wrap-style sunnies are yet another option to keep you looking fashionable, and offer more protection.

Q: Which of the following is correct according to the passage?
(a) The large-sized sunglasses once used to be in style.
(b) Black frame sunglasses are the most popular among people.
(c) Wrap-style sunglasses can keep your face from being bashed.
(d) Actors and actresses fancy wearing Classic Sunglasses.

해설
다양한 종류의 선글라스에 대해 설명해주고 있는 지문이다. 중간에 Classic Sunglass는 유명인사들 사이에 확고히 선호되는 종류라고 말하고 있다. 그러므로 '남녀 영화배우들은 Classic Sunglass를 쓰는 것을 좋아한다'는 (d)가 정답이다. 큰 사이즈의 선글라스는 여전히 유행하고 있으며, 블랙 컬러는 올해 유행할 여러 컬러들 중 하나일 뿐이기에 (a), (b) 역시 정답이 될 수 없다.

해석
훌륭한 선글라스 하나는 궁극의 패션 액세서리이다. 그러니, 2009년도에 여러분은 무슨 스타일을 찾아야 할까? 지난 몇 년 간은, "큰 것"이 최고였고, 그 유행은 계속되고 있다. 거대한 선글라스들은 올해에도 가장 섹시한 스타일 중의 하나일 것이다. 하지만, 70년대에서 영감을 받아 두꺼운 플라스틱 안경테를 가지고 있는 최신의 디자인을 눈여겨보라. 고전 선글라스들 또한 인기가 많고, 유명 인사들의 확고한 선호대상이기도 하다. 이번 시즌 안경테의 색깔은 검은색에서부터 청록색 그리고 핫 핑크까지 분포되어 있다. 극단으로 멋진 비행사 스타일 선글라스들 역시 대부분의 남성들과 여성들에게 어울린다. 이 선글라스들은 남녀 성별을 가리지 않는 훌륭한 선택이고, 무언가 다른 선글라스를 쓰고 싶을 때는 배우자와 바꿔 쓸 수도 있다. 덮는 스타일의 선글라스는 당신을 패셔너블하게 보이게 할 수 있는 또 다른 선택이고, 이는 (햇빛으로부터) 더 많은 보호를 해준다.

어휘
ultimate 최후의, 궁극의
trend 유행, 추세, 경향
latest 최근의
celeb (=celebrity) 유명인사
turquoise 청록색(의)
swap 교환하다, 바꾸다
bash 후려갈기다, 강타하다
fancy ~을 맘에 그리다, 좋아하다

정답 (d)

27 As well as the excitement and eagerness surrounding the first day at school, there are elements of stress, not only for the child, but for parents as well. When some mothers wave their children off, they find to their surprise that the joy of their new freedom is also tinged with sadness and a few regrets. Your precious baby is heading off into the big, wide world! It can be scary, handing your child over to another adult, who will have a parent-like role in his life and teach him new ways of understanding the world. You might have a few niggling doubts about child moving away from the security of his home and out into the wider community, becoming part of a "System". And there's the worry of the other children – their acceptance of your child and the potential influence they may have.

Q: Why are mothers worried about their children according to the passage?
(a) Because their children will be travelling around the world.
(b) Because it's the first time for their children to meet other grown-ups.
(c) Because their children don't know how to hang out with others.
(d) Because it's the first time for their children to experience the world outside home.

해설
아이를 처음으로 학교라는 사회적 울타리로 등교시킨 후 생길 수 있는 여러 가지 부모의 걱정들을 하나하나 설명해주고 있는 글이다. 부모 대신 아이를 맡아 가르치게 될 선생님, 집을 떠나 사회적 시스템의 일부분이 되는 아이에 대한 걱정, 그리고 친구들이 미칠 영향에 대한 걱정 등. 이 모든 걱정들이 생기는 이유는 '아이가 집 밖의 세상을 경험하는 첫 번째 일'이기 때문이다 그러므로 정답은 (d)이다.

해석
학교에서의 첫날을 둘러싼 흥분 그리고 열망과 함께, 아이들에게 뿐만이 아니라 부모에게도 마찬가지로 스트레스 요소가 있습니다. 몇몇 어머니들이 아이들에게 손을 흔들며 아이들을 떠나보낼 때, 그들은 새로 얻게 된 자유의 기쁨과 함께 슬픔과 몇 가지 후회의 증상이 나타난다는 것을 발견하고 놀라게 됩니다. 당신의 소중한 아기가 크고, 넓은 세상으로 향하는 거죠! 당신의 아이를 아이의 인생에 있어서 부모와 같은 역할을 해주고 그에게 세상을 이해하는 새로운 방식을 가르쳐 줄 다른 어른에게 건네는 것은 무서운 일일 수도 있습니다. 아이가 안전한 집에서 벗어나 더 넓은 사회로 나가서 제도의 일부분이 되는 것에 대해서 몇 가지 자질구레한 불신들이 생길 수도 있지요. 그리고 다른 아이들이 당신의 아이를 인정하는 부분과 다른 아이들이 내 아이에게 미칠 잠재적 영향력에 대한 걱정도 있습니다.

어휘
surround 에워싸다, 둘러싸다
not only A but B as well A뿐만이 아니라 B 역시도
tinge with ~의 기미를 띄게 하다
niggling 자질구레한, 하찮은 일에 신경 쓰는
doubt 의심하다
acceptance 받아들임, 수락
grown-up 성인

정답 (d)

28 The chemicals in cigaretts affect how your body works, and how well it copes during and after surgery. When you have surgery, you usually have an anesthetic drug so the operation can be performed without pain. Anaesthetic drugs can put your body under stress. They may lower your resistance to infection, and if you are unconscious, your breathing and heart need monitoring to prevent problems. If you smoke, your body is less able to cope with the stress caused by anaesthesia. Also, the nicotine in cigarette smoke increases your heart rate and blood pressure every time you smoke. Your heart works harder, and so it needs more oxygen. The carbon monoxide in cigarette smoke competes with the oxygen in your blood. If you smoke, you can have up to three times more carbon monoxide in your blood than non-smokers. This makes it harder to get the oxygen you need for your heart and body.

Q: Which of the following is correct according to the passage?
(a) Smoking reduces the effect of anesthetics.
(b) Non-smokers easily become short of breath than smokers.
(c) Smokers need more time to recover from a medical operation.
(d) Smoking elevates the level of stress in your body.

해설
담배 안의 화학물질들이 수술 후 신체 회복에 영향을 미친다고 제일 처음에 언급하고 있다. 그러므로 '흡연자들이 수술로부터 회복하기 위해 더 많은 시간이 필요하다'는 (c)가 정답이다. 흡연이 마취 효과를 줄이는 것이 아니라, 마취제로부터 얻는 스트레스를 극복할 신체적 능력을 저하시키는 것이므로 (a)는 정답이 될 수 없다.

해석
담배 안에 있는 화학제품들은 여러분의 신체의 작동과 함께 수술 중 그리고 수술 후 신체가 얼마나 잘 극복할 수 있는가에 영향을 준다. 수술을 할 때는, 수술이 고통 없이 진행될 수 있도록 보통 마취 약물을 받게 된다. 그것들은 감염에 대한 당신의 저항력을 낮추고, 만약 당신이 의식이 없다면, 당신의 호흡과 심장은 문제를 예방하기 위해서 모니터로 감시될 필요가 있다. 만약 당신이 담배를 핀다면, 당신의 신체는 마취제에 의해서 발생하게 될 스트레스를 극복할 가능성이 더 적어진다. 또한, 담배연기 안의 니코틴은 매번 당신이 담배를 피울 때마다, 당신의 심장박동수와 혈압을 증가시킨다. 심장이 더 빠르게 뛰면, 더 많은 산소가 필요하게 된다. 담배 연기 안의 일산화탄소는 당신의 혈액 속 산소와 경쟁을 하게 된다. 만약 당신이 담배를 피게 되면, 당신은 담배를 피우지 않는 사람들보다도 많게는 세 배까지 더 많은 일산화탄소가 혈액 속에 있게 된다. 이는 당신의 신체와 심장이 필요로 하는 산소를 얻는 것을 더 어렵게 만든다.

어휘
chemical 화학제품
affect ~에 영향을 주다
cope 대처하다, 극복하다
surgery 수술
anesthetic 마취의, 마취제
resistance 저항, 반대
unconscious 무의식의
monoxide 일산화물

정답 (c)

---

29 Dating back more than 100 million years, Australia's Wet Tropics Rainforests are the oldest continually surviving tropical rainforests on earth. These rainforests once covered the entire Australia continent. Today, through evolution and climate change, they cover a tiny 0.1 % of Australia's total land mass. Despite their size, they are home to an amazing diversity of plant and animal life, including over 3,000 plant species and many rare and endangered animals found nowhere else on earth. These rainforests are one of 15 natural World Heritage sites in Australia, and one of few in the world to satisfy all four of the criteria for World Heritage listing. These rainforests: represent a major stage of the earth's evolutionary history; provide outstanding examples of ongoing environmental processes; and contain the most important natural areas for the conservation of a variety of life.

Q: Which of the following is correct about Australia's Wet Tropics Rainforests?
(a) They are the only continually surviving rainforests in the world.
(b) Climate change has not affected the size of the rainforests in Australia.
(c) Many animals found in the rainforests can only be seen in Australia
(d) There is a total of 15 rainforests in Australia.

해설
지문의 중간 즈음에 'many rare and endangered animals found nowhere else on earth'라는 문장을 통해서 '강우림에 있는 많은 동물들이 오직 호주에서만 볼 수 있다'라는 (c)가 정답임을 알 수 있다. 호주의 젖은 열대성 강우림은 지구상에서 지속적으로 생존해가는 강우림 중 가장 오래되었다는 것이지, 유일한 것이라고 한 적은 없기에 (a)는 정답이 될 수 없다.

해석
1억 년 전 이상으로 거슬러 올라가는, 호주의 젖은 열대성 강우림(Wet Tropics Rainforests)은 지구상에서 지속적으로 생존해가는 가장 오래된 열대성 강우림이다. 이 강우림들은 한때 전체 호주 대륙을 뒤덮었었다. 오늘날, 진화와 기후 변화를 거쳐서, 이들은 호주 총 땅 면적의 자그마한 0.1%만을 차지하고 있다. 이들의 (작은) 크기에도 불구하고, 이 강우림들은 3,000여 종의 식물들과 지구의 다른 그 어느 곳에서도 찾을 수 없는 많은 희귀하고 멸종위기에 처한 동물들을 포함하는 놀라울 정도의 다양한 동식물들의 거주지이다. 이 강우림들은 호주의 15개 자연 세계유산 중 하나이고, 세계유산 목록에 오르기 위한 전체 4가지 기준을 모두 만족하는 세계에서도 드문 장소 중 한 곳이다. 이 강우림들은 지구의 진화 역사의 중요한 단계를 설명하고, 진행되고 있는 환경적 진행과정의 눈에 띄는 예를 제공해 주고, 다양한 생명들의 보호를 위해 가장 중요한 자연적 지역을 담고 있다.

어휘
rainforest 열대성 강우림
continually 계속적으로, 끊임없이
diversity 다양성
rare 보기 드문, 희귀한
heritage 유산

정답 (c)

30 Running a successful small business is a dream many women have. In 2006, according to the American Bureau of Statistics, nearly one in three small businesses was owned and operated by a women, the majority of them based in New York. While the motives behind women starting small businesses are endlessly varied, it is often in response to circumstances, according to Holly Kramer, American Business Women's Awards ambassador. "Many of the women I've met through the awards started their businesses in response to something that happened in their lives", she says. "Almost all of them had some kind of personal mission at the core: their primary motivation wasn't about making money." Consequently, the stories behind their business start-ups are always unique, and inspiring.

Q: Which of the following is correct according to the passage?
(a) Most of the female small business owners were born in New York.
(b) Many women start to run their own businesses to become rich.
(c) Many women are inspired to run their own businesses through events in their lives.
(d) The products sold by female business owners are very distinct from others.

해설
미국의 비즈니스 여성 시상식 대사인 Holly Kramer가 말한 문장인 'Many of the women I've met through the awards ~ in response to something that happened in their lives',을 통해서 '많은 여성들이 그들의 삶에 있어 벌어진 사건들을 통해 사업을 하기로 영감을 받는다'라는 (c)가 정답임을 알 수 있다. 대부분의 여성 사업체가 뉴욕에 위치하고 있다는 것이지 사업을 운영하는 여성들이 뉴욕 출신이라는 것은 아니기에 (a)는 정답이 될 수 없다.

해석
작은 사업체를 운영하는 것은 많은 여성들이 가지고 있는 꿈입니다. 미국 통계국에 따르면 2006년에, 거의 3개의 소규모 사업체 중 한 개가 여성에 의해서 소유되며 운영되었고, 그들 중 대다수는 뉴욕을 기반으로 두고 있다고 합니다. 여성들이 소규모 사업을 시작하는 동기는 끝도 없이 다양하지만, 미국의 비즈니스 여성 시상식 대사인 Holly Kramer에 의하면 그 이유는 종종 상황들에 대한 반응이라고 합니다. "제가 시상식을 통해 만났던 많은 여성은 그들의 삶에 일어난 무언가에 대한 반응으로 사업을 시작했습니다"라고 그녀는 말합니다. "그들 중 거의 모두가 마음 깊숙한 곳에 개인적인 사명과 같은 것을 가지고 있던 것이죠. 그들의 최우선 동기는 돈을 버는 것이 아니었습니다." 따라서, 그들의 사업 시작의 뒷이야기들은 항상 독특하고 감동을 일으키는 것들입니다.

어휘
run a business 사업을 운영하다
nearly 거의, 대략
majority 대부분, 대다수
in response to ~에 응하여, ~에 답하여
circumstance 상황, 환경
at the core 마음속이, 깊숙이
inspiring 고무하는, 영감을 일으키는

정답 (c)

---

31 The obesity explosion in recent years continues to grow and is projected by the World Health Organization to reach 1.5 billion by 2015. These staggering numbers will overwhelm medical, social and economic care-givers, creating an unparalleled chronic disease burden for the world in the next 10~20 years. Weight excess and obesity are major risk factors for heart disease, stroke, Type 2 diabetes and severe psychological conditions including depression. While the approach to combat obesity must involve a multidisciplinary collection of experts from medical, educational, governmental and social disciplines, the obesity epidemic has rapidly driven scientific researchers to understand how the brain controls human feeding behaviour.

Q: Which of the following is correct about obesity?
(a) Heart disease can contribute to the risk of obesity.
(b) Obesity is becoming a major health hazard worldwide.
(c) The number of people with obesity is higher than the number of care-givers.
(d) It requires one specialized doctor to cure obesity.

해설
비만 인구의 폭발과 관련한 글이다. 지문 초반에 국제보건기구에 의해서 비만 인구가 2015년도에 15억 명에 이를 것이라는 전망을 통해서 쉽게 '비만은 전 세계적으로 주요한 건강 위험이 되고 있다'라는 (b)가 정답임을 알 수 있다.

해석
최근년도에 비만이 폭발적으로 계속해서 증가하고 있고 국제보건기구에 따르면 2015년에는 비만 인구가 15억 명에 이를 것으로 예측된다. 이 경이적인 수치는 의학, 사회적 그리고 경제적 보호제공자들의 숫자를 압도할 것이고, 이는 다음 10~20년에 걸쳐서 전 세계에 균형 잡히지 못한 만성 질병의 부담을 만들어 낼 것이다. 체중 과다와 비만은 심장병, 뇌졸중, Type 2 당뇨병 그리고 우울증을 포함하는 심각한 정신적 상태의 주요 위험요소이다. 비만과 싸우기 위한 접근 방법이 의학, 교육, 정부, 그리고 사회 분야에서의 각 전문 분야 협력을 포함하는 한편 유행처럼 번져가는 비만은 과학 연구원들이 인간의 두뇌가 음식섭취 행동을 어떻게 통제하는지 이해할 수 있게끔 하였다.

어휘
project 예측하다
staggering 어마어마한, 경이적인
multidisciplinary 각 전문분야 협력의
overwhelm 압도하다

정답 (b)

32 Influenza is a common virus which spreads rapidly and can prove fatal to a small number of very young and elderly people. Occasionally the flu virus mutates and in a very virulent form causes high mortality. This occurred in 1918 when three waves of influenza engulfed the world in a matter of a few months. The flu appears to have originated in the US Mid-West in the spring of 1918 and to have been carried by troop movement and trade to every part of the globe. The second wave was the most lethal, resulting in high levels of mortality. Unlike previously known strains of flu, the 1918 variant universally killed proportionately larger numbers of men aged 15–40; there is no satisfactory explanation for this. Total global mortality is unknown but was probably between 30 and 100 million. However inaccurate the figures, it is clear that many more people died in the pandemic than from the direct results of the First World War.

Q: Which of the following is correct according to the passage?
(a) The virus only spreads to children or old people.
(b) Influenza sporadically turns into another life threatening ailment.
(c) The first wave of influenza was more fatal than the second one.
(d) More people died in the First World War than from the pandemic.

해설

두 번째 줄의 'Occasionally the flu virus mutates ~ causes high mortality'에서 이 감기 바이러스는 높은 사망률을 일으키는 악성의 형태로 변화될 수 있음을 알 수 있다. 그러므로 '인플루엔자는 이따금 생명을 위협하는 또 다른 병으로 변한다'라는 (b)가 정답이다.

해석

인플루엔자는 빠르게 퍼지는 일반적인 바이러스이고 적은 수의 매우 어리고 나이가 많은 사람들에게 치명적이란 것을 증명할 수 있습니다. 이따금, 이 감기 바이러스는 돌연변이를 하고 매우 악성인 형태에서 높은 치사율을 불러오기도 합니다. 이는 1918년도에 인플루엔자의 세 번의 물결이 몇 달 만에 전 세계를 삼켜버렸을 때 발생했습니다. 감기는 1918년의 봄에 미국의 중서부에서 시작된 것으로 보이며, 세계의 모든 곳으로 군대와 무역의 이동을 통해 전달되었습니다. 두 번째 물결은 가장 치명적인 것으로 가장 높은 수준의 사망률이란 결과를 낳았습니다. 이전의 감기 기질과는 다르게 1918년도의 변형체는 전 세계에서 비율적으로 더 많은 수의 15~40세 사이의 사람들을 죽였고, 이에 대한 만족스러운 설명을 밝혀내지는 못했습니다. 전체 지구의 사망률은 알려지지는 않았지만, 아마도 3000만에서 1억 명 사이일 것입니다. 이 수치가 아무리 부정확한 것이라 할지라도, 확실한 것은 1차 세계대전보다도 더 많은 사람들이 이 전염병으로 인해서 죽었다는 것입니다.

어휘

mutate 변화하다, 돌연변이를 하다
virulent 악성의, 전염성이 강한
engulf 삼켜버리다

 정답 (b)

33 One of the jobs of the noses is to warm the air we breathe up to body temperature. It does this by expanding the blood vessels in the nose so that more warm blood can warm the cold air. Those expanded blood vessels make your nose feel blocked. The blocked nose feeling causes more mucous to be produced to clear the blockage. Normally most of the mucous we produce is swept towards the back of the throat by cilia – tiny hairs on the cells in our noses – and we swallow it without noticing. But in cold weather, the cilla can't cope with the extra workload and some of the mucous runs down the nose. The drip factor is exacerbated by the effect of condensation when warm air is breathed out through the nose and comes into contact with cold air. The end result is a runny nose.

Q: What can be inferred from the passage?
(a) The air we breath up is normally warmer than our body temperature.
(b) Runny noses in cold weather show that cold weather causes colds.
(c) Runny noses in cold weather are caused by a domino effect.
(d) Running a temperature is just part of the way our body functions.

해설

겨울에 콧물을 흘리는 이유가 '혈관팽창→막힘→점액→Cilla→과다업무→흘러내림' 등의 일련의 사건들이 하나씩 이루어져 생기는 것이라고 지문은 밝히고 있다. 즉, '겨울의 콧물은 도미노 효과에 그 원인이 있다'라는 보기 (c)가 정답이다. 콧물을 통해서 추운 날씨가 감기의 원인이 된다는 내용은 지문에서 언급된 내용이 아니며, 콧물과 감기의 인과관계에 대한 설명 또한 없기 때문에 (b)는 정답이 될 수 없다.

해석

코가 하는 역할 중에 하나는 우리가 들이 마시는 공기를 우리 신체 온도로 덥히는 일이다. 이것은 코 안의 혈관을 팽창시킴으로써 더 많은 따뜻한 피가 차가운 공기를 따뜻하게 덥힘으로써 이루어진다. 이렇게 팽창된 코의 혈관들은 당신의 코가 막힌 듯한 느낌을 갖게 한다. 코가 막힌 듯한 느낌은 막힌 것을 뚫기 위해서 더 많은 점액을 불러일으킨다. 보통 우리가 만들어내는 대부분의 점액은 우리 코 안의 세포 위에 있는 작은 털들인 cilla에 의해서 목구멍의 뒤쪽으로 청소가 되고 우리는 알아채지 못한 채 이것들을 삼킨다. 하지만 추운 계절에는, cilla가 추가된 작업량을 극복하지 못하고 점액 중 일부가 코를 통해 흘러내린다. 이렇게 떨어지는 요인은 따뜻한 공기가 코를 통해서 숨 쉬어져 나와 차가운 공기와 접촉이 될 때 압축 효과에 의해서 더 심해진다. 최종결과는 콧물이 되는 것이다.

어휘

mucous 점액성의, 끈적끈적한
exacerbate 악화시키다
condensation 압축, 응축
end result 최종 결과, 결말
domino effect (하나의 사건이 다른 일련의 사건을 야기 시키는 연쇄적 효과) 도미노 효과
run a temperature 열이 나다

 정답 (c)

34 Dear Mr. Lee,

Thank you for shopping with Danoz Direct!

Our records indicate that payment on your order is now due and your product is ready and waiting to be dispatched. If the amount has already been paid, please disregard this notice. If you have not yet mailed your payment, why not make out your cheque and place it in the enclosed postage-paid envelope while this reminder has your full attention. If you use a credit card you can arrange easy monthly payments. Simply call toll free 1800 300 345 now. Thank you in advance for your anticipated cooperation in this matter.

Kind regards from Danoz Direct.

Q: What can be inferred from this letter?
(a) Mr. Lee has not paid for his order yet.
(b) The product has already been shipped to Mr. Lee.
(c) Mr. Lee can decide to pay on an installment plan.
(d) Mr. Lee should buy a reply envelope to send the payment.

해설

고객이 주문한 상품의 요금 납부와 관련하여 전달되어온 편지이다. 편지의 후반부에 'If you use a credit card you can arrange easy monthly payments.'라고 했기에, 'Mr. Lee는 할부로 금액 지불을 결정할 수 있다'는 (c)가 정답임을 알 수 있다. 초반에 만약 금액을 냈다면 이 편지를 무시하라고 했기 때문에, 아직 정확히 Mr. Lee가 돈을 납부했는지 그렇지 않은지의 여부는 확인될 수 없다. 그러므로 (a)는 정답이 될 수 없다.

해석

이 선생님께,

Danoz Direct에서 쇼핑을 해주셔서 감사드립니다.

저희 기록에 따르면 귀하가 주문하신 물품에 대한 요금이 이제 결제되어야 할 때가 되었고, 상품은 준비가 되어 배송을 기다리고 있습니다. 만약 요금을 이미 지불하셨다면, 이 통지서는 무시하셔도 됩니다. 아직 금액을 보내지 않으셨다면, 이제 생각이 나셨을 때 지금 수표를 쓰셔서 동봉되어 있는 우표가 붙은 봉투에 넣어서 보내주시는 것은 어떨까요? 만약 귀하께서 신용카드를 사용하신다면, 간단히 매달 지불하는 방식을 조정하실 수 있습니다. 요금이 들지 않는 1800 300 345번으로 지금 전화해 주십시오. 이 문제와 관련하여 귀하의 협조에 미리 감사드립니다.

Danoz Direct로부터

어휘
payment 지불, 납입
order 주문, 주문하다
due 지급기일이 된, 만기된
disregard 무시하다
postage-paid envelope 우표가 붙여진 봉투
remind 생각나게 하는 것
arrange 조정하다
in advance 미리
cooperation 협조
on installment plan 할부로

정답 (c)

---

35 Having previously instructed us on "How to Survive a Robot Uprising", robotics engineer Dr. Daniel Wilson turns his eyes to different circumstances, where robots are our only defense against alien invaders or the undead. Having scoured the archives of B-grade movies for instruction, Wilson offers up such chapters as "How to Use a Pet Robot to Terrorize Your Enemies" and "How to Command Robot Minions in Battle". The book offers no money-back guarantees should its advice fail, but it does combine some of the funniest moments in sci-fi with genuine information about the current state of robotics well.

Q: What is this passage introducing?
(a) The lecture on the latest trends in robotics.
(b) The new publication written by Dr. Wilson.
(c) The most hilarious moments from sci-fi movies
(d) Dr. Wilson's view on future developments in robotics.

해설

Daniel Wilson이 새롭게 집필한 도서를 소개하는 글이다. 로봇을 바라보는 박사의 기존의 관점을 벗어나 새로운 관점으로 책을 집필했고, 구체적으로 도서의 각 장들의 제목을 알려주며 어떤 내용일지를 독자들에게 알려주고 있다. 그러므로 이 지문이 소개하고자 하는 것은 '윌슨 박사가 쓴 새 도서'인 (b)가 정답이다.

해석

이전에 우리에게 "로봇의 반란으로부터 살아남는 방법"에 대해서 알려준 적이 있는 로봇공학자 Daniel Wilson 박사는 로봇들이 외계침략자들 혹은 완전히 죽지 못하는 자들에 대항하는 유일한 방어수단이라는 다른 상황들로 눈을 돌렸습니다. 교육을 위해 B급 영화들의 보관소를 철저히 조사한 후, Wilson은 "애완 로봇을 사용하는 방법"에서부터 "당신의 적을 겁먹게 하는 방법" 그리고 "로봇 노예들을 전투에서 지휘하는 방법" 등과 같은 장들을 제시하고 있습니다. 이 책은 이 충고들이 실패하게 되었을 때 돈을 돌려준다는 보증을 하지 않습니다. 하지만 이 책은 실로 몇 가지 공상과학에 있어서 가장 재미있는 순간들을 로봇 공학의 현 상태에 관한 진짜 정보와 잘 결합시켰습니다.

어휘
instruct 가르치다, 알리다
uprising 반란, 폭동
invader 침입자
scour 철저히 조사하다
publication 출판(물)

정답 (b)

36 You have beautiful eyes. We all do. Up close, you'll see incredible shapes, textures and colors you've probably never noticed before. Of course your eyes aren't just aesthetically amazing, they allow you to navigate around your environment with ease. You can recognize the faces of loved ones. You can also experience the splendid beauty of our world. That is why your local Eyecare Plus is focused primarily on the health and wellbeing of your eyes. Every Eyecare Plus practice is held to the highest standards of excellence in optical health care, technical expertise and customer service. We're passionate about eyes because we understand their importance. Cleary your eyes deserve to be framed in a way that enhances their natural beauty, so our range of eyewear is both fashionable and affordable.

Q: What is this passage advertising?
(a) Contact lenses
(b) Eye surgery service
(c) Affordable lasik surgery
(d) Spectacles

해설
지문의 마지막 'Cleary your eyes deserve to be framed in a way that enhances their natural beauty, so our range of eyewear is both fashionable and affordable.' 내용을 통해 광고하고 있는 것은 바로 안경임을 알 수 있다. 그러므로 정답은 (d)이다.

해석
당신은 아름다운 눈을 가지고 있습니다. 우리 모두가 그렇지요. 눈을 가까이서 보면, 여러분은 이전에는 결코 알아차리지 못했던 놀라운 모양과, 결, 그리고 색깔을 보실 수 있습니다. 물론, 여러분의 눈은 단지 미적으로만 놀라운 것은 아니지요. 눈은 여러분들이 쉽게 주위의 환경을 지나갈 수 있도록 해줍니다. 여러분은 사랑하는 사람들의 얼굴을 알아볼 수 있죠. 또한 이 세상의 놀라운 아름다움을 경험할 수도 있습니다. 이것이 바로 저희 지역의 Eyecare Plus가 여러분들의 눈의 건강과 행복에 우선적으로 중점을 두는 이유입니다. 모든 Eyrecare Plus의 실습은 눈의 건강 보호, 기술적 전문지식, 그리고 고객 서비스에 있어서 최고 수준의 우수성에 맞춰져 있습니다. 저희는 눈의 중요성을 알고 있기에 여러분의 눈에 대해서 열정적입니다. 명백히 눈은 자연스런 아름다움을 높이는 방법으로 틀이 잡혀야 될 가치가 있습니다. 그래서 저희 안경 제품들은 유행을 따르고 있고 또한 적정한 가격대입니다.

어휘
aesthetically 미적으로
wellbeing 복지, 행복
splendid 멋진, 근사한
primarily 첫째로
optical 눈의, 시각의
expertise 전문가의 의견
passionate 열정적인
frame ~에 안경테를 씌우다
eyewear 안경류
lasik surgery 라식수술
spectacle 안경

정답 (d)

37 Obesity might be a problem in the human world but a bit of extra paunch can be a godsend for corals seeking to stave off coral bleaching. With coral bleaching an increasing issue for the world's oceans, a team of international scientists claims to have shown how corals can survive world climate change. Bleaching is caused when warm water circulates over the reef, causing the corals to shed essential algae needed for energy. The corals starve if they cannot recover their algae in time. Therefore, it mostly comes down to how well-fed the corals are before the bleaching event strikes. If they have high levels of lipids or fats in their system, it gives them the energy to hang on until they can re-establish their symbiotic relationship.

Q: What can be inferred from the passage?
(a) Gaining weight is dangerous for coral's survival.
(b) Corals discard algae to get energy needed to survive bleaching.
(c) Global warming has a devastating effect on corals.
(d) Corals should be moved into cold water to avoid bleaching.

해설
살이 찌는 것은 인간에게는 문제가 될 수도 있지만, 산호초에게는 기후변화로 인해 물이 따뜻해지면서 발생하는 표백효과를 피하기 위해 충분한 영양분의 공급이 필요하다는 내용의 지문이다. 즉, 여기서 말하는 기후변화의 결과는 따뜻해진 물이기 때문에 '온난화 효과는 산호초에게 치명적인 결과를 가져온다'라는 (c)가 정답이다. 산호초를 차가운 물에 이동시켜야 한다는 보기 (d)는 지문이 언급하는 해결방안을 통해 유추할 수 있는 내용이 아닐뿐더러, 현실적으로 불가능한 방안이다.

해석
인간 세상에서 비만은 문제가 될 수도 있으나, 약간의 배가 나오는 것은 표백작용을 피하기 위해 노력하는 산호초들에게는 신의 선물일 수 있다. 세계 해양계에서 산호초의 표백작용이 점점 더 문제가 되어가는 상황에서, 국제 과학자 팀은 산호초들이 세계 기후 변화에 살아남을 수 있는 방법을 보여주었다고 주장하고 있다. 표백작용은 따뜻한 물이 암초 위를 순환함으로써 산호초의 활동력에 필요한 필수 조류(algae)를 버리게 함으로써 발생한다. 산호초들은 제때 그들의 조류를 회복하지 못하면 굶주리게 된다. 그러므로 표백작용이 발생하기 전에 산호초들이 얼마나 영양분을 잘 공급받았는지 여부가 중요하다. 산호초들이 높은 수준의 지질과 지방을 그들의 기관 내에 가지고 있다면, 이는 산호초들이 그들의 공생 관계를 재확립하기 전까지 버틸 수 있는 힘을 주는 것이다.

어휘
obesity 비만
paunch 배, 올챙이 배
godsend 하느님이 주신 선물
coral 산호초
stave off 피하다, 간신히 모면하다
bleaching 표백
reef 암초
shed 뿌리다, 버리다
algae 조류, 말무리
come down to (결국은) ~이다, ~로 귀착되다
lipid 지질
hang on 버티다, 매달리다
symbiotic relationship 공생 관계

정답 (c)

38 To. Ms. Johnson,

Although the weather was not good with a bit of drizzling, We mostly had a great time at Fun Day. (a) To tell you more about the today's get together, I think the trophy presentations went a bit quickly. (b) I have to tell you that I have absolutely no problem with moving the day for the next event after Thanksgiving Day. (c) It would have given us more chance to take photos of our kids if only we could have our kids stand and pose for pictures in front of the table a bit longer. (d) After all, it would have been much better to see their faces rather than their backs.

Best wishes,

해설
다른 문장들은 이미 벌어진 Fun Day에 관한 내용인데, (b)만 다음 행사의 일정과 관련한 얘기가 나오고 있으므로 오답이 된다.

해석
존슨 씨께,

비록 다소 가랑비로 인해 좋은 날씨는 아니었지만, 저희는 대체로 펀 데이(Fun Day)에서 좋은 시간을 보냈습니다. (a) 오늘 모임에 대해 좀 더 말씀드리기 위해, 트로피 증정식이 약간은 빨리 진행되었습니다. (b) 제가 말하고 싶은 것은 추수감사절 후에 다음 모임의 날을 옮기는데 전혀 문제없다는 것입니다. (c) 만일 우리가 우리의 아이들을 서게 해서 좀 더 긴 시간 동안 테이블 앞에서 사진을 찍을 수 있도록 포즈를 취하게만 할 수 있다면 아이들의 사진을 찍을 수 있는 기회도 많을 수 있었을 것입니다. (d) 결국, 그들의 뒷모습보다는 그들의 얼굴을 더 잘 볼 수 있었을 텐데 말입니다.

진심을 담아,

어휘
drizzle 가랑비, 이슬비, 가랑비가 내리다
get together 모임
Thanksgiving Day 추수감사절
presentation 증정식, 발표
pose for a picture 사진을 찍기 위해 포즈를 취하다

정답 (b)

39 It was once thought that the structure of our brain was incapable of further development after we reached adulthood. That's because, unlike other cells in the body, neurons do not regenerate. (a) A single thought, if repeated a few times, will build new synaptic docking points between those particular brain cells that can last indefinitely. (b) This seemed to support the view that what happens in childhood is our destiny – that the thought and behaviour that define our character are basically fixed by the age of twenty. (c) That view now seems to be a myth. (d) The cells are not like inert electrical wiring, because, while no new brain cells are born in adulthood, each cell is capable of establishing thousands of new connections with its neighbours, given the opportunities.

해설
지문의 내용과 각 문단에서 말하고자 하는 뉘앙스를 명확히 파악해야지 풀 수 있는 문제다. 인간의 뇌구조가 더 멀리 발전 할 수 없는 이유로 뇌세포가 재생산이 되지 않기 때문이라는 이유를 들고 있다. (b)는 이로 인해 기존에 생각되어지던 고정관념을 언급하고, (c)는 이 고정관념이 사라졌음으로 그리고 (d)에서 이에 대한 근거로 세포가 서로 간에 새로운 결합을 만들어 낼 수 있음을 언급하고 있다. 반면 보기 (a)는 앞에서 나온 세포의 재생과 관련 없이 마지막 보기에서 언급되는 두뇌 세포들 간의 결합과 관련한 이야기를 하고 있기 때문에 맥락에서 벗어난다.

해석
우리의 뇌 구조가 우리가 성인에 도달한 이후에는 발전할 수는 없다고 한때 생각되었었다. 그 이유는 신체의 다른 세포들과는 다르게, 신경단위들은 재생을 하지 않기 때문이다. (a) 하나의 생각이 몇 번 반복이 된다면 무기한으로 지속되는 특정 두뇌 세포들 간에 새로운 시냅스 결합을 만들어 낼 것이다. (b) 이것은 어린 시절 벌어지는 일들은 우리의 운명이고, 우리의 성격을 정의하는 생각과 행동은 기본적으로 20살이 되면 고정이 된다는 관점을 뒷받침 해주는 것처럼 보인다. (c) 그 관점은 이제 과거의 이야기다. (d) 두뇌세포들은 활동을 못하는 전기 배선과 같은 것이 아니다. 왜냐하면, 성인기에 새로운 두뇌세포가 만들어지지는 못하는 반면, 각각의 세포들은 서로 인접해있는 세포들과 함께 기회가 주어진다면 수천 개의 새로운 연결고리를 확립할 수 있기 때문이다.

어휘
be incapable of ~을 할 수 없는
adulthood 성인
neuron 신경단위
regenerate 재생하다
synaptic 연접(의)
indefinitely 무기한으로
inert 활발하지 못한, 활동을 못하는

정답 (a)

40 A hot cup of tea causes throat cancer. (a) Iranian researchers studying tea-drinking habits found that drinking very hot tea was associated with an eight-fold increase in the risk of throat cancer compared with sipping warm or lukewarm tea. (b) Both smoking rates and alcohol consumption are associated with the throat cancer. (c) People who regularly drank tea less than two minutes were five more times likely to develop the cancer compared with those who waited four or more minutes. (d) The research suggests people should let their drinks cold before consuming them.

해설

뜨거운 차를 마시는 것과 식도암 간의 관계를 설명한 글이다. (a)에서는 뜨거운 차를 마시는 것이 그렇지 않은 것보다 식도암을 발생시킬 확률이 높다고 이야기하고, (c)에서는 구체적으로 차를 마시는 시간을 기준으로 설명해주고 있다. (d)에서는 이를 바탕으로 건강을 위해 차를 천천히 마시는 것이 좋다는 결론을 내리고 있다. 반면, (b)는 차와는 상관없는 흡연과 음주 그리고 식도암 간의 관계를 언급하고 있으므로 전체 문맥상 어울리지 않는다. 정답은 (b)이다.

해석

뜨거운 차 한 잔이 식도암을 일으킬 수 있다. (a) 차 마시는 습관을 연구한 이란 연구원들은 매우 뜨거운 차를 마시는 것이 따뜻하거나 미지근한 차를 마시는 것과 비교했을 때 식도암의 위험이 8배 증가하는 것과 관련이 있음을 밝혀냈다. (b) 흡연율과 알코올 소비액은 둘 다 식도암과 관련이 있다. (c) 차를 2분보다 적은 시간에 규칙적으로 마시는 사람들은 4분에서 5분 동안 기다려서 차를 마시는 사람들보다 5배나 더 암에 걸릴 확률이 높았다. (d) 이 연구조사는 사람들에게 차를 마시기 전에 차가 차가울 때까지 놔둬야 함을 암시한다.

어휘

throat cancer 식도암
habit 습관
be associated with ~와 관련이 있다
lukewarm 미지근한
consumption 소비(액)
consume 마셔버리다, 소비하다

✓ 정답 (b)

Actual Test ·3 Answers

1. (c)	2. (c)	3. (b)	4. (d)
5. (c)	6. (b)	7. (d)	8. (c)
9. (c)	10. (c)	11. (b)	12. (c)
13. (d)	14. (d)	15. (a)	16. (d)
17. (c)	18. (c)	19. (c)	20. (d)
21. (d)	22. (c)	23. (c)	24. (b)
25. (d)	26. (b)	27. (c)	28. (c)
29. (d)	30. (c)	31. (b)	32. (d)
33. (c)	34. (c)	35. (d)	36. (b)
37. (c)	38. (d)	39. (d)	40. (b)

1 We all know that stopping smoking is good for our health at any time of our life. Especially, it _____ before you have an operation. Why do you have to wait and increase your risks when you have surgery? You will not be able to smoke immediately after surgery, so you can make this a good opportunity for you to stop for good. Quitting completely is the only way to stop and reverse the damage done by cigarettes. You can cut down before stopping smoking completely, but the recovery of your body will only start from the time you stop completely.

(a) is too late to stop smoking completely
(b) can be too dangerous to stop smoking
(c) might be the best time to quit smoking
(d) might be considered inappropriate to quit smoking

해설

빈칸 뒤의 문장에서 수술 후에는 바로 담배를 피울 수가 없기 때문에 이것을 영원히 담배를 끊기 위한 좋은 기회로 만들 수 있다고 말하고 있다. 그러므로 '수술을 하기 전이 담배를 끊기 위한 최고의 시간일 수도 있다'는 내용의 (c)가 정답이다. 나머지 보기들은 지문이 의도하는 바와 상반되는 내용의 보기들이다.

해석

우리는 모두 우리 삶의 어느 때이던 간에, 담배를 끊는 것이 우리의 건강을 위해 좋다는 것을 알고 있다. 특히, 당신이 수술을 하기 전이 담배를 끊기 위한 최고의 때일 수 있다. 수술을 받게 될 때, 왜 (담배 끊는 것을) 기다려서 수술시 위험을 증가시키는가? 수술 후에 당신은 곧바로 담배를 피울 수 없으니 이것을 영원히 담배를 끊기 위한 좋은 기회로 만들 수 있을 것이다. 담배를 완전히 끊는 것만이 담배에 의해서 행해진 신체의 손상을 멈추고 되돌릴 수 있는 유일한 방법이다. 담배를 완전히 끊기 전에 조금씩 줄일 수도 있다. 하지만 당신의 신체의 회복은 오직 담배를 완전히 끊은 순간부터 시작될 것이다.

어휘
operation 수술
for good 영원히
reverse 뒤엎다, 뒤집다
cut down 줄이다
completely 완전히
quit 그만두다

정답 (c)

---

2 Taking the boss hostage as a means of resolving an industrial dispute is popular in France. Earlier this month the head of Sony France was kidnapped by factory workers demanding a better severance deal. He was locked in a meeting room while the plant was barricaded with large tree trunks before being freed the following day after workers' demands were met. In January 2008 the British boss of an ice-cream factory was held hostage after announcing plans to fire more than half the workforce. Kidnapping the boss _____ in the next few months as more companies plan to lay off their workers.

(a) is believed to diminish
(b) will rarely happen
(c) is expected to increase
(d) might become an obsolete tactic

해설
프랑스에서 벌어지고 있는 직원들에 의한 사장 납치 사건들을 설명하고 있는 글이다. 빈칸이 포함된 문장에는 사장을 납치하는 것이 다음 몇 달 동안 어떤 상황이 될 것인지에 대한 적절한 내용이 들어가야 한다. 빈칸 뒤의 문장에서 앞으로도 회사들의 직원 해고가 많을 것이라는 원인이 주어졌기에 사장 납치 범죄 역시 '증가될 것으로 예상된다' 인 (c)가 문맥상 가장 적절하다.

해석
프랑스에서는 산업논쟁을 해결하는 방법으로 사장을 인질로 잡는 것이 인기이다. 이번 달 초에, Sony France의 사장이 더 나은 퇴직정책을 요구하는 공장 직원들에 의해서 납치되었다. 공장이 큰 나무통들로 바리케이드가 쳐져 있는 동안 사장은 노동자들의 요구가 수용된 후 다음 날 자유롭게 풀려나기 전까지 회의실에 갇혀 있었다. 2008년 1월에는 아이스크림 공장 영국인 사장이 전체 노동자의 절반을 해고하는 계획을 발표한 후 인질로 잡히기도 했다. 사장을 인질로 잡는 행위는 더 많은 회사들이 문을 닫게 되면서 다음 몇 달 동안 증가할 것으로 예상된다.

어휘
take a person hostage 누구를 인질로 잡다
means 수단, 방법
resolve 풀다, 해결하다
kidnap 유괴하다, 납치하다
severance deal 퇴직정책
barricade 바리케이드를 쌓다
workforce 총 노동인구
obsolete 시대에 뒤진, 진부한
lay off 해고하다

정답 (c)

---

3 Adding dairy products to your diet is the easiest way to get your daily requirement of calcium, as well as plenty of other beneficial nutrients. But what if you're intolerant to lactose? The symptoms of lactose intolerance affect different people in different ways and can range from mild discomfort to abdominal pain. Lactose is the sugar found in milk. When we consume milk, an enzyme called lactase in the small intestine splits lactose into its two component sugars, called glucose and galactose, which the body uses for energy. Without sufficient quantities of lactase in the small intestine, lactose _____ and passes to the large intestine where it ferments and produces gases that may cause pain, bloating, and sometimes diarrhea. This is called lactose intolerance and almost all cases are permanent, usually because the production of lactase in the body has ceased.

(a) will remain as glucose and galactose
(b) can't be digested
(c) will be absorbed to the body
(d) can't produce enzyme

해설
유당인 lactose는 소장에 있는 lactase에 의해서 분해되어 소화가 되는데, 이 lactase가 없으면 유당 분해효소 결핍증에 걸려 우유를 소화시키지 못한다는 내용의 글이다. 빈칸 앞에서 소장에 충분한 lactase가 없는 경우를 얘기하고 있으므로, lactose는 소화가 될 수 없다는 (b)가 정답이다.

해석
유제품을 식단에 더하는 것은 다른 많은 유익한 영양분들과 함께 하루 필수 칼슘 양을 얻는 가장 쉬운 방법이다. 하지만 만약 당신이 유당을 섭취할 수 없다면 어떻게 해야 하나? 유당 분해효소 결핍증의 증상들은 여러 사람들에게 여러 방식으로 영향을 미친다. 그리고 가벼운 불쾌함에서부터 복부통증까지 다양할 수 있다. 유당은 우유에서 발견되는 설탕이다. 우리가 우유를 섭취할 때, 소장 안에 락타아제라고 불리는 효소가 유당을 신체가 에너지를 위해서 사용하는 글루코스와 갈락토스라는 두 가지 성분 설탕으로 분리시킨다. 소장 내의 충분한 양의 락타아제가 없으면, 유당은 소화가 될 수가 없고, 대장으로 전달되어 발효되고 통증과, 복부팽창 그리고 때때로 설사를 일으키는 가스를 생산한다. 이것이 유당 분해효소 결핍증이라고 불리고 거의 대부분의 경우 신체 내의 락타아제의 생산이 멈추었기 때문에 영구적이다.

어휘
dairy product 유제품
requirement 요구, 필요조건
beneficial 유익한
lactose intolerant 유당 분해효소 결핍증
what if ~ 만약 ~라면 어쩌지?
abdominal 복부의
split 쪼개다, 분할하다
sufficient 충분한
ferment 발효하다
small intestine 소장
cease 그만두다, 멈추다

정답 (b)

4 It's no secret that the hardest thing about a fitness regime is not the sit-ups, push-ups or even the long sessions on a bike. Anyone with an exercise routine knows _____ is the toughest part of all. Once summer is over, the motivation of getting into shape for the days on the beach disappears as the winter months loom. Suddenly, going out for a run or doing laps of the swimming pool doesn't seem so important. The exercise shoes are quietly packed away, with the promise to pull them out in October in time for next summer. "We see this happening every year, and it is a natural tendency for people to stop paying so much attention to not only their physical appearance but their fitness level as well." says Alicia Gibson of the American Fitness network.

(a) being on good terms with trainers
(b) resisting food temptations
(c) finding the right place to work out
(d) making exercise a part of your life

해설
운동을 정기적으로 함에 있어서 가장 어려운 것이 무엇인가를 보기 중에 골라야 한다. 빈칸 뒤의 문장에서는 여름이 끝나고 난 뒤, 운동을 하고자 하는 동기가 사라진다는 예를 들고 있다. 즉, 운동을 함에 있어 가장 어려운 것은 '운동을 삶의 일부분으로 만들어야 하는 것'이라는 (d)가 정답이다.

해석
건강관리요법에 있어서 가장 어려운 일은 윗몸 일으키기도 아니고, 팔굽혀 펴기도 아니고, 자전거를 오랜 시간동안 타는 것조차도 아니라는 것은 비밀스러운 사실이 아닙니다. 운동을 정기적으로 하고 계신 분이라면 누구라도 운동을 지속적으로 하고, 운동을 삶의 일부분으로 만드는 것이 무엇보다도 가장 어려운 일이라는 것을 알고 있습니다. 일단 여름이 끝났을 때, 해변에서의 날들을 위해 몸매를 관리하려던 동기가 겨울이 오면서 사라져 버립니다. 졸지에 뜀박질을 하러 나가고, 수영장을 돌고 하는 것들이 그다지 중요하지 않게 됩니다. 운동 신발은 내년 여름을 위해 10월 달쯤 다시 꺼내겠다는 약속과 함께 조용히 싸서 치워져버립니다. "우리는 이런 상황을 매년 겪게 됩니다. 사람들은 외모뿐 만이 아니라 건강 상태에 대해서도 큰 관심을 기울이지 않게 되는 것이 자연스러운 경향이죠."라고 미국 건강 네트워크의 Alicia Gibson은 말하고 있습니다.

어휘
fitness regime 건강관리요법
motivation 자극, 동기
get into shape 몸매를 가꾸다
loom 아련히 나타나다
pack away 포장해서 치우다
tendency 경향, 추세
on good terms with ~와 친밀한
temptation 유혹

정답 (d)

---

5 Malaysian police fired tear gas to disperse more than 2,000 protesters in the capital, Kuala Lumpur. The demonstrators attempted to present a petition to the Malaysian king, calling for the reinstatement of Bahasa Malay in the teaching of science and math. The government of former prime minister Mahathir Mohamad _____, concerned that poor English-language skills were undermining student performance. But activists and opposition politicians are concerned at the impact on the Malay language.

(a) opposed to the idea of teaching the foreign language in classes
(b) prohibited learning science and math in English
(c) mandated teaching these subjects in English
(d) supported the demonstrator's petition

해설
빈칸은 전 국무총리인 Mahthir Mohamad가 무엇을 했는지에 대한 서술 내용이 나와야 한다. 빈칸 뒤에는 낮은 영어 실력이 학생들의 성취도를 손상시키고 있다는 걱정을 했다는 내용이 언급되므로, 이를 막기 위해, 영어로 학교에서 수업을 하도록 지시했다는 내용이 나와야 한다. 그러므로 정답은 (c)이다.

해석
말레이시아 경찰은 수도 Kuala Lumpur에 모인 2000여 명의 시위자들을 분산시키기 위해서 최루탄을 발사했습니다. 시위자들은 과학과 수학을 가르침에 있어서 말레이시아 공용어를 재사용하는 것을 요청하는 탄원서를 말레이시아 국왕에게 제출하기 위한 시도를 했습니다. 전 총리인 Mahathir Mohamad 정부는 낮은 영어 실력이 학생들의 성취도를 손상시키고 있다고 걱정해, 이 과목들을 영어로 가르치도록 명령했습니다. 하지만 운동가들과 야당 정치인들은 이것이 말레이시아 언어에 미칠 충격을 걱정하고 있습니다.

어휘
fire 발사하다
tear gas 최루탄
disperse 흩어지게 하다
demonstrator 시위자
petition 청원, 탄원
reinstatement 회복, 복원
concern 관심을 갖다, 염려하다
undermine 훼손하다, 손상시키다
Bahasa Malay 말레이시아 공용어

정답 (c)

6 When was the last time you truly got away from it all? With the ever-increasing demands of work, finances, and family, chances are the answer is "I can't remember". You need to be connected, every day, in more places, and that's where WestNet Wireless Broadband _____. Whether you're trapped in a corporate board room or holidaying up the coast, WestNet Wireless Broadband is as mobile as you are—and as flexible, reliable and accessible as you're expected to be. As well as having faster speeds in more places, America's greatest wireless broadband coverage and best value for money, WestNet Wireless Broadband has another great advantage: It is part of WestNet, so it's backed by the reliability and security of the country's largest internet service provider.

(a) can help you take a rest at work
(b) can give you the edge
(c) can guarantee you the fastest speed
(d) can prevent you from having a bill blow-out

🔓 해설

빈칸의 앞뒤 문장의 흐름을 이해하고 있는지 묻고 있다. 바쁜 세상 속에서 사람들은 매일, 그 어떤 장소에서도 인터넷에 연결이 되어 있어야 한다고 언급되고 있고, 그것을 해결해 줄 수 있는 것이 WestNet Wireless Broadband라는 것이 글의 전체 흐름인 광고글이다. 직장에서 휴식을 취할 시간을 주겠다는 것이 아니라 직장에서든 어디든 인터넷에 연결할 수 있다는 것이 요점이므로 (a)는 정답이 될 수 없고, 빠른 스피드는 뒤에서 추가로 언급되는 상품의 장점일 뿐이지, 빈칸의 앞뒤 내용과는 관련이 없다. 그러므로 정답은 '강점을 줄 수 있다'는 (b)이다

🔓 해석

모든 것으로부터 진정 떠나 있었던 때가 마지막으로 언제였나요? 어느 때보다도 더 증가하고 있는 일, 재정 그리고 가족들의 요구들을 생각할 때, 대답은 "전 기억이 나지 않아요"일 가능성이 높겠죠. 여러분은 매일, 더 많은 장소에서 (인터넷에) 연결되어 있을 필요가 있습니다. 바로 이 부분이 WestNet Wireless Broadband가 여러분에게 강점을 드릴 수 있는 부분이죠. 여러분이 회사 회의실에 갇혀 있든, 해변에서 휴일을 보내고 있든, WestNet Wireless Broadband는 여러분만큼이나 이동성을 가지고 있습니다. 그리고 여러분들 만큼이나 융통성이 있고, 믿음직하고, 접근성이 높지요. 더 많은 장소에서 더 빠른 스피드와 미국에서 가장 큰 무선 광대역 범위, 그리고 가장 최상의 가격뿐만이 아니라, WestNet Wireless Broadband는 또 다른 훌륭한 장점을 가지고 있습니다. 그것은 바로 본 서비스가 WestNet의 일부분이라는 것입니다. 그러므로 저희는 나라에서 가장 큰 인터넷 서비스 제공자의 신뢰성과 안정성에 의해 지원받고 있다는 것이지요.

🔍 어휘

get away from ~으로부터 도망치다
finance 재정, 재무
chances 가능성
edge 강점, 우세
holiday 휴일을 보내다
mobile 움직이기 쉬운, 이동성이 있는
wireless 무선의
coverage 적용범위, 유효 도달 범위
back 후원하다, 지원하다

✓ 정답 (b)

7 Despite the recession, sales of guitars are booming, says Dominic White in The Canadian Financial Review. Imports of guitars and guitar amplifiers continue to grow and have almost doubled in the past five years. This increase in sales is partly due to a drop in the price of guitars as more are now made in China. Decent quality electric and acoustic guitars have collapsed in price from 1,000 dollars to 300 dollars. The surge in interest is being attributed to the "cocooning effect" which encourages people to stay at home and spend their spare cash on entertaining themselves. Manufacturers _____, offering starter packs and replicas of stars' instruments.

(a) are struggling to survive the recession
(b) have tried to export their guitars to China
(c) raised the prices of guitars
(d) have been quick to spot the trend

🔓 해설

글의 주제는 경기후퇴에도 불구하고, 기타 판매 사업이 어떻게 호황을 누리고 있는지를 설명해주고 있다. 그러므로 제조업체들이 경기후퇴에서 살아남기 위해 악전고투하고 있다는 내용인 (a)는 정답이 될 수 없고, (b), (c) 역시 현재의 기타 산업 특성과는 전혀 상반되는 내용이므로 정답이 될 수 없다. 제조업체들이 현 추세를 잘 파악해서 추가 상품을 내놓고 있다는 내용의 (d)가 정답으로 나와야 한다.

🔓 해석

경기후퇴에도 불구하고 기타 판매가 폭등하고 있다고 Canadian Financial Review 지의 Dominic White 씨가 말합니다. 기타와 기타 앰프의 수입이 지속적으로 증가하고 있고, 지난 5년간 거의 두 배 가까이 늘었습니다. 이러한 판매의 증가는 일정 부분 기타의 가격 하락에 기인하는 데, 이는 더 많은 기타들이 이제 중국에서 만들어지고 있기 때문입니다. 일정 수준의 품질의 전자 및 어쿠스틱 기타들의 가격은 1000달러에서 300달러로 폭락했습니다. (기타에 대한) 관심도의 증가는 사람들이 집에서 머물며 여유 돈을 스스로를 즐겁게 하는데 쓰도록 조장하는 일명 누에고치 효과 덕분으로 여겨지고 있습니다. 기타제조사들은 이러한 트렌드를 알아차리고, 초보자들을 위한 패키지와 스타들의 장비 복제품을 팔려고 내놓고 있습니다.

🔍 어휘

boom 폭등하다, 경기가 좋아지다
import 수입(품), 수입하다
due to ~ 때문에
decent 훌륭한
collapse 폭락하다, 무너지다
cocooning effect 누에고치 효과

✓ 정답 (d)

8 If your child has an allergy or food intolerance, there are plenty of food alternatives _____ _____. Finding replacements for dairy and wheat products can be especially difficult when it seems to creep into the normal diet so readily. Children have special daily requirements for growth, brain function and energy, so it is important to encourage replacing healthy foods with those you are eliminating. If your child has lactose intolerance you can easily replace dairy milk with oat milk or rice milk. Here's the key. Don't tell them. Serve it differently, such as in a banana smoothie with honey and vanilla. They won't even notice the difference.

(a) that can help cure their diseases
(b) to be cultivated domestically
(c) to make up for what they can't have
(d) that add flavors to milk and wheat

9 When you have young children in your family, it's _____, both indoors and out. Just as we use a wide range of devices, such as safety latches and covers for electrical outlets, to help prevent accidents occurring inside the home, in the backyard, the right fence can provide peace of mind. Here is a smart and practical solution. Fencing made from COLORBOND steel gives you added protection against unwanted entry and unwelcome eyes. As it has no footholds, it's hard to climb and as the panels can't be loosened or removed, fencing made from COLORBOND steel turns your backyard into a secluded and safer space.

(a) important to turn your home into the kids playground
(b) significant to buy lots of safety home gadgets
(c) vital to childproof your home
(d) important to have child-friendly fencing

해설

단락의 첫 문장이 주제문인 경우이다. 지문은 음식, 그 중 우유나 밀 제품에 대해서 알레르기나 과민성이 있는 아이들을 위해서 대체음식들을 찾아서 대신 섭취하게끔 해야 한다고 말하고 있다. 따라서 정답은 '그들이 먹을 수 없는 것을 보충해 줄 수 있는' 이란 (c)가 정답이다. 이러한 대체 음식은 말 그대로 영양분을 대체하기 위함이지, 대체 음식 자체가 아이들의 병을 치료할 수 있는 것은 아니므로 (a)는 정답이 될 수 없다.

해석

만약 당신의 아이가 알레르기나 음식에 대한 과민성이 있다면, 아이들이 먹을 수 없는 음식을 대신할 수 있는 수많은 대체 음식들이 있습니다. 낙농음식과 밀 제품을 대체할 음식을 찾는 것은 그것이 즉시 정규 식단에 몰래 들어가려 할 때는 굉장히 어려울 수가 있습니다. 아이들의 성장과, 뇌기능, 그리고 에너지를 위한 특별한 하루의 섭취량이 있습니다. 그러므로 여러분이 제거하려는 음식을 대체할 건강한 음식을 찾도록 권장되는 것은 중요한 일입니다. 만약 여러분의 아이가 유당 분해효소 결핍증을 갖고 있다면 여러분은 쉽게 유제품 우유를 보리 우유나 쌀 우유로 대체하실 수 있습니다. 여기서 중요한 점이 있는데요. 아이들에게 말하지 마세요. 꿀과 바닐라를 함께 탄 바나나 스무디와 함께 타서 다르게 아이들에게 먹이세요. 아이들은 차이점을 알아차리지도 못할 겁니다.

어휘

intolerance 과민성
replacement 대체(자)
dairy 낙농(의)
creep into ~에 몰래 들어가다
requirement 요구, 필요(물)
lactose intolerance 유당 과민성
oat 귀리
notice 알아차리다
cultivate 재배하다, 경작하다

정답 (c)

해설

만약 집안에 어린아이들이 있다면 집 안팎을 어떻게 해야 하는가에 대한 빈칸 넣기 문제이다. 빈칸 뒤의 내용들은 아이들의 안전을 위해 집 안에 준비해 놓는 여러 장치들과 함께, 집 밖의 안전을 위해서 본 지문이 광고하고 있는 울타리를 설치할 것을 권하는 내용이다. 그러므로 정답은 (c)이다. 보기 (a)의 집을 아이들의 놀이터로 만드는 것과 뒤에 나오는 펜싱 광고를 통한 안정성은 직접적인 연관성이 떨어지고, 집 내부에도 펜싱을 치자는 것이 아니므로 (d)는 정답이 될 수 없다.

해석

당신의 가족들 중에 어린아이들이 있을 때, 당신의 집 안팎 모두 아이들에게 안전하게 하는 것은 극히 중요한 일입니다. 우리 집 안에서 사고가 일어나는 것을 예방하기 위해서 안전 걸쇠나 전기 콘센트 덮개와 같은 다양한 종류의 장치들을 사용하는 것처럼, 뒤뜰에서는 올바른 울타리가 마음의 안정을 가져다 줄 수 있습니다. 여기 현명하고 실용적인 해결 방법이 있습니다. COLORBOND 강철로 만들어진 울타리는 불필요한 출입과 달갑지 않은 시선들로부터 추가적인 보호망을 당신께 드릴 수 있습니다. 그것은 발판이 없기 때문에, (울타리를) 타고 오르는 것이 어렵습니다. 그리고 벽판이 느슨해진다거나 제거가 되지 못하기 때문에, COLORBOND 강철로 만들어진 울타리는 당신의 뒤뜰을 세상과 격리된 그리고 더 안전한 공간으로 바꾸어 드립니다.

어휘

childproof (물건, 장소 등을) 어린아이에게 안전하게 하다
latch 걸쇠, 빗장
electrical outlet 전기 콘센트
fencing 울타리, 담
foothold 발판, 발디딤
secluded 격리된, 외딴

정답 (c)

10

Most of us aren't perfectly symmetrical. For instance, one leg might be a tiny bit shorter than the other. Even this slight discrepancy adds pressure to the musculoskeletal system and impacts on how we use our muscles. Adding to the effect is the fact that _____, so we tend to use one side of our bodies much more than the other. For example, have you ever noticed that you always lead off with your right foot? Decades later it's not surprising that we end up with unbalanced bodies.

(a) we can use both our right and left hands equally skillfully
(b) most of our bodies are not proportionate
(c) few of us are ambidextrous
(d) most of us discriminate against people based on their looks

해설

인간의 신체는 균형이 잡히지 않았다는 것이 본 글의 주제이다. 빈칸에 들어갈 내용은 이러한 결과에 더 영향을 주는 사실로, 결국 우리들이 신체의 한쪽을 다른 쪽보다 더 사용하는 경향이 있다는 내용으로 연결이 되어야 한다. 그러므로 '우리들 중 극소수만이 양손잡이다' 라는 의미의 (c)가 정답이다. 우리의 신체가 균형적이지 못하다는 내용의 (b)는 우리가 신체의 한쪽을 더 많이 사용함으로써 생기는 결과지 원인이 아니므로 정답이 될 수 없다.

해석

우리 대부분은 완벽하게 대칭적이지 않다. 예를 들어, 한 쪽 다리는 아주 조금 다른 쪽보다 짧을 수 있는 것이다. 이렇게 자그마한 불일치조차도 근육 골격 계통에 압박을 더하고 우리가 근육을 사용하는 방식에 영향을 줄 수 있다. 이러한 결과를 더해 주는 것은 우리들 중 거의 극소수가 양손잡이라는 사실로 우리는 다른 쪽보다 우리 신체의 어느 한 쪽을 더 많이 사용하는 경향이 있다. 예를 들어, 당신은 항상 당신의 오른쪽 발을 먼저 내딛는다는 것을 알아챈 적이 있는가? 수십 년이 지나서 우리가 균형이 잡히지 않은 신체를 갖게 되더라도 놀라운 일이 아닌 것이다.

어휘

symmetrical 균형 잡힌, 대칭의
discrepancy 불일치
musculoskeletal system 근육 골격 계통
ambidextrous 양손잡이의
proportionate 비례하는, 균형이 잡힌

정답 (c)

11

Dear editors,

Knowing that we were going to be facing two weeks of more than 40 degrees celsius weather this summer, I was at a loss for meals to make for my family in the heat. That was until I read your January issue, which was full of lots of fresh, filling and delicious recipes _____.
The meals are really quick to prepare, which means I've spent very little time at the stove on these hot days. Among the recipes, the Asian-Style Chicken Salad has become an instant favourite. Thank you Lovely Meals for helping me to survive the heat-wave with delicious meals!

Sincerely,

(a) that needed a good budget
(b) that required little or no cooking
(c) that needed meticulous accuracy
(d) that required melting, boiling and frying

해설

필자가 감사하는 조리법에 대한 추가설명으로 가장 적절한 내용이 빈칸 안에 들어가야 한다. 빈칸 뒤에 이어지는 문장을 통해 조리법을 사용해 만든 음식들이 빠르게 준비할 수 있기에 더운 날씨에 스토브 앞에서 서 있을 필요도 거의 없었다는 것을 알 수 있다. 즉, 잡지에서 제공한 조리법들은 '요리를 할 필요가 거의 또는 전혀 없는 조리법' 이란 의미가 되는 보기 (b)가 정답으로 가장 적절하다.

해석

편집자님께,

이번 여름에 섭씨 40도가 넘는 날씨를 두 주 동안 맞이해야 한다는 것을 알기에, 저는 이 더위 속에서 가족들을 위한 음식을 무엇을 해야 할지 어쩔 줄 몰라 하고 있었습니다. 이러한 걱정은 요리 자체가 거의 또는 전혀 요구되지 않는 신선하고, 배부르고 맛있는 요리법으로 가득 찬 귀사의 1월호 잡지를 보기 전까지였습니다. 그 음식들은 준비과정이 정말 빨랐기에 이 더운 날씨에 오븐 앞에서 보내는 시간이 굉장히 짧았습니다. 조리법들 중에서 아시아 스타일 치킨 샐러드는 바로 제가 가장 선호하는 조리법이 되었습니다. 이 혹서기간을 맛있는 음식으로 살아남도록 절 도와주신 Lovely Meals에 감사드립니다.

진심을 담아서,

어휘

face 직면하다, 맞이하다
at a loss 난처하여, 어쩔 줄 몰라서
recipe 조리법
prepare 준비하다
instant 즉시, 즉각
heat wave 혹서, 열파
budget 예산
meticulous 세심한
accuracy 정확, 정밀도

정답 (b)

12 A young woman was stripped naked, bound and gagged, tied to a log and set on fire by a band of villagers. she burnt to death in the blaze. Her crime was that she was suspected of being a witch. Belief in witchcraft is popular in rural Papua New Guinea, and _____ is a common practice. Last year alone some 50 people were victims of witchcraft-related murder in the Highlands provinces, and there were over 500 attacks linked to witchcraft throughout the entire country. However, these are only the deaths and attacks that are recorded. There is no precise figures as many incidents occur in remote areas and often go unreported. Furthermore, the locals often refuse to cooperate with the authorities when a death occurs. It is notoriously difficult to find eyewitnesses who are willing to talk. Therefore, it is difficult to apprehend the offenders and to solve these covert crimes.

(a) exorcism for the evil spirits
(b) extracting a confession of sorcery
(c) homicide against suspected sorcery
(d) using magic to slaughter people

13 The global financial crisis _____, especially in Asia, and women–as always–are the ones who suffer the most. The major reason is that female workers are concentrated in labor-intensive export industries. They are generally clustered at the lower levels in casual, temporary, sub-contracted and informal employment, The work is insecure, wages low and conditions poor. Women in the clothing, textiles and electronics industries will be the first to go. We know this from 1997 economic crisis: in Thailand 98% of those laid off from the garment sector were women and in the toys sector it was 88%. In Korea, 85% of those who lost jobs in financial services and banking were female. Failure to recognize this gender crisis could be worsening the working and living conditions of millions.

(a) is gender blind
(b) is adversely affecting every sector
(c) is a man-made catastrophe
(d) has a certain bias

해설
파푸아뉴기니에서 벌어지고 있는 마녀사냥에 대한 글이다. 초반에 마녀로 의심받아 살해당한 한 여성의 예가 등장한다. 그리고 빈칸 뒤의 문장에서, 마술과 관련한 살해행위의 피해자가 작년에만 50여 명 된다는 내용을 파악할 수 있다. 즉 빈칸에는 '의심되는 마술행위에 대한 살인행위' 인 (c)가 정답으로 가장 적절하다.

해석
젊은 여성이 발가벗겨진 채로, 재갈이 물려 통나무에 묶인 채로 마을 사람들에 의해서 불 질러졌고 화염 속에서 타 죽었습니다. 그녀의 죄는 그녀가 마녀라는 의심을 받았다는 것이었습니다. 주술에 대한 믿음은 파푸아뉴기니의 시골 지방에서는 널리 퍼져있습니다. 그리고 의심이 되는 마술행위에 대해서는 살인을 저지르는 것이 일반적인 관행입니다. 작년에만 고지 지방에서 마술과 관련해 벌어진 살인의 희생자 수가 50여 명 정도였습니다. 그리고 국가 전체에 걸쳐서 마술과 관련해 벌어진 500개가 넘는 공격사건이 있었습니다. 하지만, 이 죽음과 공격사건의 수는 기록이 된 것들일 뿐입니다. 많은 사건들이 멀리 떨어진 지역에서 벌어지고 종종 신고가 되고 있지 않기 때문에 정확한 수치는 존재하지 않습니다. 게다가, 지역민들은 종종 사망사고가 발생했을 때, 당국에 협조하는 것을 거부하곤 합니다. 기꺼이 말을 하겠다고 나서는 증인을 찾는 것도 악명 높을 정도로 힘듭니다. 그래서 범인을 체포하는 것도 어려워 이 은밀한 범죄들을 해결하는 것이 어렵습니다.

어휘
gag 재갈을 물리다
band 무리, 한 무리의 사람들
blaze 불길, 화염
be suspected of ~으로 의심받다
witch 마녀
witchcraft 마법, 주술
murder 살인
homicide 살인행위
eyewitness 증인
apprehend 체포하다
covert 암암리의, 은밀한
exorcism 귀신 쫓아내기, 구마주문
extract 뽑아내다, 캐내다
confession 자백
sorcery 마법, 마술
slaughter 대량 학살하다

 정답 (c)

해설
빈칸이 포함된 문장의 뒤쪽에서 가장 많은 고통을 겪는 것은 여성이라고 말하고 있다. 이어지는 내용들을 통해서도 몇 나라의 예를 들어, 금융위기 시 비율적으로 더 많은 여성들이 해고를 당했음을 알려주고 있다. 이를 통해서, 빈칸은 세계 금융위기가 '특정하게 치우쳐 있다' 라는 (d)가 정답임을 알 수 있다.

해석
세계 금융위기는 특히 아시아에서 뚜렷한 편견을 보이고 있고, 항상 그랬듯이 가장 많은 고통을 겪게 되는 것은 여성들이다. 중요한 이유는 여성 근로자들이 노동 집약적인 수출 산업에 집중되어 있다는 것이다. 그들은 일반적으로 낮은 수준의 평범하고, 일시적이며, 도급 계약되고 비형식적인 고용에 밀집되어 있다. 일자리는 불안정하고 임금은 낮으며 환경은 열악하다. 의류 옷감과 전자 산업에 종사하는 여성들이 우선적으로 해고될 것이다. 우리는 이것을 1997년 경제위기로부터 통해서 알 수 있다. 이 당시 태국에서는 의복 분야에서 해고된 98%가 여성이었고, 완구 분야에서는 해고된 88%가 여성이었다. 한국에서는 금융서비스와 은행업 분야에서 일자리를 잃은 사람들의 85%가 여성이었다. 이러한 성별 위기를 알아차리지 못하는 것은 수백만 명의 일자리와 생활 상황을 더욱 악화시키게 될 것이다.

어휘
global financial crisis 세계 금융위기
labor-intensive 노동집약적인
cluster 밀집하다
temporary 일시적인, 임시의
sub-contract (도급) 계약을 하다
garment 의복
worsen 악화시키다
man-made 인간이 만들어 낸
bias 편견, 치우침

정답 (d)

14 An angry chimp has proved humans aren't the only ones _____. When Santino, a chimpanzee at the Furuvik Zoo in Sweden, started pelting zoo visitors with stones and his keepers were puzzled. Chimps are often aggressive and this 31-year-old was a dominant male, so the behaviour was no surprise. But where was he finding his missiles? A search revealed that Santino had been stockpiling rocks. He'd fished stones from the land surrounding his enclosure and even shaped pieces of concrete into disc-shaped missiles. Fortunately for visitors he wasn't very good at throwing, so no one was badly hurt, but his behaviour has led scientists to conclude that planning ahead is not a uniquely human trait. It seems chimpanzees also have a sophisticated understanding of the past and future.

(a) who can guess what others are thinking
(b) capable of making an instrument
(c) resorting to violence as a solution
(d) who can premeditate

15 Skin cancer is caused by exposure to ultraviolet radiation from the sun. Experts say that ultraviolet radiation is strongest between 11 in the morning and 3 in the afternoon and is present all year. Boaters are particularly susceptible, as reflected radiation from the water gives an additional radiation effect. Preventive measures are very important and clothing provides the best protection. _____, They should cover areas of their bodies with a hat. A hat will cover their faces, ears and necks. They should wear a long-sleeved shirt. It is also essential to apply sunscreen to exposed areas with a maximum sun protector factor. It's important to apply the sunscreen 15 minutes before going out reapply every two and a half hours.

(a) Therefore
(b) In the end
(c) Moreover
(d) Unfortunately

해설

지문 속에서 침팬지가 어떠한 행동을 했는지를 파악하면 답을 찾을 수 있다. 침팬지는 사람들에게 돌을 던지기 위해 사전에 돌들을 모아서 비축해 놓았다고 한다. 또한 마지막 문장에서도 사람만이 앞서서 계획을 할 수 있는 존재가 아니라고 과학자들이 결론을 내렸다고 하는 것을 봐서 정답은 '사전 계획을 할 수 있는'인 (d)가 정답이다.

해석

화가 난 한 침팬지가 인간들이 앞서 계획을 할 수 있는 유일한 존재가 아님을 증명하였다. 스웨덴의 Furuvik Zoo에 있는 침팬지 Santino는 방문객들에게 돌멩이를 내던지기 시작했고 이로 인해 그의 사육사들이 당황했다. 침팬지들은 종종 공격적이고, 이 31살의 침팬지는 무리를 지배하는 수컷이다. 그래서 그 행동은 놀라울 것이 없었다. 하지만, 그는 어디서 그의 미사일을 찾았던 것일까? 탐색 결과 Santiano는 돌멩이들을 비축해 왔던 것으로 밝혀졌다. 그는 그의 울타리를 둘러싸고 있는 땅에서 돌멩이들을 찾아냈고, 콘크리트 조각들을 원형 모양의 미사일로 만들기까지 했다. 방문자들에게는 다행히도, 그는 던지기를 그다지 잘하지 못했고, 아무도 심하게 다치지는 않았다. 하지만 그의 행동은 과학자들에게 사전 계획이란 것이 인간의 독특한 특성이 아니라는 결론을 내리도록 만들었다. 침팬지들 또한 계획을 할 수 있는 능력이 있고 과거와 미래에 대한 섬세한 이해력을 가지고 있는 것처럼 보인다.

어휘

prove 증명하다
pelt 공격하다, 내던지다
stockpile 비축하다
enclosure 울타리
fortunately 다행히도
planning 계획
trait 특성, 특징
sophisticated 정교한, 고급인
capable of ~을 할 능력이 있는
instrument 기구, 도구
resort to ~에 의존하다
premeditate 사전에 계획하다

정답 (d)

해설

연결사 문제이다. 지문은 태양의 자외선에 노출이 될 시 생기는 피부암에 대해서 이야기하고 있다. 빈칸 앞의 문장에서는 특히 배를 타는 사람들이 추가적인 열 효과를 받는다고 언급하고 있다. 그리고 빈칸 뒤에서는 이들이 모자로 그들의 신체 부위를 덮어야 한다고 말하고 있다. 태양열을 많이 받는 결과로 모자로 덮어야 한다는 것이기에 연결사는 (a) Therefore가 위치해야 한다. 정답은 (a)이다

해석

피부암은 태양으로부터의 자외선 열에 노출됨으로써 발생된다. 전문가들은 자외선 열이 아침 11시와 점심 3시 사이에 가장 강력하며, 일 년 내내 나타난다고 말한다. 배를 타는 사람들의 경우 물에서 반사된 열이 추가적인 열 효과를 내게 되므로, 특히나 더 영향을 받게 된다. 그러므로 그들은 신체의 부분들을 모자로 덮어야 한다. 모자는 그들의 얼굴과, 귀, 그리고 목을 덮어줄 것이다. 그들은 긴 팔 셔츠도 입어야 한다. 가장 강력한 태양 보호 요소를 가진 선 스크린을 노출이 되는 부위에 바르는 것은 필수다. 또한, 외출하기 15분 전에 선 스크린을 바르는 것과 매 두 시간 반마다 다시 발라주는 것 또한 중요하다.

어휘

skin cancer 피부암
ultraviolet 자외선(의)
radiation 방사, 복사선
be susceptible to ~에 걸리기 쉬운, ~에 영향 받기 쉬운
preventive 예방하는, 예방적인
apply (약 따위를) 바르다, 적용하다

정답 (a)

16 Nocturnal cramps in the calf or foot are the most common in both pregnant women and the elderly, suggesting there's a connection with reduced blood circulation. However, research hasn't uncovered any underlying medical problem or sleep disorder that can account for the cramping. Dehydration can be a risk factor for cramps because it plays havoc with your electrolyte levels. _____, a diet lacking in essential minerals, especially potassium, which is found in fruits and vegetables, fish, meet, dairy and whole-grain foods, may make cramps more likely.

(a) On the contrary
(b) For instance
(c) Thus
(d) Likewise

해설
야간에 발생하는 경련과 관련한 내용의 지문이다. 중간에 however가 포함된 문장에서 구체적으로 이러한 현상이 일어나는 원인을 밝혀내지는 못했다고 말하고 있다. 그 뒤의 문장은 정확한 이유는 아니지만 탈수가 이러한 현상에 위험 요소가 될 수 있다고 말하고 있고, 빈칸 뒤의 문장에서는 필수 미네랄 섭취의 부족이 경련을 불러일으킬 수도 있다고 말하고 있다. 즉, 빈칸으로 연결된 앞뒤의 두 문장은 야간 경련을 일으킬 수 있는 두 가지 가능한 요소로 동등한 성격의 문장이다. 그러므로 정답은 (d) Likewise(마찬가지로) 이다.

해석
종아리 혹은 발 부분에 나타나는 야간의 경련은 임산부와 나이 드신 분들 양쪽 모두에 가장 흔하게 나타남으로 이것이 혈액순환의 감소와 연관이 있음을 추측할 수 있다. 하지만, 연구는 어떠한 근원적인 의학적 문제나 경련을 일으키는 원인이 될 수 있는 수면장애를 밝혀내지는 못했다. 탈수는 위험 요소인데, 왜냐하면 이는 당신의 전해질 수준을 파괴시킬 수 있기 때문이다. 마찬가지로, 특히 과일과 야채, 생선, 고기, 낙농 및 정백하지 않은 음식에서 발견되는 칼륨을 비롯한 필수 미네랄의 부족은 더 많은 경련을 불러일으킬 수도 있다.

어휘
nocturnal 밤의, 야간의
cramp 경련
underlying 근원적인
sleep disorder 수면 장애
dehydration 탈수
electrolyte 전해물, 전해질
potassium 칼륨

정답 (d)

---

17 Argentina's farmers' organizations halted sales of grains and livestock in a week-long strike against the government's export tax on soybean. They argue they're being penalized at a time when the country is in the grip of drought. The government said it could not forgo the revenue in the current economic crisis. But on the eve of the strike it announced that 30% of the export tax revenue would go to regional governments for infrastructure.

Q: What is the main topic of the passage?
(a) How unfair it is to tax the farmers.
(b) Difficult economic conditions in Argentina.
(c) A new duty imposed on an agricultural product.
(d) The government's long-term plan to build infrastructure.

해설
전체 지문을 통해서 문제가 되는 것은 정부가 콩에 수출세를 매겼다는 것이다. 농부들은 이로 인해 파업을 했지만, 정부를 이 세를 통해서 기간 사업에 투자를 하겠다고 밝혔다는 내용의 글이다. 그러므로 '한 농업 상품에 매겨진 새로운 세금' 인 (c)가 정답이다.

해석
아르헨티나 농부 조합은 정부의 콩에 대한 수출세에 대항한 일주일간의 파업에서 곡물과 가축의 판매를 중단시켰다. 이들은 현재 국가가 가뭄에 빠져 있는 시기에 궁지에 몰리게 되었다고 주장한다. 정부는 현재의 경제 위기에서 세입 없이 버틸 수는 없었다고 말했다. 하지만 파업 전날 정부는 수출 세입의 30%가 기간 시설 투자를 위한 지역 정부에 들어가게 될 것이라고 발표했다.

어휘
halt 정지하다
grain 곡물, 곡류
livestock 가축
strike 파업, 노동쟁의
soybean 콩
penalize 벌하다, 궁지에 몰아넣다
in the grip of ~에게 잡혀, ~에 걸려
drought 가뭄
revenue (국가의) 세입, 소득
forgo ~없이 때우다, 보류하다
on the eve of ~의 직전에, ~에 임박하여
condemn 비난하다
stunt 이목을 끌기 위한 행위

정답 (c)

18 As Easter approaches, we need to be aware that chocolate is not suitable for dogs and cats; it results in a serious risk to their health. The problem is that the body systems of dogs and cats cannot handle the key ingredient in chocolate, theobromine, as well as humans can. Theobromine can cause a range of problems in domestic animals because it triggers the release of adrenaline and can lead to a greatly accelerated and irregular heart rate. In high dosage situations, pets can begin to vomit, suffer diarrhea and excessive urination. This can be followed by depression, coma, seizure and death.

Q: What is the main idea of the passage?
(a) People eat chocolate on Easter day.
(b) Theobromine can bring negative effects to both humans and pets.
(b) Chocolate poses a great threat to pets.
(c) There are diseases that pets can transmit to humans.

해설

첫 번째 문장의 'we need to be aware that chocolate is not suitable for dogs and cats'를 통해서 이어질 내용을 충분히 짐작할 수 있다. 마지막 두 문장인 'pets can begin to vomit, suffer diarrhea and excessive urination. This can be followed by depression, coma, seizure and death'을 통해서도 지문의 주제가 (c)임을 확인할 수 있다.

해석

부활절이 다가옴에 따라, 우리는 초콜릿이 강아지나 고양이들에게 적합하지 않다는 것을 알고 있을 필요가 있습니다. 왜냐하면 그것은 그들의 건강에 심각한 위험의 결과를 낳기 때문이죠. 문제는 강아지와 고양이들의 신체 체계가 초콜릿의 주요 성분인 theobromine을 사람들만큼 잘 처리할 수 없다는 것입니다. theobromine은 가정용 동물들에 있어 여러 가지 문제들을 일으킬 수 있습니다. 왜냐하면 그것은 아드레날린의 분비를 일으키고 매우 가속화되고 불규칙한 심장 박동을 이끌 수 있기 때문이죠. 많이 투약된 상황에서, 애완동물들은 토를 하기 시작하거나, 설사 그리고 과도 소변으로 고생할 수 있습니다. 이러한 것들은 우울증, 혼수상태, 발작, 그리고 죽음으로 이어질 수도 있지요.

어휘

be aware 알고 있다, 깨닫고 있다
pose a threat to ~에게 위협을 준다
trigger 일으키다, 유발하다
irregular 불규칙한
heart rate 심장 박동수
theobromine 테오브로민(카카오의 알칼로이드)
urination 소변보기, 배뇨
depression 우울증
seizure 발작

✓ 정답 (c)

---

19 Dear Max,

You've received this email from Amazon.com because your email address was used to register on our website. If you did not register at our site, please disregard this email. You do not need to unsubscribe or take any further action. Otherwise, You need to "validate" your registration to ensure that the email address you entered was correct. This protects against unwanted spam and malicious abuse. To activate your account, simply click on the link provided or depending on your email client you may need to cut and paste the link into your web browser. Thank you for registering and we hope you enjoy the site!

Kind Regards,

Q: What is the purpose of this letter?
(a) To confirm the email address change.
(b) To notify of safety concerns to its members.
(c) To help its members finish singing up for the website.
(d) To thank its members for their support.

해설

편지 초반에 편지를 받는 사람이 편지를 보낸 회사의 사이트에 본 이메일을 등록했기 때문에 본 메일을 보냈다고 밝히고 있다. 뒤에서 간단한 절차를 통해 계정이 활성화 될 수 있음을 밝히고, 즐겁게 사이트를 이용하라고 하는 것으로 보아, 본 메일의 목적은 직접 메일 수신을 통해 최종 등록절차를 마무리 짓도록 하는 이메일임을 알 수 있다. 그러므로 정답은 (c)이다.

해석

맥스 씨에게,

귀하께서는 본 이메일 주소를 저희 웹사이트에 등록하기 위해서 사용하셨기에 본 메일을 Amazon.com으로부터 받으시는 겁니다. 만약 귀하께서 저희 사이트에 등록을 하신 적이 없다면 본 메일을 무시하십시오. 등록을 취소한다거나 그 밖의 다른 행동을 취하실 필요가 없습니다. 만약 그렇지 않다면, 입력한 이 이메일 주소가 맞는지 확인하기 위해서 귀하의 등록사항을 확인해 주실 필요가 있습니다. 이것이 원치 않는 스팸이나 악의적인 사용으로부터 보호해 줄 겁니다. 계정을 활성화하기 위해서, 간단히 제공된 링크를 클릭하시거나 혹은 귀하의 이메일 서버가 무엇이냐에 따라 링크를 웹 브라우저에 잘라서 붙여넣기를 하실 필요가 있을 수도 있습니다. 등록을 해주셔서 감사하고 저희 사이트를 즐기시기를 바랍니다.

어휘

register 등록하다
disregard 무시하다
validate 확인하다, 유효하게 하다
malicious 악의 있는
activate 활성화하다
cut and paste (컴퓨터 사용 시) 잘라서 붙여 넣다
notify 통보하다
sign up for 등록하다, 참가하다

 정답 (c)

20 A strong muscle jerk just after you've fallen asleep is called a hypnagogic jerk. It's thought to be caused by the brain misinterpreting sensations from your muscles. As you fall asleep your muscles relax and go slack, and sometimes the brain interprets this as falling. An actual sensation of falling may accompany the jerking as the muscles try to get you upright again, or you may simply experience the jerk of the muscles. Hypnagogic jerks are most likely to occur when you're trying to fight off sleep or when you haven't slept for more than 24 hours. Stress, intense physical exercise or a high intake of caffeine or other stimulants can also increase your chances of experiencing a hypnagogic jerk.

Q: What is the best title for the article?
(a) Why these jerks need fixing.
(b) How muscle jerks affect people's health.
(c) A reminder of how powerful our brain is.
(d) Why our bodies twitch during slumbering hours.

해설
수면 시 나타나는 근육경련 현상의 의학적 용어를 알려 준 후, 왜 그런 현상이 일어나는지에 대해서 예를 들어 자세히 설명해 주고 있다. 그러므로 이 기사의 제목은 '신체가 수면 시간 동안 경련을 일으키는 이유'인 (d)가 가장 적절하다.

해석
당신이 잠에 든 후의 강력한 근육 경련은 최면경련이라고 불립니다. 이것은 두뇌가 당신의 근육으로부터의 감각을 잘못 해석함으로써 생긴다고 알려져 있습니다. 당신이 잠이 들게 되면, 당신의 근육들도 긴장을 풀고 느슨해집니다. 그리고 가끔 두뇌는 이것을 넘어지는 것으로 해석을 해버리지요. 넘어질 때 생기는 실제의 감각은 근육들이 당신을 다시 똑바로 세우기 위해서 노력함으로써 생기는 경련을 수반하거나 또는 당신은 그냥 단순히 경련을 경험하게 되기도 하지요. 최면경련은 당신이 잠에서 벗어나려 한다거나 혹은 24시간 이상 동안 잠을 자지 않았을 때 가장 발생할 확률이 높습니다. 스트레스, 격렬한 육체 운동 혹은 카페인의 높은 섭취 또는 다른 각성제들 또한 당신이 최면경련을 경험할 확률을 증가시킵니다.

어휘
jerk 경련
hypnagogic 최면의
misinterpret 잘못 해석하다, 오해하다
malfunction 기능장애, 고장
muscle 근육
slack 느슨한
stimulant 흥분제, 자극물
twitch 경련을 일으키다
slumber 수면을 취하다, 자다

정답 (d)

21 China's leaders are touchy about Tibet, and in scrapping a major summit with the EU they have let their anger boil over. A team of 150 political and business leaders was to meet in Lyon on 1 December, an annual fixture of ten years' standing. But the Chinese are furious that France's President agreed to meet the Dalai Lama during a trip to Poland. In response, they pulled out of the summit at the last moment, saying that the bad atmosphere meant nothing could come of it. After Dalai Lama said China's lack of moral authority made it unfit to be a super power, they are even threatening to cut trade with France. However, the Chinese didn't go overboard when England's prime minister gave the Dalai Lama the red carpet treatment this year. Nor did they do more than complain when President Bush awarded him the Congressional Medal of Honour. So, why are they picking on the France's president?

Q: What is the main topic of the passage?
(a) China's meticulously planned withdrawal from the summit.
(b) The imprudent decision made by French President.
(c) Dalai Lama's popularity among many Western countries.
(d) China's inconsistent reactions toward matters concerning Tibet.

해설
마지막의 "So, why are they picking on the France's president?"란 문장을 통해 주제가 드러난다. 프랑스 대통령이 티베트의 지도자인 달라이 라마를 만나기로 한 것에 회담까지 참여하지 않은 중국을 두고, 미국과 영국이 그랬을 때는 별 다른 행동을 취하지 않던 중국이 왜 프랑스에게는 민감하게 대하는가가 전체 글의 논지다. 그러므로 '티베트와 관련한 문제에 대해서 중국의 일관성 없는 반응'인 (d)가 정답이다.

해석
중국의 지도자들은 티베트에 관해서 과민반응을 보이는데, 유럽연합과의 주요 수뇌회의를 버리는 것으로 그들은 그들의 분노가 끓고 있다는 것을 표출했다. 150명의 정치인 그리고 비즈니스 지도자들이 10년간 지속되어온 연중 고정행사로 12월 1일 Lyon에서 만나기로 되어 있었다. 하지만 중국인들은 프랑스의 대통령이 달라이 라마의 폴란드 여행 중에 그를 만나기로 합의하면서 분노했다. 이에 응하여, 중국인들은 이러한 분위기에서 그 무엇도 건질 것이 없다고 말하며 마지막 순간에 수뇌 회의에서 철수했다. 달라이 라마가 중국의 도덕적 권위의 부족이 초강대국이 되기에 적합하지 않다고 말한 이후에, 중국은 이제 프랑스와의 무역을 끊겠다고까지 협박하고 있다. 하지만, 중국인들은 영국의 수상이 올해 달라이 라마에게 빨간 카펫까지 깔아주는 대접을 해주었을 때, 이렇게 극단적으로 가지 않았었다. 또한 그들은 미국 부시 대통령이 그에게 의회 명예의 메달을 수여했을 때도 불만을 표출하는 것 이상의 행동을 하지 않았었다. 그러면 왜 그들은 이렇게 프랑스 대통령만을 괴롭히고 있는 것일까?

어휘

touchy 과민한
scrap 찢어발기다, 버리다
summit 수뇌회의
fixture 고정행사
at the last moment 마지막 순간에
go overboard 극단으로 가다
pick on ~를 괴롭히다
meticulously 세심하게
imprudent 경솔한
inconsistent 일관성이 없는

정답 (d)

---

22 MRI is a form of imaging which uses a large magnet and radio waves. There is no X-ray radiation. A radiographer will perform the examination. They will position you on a MRI table. The Radiologist will supervise and report on the images. Depending on the body part scanned a separate "coil" maybe placed on the region to be imaged before you are moved into the open tunnel. The MRI scanner makes a loud knocking sound while the imaging occurs and you will be given earplug or earphones. You may feel quite warm as a normal response to the scan.

Q: What is the best title of the passage?
(a) How MRI helps in diagnosis.
(b) Possible risks when taking a MRI scan.
(c) How the MRI examination is performed.
(d) Different roles between radiographers and radiologists.

해설

지문의 주제를 파악해야 하는 데, 글의 내용은 MRI에 대한 설명 이후, MRI 촬영이 진행되기 전까지 발생하는 준비과정들을 순서대로 설명해주고 있다. 그러므로 정답은 (c)이다.

해석

MRI는 자력과 전파를 사용하는 화상진찰의 형식이다. X-선 방사는 일어나지 않는다. 방사선 사진사가 검사를 실행한다. 그들은 당신을 MRI 테이블 위에 위치시킬 것이다. 방사선과 의사가 감독을 하고 영상에 대해서 보고를 할 것이다. 영상이 주사된 신체 부위가 어디냐에 따라서, 분리된 전기장치가 당신이 열린 터널 안으로 이동하기 전에 촬영이 되어야 할 부위에 놓일 수도 있다. MRI 스캐너는 촬영이 발생할 때 시끄러운 두들기는 소리를 내고, 당신은 귀마개나 이어폰을 받게 될 것이다. 당신은 스캔에 대한 정상적인 반응으로 꽤 따뜻함을 느낄 수도 있다.

어휘

magnet 자력, 자석
radio wave 전파
radiographer 방사선 사진사
radiologist 방사선과 의사
region 신체의 국부, 부위

정답 (c)

---

23 Sir Andrew Lloyd Webber has announced that the button is pushed on a sequel to The Phantom of the Opera. The new musical, entitled Phantom: Love Never dies, hopes to make theatrical history by opening in three cities simultaneously at the end of 2009. Theaters in New York's Broadway and London's West End will be joined by a venue in a yet undecided Asian city, possibly Shanghai. The Phantom sequel will be set in Coney Island, Brooklyn, and fast-forwarded a decade after the events at the Paris Opera described in Gaston Leroux's original novel. The most likely candidates for the lead role are Australian Hugh Jackman and Scotsman Gerad Butler. The original Phantom of the Opera has been seen by more than 80 million theatergoers in 124 cities, and has taken more than US$ 5 billion at the box office.

Q: Which of the following is correct according to the article?
(a) The sequel to The Phantom of the Opera has finished filming.
(b) Phantom: Love never dies will be opening exclusively in London.
(c) One of the three venues for the musical's opening is yet to be decided.
(d) The lead role for the sequel will be played by two different actors.

해설

뮤지컬 '오페라의 유령'의 후속 작품에 관한 기사이다. 2009년 말에 세 개의 도시에서 동시에 개봉할 계획이라는 내용이 언급되고, 두 개의 장소는 결정되었지만 한 곳은 아직 결정된 바가 없다고 말하고 있다. (상하이는 가능성일 뿐이다) 그러므로 '이 뮤지컬 개봉의 세 군데 장소 중 한 곳은 아직 결정된 바가 없다' 라는 (c)가 정답이다.

해석

앤드류 르로이드 웨버 경은 오페라의 유령의 후속편을 위한 단추가 눌러졌다고 발표했습니다. "유령, 사랑은 결코 죽지 않는다"로 제목이 붙여진 새로운 뮤지컬은 2009년 말에 세 개 도시에서 동시에 개봉함으로써 연극 역사를 만들어 갈 것으로 기대됩니다. 뉴욕의 브로드웨이 극장들과 런던의 West End 이외에 아직 결정되지 않은 한 곳은 아시아 도시가 개봉장소가 될 것인데, 아마도 상하이로 결정될 가능성이 있습니다. 유령 후속편은 브룩클린의 Coney 섬을 무대로 차려질 것입니다. 그리고 Gaston Leroux의 원작 소설에서 묘사된 파리 오페라에서의 사건들이 벌어진 시점으로부터 10년 후로 건너 뛸 겁니다. 주인공 역할로 가장 가능성 있는 후보는 호주의 휴 잭맨과 스코틀랜드인 제라드 버틀러 입니다. 원작 오페라의 유령은 124개 도시의 8000천만 연극광들이 지켜봤고, 박스오피스에서 50억 달러 이상을 벌어 들였습니다.

어휘

sequel 속편
entitle ~에게 제목을 붙이다
theatrical 극장의, 연극의
simultaneously 동시에, 일제히
venue 개최지, 지정지
theatergoers 연극광
exclusively 독점적으로
lead role 주인공

정답 (c)

24. Sharia is the Islamic system of law. Sharia derives from the teaching of the Koran and from the Prophet Mohammed's precepts and example. Unlike Western systems of law, sharia is regarded as the expression of the divine will. Some commentators believe that since much of the process of interpreting the divine word had, in theory, been concluded by the end of the tenth century, it is a static system. Rather than change with society. However, there are many modern developments in sharia which demonstrate otherwise, for example Islamic banking and finance principles to accommodate the prohibition on charging and earning interest. Its other main distinction is the way it regulates every area of life – not just the criminal and civil law, but ritual and custom from prayer to dress, and personal hygiene. And unlike Western law, it isn't confined to man's relationship with his neighbours and the state, but also covers his relationship with God. It not only categorizes acts according to whether they're permissible or forbidden, but also whether they are praiseworthy or blameworthy.

Q: Which of the following is correct about Sharia?
(a) It has never been changed since the end of the 10th century.
(b) It also deals with matters concerning business.
(c) It has always been a cause of major controversy in Islamic countries.
(d) It has a lot in common with Western systems of law.

어휘
Sharia 이슬람 법
derive 끌어내다, ~의 유래를 찾다
prophet 예언자
precept 가르침, 교훈
static 정적인
demonstrate 증명하다, 설명하다, 밖으로 나타나다
criminal law 형법
civil law 민법
praiseworthy 칭찬할 만한
blameworthy 비난받을 만한

정답 (b)

25. You might look back and laugh at the outdated outfits and hairdos in old photos. But it does make you realize how quickly time passes. Just as life changes, so do your savings needs. And if you haven't reassessed these in a while, perhaps it's time to bring them up to date. We offer a range of savings and investment options to suit you, no matter what type of saver you are. Are you the type who needs access to your money at anytime? Or are you prepared to pop your money away for a while? Do you prefer to manage your financial affairs online? Or do you simply need to be more disciplined? The answer to all these questions and more is simple. To find the savings product that's right for you, go to our website. Alternatively, visit your local branch or call 1800 384 345.

Q: What is being promoted in the advertisement?
(a) Personalized fashion and style advice.
(b) A confidential stock tip.
(c) A newly introduced savings option.
(d) Financial consultation services.

해설
이슬람의 법 체계인 Sharia의 특징에 대해서 설명해주고 있는 글이다. 지문 중 'However, there are many modern developments in sharia which demonstrate otherwise, for example Islamic banking and finance principles to accommodate the prohibition on charging and earning interest'를 통해서 sharia가 은행, 재정 원칙에 관여하고 있음을 알 수 있다. 그러므로 '그것은 비즈니스와 관련한 문제들도 다룬다' 라는 (b)가 정답이다.

해석
Sharia는 이슬람의 법 체계이다. Sharia는 코란의 가르침과 예언자 Mohammed의 교훈과 예에서 기원을 찾을 수 있다. 서양의 법 체계와는 다르게, Sharia는 신성한 의지의 표현으로 여겨진다. 몇몇 주석자들은 이 신성한 말들에 대한 해석의 과정이 이론적으로 10세기 말에 종료가 되었으므로, 이는 이제 정적인 체계라고 믿고 있다. 사회와 함께 변하는 것이라고 보기보다는 말이다. 하지만, 이와는 다르다는 것을 증명해주는 Sharia에서의 많은 현대적인 발전이 있다. 예를 들어, 이자를 부과하고 이자를 벌어들이는 것에 대한 금령을 조정하기 위한 이슬람의 은행과 재정의 원칙을 들 수 있겠다. 또 다른 특성은 이 법이 모든 삶의 범위를 규정하는 방식이다. 이는 형법과 민법만이 아니라 기도와 복장, 그리고 개인위생에 이르는 의식과 관습도 규정한다. 그리고 서양의 법과는 다르게, 이 법은 인간들의 이웃과 국가에의 관계에만 한정되어 있는 것이 아니라, 인간들의 신과의 관계 또한 포괄하고 있다는 것이다. 이 법은 그것들이 허용할 수 있는가 금지되어야 하는가와 관련한 행동들만을 분류하고 있는 것이 아니라, 그것들이 칭찬할 만 것인가 혹은 비난받아야 할 것인가에 따른 행동도 분류하고 있다.

해설
지문 전체의 내용을 이해해야지만 정답을 찾을 수 있는 문제이다. 과거의 저축 방식을 새롭게 바꿀 필요가 있다는 것이 본 광고 글이 말하고자 하는 내용으로, 개인에게 적합한 저축 및 투자 관련 옵션들을 제공하겠다고 언급하고 있다. 그러므로 '재무 상담 서비스'인 (d)가 정답이다.

해석
여러분은 과거를 회고해보고 오래된 사진에 있는 촌스런 복장과 머리 스타일에 웃음을 터트릴 수도 있습니다. 하지만, 이러한 것들은 여러분에게 시간이 얼마나 빨리 흘러가는지를 깨닫게 해주죠. 삶이 변화하는 것처럼, 당신의 저축도 변화할 필요가 있습니다. 그리고 만약 여러분이 한동안 이 부분을 재평가해보지 않으셨다면, 이제 이것들을 최신의 것으로 변화시킬 시간이 되었습니다. 저희는 여러분의 저축 스타일에 관계없이 여러분에게 적절한 다양한 종류의 저축과 투자 옵션을 가지고 있습니다. 언제 어느 때라도 저축한 돈에 접근할 필요가 있으신가요? 아니면 당신은 당분간은 돈을 멀리 치워두실 준비가 되신 분인가요? 당신은 온라인으로 재정적 문제를 처리하기를 원하시나요, 아니면 단순히 좀 더 재정적으로 훈련을 받을 필요가 있으신가요? 이러한 질문들과 더 많은 질문들에 대한 답변은 간단합니다. 여러분에게 적절한 저축상품을 찾고 싶으시다면, 저희 웹사이트를 방문하세요. 아니면, 여러분의 지역 지점을 방문하시거나 1800 384 345로 전화주십시오.

어휘
look back 뒤돌아보다, 회상하다
outdated 구식의, 철이 지난
hairdo 머리 스타일
savings 저금, 저축
reassess 재평가하다
up to date 최신의, 현대식의

정답 (d)

26 In Manchester, England, the final of the street soccer competition saw the Zambian women's team beat Liberia 7-1. In the men's round, Afghanistan beat Russia 5-4. The Cup began in Graz, Austria, in 2003, with 18 nations taking part. It has since grown to 56 teams. The tournament is credited with raising the esteem of the homeless while helping many to get off drugs and alcohol and find housing and jobs. At the end of the games, 15 Zimbabwean and Afghani players sought asylum and the entire Liberian women's team, as well as a Kenyan player, went missing.

Q: Which of the following is correct according to the article?
(a) The woman's Cup was won by Liberia.
(b) Afghanistan beat Russia by one goal.
(c) The street soccer competition was first launched in England.
(d) A number of players disappeared after they returned to their countries.

27 Acclaimed director Clint Eastwood focuses on the plight of a woman in this true story of single mother Christine Collins taking on the Los Angeles police force as she tries to find out what happened to her missing son. Set in 1928, when police corruption was rife, a police captain tries to foist another nine-year-old boy on Christine, claiming he's her son when she knows he's not. Malkovich co-stars as a Protestant minister who decides to support Christine in her cause. The discovery of a serial killer of young boys may hold the answer to Christine's agony. It's a fine film, beautifully realized by a Hollywood legend.

Q: Which of the following is correct about the movie?
(a) The story of the movie is fictional.
(b) The heroine of the movie is a police officer in Los Angeles.
(c) The level of depravity was high among police officers in the late 1920's.
(d) The main character in the movie was acted by a Hollywood legend.

해설

집 없는 자들을 대상으로 한 거리 축구시합과 관련한 뉴스 기사이다. 각 선택지의 내용과 본문의 내용을 꼼꼼히 맞춰 가며 정답을 골라내야 한다. 지문 중 'Afghanistan beat Russia 5-4'를 통해서 아프가니스탄이 러시아를 한 골 차이로 이겼음을 알 수 있다. 그러므로 정답은 (b)이다. 거리축구 시합이 최초로 시작된 것은 오스트리아이고, 사라진 선수들은 대회가 치러진 영국에서 이지 자신의 고국에서 사라진 것이 아니므로 (c), (d)는 정답이 될 수 없다.

해석

영국의 맨체스터에서 열린 거리축구대회 결승전에서 잠비아 여성팀이 리베리아를 7-1로 이겼습니다. 남자부 경기에서는 아프가니스탄이 러시아를 5-4로 이겼습니다. 이 대회는 2003년도 오스트리아의 Graz에서 18개 국가가 참여하며 시작되었습니다. 그 이후로 대회는 56개의 팀으로 성장했습니다. 본 경기대회는 많은 사람들이 마약과 술을 끊고, 집 없는 사람들이 거주할 곳과 일자리를 찾도록 하는 반면 그들의 존경심을 높이는 역할을 해왔습니다. 게임이 끝나고 나서 15명의 잠비아와 아프가니스탄 선수들이 망명을 요청했고, 전체 리베리아 여자 팀과 한 명의 케냐 선수는 사라져버렸습니다.

어휘

the final 결승전
beat ~에게 이기다
take part 참여하다
esteem 존중, 존경
homeless 집 없는 사람, 부랑자
get off ~에서 벗어나다
seek asylum 망명을 요청하다

정답 (b)

해설

클린트 이스트우드에 의해서 감독된 영화의 내용에 대한 글이다. 지문 중 'Set in 1928, when police corruption was rife'를 통해서 1928년도에 경찰의 부패가 성행했음을 알 수 있다. 그러므로 '부패행위의 수준이 1920년 후반에 경찰들 간에 높았다' 라는 (c)가 정답이다. 영화는 실화이고, 할리우드의 전설은 영화의 주연이 아니라 감독이기 때문에 (a), (d) 모두 정답이 될 수 없다.

해석

갈채를 받는 감독인 Clint Eastwood는 잃어버린 아들에게 무슨 일이 생긴 건지 알아내고자 로스앤젤레스 경찰과 싸우는 싱글 맘 Christine Collins의 실화에서 한 여성의 곤경에 초점을 모은다. 경찰의 부패가 성행하던 1928년에, 한 경찰 서장이 또 다른 9살짜리 소년을 Christine을 속여 떠맡기려 합니다. 그녀는 그 아이가 아들이 아님을 아는데도, 그 아이가 그녀의 아들이라고 주장하면서 말이다. Malkovich는 그녀의 주장을 지지하기로 결정하는 신교도 목사로서 공동 주연을 맡았다. 어린 아이들에 대한 연쇄 살인범의 발견이 Christine의 고통에 대한 대답을 쥐고 있을 수도 있다. 이 영화는 할리우드의 전설에 의해서 아름답게 실현된 괜찮은 작품이다.

어휘

acclaimed 갈채를 받는, 환호를 받는
plight 곤경, 궁지, 어려움
take on ~에 도전하다 ~와 싸우다
foist 속이다, 억지로 떠맡기다
agony 고민, 고통
depravity 악행, 부패행위

정답 (c)

28 For over 50 years, Biotherm has studied the skin's natural mechanisms to deliver innovative and effective skincare solutions. Biotherm's biologists have discovered Pure Thermal Plankton, a natural agent located deep in the thermal springs of the French Pyrenees. Pure Thermal Plankton rejuvenates the appearance of the skin, leaving it radiant and glowing with health. Plus, it helps stimulate the skin's natural self-renewal process, improving your skin's natural defence mechanisms against the signs of ageing and helping control skin sensitivity.

Q: What can Pure Thermal Plankton do to skin?
(a) It warms up skin to prevent itching.
(b) It stimulates breaking out under skin on face.
(c) It makes skin visibly younger on the outside.
(d) It protects skin from sun damage.

해설
피부 화장품에 관한 광고의 글로 비교적 쉽게 정답을 고를 수 있는 문제이다. 지문에서 언급되고 있는 Pure Thermal Plankton이 피부에 무엇을 하는지 지문을 통해 알아내어야 한다. 본문 중 'Pure Thermal Plankton rejuvenates the appearance of the skin, leaving it radiant and glowing with health.'를 통해서 피부가 젊어지도록 한다는 것을 알 수 있다. 그러므로 정답은 (c)이다.

해석
50년이 넘는 시간 동안, Biothem은 혁신적이고 효과적인 피부 관리 해결책을 전달하기 위해서 피부의 자연적 구조를 연구해왔습니다. Biothem의 생물학자들은 프랑스의 피레네 산맥의 열 온천 안의 깊은 곳에 위치한 자연약품인 순수 열 플랑크톤을 발견했습니다. 순수 열 플랑크톤은 피부의 외관이 활기를 띠게 해주고, 피부가 건강과 함께 타오르고 빛을 발하게 해줍니다. 게다가, 그것은 피부의 자연적 자가 재생 과정을 촉진하여, 피부의 노화의 징후에 대한 자연적 방어 구조를 발달시키고 피부 민감함을 통제하는 것을 도와줍니다.

어휘
mechanism 과정, 구조, 기구
innovative 혁신적인
thermal 열(의), 열량의
biologist 생물학자
plankton 플랑크톤, 부유생물
agent 약품
rejuvenate 젊어지게 하다, 활기를 띠게 하다
renewal 부활, 재생, 갱생
aging 나이를 먹음, 노화
break out 여드름이 나다

정답 (c)

29 Sleepwalking is a misnomer because it often involves more than walking. The sleeper may also talk, cook, rearrange the furniture or even drive. Sleepwalking occurs during the deep stages of sleep so it can be hard to wake sleepwalkers, and when you do they will feel groggy and disoriented. If you find your kids sleepwalking at home, the best thing to do is to gently guide them back to bed. The condition is most common in primary school aged children, and usually gets better as the child ages. It's usually associated with overtiredness or a full bladder, so good sleep hygiene, which means going to bed at the same time every night in a dark quiet room and a comfortable bed, helps reduce the risk. Adult sleepwalking may be caused by fever, illness, stress or alcohol intake. It also seems to be hereditary.

Q: Which of the following is correct according to the passage?
(a) Sleepwalking is common in teenagers.
(b) Sleepwalkers will feel exuberant if they're woken up.
(c) A quiet bedroom would not be good for sleepwalkers.
(d) Sleepwalking can run in the family.

해설
지문의 맨 마지막 문장 'It also seems to be hereditary'를 통해서 몽유병이 유전될 수 있음을 알 수 있다. 그러므로 '몽유병은 유전 될 수 있다'인 (d)가 정답이다.

해석
몽유병(sleepwalking)은 그것이 단순히 걷는 것(walking)보다도 더 많은 것을 포함하고 있기에 잘못 붙여진 이름이다. 몽유병 상태인 사람은 말도 하고, 요리도 하고, 가구를 재배치하기도 하고 혹은 운전도 할 수 있다. 몽유병은 깊은 수면 단계 중에 발생하고, 몽유병 상태인 사람을 깨우는 것은 어려운 일이다. 그리고 그들을 깨우게 될 시, 이들은 비틀거림과 혼란스러움을 느끼게 될 것이다. 만약 당신의 아이가 집에서 몽유병 상태에서 돌아다니는 것을 보게 되면, 최선의 행동은 그들을 자연스럽게 침대로 인도하는 것이다. 몽유병은 초등학교 나이의 어린이들에게 가장 일반적이고, 보통 아이가 나이가 들수록 상태는 호전된다. 몽유병은 보통 지나친 피로 혹은 방광이 가득 찬 것과 관련이 있다. 그러므로 매일 밤 같은 시간에 어둡고 조용한 방의 편안한 침대에서 잠을 자는 이른 바 좋은 수면 위생상태가 몽유병의 위험을 덜어줄 수 있다. 성인 몽유병은 열이나, 질병 스트레스 혹은 알코올 섭취로 인해서 발생될 수 있다. 이는 또한 유전적인 것으로 보이기도 한다.

어휘
sleepwalking 몽유병
misnomer 틀린 이름, 잘못 부름
groggy 비틀거리는, 휘청거리는
disoriented 어리둥절한, 분별력을 잃은
age 나이를 먹다
bladder 방광
hereditary 세습의, 유전의
common 일반적인
exuberant 열의가 넘치는, 원기 왕성한
run in the family 유전하다, 혈통을 물려받다

정답 (d)

30 Teaching about long-term water efficiency and educating children on the value of water is the main aim of Seqwater's dedicated water education program for primary and secondary school students. Seqwater is the single treated and bulk water service provider for the southeast Queensland region. It has responsibility for managing physical assets worth $1.8 billion comprising 24 dams and 49 weirs across the southeast. Seqwater currently operates 46 water treatment plant facilities. Schools can now enroll to take conducted tours and learn valuable insights about dam operations, links between catchment areas and the treatment of water. Education programs can also be customized for each school.

Q: Which of the following is correct about Seqwater?
(a) It manages personal assets and provides consulting assistance.
(b) It is an education institute that instructs students on water management.
(c) It offers programs that help students learn more about water supplies.
(d) It is a personalized tour agency based in Queensland.

31 A research, carried out on people who'd attended business conferences in the last three months, found that 71% of respondents rated the general standard of business presentations to be below average or poor. Only 9% said they had seen a presentation they rated as excellent. The standard bullet-point presentation was ineffective, especially when the speaker read each bullet point aloud. Other things to avoid when giving a presentation include delivering too much information, overuse of industry jargon and acronyms, hiding behind the lectern, avoiding eye contact with the audience, and using a monotone voice. Also, more than half said they preferred to receive the PowerPoint material via email prior to the presentation.

Q: Which of the following is correct according to the passage?
(a) Most of people think the general level of presentation skills is high.
(b) Many people prefer receiving presentation materials in advance.
(c) Speakers should speak with a constant, loud voice during presentations.
(d) The common response to a boring presentation is checking their e-mails.

해설
첫 번째 문장 'Teaching about long-term ~ for primary and secondary school students'를 통해서 Seqwater가 물과 관련한 교육 프로그램을 진행하고 있음을 알 수 있다. 그러므로 정답은 '물 공급과 관련해 학생들에게 더 배울 수 있는 프로그램을 제공한다'는 보기 (c)가 정답이다. Seqwater는 물 공급 회사로 학생들을 위한 물 교육 프로그램을 제공하는 것이지 교육업체는 아니기에 (b)는 정답이 될 수 없다.

해석
장기간의 물 효율과 물의 가치에 대해서 아이들을 교육하는 것은, Seqwater의 초등과 중등학교 학생들에 대한 헌신적인 물 교육 프로그램의 주요목표이다. Seqwater는 남동 퀸즐랜드 지역의 정수된 물과 덩어리 물의 단독 공급자이다. 본 회사는 남동지방에 걸쳐서 24개의 댐과 49개의 둑으로 이루어진 18억 달러의 가치에 해당하는 실질자산을 관리할 책임을 가지고 있다. Seqwater는 현재 46개의 정수처리공장시설을 운영하고 있다. 학교들은 이제 안내 여행을 등록할 수 있고 댐의 운영, 저수지 지대와 물의 처리 간의 고리에 관해서 소중한 통찰력을 배울 수 있다. 교육 프로그램은 또한 각각의 학교들이 개별적으로 희망하는 대로 맞춰질 수 있다.

어휘
efficiency 능률, 효율
treated 처리된
weir (물레방아용) 둑
responsibility 책임, 의무
asset 자산
facilities 시설
catchment 집수, 저수지
customize 개인의 희망에 맞추다

정답 (c)

해설
한 조사 결과를 통해 프레젠테이션 시 피해야 할 내용들에 대해서 설명해 주고 있는 글이다. 마지막 문장 'more than half said ~ prior to the presentation'을 통해서 많은 사람들이 사전에 프레젠테이션 자료를 받는 것을 선호함을 알 수 있다. 그러므로 정답은 (b)이다.

해석
지난 3개월간 사업 회의에 참석했던 사람들을 대상으로 실시한 조사에서 응답자의 71%가 사업 발표의 일반적인 수준이 평균보다 낫거나 형편없는 수준이라고 평가했다. 단지 9%만이 훌륭하다고 평가받을 만한 수준의 발표를 봤다고 답했다. 일반적인 bullet point 발표는 효과가 없었다. 특히 발표자가 각각의 포인트 내용을 큰 소리로 읽기만 할 경우에는 더했다. 발표를 할 때 피해야 할 다른 것들은 너무 많은 정보를 전달하려는 것이나, 산업용 전문용어와 약어의 지나친 사용, 연설용 탁자 뒤에 몸을 가리는 것, 청중과의 눈 맞춤을 피하는 것, 그리고 단조로운 음성을 사용하는 것 등이 포함된다. 또한, 절반 이상은 그들이 발표 이전에 이메일을 통해서 파워포인트 자료를 받는 것을 선호한다고 말했다.

어휘
carry out 실시하다
conference 회의
rate 평가하다, 등급을 매기다
bullet-point 프레젠테이션 파일에서 동그라미 기호 표시
deliver 전달하다
jargon 전문(특수) 용어
acronym 약어
lectern 연설용 탁자
monotone 단조로운

정답 (b)

32 Many new cars have onboard sensors that indicate when you're at risk of getting a flat tyre. Wouldn't it be good if your body had the same level of tech support? Proteus Biomedical, a Californian company, is working on "smart pills" – internal sensors that monitor health. The plan is for these sensors to be linked to a computer hub that wirelessly broadcasts a stream of diagnostic data. The company likens the benefits of the systems to telling you to get a tune-up before you have an expensive breakdown. For the moment, the smart pills are being designed to help monitor mechanical and electrical devices rather than vital body parts, but its developers believe the market for smart "pharmacy technology" is already large enough to create a whole new industry.

Q: Which of the following is correct according to the article?
(a) Smart pills can examine people's health by their looks.
(b) Smart pills will transmit gathered data through landline to the hub.
(c) Car sensors were designed after the mechanisms behind how the smart pills work.
(d) Smart pills are not being produced for the purpose of pharmaceutical use yet.

해설

자동차의 고장과 관련한 사전지시 센서를 언급하며, 신체에도 이러한 기술이 적용될 가능성에 대해서 언급하는 내용의 글이다. 'For the moment ~ vital body parts'란 문장을 통해서, smart pills는 현재 사람의 신체가 아닌 기계와 전기 장치들의 감시를 위해서 제작되고 있음을 알 수 있다. 그러므로 'Smart pills는 제약의 용도를 목적으로 아직 생산되어지고 있는 중이 아니다'라는 (d)가 정답이다.

해석

많은 신차들은 타이어에 바퀴가 생길 위험에 있을 때 이를 알려주는 차 내에 탑재된 센서를 가지고 있습니다. 만약 여러분의 신체에도 이러한 수준의 기술적 지원을 가지고 있다면 좋지 않겠습니까? 캘리포니아 회사인 Preoteus Biomedical은 건강을 감시해주는 내부 센서인 "Smart pills"를 연구중에 있습니다. 계획은 이 센서들을 컴퓨터 허브 장치에 연결해 건강진단 자료들을 무선으로 방송하게끔 하는 것입니다. 이 회사는 이 시스템의 이점을 마치 돈이 많이 드는 고장이 나기 전에 엔진 등의 철저한 조정을 하라고 알려주는 것에 비유합니다. 당장은 이 "smart pills"는 절대적으로 필요한 신체 부분보다는 기계와 전기 장치들을 감시하기 위해 제작되고 있습니다. 하지만 개발자들은 현명한 "제약업의 기술"은 이미 완전한 새 산업을 만들어 낼 만큼 충분히 규모가 크다고 믿고 있습니다.

어휘

onboard 내부에 장착한
flat tyre 펑크 난 타이어
liken 견주다, ~에 비유하다
hub 중앙, 중심
broadcast 방송하다
diagnostic 진단상의
tune-up 조정
for the moment 당분간은, 당장은
transmit 보내다, 전파하다

정답 (d)

33 A car billed as the world's cheapest was launched by Tata Motors in India's financial capital, Mumbai. The launch has been delayed when protests by farmers over land seizures for the Tata factory in West Bengal forced the company to relocate to other region. The car, which will sell for 2,800 dollars, is seen as an affordable people's car and an alternative to unsafe motorcycle use. But critics argue it will contribute to increased pollution and road congestion. A version of the car may eventually be marketed in Europe and the US.

Q: What can be inferred from the passage?
(a) Tata Motors has cancelled its plan to build a new factory.
(b) The launch of the car was scrapped due to protests by farmers.
(c) The car's safety features are better than those of motorbikes.
(d) The car has been launched in the US.

해설

본문 중 'The car~alternative to unsafe motorcycle use'이란 문장을 통해 이 자동차가 오토바이를 타는 것보다 안전하다고 여겨짐을 유추해 낼 수 있다. 그러므로 정답은 '자동차의 안전 특징이 오토바이의 그것보다 낫다'라는 (c)가 정답이다.

해석

타타 자동차 회사에 의해 만들어진 세계에서 가장 저렴한 것으로 발표된 차가 인도의 금융 수도인 뭄바이에서 출시되었습니다. 본 자동차의 출시는 West Bengal에 있던 타타 공장의 땅 압수로 인해서 벌어진 농부들의 항의로 회사가 다른 지역으로 이전됨으로써 연기되었습니다. 2,800달러에 팔리게 될 이 자동차는 가장 구입 가능한 서민의 자동차이고 안전하지 못한 오토바이의 대체품으로 여겨지고 있습니다. 하지만 비평가들은 이 자동차가 공해와 도로 혼잡의 증가를 가져올 거라고 주장합니다. 이 자동차의 한 버전이 최종적으로 유럽과 미국의 시장에 출시될 것입니다.

어휘

bill 광고하다, 발표하다
seizure 강탈, 점령, 압수
relocate 이전시키다
affordable 구입가능한
critic 비평가
congestion 혼잡
market 시장에 내놓다

정답 (c)

34. Indicting Omar al-Bahir for war crimes is a big step for international justice. An arrest warrant has been issued for Sudan's president by the International Criminal Court in The Hague accusing him of orchestrating the violence in Darfur, where an estimated 300,000 have died and nearly three million left homeless in an orgy of government-sponsored rapes and killings. Chief prosecutor Luis Moreno-Ocampo says more than 30 witnesses will testify against Bashir, although the genocide charge has been dropped because it was judged too hard to prove. But there is little prospect of anyone arresting Bashir, who has significant support from other African countries as well as China and Russia. He dismissed the warrant as a colonialist plot. Barshir also expelled eleven international aid agencies.

Q: What can be inferred from the passage?
(a) Sudan's president is under arrest for criminal offences.
(b) There is enough evidence to prove the charges of mass murder against Bashir.
(c) Sudan's neighboring countries are looking after Bashir's back.
(d) It's only a matter of time before the Court brings him to trial.

해설
'there is little prospect of anyone arresting Bashir, who has significant support from other African countries' 문장을 통해서 아프리카의 다른 국가들이 그를 지지하고 있음을 알 수 있다. 그러므로 '수단의 근처 국가들이 Bashir의 뒤를 봐주고 있다'는 보기 (c)가 정답이다. 수단의 대통령은 현재 체포된 상태가 아니고, 그가 재판에 회부될 가능성은 적다고 했기 때문에 (a), (d)는 모두 정답이 될 수 없다.

해석
Omar al-Bahir를 전쟁 범죄로 기소하는 것은 국제 정의를 위한 큰 걸음이다. 수단의 대통령에 대한 체포 영장이 헤이그에 위치한 국제 범죄 재판소에 의해 발행되었고 이는 정부에 의해 지원된 강간과 살인의 혼란에 의해 거의 3백만 명이 집을 잃고 약 30만 명이 죽은 Darfur에서의 폭력을 지휘한 그를 고발하기 위함이다. 주 검찰관인 Luis Moreno-Ocampo 씨는 비록 대학살에 대한 고발 건은 증명하기 너무 힘들다는 판단에 의해서 기각되었음에도 불구하고, Bashir에 대항하여 30여 명이 넘는 증인들이 증언을 할 것이라고 말했다. 하지만, 다른 아프리카 국가들 및 중국과 러시아의 중대한 지지를 받고 있는 그를 누군가가 체포하는 것은 가능성이 낮다. 그는 영장이 식민지주의자들의 음모라고 간단히 치부해 버렸다. Bashir는 또한 11명의 국제 원조 단체들을 추방해버렸다.

어휘
indict 기소하다, 고발하다
justice 정의
arrest warrant 체포 영장
orchestrate 조직하다
orgy 법석대기, 유흥, 방탕
testify 증언하다
dismiss 간단히 치부해 버리다, 해고하다
genocide 계획적 대학살
prospect 전망, 예상

 정답 (c)

---

35. Analysis of more than 1500 coprolites, or fossilized dung, has revealed the diet of several moa species, throwing light on the ecology of New Zealand prior to human settlement. Moa dominated New Zealand prior to human arrivals, with almost a dozen species making up virtually the entire local mega-fauna. The females of the largest moa species were 3 meters tall and weighed 250 kg. Some of the droppings studied were 15 cm long. Surprisingly for such large birds, over half the plants that were detected in the feces were under 30 cm in height. This suggests that some moa grazed on tiny herbs, in contrast to the current view of them as mainly shrub and tree browsers. There is no satisfactory answer as to why these species with few predators would need to grow so big if they were largely living off low-growing herbs.

Q: Which of the following can be inferred from the passage?
(a) The dissection of Moa revealed their dietary intake.
(b) Moa became extinct due to indiscriminate hunting by humans.
(c) The reasons to why Moa was so small in size were finally uncovered.
(d) Moa was rarely attacked by other species of animals.

해설
모아란 동물에 대한 설명글이다. 지문 중 'There is no satisfactory answer as to why these species with few predators ~ largely living off low-growing herbs.'를 통해서 모아를 잡아먹는 육식동물이 거의 없었음을 알 수 있다. 그러므로 '모아는 다른 종의 동물들에 의해 공격을 받은 적이 거의 없다'는 (d)가 정답이다. (b)는 역사적으로 맞는 사실이지만 지문을 통해서 알아낼 수 있는 내용은 아니다.

해석
1,500개 이상의 Coprolite(화석이 된 똥)의 분석은 몇 가지 Moa 종의 식습관을 밝혀냈고 이는 인간의 정착 이전에 생태학에 빛을 밝혀주고 있다. Moa는 인간이 도착하기 전 거의 12개의 종들이 사실상 전체 지역의 대형 동물군을 이루면서 뉴질랜드를 지배했었다. 가장 큰 Moa 종의 암컷들은 키가 3미터 정도에 250킬로그램의 몸무게가 나갔다. 연구된 배설물들의 몇몇은 길이가 15cm이었다. 이렇게 큰 새들에게 있어서 놀랍게도, 이 배설물들 내에서 탐지된 절반 이상의 식물들의 높이가 30cm 이하였다. 이것은 몇몇 Moa들이 작은 나무나 나뭇잎을 주로 먹었을 거라는 현재의 그들에 대한 견해와는 다르게 자그마한 풀잎들을 뜯어먹었다는 것을 암시한다. 거의 약탈자가 없던 이 종들이 만약 주로 낮게 자라는 풀잎들을 먹으며 살았다고 한다면 왜 그렇게까지 크게 자랐을 필요가 있는가에 대해서는 만족스러운 정답이 없다.

어휘
dissection 절개, 해부
coprolite 똥의 화석
ecology 생태학
mega-fauna 대형 동물군
shrub 키 작은 나무
predator 약탈자, 육식동물
intake 섭취량
indiscriminate 무차별의

 정답 (d)

36 In Denmark, the family farm has traditionally passed from one generation to the next. Each successive heir would try to expand upon the work already put in by their parents, their grandparents, sometimes even their great-grandparents. As agriculture and animal husbandry have become more scientific over the past 50 years, sons and daughters have gone off to college and brought home new methods to cut costs and increase output, and the family farm has evolved into a business like any other, requiring accountants and financial planners. For many, this was a blessing that helped reduce overheads, increase profits and maximize return. However, these days, the youngsters going off to further their education often don't come back – at least not to work. They find careers in the city and build lives for themselves that are different to that of their forefathers.

Q: What is the next paragraph likely to be about?
(a) How Danish family farms prospered over the past 50 years.
(b) The difficulties Danish family farms are currently going through.
(c) The merits and demerits of further education.
(d) The increasing rate of family collapse in Denmark.

해설
덴마크의 가족 농장과 관련한 글이다. 마지막에 등장하는 접속사 'However' 이하의 문장 내용이 문제 해결의 핵심이다. 그동안 대대로 내려오면서 진화해온 가족 농장의 모습과 반대로 요즈음에는 젊은이들이 도시로 가 거기서 정착을 하고 기업을 물려받기 위해서 돌아오지는 않는다는 내용이다. 그러므로 뒤이어 이어질 내용은 이러한 현상으로 인한 '덴마크의 가족 농장들이 현재 겪고 있는 어려움'이라는 (b)가 정답이다. 아이들이 최소한 기업을 잇기 위해 돌아오지 않는다고 한 것을 가족의 붕괴라고 하는 것은 지나친 비약이기에 (d)는 정답이 될 수 없다.

해석
덴마크에서, 가족 농장은 전통적으로 한 세대에서부터 다음 세대로 이어져 왔습니다. 각각의 이어지는 후계자들은 그들의 부모, 조부 그리고 가끔은 그들의 증조부, 조모에 의해서 이미 투입된 과업 위에서 (농장을) 확장하려고 할 것입니다. 농업과 농축업이 지난 50년에 걸쳐서 더 과학적이 됨에 따라서, 아들과 딸들은 대학을 가고 비용을 줄이고 생산량을 늘릴 수 있는 새로운 방법들을 집으로 가져왔습니다. 그리고 가족 농장은 회계사와 재정관리사들을 필요로 하는 여느 다른 사업체들처럼 진화되어 왔지요. 많은 사람들에게 있어서, 이것은 간접비를 줄이고, 이익을 늘리고, 수익을 최대화할 수 있도록 도와주는 축복이었습니다. 하지만, 오늘날, 젊은이들은 교육을 더 받기 위해서 떠나지만 종종 돌아오지는 않습니다. 최소한 일하려고 오지는 않지요. 그들은 도시에서 그들의 직업을 찾고, 그들의 선조들과는 다른 그들을 위한 삶을 세워갑니다.

어휘
successive 잇따른, 연속하는
heir 상속인, 후계자
agriculture 농업, 농경
husbandry 농업, 경작
scientific 과학적인
accountant 회계사
overhead 간접비, 제 경비
maximize 최대화하다
forefather 조상, 선조
prosper 번영하다, 성공하다

정답 (b)

---

37 Most of us have our own precious memories growing up climbing trees, walking pet or playing on swings. Kids are naturally energetic and their parents should take advantage of their youngsters' inbuilt need for fun and activity. Some parents may even find it's contagious and start moving about more themselves. South African families are some of the luckiest in the world because their splendid climate lets them spend much of the year outside. Not only does outdoor play encourage activity that strengthens and helps young bodies to grow, it also gets them off the sofa, away from computers and television screens, into fresh air and sunshine. Initially, some kids may complain this simpler playtime is a bit boring, but there's so much to do out there that most kids quickly embrace a change of scene. Planting a herb or vegetable patch, weeding, watering and picking the produce is a great way to involve young children with nature and reap the rewards with some health-giving goodies as well.

Q: What can be inferred from the passage?
(a) The weather in South Africa is very sunny but stormy.
(b) Children can receive manufactured goods by doing outdoor activities.
(c) It's healthy for kids to venture out into the great outdoors.
(d) Many people have memories of either watching television or playing computer games.

해설
본문의 내용은 아이들을 집에만 있게 하지 말고 야외에서 놀면서 자연을 느끼도록 해야 한다고 역설하고 있으므로 야외에서 활동하도록 하는 것으로 건강하게 자랄 수 있다고 답한 (c)가 답이다.

해석
우리들 대부분은 자라면서 나무를 오른다거나, 애완동물을 산책시킨다거나, 그네를 타는 등의 자신들만의 소중한 추억을 가지고 있다. 아이들은 본래 에너지가 넘치며, 그들의 부모들은 어린 자식들의 즐거움과 활동에 대한 타고난 욕구를 잘 활용해야 한다. 일부 부모들은 이러한 욕구가 전염성이 강해 오히려 본인들이 신나게 뛰어 돌아다니기도 한다. 남아공의 가정들은 세계에서 최고의 행운을 갖는 집단일 수 있는데 왜냐하면 우리의 멋진 기후로 인해 연중 대부분의 시간을 야외에서 보낼 수 있기 때문이다. 야외에서 하는 놀이는 활동을 증진시킬 뿐만 아니라 한창인 신체를 강하게 성장할 수 있도록 돕는다. 또한 소파에서 일어나게 하고, 텔레비전과 컴퓨터 스크린에서 눈을 떼게(멀리 하게) 해서 신선한 공기와 햇볕을 쐬게 한다. 처음에, 일부 아이들은 이러한 좀 더 소박한 놀이 시간이 지루하다고 불평을 할 수도 있겠으나, 그곳에서 많은 할 것이 있어서 대부분의 아이들은 재빨리 이런 변화를 수용하게 된다. 약초를 심거나 야채밭을 일구고 잡초도 뽑고 농작물의 과실을 따게 하는 것과 몸에 좋은 간식거리를 보답으로 수확하도록 하는 것은 모두 그들로 하여금 자연에 참여하게 하는 훌륭한 방법이 된다.

어휘
memory 추억, 기억
walk pet 애완동물을 산책시키다
inbuilt 타고난
contagious 전염성의
splendid 훌륭한, 멋진
encourage 장려하다
outdoor play 야외놀이

✓ 정답 (c)

38 Like most experiences with your first child, our first trip overseas with our 18 month old daughter was a major learning curve. (a) Both of us have globe-trotted many times but nothing could prepare us for the trepidation of taking our daughter with us on a trip to France. (b) It started really well. (c) She handled the two flights there with no difficulty and received compliments from all the flight crew for being so well behaved. (d) It was a major clean up operation and throughout it all we awkwardly smiled at our fretful baby.

해설
아이와 비행기를 타고 간 첫 해외여행에서의 에피소드를 작성한 에세이 글이다. (a)에서는 아이와의 첫 번째 해외여행에서 오는 불안감을 설명했고, (b)에서는 시작이 아주 좋음을 알려주고 있다. (c)에서는 부연설명으로 큰 문제가 없이 비행을 한 아이에 대한 설명을 하고 있다. 하지만 (d)는 청소작업과 함께 까다로운 자신들의 아이에 대한 내용을 언급하고 있으므로 전체 문맥과 어울리지 않는다. (c)와 (d) 사이에는 초반과는 달리 결국 문제를 일으킨 아이에 대한 설명의 글이 위치해야 할 것이다. 그러므로 정답은 (d)이다.

해석
처음으로 아이를 낳았을 때 대부분의 경험이 그러하듯이, 저희도 18개월 된 딸과 함께 한 첫 번째 해외여행은 중요한 학습곡선이었다. (a) 우리 부부는 여러 번 전 세계를 돌아다녀 봤지만, 그 무엇도 우리 딸을 프랑스로의 여행에 함께 데려감에 있어서 생기는 걱정을 덜어주지는 못했다. (b) 시작은 좋았다. (c) 딸은 그곳으로 가는 처음 두 번의 비행을 어려움 없이 잘 견뎌 내었고 너무 착하게 행동함으로서 모든 승무원들로부터 칭찬을 받았다. (d) 이것은 큰 청소 작업이었고, 청소가 진행되는 동안 우리는 우리의 까다로운 아이를 보며 어색하게 미소를 지었다.

어휘
learning curve 학습곡선
trepidation 공포, 전율, 걱정
glob-trot 전 세계를 돌아다니다
awkwardly 어색하게
fretful 까다로운, 불평이 많은

✓ 정답 (d)

39 Whooping cough is a highly contagious respiratory infection that is particularly dangerous for young babies. (a) The symptoms are similar to a cold but they quickly progress to a severe cough which includes the characteristic whooping sound and vomiting at the end of a bout of coughing. (b) Babies under 6 months are more at risk because they are more seriously affected by the disease than older children or adults. (c) One in every 200 babies who contract whooping cough will die and it is most often spread to babies from family members who are not immunized. (d) It was the first death in America from this disease since the early 1990's.

해설
어린 아기들에게 위험한 호흡기 질병인 백일기침에 대해 설명하는 글이다. (a)에서는 백일기침의 증상과 특징 (b)에서는 이 질병에 가장 위험한 그룹에 대한 설명, 그리고 (c)에서는 (b)에 대한 부연 설명으로 매 200명의 아기들 중 한 명이 이로 인해 사망함을 알려주고 있다. 반면, (d)는 '이것이 미국에서의 첫 번째 죽음이다' 라고 얘기하고 있는 데, 이는 (C)에서 평균적으로 사망하는 아이들의 수를 마치 정말 한 명이 죽은 것으로 해석해서 작성한 것으로 전체 문맥과 어울리지 않는 문장이다. 정답은 (d)이다.

해석
백일기침은 특히 어린 아기들에게 위험한 전염성이 높은 호흡기 질병이다. (a) 이 증상들은 감기와 비슷하지만 그르렁 거리는 소리와 한 차례의 기침 끝에 토를 하게 되는 특징들을 포함하는 심한 감기로 빠르게 전개된다. (b) 6개월 미만의 아기들은 나이가 있는 어린이들이나 성인들에 비교해서 병에 더 심각하게 영향을 받기 때문에 더 위험하다고 할 수 있다. (c) 백일기침에 감염된 매 200명의 아기 중 한 명이 죽게 되고, 이는 종종 면역성을 투여 받지 못한 가족 구성들의 아기들에게 퍼져나간다. (d) 이는 1990년 초기 이후 이 병에 의한 미국에서의 첫 번째 죽음이다.

어휘
whooping cough 백일기침
contagious 전염성의 respiratory 호흡기의
infection 전염(병)
symptom 증상
vomit 토하다
a bout of 한 차례의
spread 퍼지다
immunize 면역이 되게 하다, 면역성을 주다

✓ 정답 (d)

40 The right of women to vote had been demanded by feminist movements in Europe and the USA in the nineteenth century but made little headway before the first world war, as most males were hostile or indifferent. (a) New Zealand was the first country to give the vote to women in 1893, followed by the states of Australia between 1893 and 1909. (b) Israeli women serve two years of mandatory military service. (c) In Europe the only countries to enfranchise women before 1914 were Finland and Norway. (d) The important role played by women during the war, far more than the activities of the suffragettes, helped to persuade the British Parliament to give the vote to women over thirty in 1918 and women over twenty-one in 1928.

해설
여성의 참정권이 주어진 나라들을 차례대로 열거하며 설명해 주고 있는 지문이다. (a), (c), (d)에서는 각각 어떤 국가들이 차례대로 자국의 여성들에게 참정권을 주었는지 설명해주고 있다. (b)는 참정권과는 관련 없이 이스라엘 여성들이 2년의 군복무를 한다는 내용으로 전체 맥락에서 벗어나고 있다. 그러므로 정답은 (b)이다.

해석
여성들의 참정권은 19세기 미국과 유럽의 여성운동에 의해서 요구되어졌습니다. 하지만 1차 세계대전에 이전에는 대부분의 남성들이 이에 대해서 적대적이고 무관심했기 때문에 거의 진척이 되지 못했지요. (a) 뉴질랜드는 1893년에 여성들에게 참정권을 준 첫 번째 나라였고, 뒤 이어서 1893년과 1909년 사이에 호주의 여러 주들이 여성에게 참정권을 주었습니다. (b) 이스라엘의 여성들은 2년간의 의무 군복무를 합니다. (c) 유럽에서 1914년 이전에 여성들에게 선거권을 준 유일한 나라는 핀란드와 노르웨이였습니다. (d) 여성 참정권자들의 활동보다는 여성에 의해서 전쟁기간 동안 행해진 훨씬 더 중요한 역할들은 영국의회가 1918년도에 30세가 넘은 여성들에게 그리고 1928년도에는 21살이 넘는 여성들에게 투표권을 주도록 설득하는데 도움을 주었습니다.

어휘
right 권리
vote 투표하다
make headway (일이) 진척되다
hostile 적대적인
indifferent 무관심한
mandatory 의무적인, 강제적인
enfranchise 선거권을 주다
suffragette 여성 참정권론자

정답 (b)

J&L English Lab 정기 TOEIC 시험 만점자이며 TEPS 1+ 등급의 소유자들이 뭉쳐서 만든 전문 컨텐츠 개발 팀이다. 에듀조선 출판사의 TEPS 문항 개발 작업을 담당하기도 했던 이들은 해외유학생활의 경험과 학원 강의, 영어연구원 등의 경력을 바탕으로 현재 호주에 거주하며 다양한 수험서들의 집필과 문제개발을 진행하고 있다.

표현 하나를 들으면 대답 세 개가 보이는
1+3 미드 English

표현 하나를 들으면 대답 세 개가 보이는

1+3 미드 English  ❶ 젊은이들의 일상회화

청소년들의 사랑과 우정 그리고 배신을 그린 **The O.C**
전 세계 젊은이들을 매료시킨 최고의 트렌디 미드 **Gossip Girl**
당찬 4명의 여성이 펼치는 화려한 리얼리티 쇼 **The Hills**
청소년들에게 벌어지는 다양한 주제를 다룬 **One Tree Hill**

260쪽 / 12,000원 / MP3 CD

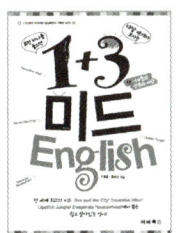

표현 하나를 들으면 대답 세 개가 보이는

1+3 미드 English  ❷ 여자들의 성공과 사랑

전 세계 여성들에게 뉴욕 열풍을 가져온 **Sex and the City**
잘 나가던 커리어 우먼의 자아 찾기 여행 **Samantha Who?**
커리어 우먼들의 사회 속 생존법칙을 그린 **Lipstick Jungle**
아줌마 파워는 한국뿐 아니라 미국에서도 통한다 **Desperate Housewives**

260쪽 / 12,000원 / MP3 CD

표현 하나를 들으면 대답 세 개가 보이는

1+3 미드 English ❸ 남자들의 삶과 로망

천재소년 두기가 돌아왔다 **How I met your mother**
범죄수사 미드의 최고봉 **CSI Las Vegas**
버락 오바마 대통령도 팬이라고 자처한 남성 드라마 **Entourage**
2009년 전미 시청률 1위를 빼앗은 다크호스 **The Mentalist**

260쪽 / 12,000원 / MP3 CD

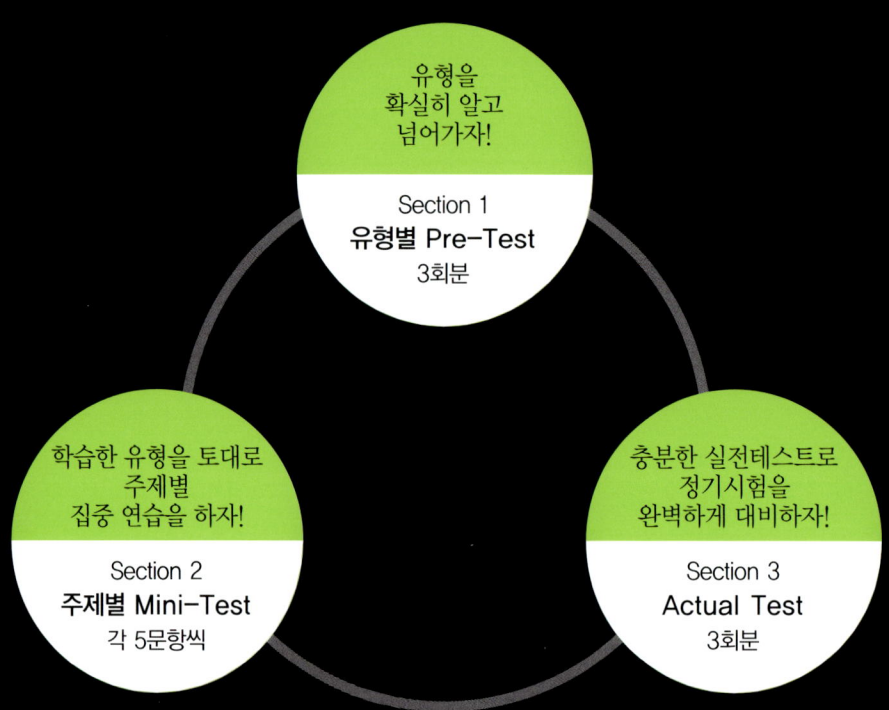